The Seattle School Library
2501 Elliott Ave
Seattle, WA 98121
theseattleschool.edu/library

D1790531

DATE DUE

THE POISONING OF EROS

SEXUAL VALUES IN CONFLICT

Raymond J. Lawrence, Jr.

Augustine Moore Press
New York

Copyright © 1989 by Raymond J. Lawrence Jr.
All rights reserved.

SECOND PRINTING — JANUARY, 1990

Published by:
Augustine Moore Press
P.O. Box 235, Times Square Station
New York, New York 10108

International Standard Book Number 0-9623310-0-7
Library of Congress Catalogue Card Number: 89-92038

For my Father
for obvious reasons
and some not so obvious.

And for
John Wesley Lawrence
who in my youth
showed me the ways of the spirit.

"Christianity gave Eros poison to drink
He didn't die but degenerated into vice."

Nietzsche

Contents

Introduction 1
1. Religious and Philosophical Origins 5
2. Sexual Valorization in the Jesus Movement 31
3. The First Four Hundred Years:
    The Victory of Syncretism 87
4. The Medieval Synthesis 134
5. The Tide Turns: Luther and the Reformation 166
6. From Luther to the Sexual Revolution 196
7. Toward a New Sexual Ethics
    of Carnal Reciprocity 247
Acknowledgements 278
Biblical Index 281
General Index 283

INTRODUCTION

The history of Western sexual values is profoundly equivocal; the tradition is divided against itself. We know why this is so. The West has drunk almost equally from two quite different wells. On the one hand we have inherited a powerfully sex-affirming biblical tradition, and on the other hand a deep suspicion of sex, acquired mainly from the Greco-Roman tradition. The latter has achieved ascendancy in Christendom, but it has never fully succeeded in quashing the former.

Popular opinion holds that Christianity brought a new sex ethics of chastity to a debauched Greco-Roman world. Michel Foucault and others have already shown the error of that opinion. The conflict was not between the orgiastic classical pagan culture and the chaste church, but between a sex-affirming Hebraic and a sex-negating Greco-Roman culture. Furthermore, that conflict has been brought forward into the present through the strange marriage of Christendom's baptized platonist ideology and its venerated Hebrew scriptures.[1] Western religious tradition has generally dealt with this unlikely marriage by interpreting the biblical texts as if they were written by sexually suspicious platonists. Hence the uniquely Hebraic way of seeing and valuing sexuality has been obfuscated by subsequent translation and interpretation.

Thus the biblical texts are commonly viewed through the distorting prism of platonism. For example, the biblical literature is read as if it endorses monogamy, which it does not. The story of Sodom is metamorphosed from a cautionary tale about inhospitality into one about sexual sins. Onan is similarly reworked, distorted into a concern about masturbation. The New Testament texts, however, are the most distorted. The presumption that Jesus and Paul were sexual celibates has no foundation in biblical material and in fact flies in the face of strong circumstantial evidence to the contrary. The refusal even to give a footnote to the

---

1 I am using platonism in the broad sense of that body/soul dualism that has been inherited from the Greco-Roman world; Plato himself is not entirely responsible for its various permutations. I also follow the direction of modern biblical scholarship which views the New Testament as Hebraic literature which happened to be written in Greek.

The Poisoning of Eros

strong possibility that Paul was addressing his wife in the Philippian letter demonstrates the bias inherent in most translations and interpretations of the texts. Even such a reputable scholar as Philippe Ariès assumes Paul's sex-negativism, a view that has been undermined by recent scholarship.[2] The appearance of the word "fornication" in the English translations of the New Testament provides the strongest distortion in favor of Greco-Roman sexual values. As a translation of the Greek *porneia*, "fornication" is perhaps the most deliberately mistranslated word in the biblical literature, a literature that demonstrates no interest in the modern concern about "sex outside the bounds of marriage."

This book traces from the beginning the major events and turning points in the struggle in Christianity between the Hebraic and the Greco-Roman way of seeing and valuing sexuality. The four hundred years between Jesus and Augustine demonstrate the gradual but ineluctable process of jettisoning a Hebraic anthropological construct that affirmed sex in favor of a platonic construct that was sex-negating. Whatever wisdom Augustine possessed---and he possessed much---he crowned Western theology with a negativity toward sex. Another six hundred years passed before Augustine's error fully bore fruit, the kind of fruit that likely would have troubled Augustine himself. The middle of the eleventh century witnessed the bloody campaign to abolish clerical marriage, a campaign that lasted two centuries. Clerical celibacy and widespread monasticism were the results. The ideal of chastity had reached its point of greatest influence and power.

In the early sixteenth century Martin Luther offered the strongest reassertion of Hebraic sexual affirmation in all of Christian history. The rhyme attributed to him, "Who loves not wine, women, and song remains a fool his whole life long," may or may not be authentic, but he would have been delighted to have it attributed to him in either case. Karl Barth and Paul Tillich in the twentieth century are in this respect Luther's progeny. Each in his own audacious personal life demonstrated an unabashed affirmation of sexuality, one that was not constrained by the strict boundaries of monogamy.

In our own generation many continue to reenact the struggle between Hebraic and Greco-Roman ways of seeing and valuing sexuality. Paul Moore, the Episcopal Bishop of New York, is an example. In 1979, he published an autobiographical account of his own struggles with certain behavior and values promoted by the sexual revolution. The conflict was

---

2 Philippe Ariès, *Western Sexuality*, Philippe Ariès & André Béjin, eds., Anthony Foster, trans., New York: Basil Blackwell, 1985, p. 38.

Introduction

most personalized by the obvious premarital sex engaged in by his own children. His initial response to their behavior was what one would expect from a liberal cleric. He was tolerant, but he established a rule that no unmarried cohabitation would be permitted under his roof, regardless of what his guests were doing elsewhere. Moore's household rule was put to the test at a vacation cabin episode in which his children arrived early and set up sleeping arrangements according to their own wishes. On his arrival the Bishop then faced the dilemma of whether to exercise his authority and enforce the rule he had enforced at home. This decision confronted Moore with his own uncertainty about whether "the old way was better or even more moral than the new way." He decided to rescind his rule. However, as he put it, he did not go lightly against "the venerable traditions of the church."[3]

In his deference to venerable tradition and in acknowledging his alienation, Moore inadvertently gave away more than he needed to. The venerable tradition is a deeply divided one. Moore placed himself in opposition to a large part of the venerable tradition, especially the part that has dominated the last thousand years. However, we can confidently presume that Moore would have had the support of a venerable tradition that is represented by Paul Tillich, Karl Barth, Martin Luther, Heloise and Peter Abelard, Norman Anonymous, Julian of Eclanum, Theodore of Mopsuestia, and countless other lesser-knowns whose spoken or written words have been expunged from history. Not least of all, Moore has the implied support of the biblical literature.

This book is the story of that "other" venerable tradition of which Moore seems unaware, that persisting trail of those in the West who in faithfulness to Hebraic or biblical tradition have affirmed human sexuality as a good in and of itself, requiring no extrinsic justification. In the last chapter I propose a new basis for sex ethics, one that is indebted mostly to the basic assumptions of Hebraic thought.

If this book seems to be written for Christians, that is not my intention. Western culture is largely shaped in its sex values by Judaeo-Christian myths and symbols. The age of Christendom may be over, but the values it has bequeathed remain. The mythmakers of the past belong to us all, not just to the subgroups who praise their names.

If I seem critical of the dominant Western religious tradition, especial-

---

3   Paul Moore, *Take a Bishop Like Me*, New York: Harper & Row, Publishers, 1979, p. 77.

ly the more recent, that is as I intended. History is the story of winners and losers, and as is often said, the winners have written the history---their way.[4] This book is in large part a challenge to the way the winners have written history. It is also an attempt to rectify the wrongs done to the losers, or some of them. Sometimes losers, once they are dead and buried, are transformed like Jesus into winners by subsequent interpretation. More often, like Theodore of Mopsuestia, they remain pale shades and the truth to which they testified forgotten. This is an attempt to restore our collective memory.

I began this work intending to propose a new basis for sexual ethics. As a result I was driven to dig through history. This was a course that was forced on me when I gradually discovered, as Teilhard de Chardin said, "Everything is the sum of the past, and nothing is comprehensible except through its history."[5] In the process I discovered that the so-called "sexual revolution," for all its banality, is at its source a bold reassertion of the Hebraic/biblical affirmation of sexuality.

---

4   Elaine Pagels, *The Gnostic Gospels*, New York: Vintage Books, 1979, p. 170.
5   Pierre Teilhard de Chardin, *The Future of Man*, Norman Denny, trans., New York: Harper & Row, Publishers, 1964.

Chapter One
Religious and Philosophical Origins

*Both read the Bible day and night
But thou read'st black where I read white.*
-- William Blake*

I

The roots of Western sexual valorization[1] are a tangle of two old and differing traditions, the Hebrew and the syncretistic Greco-Roman. Although practically all Western myths and values have developed from the converging of these two traditions, their intersection has not been peaceable but a polemical one.

While there are points of agreement in the two traditions, in particular the passion for justice, their antithetical character is basic and profound, expressing conflicting views of the nature of personhood.

It perhaps goes without saying that variants exist within each of the two traditions. Though Plato remains today the preeminent representative of the Greco-Roman tradition, there is diversity within that tradition. Not everyone who shares Plato's basic assumptions is entirely faithful to Plato. Nevertheless, in this discussion I am using "platonic" as a convenient epithet for Greco-Roman philosophy and religion as a whole.

Hebrew tradition, which has been transmitted to the West through the polymorphic biblical literature, is similarly marked by diversity. Nevertheless, certain generalizations about Hebrew tradition can be made, particularly as that tradition confronts Greco-Roman tradition.

Syncretistic Greco-Roman civil religion was a mishmash of collected gods, rituals, and philosophies.[2] This conglomeration seems to have been in agreement, however, on an understanding of personhood

---

* "The Everlasting Gospel," IV, 13-14, *Blake*, W. H. Stevenson, ed., New York: W.W. Norton & Co., Inc., 1971, p. 850.
1. "To valorize" is a verb given prominence recently by the translators of Michel Foucault's volume on the history of sexuality. The meaning is essentially the same as "to valuate" or "to give a value to", but "valorize" seems to connote a valuing process somewhat more removed from commercial and commodity processes and is no doubt why Foucault translators used the word.
2. "The tendency to identify the deities of various people and to combine their cults." Frederick C. Grant, *Hellenistic Religion: The Age of Syncretism,* New York: The Bobbs Merrill Company, Inc., 1953, p. xiii. Also, *Ancient Roman Religion,* New York: The Liberal Arts Press, 1957, p. 215: "The chief characteristic of religious history in the imperial period was the influx of foreign deities and cults into Rome."

that was essentially platonist in construct, a dualism of the exiled soul implanted in a body that is its tomb.[3] As Plato puts it alliteratively, the body (*soma*) is the tomb (*sema*) of the soul (*psyche*).[4] This "fallen" soul longs for liberation, its return to the divine sphere, the "flight of the alone to the alone," or what Paul Henry calls an individualist and intellectualist salvation sought in flight and union with God in solitude.[5] In this anthropology the soul is the spark of divinity and the body its impediment, even its defilement. The worldly activities of the soul are thinking, reflecting, and speculating, activities which create an affinity between soul and mind. In the course of Christian history it is therefore the Gnostics (those who know in contrast to those who believe/have faith), who are the chief perpetuators of the platonic tradition and it is they who represent platonism's full spiritualistic dualism in Christian garb.

As Paul Ricoeur puts it somewhat hyperbolically, the Hebrew prophets do not think, reflect, or speculate. Rather they cry out, threaten, groan, and exult.[6] In the Old Testament tradition it is not souls and minds that belong to God, but the whole created being, as well as the entire created order. ("The whole creation groans and travails together until now," says Paul in Rom. 8:23.) Jewish anthropology is not marked by dualism, but by psychosomatic unity.

II

Platonic and Hebrew anthropology clearly vary in their language. The ways the two cultures describe personhood are semantically quite different and revealing. There is no word in Hebrew that quite corresponds to the Greek "soul" (*psyche*). There is no divine "something" in the individual which returns to God at death. Unlike the dualistic body/soul construct of platonism, Jewish anthropology uses a variety of concepts to describe the human experience, each simply an aspect of the whole. In Hebrew *nephesh* bears some similarities to and is often translated "soul". It is the essential and vital quality of life itself and often associated with breathing. But it embraces the whole of existence and for that reason is usually better translated as "person" than

---

3 Paul Ricoeur is particularly helpful here, see esp. *The Symbolism of Evil*, Boston: Beacon Press, 1967, p. 279.
4 *Cratylus*, 400 C.
5 *Plotinus: The Enneads*, Stephen MacKenna, trans. London: Faber and Faber, 1956, p. xxxix.
6 Ricoeur, *op. cit.*, p. 53.

"soul". Further, *nephesh* is neither antithetical nor in polar relation to the body.

Jewish and Greek constructs vary even further: the Hebrew promotes the idea of the divine spirit (Heb. *ruach*), a word etymologically related to "wind" or "gust of air", hence "breath", referring to God's dynamic and creative activity, and culminating in the Jewish-Christian metaphor of the Holy Spirit. In sheol, the Hebrew underworld or place of the dead, there is life but little spirit. While spirit, even divine spirit, is also a Greek concept, especially among the Stoics, it is a metaphor that never quite took root, whereas for the Jews it became the primary metaphor in the God/man encounter, as evidenced so powerfully in the early church. "Spirit" therefore assumed in Jewish tradition the main function of "soul" in Greek tradition. The major difference between Greek "soul" and Hebrew "spirit" is that the latter is not an intrinsic part of personhood or a divine substance within the human construct, but rather the animating or lifegiving power of which persons are the recipient. In the second, or Yahwist, creation account God breathes into the nostrils of man and he lives, (Gen 2:7) but there is no substance in him that is sacred, that is, no human spirit that represents the divine part of human personality. In Hebrew theology the only divine "substance" in man, though hardly a substance, is his own miraculous existence. Of this, man is wholly recipient; no particular piece of him is divine. In both accounts in Genesis the human species is in every respect creature, the one addressed. Persons in their totality are addressed by God. The focus of religion is therefore on the relationship between the human creature and the creating God, not on any division of personhood into divine and earthly components.[7]

In the New Testament only Mt 10:28 ("Do not fear those who kill the body but cannot kill the soul . . .") makes use of soul (*psyche*) in its platonic sense. In more than 60 other instances psyche is used as if it were a translation of the Hebrew nephesh, meaning "life" or "person". Matthew even uses the word in this sense several times, as, for example, in 2:20, "the men who threatened the child's life (*psyche*) are dead." Furthermore, "life" (*psyche*) in this sense means natural life, that which ends in death. *Psyche* in this sense is even juxtaposed to "spirit". So James 3:15: "This is not the wisdom that comes from above; it is

---

7   Herbert N. Schneidau (*Sacred Discontent,* Baton Rouge: LSU Press, 1976.) is very helpful in this respect, showing the consistent deracinating character of Hebrew religion which challenged every attempt of the various syncretistic mythologies to create a divine beachhead on the earth or in the psychological make-up of human beings.

earthbound, "sensual" (*psychichos*),"demonic." (N.E.B.) *Psychichos* is the adjectival form of *psyche,* or "soul-ish". And Paul writes (1 Cor. 2:14): "A man who is unspiritual (*psychichos*) refuses what belongs to the spirit of God." As if to confuse the platonists in their own language, Paul writes in 1 Cor. 15:44ff that the "soul-ish" (*psychichos*) body dies and the spiritual (*pneumatikos*) body is raised up.

The juxtaposition is a double one. Paul is denying the immortality of the soul on the one hand, and, as Birger Pearson has demonstrated, he is also repudiating mind (Gr. *nous*) as the divine substance in persons, and affirming spirit (breath) as the divine connection.[8] In Hellenistic philosophy at the time of Paul, soul as a concept had evolved into a kind of doublet of soul/mind, respectively the lower and higher divine substances in persons. As a result, the immortality of the soul came to mean something like the immortality of the mind and was related to wisdom. In a Hellenistic-Jewish context those more faithful to Jewish tradition replaced mind with spirit. It was apparently in this arena that Paul and his Corinthian opponents were engaged. Paul's opponents appear to have held the view that wisdom warranted immortality. Hellenistic-Jewish wisdom mysticism, a kind of pre-gnosticism, was essentially a revolt against Hebrew theology, specifically against the notion of human creatureliness. Paul was attempting to counter this rebellion. The unfortunate fact that in modern English the word "spirit" has evolved since into "mental incorporeality" makes this entire exposition itself problematic.[9] Paul's "spiritual" (*pneumatikos*) as rooted in breathing or wind is not carried into modern English. Ironically, the contemporary definition of "spirit" actually seems to transpose Paul into the camp of those against whom he was contending. "Spirit" has taken on some of the attributes of Greek "soul" in modern English. Its bodily locus is the mind rather than the whole person. It has developed an antithetic relationship to the body---incorporeality. It has lost the meaning of life-giving animation. Hence Tillich says the only modern remnant of the New Testament meaning of "spirit" is in the use "spirited", as in "a spirited horse."[10]

Similarly, the antithesis of body/flesh on the one hand and soul/mind on the other, which was promoted by Greco-Roman syncretistic religion, is not a part of Jewish scripture tradition.

---

8   Birger Albert Pearson, *The Pneumatikos-Psychikos Terminology*, Missoula, Montana: The Scholars Press, 1973.
9   Cf. Norman O. Brown, *Love's Body,* New York: Vintage Books, 1966.
10 *Systematic Theology*, Vol. III, Chicago: University of Chicago Press, 1963, p. 23.

Religious and Philosophical Origins

Whereas flesh becomes among the syncretists the evil principle, in Jewish theology flesh is neither evil nor antithetical to the "higher" parts of man. Flesh is rather the whole of man's creaturely experience, physical and mental. Flesh is "the situation of man before God", the whole "earthly sphere".[11] When Paul says flesh and blood cannot inherit the kingdom (1 Cor. 15:50) he is misunderstood in modern English. He is heard as if he were a syncretist who pits the flesh/body against the soul/mind, semantic evidence itself of the covert victory of syncretism in the modern West. Within the category of flesh and blood Paul includes every aspect of human creatureliness, including mind and soul, and especially including wisdom.[12]

III

These mythical constructs and metaphors of the shape of human personality have quite concrete implications. While the Jews seek the land of milk and honey for the nurture and fulfillment of the whole person, the Greeks speculate about the Utopian republic and cultivate the contemplative life for the sake of the soul and mind. In their respective myths dealing with death, the Greeks create the immortality of the soul, the survival of the divine substance in persons, while the Jews announce the resurrection of the body, the "standing up again"[13] of the whole person.[14]

The platonic dualism which philosophically undergirded Roman syncretism actually reached further back beyond Plato himself, who has become the convenient symbol of dualism. Pythagoras before him demonstrated the same dualism. As the soul gains, the body loses, he said. Stoicism, the preeminent philosophy of the empire at the beginning of the Christian movement, was similarly dualistic in its anthropological construct.

The implications for sexual valuation in this dualistic anthropology

---

11 Edward Schweitzer, *Theological Dictionary of the New Testament,* Gerhard Friedrich, Geoffrey W. Bromiley, ed. & trans., Grand Rapids, MI: Wm. B. Eerdmans Publishing Co., 1968, Vol. VII, p. 123.
12 E. P. Sanders suggests it would be appropriate to capitalize Spirit and Flesh in Pauline usage as a way to clear up misunderstandings in English. See *Paul and Palestinian Judaism,* London: SCM Press, 1977, p. 553.)
13 The prefix "ana" in the Greek word "*anastasis*" (resurrection) means either "up" or "again" and probably connotes both in this compound word. Hence I use both.
14 For further discussion here see Martin Hengel, *Judaism and Hellenism I.* Philadelphia: Fortress Press, 1974, pp. 198 ff.

The Poisoning of Eros

are not difficult to decipher. Sex was associated with the body and shared its low status. Sex was part of the encumbrance the soul jettisons as it rises to the divine, or as divine power increases. This devaluing of sex led in two directions, toward asceticism on the one hand, and toward orgiastic sado-masochism on the other, each motivated by contempt for the flesh.

The Stoics themselves were particularly suspicious of sex, not only for reasons mentioned above, but because the ecstasy of coitus seemed to them subversive to the rule of reason. The philosopher Seneca, contemporary of Jesus, tutor to the emperors and preeminent Stoic of his day, characterized sexual desire as "friendship gone mad."[15] On the question of whether "Sappho slept with anyone who asked her," he thought it "better unlearned if one actually knew."[16] He also wrote that the best women, like other animals, do not indulge in further sex when they have conceived. Contraception was excluded by Stoic doctrine.[17]

Among certain later Christians the most widely admired Stoic of all was Musonius Rufus. He was contemporaneous with Jesus, reaching the peak of his influence during the time of Nero. Origen considered him one of two pagan models of the highest types, Socrates being the other.[18] Pliny expressed admiration for him. He finally became one of Nero's many political victims, though he escaped execution and suffered only banishment.

Musonius Rufus was considerably more sympathetic to women than most of the other philosophers of the time. Contrary to most, he argued that marriage did not handicap the pursuit of philosophy.[19] In his view the primary end of marriage was "community of life with a view to the procreation of children."[20] He also argued against the propriety of a man having sexual relations with an unmarried slave. "How would the same man like it if his wife had sexual relations with a male slave?" he asked.[21] Men, he said, should expect to be more moral than women if they expect to be superior. Perhaps most remarkable is

---
15   Seneca: *Letters from a Stoic*, Robin Campbell, ed./trans., New York, Penguin Books, 1969, p. 50.
16   *Ibid*, p. 159.
17   John T. Noonan also supports this conclusion. See *Contraception*, Cambridge: Harvard University Press, 1986 ed., pp. 48 & 77.
18   *Contra Celsum* III, 66.
19   *Musonius Rufus, "The Roman Socrates"*. Cara E. Lutz, trans./ed., New Haven: Yale University Press, 1947, p. 91.
20   *Ibid*, p. 89.
21   *Ibid*, p. 87.

Religious and Philosophical Origins

his opinion that women as well as men should study philosophy. Cara Lutz contends that Musonius Rufus represented the greatest heights Stoicism ever reached.[22]

However humanistic his attitudes toward women, he relegated sexual relations strictly to the purposes of procreation. "Men who are not wantons or immoral are bound to consider sexual intercourse justified only when it occurs in marriage and is indulged in for the purpose of begetting children, since that is lawful, but unjust and unlawful when it is mere pleasure-seeking, even in marriage."[23]

In ritual support of Stoic ideology, continence was required for many pagan temple rituals. The Eleusinian rite, for example, required sexual abstinence of hierophants before and during celebrations.[24] Perhaps of the most important symbolic significance were the virgins of the Roman goddess Vesta, who for a thousand years of Roman history held the most sacred of priestly offices.[25] So seriously regarded was their sexual purity that they risked the specific death penalty of being buried alive if they defiled themselves by sexual intercourse during their 30 years of obligation. Some of them paid the penalty of this capital offense, proof of the seriousness with which the Romans viewed this matter.[26]

IV

A commonplace notion in the modern world, one promoted by numerous Hollywood films, is that the Roman world at the beginning of the Christian era was marked by uninhibited sexual promiscuity and that the Christian religion introduced and promoted sexual restraint. Nothing could be farther from the truth. (See pp. 89ff.) There is, of course, evidence of sexual excess such as Nero demonstrated. However, Nero and his kind deeply offended the philosophers and moralists of the age at least as much and perhaps

---

22   *Ibid*, p. 30.
23   *Ibid*, p. 87.
24   Albrecht Oepke, *Theological Dictionary of the New Testament,* Gerhard Kittel, Geoffrey W. Bromiley, ed. and trans., Grand Rapids, Mich: Wm B. Eerdmans Publishing Company, 1964, under *gyne*. Even though very little is known about Eleusinian and Orphic rituals, it is clear, according to Mircea Eliade, that they reflect the mythology of gnosticism. (*A History of Religious Ideas,* Vol. 1, Chicago: University of Chicago University Press, 1978, p. XIV.)
25   Cicero: *De Domo Sua* 53, 136, *De Haruspicum Responsis* 7.13.
26   Otto Kiefer, *Sexual Life in Ancient Rome,* London: George Routledge & Sons, Ltd., 1934, p. 113. Kiefer says three Vestal Virgins were condemned to death in 114 BCE, but does not cite his source.

The Poisoning of Eros

more than he would have offended the 20th century West.

Greco-Roman tradition had a long history of careful and reflective, and even fearful attitudes toward sexual pleasure, a response that was anything but uninhibited. Philospher George Boas says that pre-platonic writers do not hold to the notion that love might reinforce the human element in human interactions. He points out that as far back as Hesiod (circa 800 BCE [Before Common Era]) Eros is himself associated with the irrational, the uncontrollable, the mad, and the foolish. This very early Greek thought conveys the notion that, whether one surrenders to Eros or refuses to capitulate, either way one is doomed.[27] What constituted promiscuity in the Greco-Roman world was shaped by an entirely different construct from that of the modern world. Michel Foucault points out that antiquity failed to invest sexuality with positive values and that a fear of sex and a model of abstention shaped sexual value formation in the classical world.[28] The sexual attitudes that were often correctly attributed to later Christians were actually antedated by the Greco-Roman philosophical tradition. For example, the so-called "missionary position" was not invented by missionaries, but by the 2nd century (CE) Greek philosopher and dream interpreter, Artemidorus. He proposed the face-to-face man-on-top position as the only proper one, and that oral eroticism was "an awful act."[29] Much of what gets interpreted as orgiastic in classical Greek times is a misreading of the signs. The extensive phallic imagery on Greek pottery, for example, is in large part symbolic of the domination of men over women rather than an affirmation of phallic eroticism.[30] Similarly, the numerous phallic effigies in Athens, called Herms, the huge phalluses still standing on the island of Delos, and the Dionysian cultic processions in which phalluses were paraded as Christians later paraded the cross, are subject to misunderstanding. They demonstrated a veneration of the male generative principle and of the domination of men over women and as such were more an affirmation of male power than of sexual eroticism.

This is not to suggest that orgiastic sexual practices in religious

---

27 George Boas, "Love", Vol. 5, *Encyclopedia of Philosophy,* Paul Edwards, ed., NY: The MacMillan Co., 1967, p. 89.
28 *The History of Sexuality, Vol 2, The Use of Pleasure,* Robert Hurley, trans, NY: Pantheon Books, 1985, p. 14.
29 See Michel Foucault, *The History of Sexuality, Vol. 3, The Care of the Self,* Robert Hurley, trans., New York: Pantheon Books, 1986, p.23.
30 For a thorough examination of this theme, see the brilliant work by Eva C. Keuls, *The Reign of the Phallus: Sexual Politics in Ancient Athens,* New York: Harper & Row, Publishers, 1985.

Religious and Philosophical Origins

observances were unknown in Athens and Rome. The evidence is scanty, but the Dionysian cult itself, the cult of intoxication and ecstasy, even raving, had at various times some form of liturgical sex, pederasty in particular. The practices of the cult seem to have been highly variable at different times and places. However, when its "secret" liturgical sexual practices became public knowledge, they seem to have been treated as scandalous. The Bacchic mysteries were an Italian version of the Dionysian cult. In 186 (BCE) the Roman government laid aside its customary tolerance toward a wide range of religious cults and supressed the Bacchanalia in Italy with extreme and unprecedented brutality. Contrary to popular opinion, an unabashed acceptance of sexuality was not a characteristic of the classical world.[31]

Similarly, male homosexuality of the classical Greek period is popularly misunderstood today. Socrates and Plato would likely not have been pleased with the physicality of a late 20th century gay liberation parade or one of the gay baths that became so popular in San Francisco in the 70 s. We can conjecture that each of them participated personally in some kinds of homosexual behavior, either with "boys" they were rearing, with other adult males, or both. However, as we see from the *Symposium*, they approached the matter of sexuality from a radically different philosophical basis than the gay movement of the 20th century.

Plato's well-known discussion of love in the Symposium is an affirmation of love and of the Goddess of Love, Aphrodite. However, it should be noted that Plato affirms chiefly the love of souls rather than bodies, just as he seems to value homosexual above heterosexual love. He distinguishes between the Common Aphrodite and the Heavenly Aphrodite. The love of the former, which inferior men feel, is principally toward women and boys, but in any case, prefers bodies rather than souls. The love of the Heavenly Aphrodite has no share in the female. It is love only of what is stronger and has more mind. Beauty of souls is more precious than the beauty of the body. Thus we have an affirmation of male homosexual love combined with a disdain for the physicality of sex.

A superficial reading of the Symposium dinner party suggests something of a homosexual orgy, the all-male party, with eating and drinking until dawn, participants half-lying on each other on couches around a low table, as was the custom. Socrates himself chooses, "as

---

31 See Walter Burkert, *Greek Religion,* John Raffan, trans., Cambridge, Mass.: Harvard University Press, 1985, pp. 108-109, 290-293.

The Poisoning of Eros

usual", Plato notes, a seat next to Agathon, "the handsomest beauty of the party." But it is made very clear by Plato that this was not for purposes of satisfying himself physically. The climax of the Symposium is a long speech by Alcibiades in which he tells how he previously had courted Socrates as a lover, invited him to dinner alone, even slept the entire night in his embrace, "but got nothing from it". Alcibiades seems to be building a complaint against Socrates, but he turns his argument in the end toward an expression of profound admiration for Socrates, particularly for his restraint. "I thought I had been disgraced. . . and yet I admired his temperance and courage . . . I had met such a human being for wisdom and endurance as I never expected to find in the world . . . " The thrust of Plato's dialogue is to show at once both Socrates' intense love of beautiful men and his physical abstinence under the most severe temptation. It is souls he loves rather than bodies.

In *The Laws* for his Utopian state, Plato is even more explicit. The "world would benefit enormously," he says, if the sexual pleasures were starved.[32] He argues that the natural purpose of the sexual act is procreation and that ideally all sexual relations that are not directed toward procreation are forbidden. He admits that such restraint would be too idealistic even in his perfect state, so he grants a concession to human recalcitrance: though ideally a man would have intercourse only with "the wife he wed in holy marriage," intercourse with another woman would be tolerated so long as he kept the affair secret. Otherwise the man would be treated as an alien.

Thus Socrates and Plato viewed all physical sexuality in any form as ontologically and qualitatively inferior to abstinence simply because it involved the body rather than the soul. Though they were quite tolerant of both homosexuality and extramarital heterosexuality, they held the opinion that neither was beneficial to the soul's health. Socrates recommended fleeing from the sight of a handsome boy, even if that meant a year of exile. It takes at least a year, he is reported by Xenophon to have said, "to recover from the scorpion's bite," the metaphor he used to describe the lust for a boy with a pretty face.[33] The homosexual liaisons that were established between men and boys were in large part directed toward initiating boys to the power of the male fraternity. That relationship was supposed to terminate when the boy reached adulthood, at which point he became even more attractive

---

32 *The Laws,* sect. 841.
33 Xenophon, *Memorabilia* I, III, 13.

because he was developing mind and strength. This intimate initiation was apparently part of the profound war of the sexes that marked classical Greece. Athens was, as Vern Bullough put it, one big men's club.[34]

Eva Keuls thinks that Socrates' deathbed remark, "We owe a cock to Asclepius; pay it and do not forget," is a sexual pun and double-entendre. The rooster was a conventional homosexual love gift and also a standard offering to Asclepius, the god of health, who was at that moment curing Socrates of the sickness called life. Socrates had just uncovered himself and the jailer was feeling his feet and legs to check for the effects of the hemlock. Keuls conjectures that Socrates is displaying and commenting on an erection caused by the poison, or the jailer's touch, or both. This interpretation is congruent with consistent portrayals of Socrates as satyr-like and perpetually randy, though perhaps resolutely abstemious as well.[35]

Perhaps the reason for the lack of evidence of the physical expression of adult homosexuality in Greek culture is that the two main principles of immorality in sexual behavior were excess and passivity.[36] An effeminate man was viewed with contempt. If homosexuality was tolerated, softness and submissiveness were not, an attitude which would have inhibited the kind of homosexual expression that has emerged in the 20th century. The classical Greek valorization of sexuality in general was profoundly paradoxical. On the one hand, the Greeks were quite tolerant of homosexuality and extramarital heterosexuality, provided the marks of excess and submissiveness were avoided. On the other hand, they worried about the ill effects of any kind of sensual pleasure on one's health. By the beginning of the Christian era the Stoic men of letters were generally less tolerant of sex in any form and continued to emphasize an assessment of sex as potentially damaging to one's spiritual and physical health.

V

It would be a mistake to assume that body/soul dualism *led* to a demeaning of sexuality in the Greco-Roman tradition. The process may just as well have worked the other way. Or perhaps the two are

---

34 Vern L. Bullough, *Sexual Variance in Society & History,* Chicago: University of Chicago Press, 1976, p. 106.
35 Keuls, *op. cit.*, pp. 79-80.
36 Foucault, *op. cit.,* p. 47.

synergistically related. In any case, one of the great puzzles in human history, as Paul Ricoeur points out, is the persistent association of sexuality with defilement, which he defines as a "quasi-material something that infects as a sort of filth, that harms by invisible properties . . . [and] works in the manner of a force in our psychic and corporeal existence."[37] He calls this "indissoluble complicity between sexuality and defilement" very strange, pre-ethical and primitive in character. We must not be governed by it, and yet we are.[38] We certainly cannot build an ethics on it, but it remains something deep in human memory, perhaps in the unconscious of us all, and constitutes "an archaism that is most resistant to criticism."[39] Sexual purity, virginity, and celibacy apparently have the power to ward off these ghosts of defilement that prowl our inner recesses. The constraints of monogamy also minimize the power of these ghosts. Marital sex whose only purpose is procreation further reduces contamination. Perhaps sexual experience is so intimate and has such power to dissolve one's identity that we are driven from some unconscious level to make it a sacrament either of God or the Devil. The Jews, however, steadfastly refused to permit such a sacralization or demonization of sex.

VI

In Jewish tradition sexuality is simply another, but highly valued, piece of the human experience, a part of the divine creation. It is neither divinized nor demonized. Jewish tradition abhorred the divinization of sex by the Palestinian fertility cults and their orgiastic religious practices. Equally anathematic were celibacy and virginity. Jephthah's daughter mourns her virginity when she discovers she is to be made a human sacrifice. The Temple of the Virgins (Parthenon) stands on the best ground in Athens, but it could never have been built in Jerusalem. Virginity and celibacy in Israel are viewed as a rebellion against the divine command, a rejection of creation itself.

Rabbi David M. Feldman clearly documents the ongoing and consistent affirmation of sexuality among the Jews. Unlike later Christianity, sexual asceticism was at no time accorded the dignity of a religious value. Sexual intercourse was even granted in certain circumstances the status of *mitzvah*, a religious duty that has connotations

---
37 Ricoeur, *op. cit.*, p. 26.
38 *Ibid.*, p. 28.
39 *Ibid.*, p. 29.

Religious and Philosophical Origins

of meritorious performance, a charitable and humanitarian act. Sexual intercourse is *mitzvah*, for example, when performed in response to a woman's yearning, as when she is nursing or prior to a journey separating her from her husband. In Jewish history coitus has been consistently and unambiguously valued for the sheer joy and pleasure of it, even where procreation was obviously impossible.[40]

Even so, there are hints, however meager, of sex as defilement in the Old Testament, and to that extent the Jews share with the Greco-Roman tradition that sense of sex as contamination. During the exodus Moses prepares the people for a theophany by requiring them to wash their clothes and abstain from sex for three days (Ex 19:15). David was permitted to eat the hallowed liturgical showbread after he had kept himself from women the required three days (I Sam 21:5-7). An emission of semen required bathing and rendered whomever it touched unclean until evening (Lev 15:16 ff., 22:4). Menstruation also rendered a woman unclean for seven days and did the same for anyone who had intercourse with her during that period (Lev 15:19 ff.). The high priest in Jerusalem was also prohibited from having more than one wife, the only one in Israel required to be monogamous. Finally, there is the presence of the serpent in the Garden of Eden. While the Hebrew version of the sin of Adam is clearly not sexual, the serpent remains, a remnant of the adopted Babylonian or pre-Babylonian creation myth, and, at least unconsciously, carries sexual connotations.[41] What is remarkable, however, is not the existence of these few traces of sex as defilement, but that there are relatively so few of them in the biblical tradition.

Jewish tradition, like all others, has been affected, at least to some extent, by other cultures with which it interfaced. For survival, if for no other reason, modern Jewish tradition in the West has taken on a certain Christian coloration. This is clearly demonstrated in contemporary Jewish marriage practice. The Ashkenaze Jews of the West

---

40 David M. Feldman, *Marital Relations, Birth Control and Abortion in Jewish Law*, New York: Schocken Books, 1974, p. 67.
41 Ricoeur, *op. cit.*, pp. 233 ff. But see also Claus Westermann (*GENESIS 1-11: A Commentary*, Minneapolis: Augsburg Publishing House, 1984), who argues against the sexual symbolism of the serpent on the grounds that it would not be consistent with Genesis theology. Ricoeur's point is that certain inconsistencies do find their way into the texts, this being a case in point. Furthermore, to argue that the snake cannot carry sexual connotations seems psychoanalytically naive.

have mimicked Christian practices more than the Sephardic Jews living as they do mainly in a Moslem culture. The practice of rabbis' officiating at marriage ceremonies originated in medieval Europe as the Jews aped Christian custom.[42] Unlike the Sephardim, the Ashkenazim also adopted monogamy in the early medieval period. The Torah[43] neither legislates monogamy nor prohibits polygamy, a fact which often comes as a surprise to middle class Westerners. The first authority in Jewish history to call for a ban on polygamy was Rabbi Gershom ben Judah of Worms in 1040 CE (Common Era). It is no coincidence that Gershom proposed this innovation at the onset of the genocidal Gregorian campaign against married clergy in the Western church. The Gregorian religio-political campaign, ultimately successful, universally proscribed marriage for clerics, who made up practically the entire intelligentsia of medieval western Europe. The Jews of Germany and France no doubt understood quite well the risks of continuing polygamy in such an environment.

Gershom's ruling affected only German and French Jews at first. Spanish Jews were not immediately affected, nor were other Sephardic Jews.[44] Only in the mid-20th century did the Chief Rabbinate of the State of Israel extend Gershom's ban to the Sephardic Jews of the East,[45] but even then exemptions were granted to polygamous immigrants entering Israel.[46]

Gershom's ruling, of course, allowed for certain exceptions, as in the case of the levirate law and in the cases of barren women. Even so, he did not have universal support for his ban. It was, after all, an innovation in the context of at least two thousand years of Jewish tradition. Discussions arose about the ruling's being contrary to the Torah. While Genesis 2:24 may seem to imply monogamy, it is hardly explicit. The book of Deuteronomy, itself a document of religious and moral reform, inveighs against "a man who multiplies wives to himself" (17:17), but the context is a criticism of one who multiplies to himself

---

42 Adin Steinsaltz, *The Essential Talmud.* Chaya Galai, trans., New York: Basic Books, 1976, p. 130.
43 Torah is the Law and consists of the first five books of what Christians call the Old Testament.
44 Robert Gordis, *Love and Sex,* New York : Farrar, Straus & Giroux, 1978, p. 34.
45 Isaac Klein, *Code of Maimonides, Book Four, The Book of Women,* New Haven: Yale University Press, 1972, p. xxiv.
46 Moshe David Herr, *Encyclopedia Judaica,* Vol. 12, p. 259.

Religious and Philosophical Origins

horses, and one who multiplies greatly to himself gold and silver. This is clearly a criticism of excessive polygamy, not an advocacy of monogamy. Deuteronomy 21:15 explicitly accepts polygamy, and the lives of the patriarchs demonstrate indisputably its acceptance.[47]

Hillel, who was the preeminent rabbi of the first century, witnesses to the practice of polygamy and to Jewish sexual permissiveness about certain kinds of relationships outside of marriage---at least for men. As he wistfully puts it: "The more flesh, the more worms: the more property, the more anxiety; the more wives, the more witchcraft; the more slave girls, the more lewdness; the more slaves, the more thievery."[48] Hillel appears to have discovered the recently popularized axiom, "less is more," but even that does not lead him to advocate monogamy. The schools of Hillel and Shammai entered into a dispute on the subject of the treatment of the children of rival wives.[49]

The Mishna and the Talmud both testify clearly to the practice of polygamy. The Mishna was written about 200 CE and was to some extent drawn from the longstanding oral tradition interpreting the Torah. The Pharisees in the 1st century BCE had already decided to teach in the Mishna form.[50] The Talmud is an extensive commentary and discussion of the Mishna. There are actually two Talmuds, the Babylonian, compiled by the end of the 4th century CE, and the less important Jerusalem, by the end of the 5th century CE. The Mishna and Talmud together comprise the authoritative post-biblical commentary on the Torah and have weight as sacred writings for the Jews. In common usage "Talmud" includes both Mishna and the interpretation of it, referred to as "Gemara". It should be noted that these writings are dialectic in construct. They contain discussions of varied opinion and can be quoted to support quite contradictory positions. Polygamy, however, is given more than a passing nod---there are quite elaborate guidelines on its various aspects.

The Babylonian Talmud, for example, specifically permits a man as many as four wives. In such polygamous marriages each wife is guaranteed sexual intercourse at least once a month.[51] (This is probably the

---

47 For a discussion of this see Ze'ev W. Falk, *Jewish Matrimonial Law in the Middle Ages,* Oxford: Oxford University Press, 1966, p. 27; and Marcus Cohn, *The Universal Jewish Encyclopedia in Ten Volumes,* Isaac Landman, ed., New York: 1942, Vol. 7, pp. 370 ff.
48 Mishna. Aboth 2:7.
49 TB (Babylonion Talmud) Yabamoth 15a.
50 Simon Cohen, *Universal Jewish Encyclopedia* Vol. 1, p. 148.
51 TB (Babylonian Talmud) Kethuboth 5;10.

The Poisoning of Eros

source of a similar rule in Islam.) In the Mishna, the various rights of inheritance are spelled out for each of the maximum four widows of one man,[52] and certain limitations are instituted for polygamous marriages. A man is prohibited from betrothing a woman and her daughter or sisters at the same time.[53] These restrictions were clearly attempts to humanize polygamy by eliminating some of the aspects of it which were especially degrading to women.

Josephus, writing in the 1st century CE, tells his Roman readers of the longstanding Jewish custom of marrying many wives.[54] The Talmud records an inquiry of the chief steward of King Agrippa II (27?-93 CE),[55] a certain Joseph ben Simai, who asked Rabbi Eliezer if he could observe two Sukkas (a Jewish religious feast) since he had two wives, one in Tiberias and one in Sepphoris. Eliezer answered in the negative on the grounds that to go from one Sukkah to another nullifies the blessing.[56] Even the New Testament appears to support the fact of polygamy in the story of the woman who married seven brothers (Mt 22:23; Mk 12:18; Lk 20:27) and in the Pastorals (I Tm 3:4;12 & Ti 1:6). Note also that John the Baptist, in attacking Herod Antipas, focuses exclusively on the fact that he married his brother's wife (Mt 14:3-12; Mk 6:17-28). Marriage to a brother's wife was a capital crime in the Torah, except when the levirate law came into play.[57] Justin Martyr, the Christian apologist of the second century, attempts to discredit Jews by pointing out that their sages permitted polygamy and that they defended their polygamy by pointing to the example of the Patriarchs.[58] "You should obey God rather than your blind and stupid teachers . . . who aspire to be called Rabbi . . . [and] who even now permit each of you to have four or five wives." Then Justin goes on to add that the Patriarchs took many wives not to commit adultery, "but that certain mysteries might thus be indicated by them."[59] In 285 the Emperor Diocletian forbade bigamy in the provinces, presumably includ-

---

52 TB Kethuboth 10:1-5.
53 TB Kuddushim 2:7.
54 Josephus, *The Jewish War,* G. A. Williamson, Trans., New York: Penguin Books, 1959, p. 86. See also *Antiquities,* Vol. 17:1:3
55 Son of Herod Agrippa I, who was grandson of Herod I, the Great. Agrippa I succeeded Herod Antipas, Jesus' adversary, the "fox", as tetrarch of Galilee in 39 CE.
56 TB Sukkah 27a.
57 Harold W. Hoehner, *Herod Antipas,* Cambridge: Cambridge University Press, 1972, p. 137.
58 *Dialogue with Trypho,* 112 and 134.
59 *Ibid.,* p. 141.

ing the Jews. In 393 the Emperor Theodosius voiced opposition to Jewish polygamy.[60]

The actual extent to which polygamy was practiced by Palestinian Jews at the beginning of the Christian era is simply not known for certain and is a matter of some dispute among scholars.[61] That it was practiced to some extent at the time of Jesus seems incontrovertible. It may have been limited mostly to the affluent, especially since additional wives were an additional cost to the household. The highly regarded George Foot Moore may be correct in his judgment that polygamy "was evidently not common among Palestinian Jews" of this period.[62] However, he makes this claim partly on the questionable grounds that the Gospels "suppose a practically monogamous society." However much or little it was practiced, there is no evidence of religious or moral sanctions levied against those who did practice it. The prophetic confrontation of those who multiply their wives is of the same order as the criticism of those who multiply their homes, and should not be taken as an advocacy of monogamy. Christian scholarship especially has shown a tendency to wish away first century Palestinian polygamy.[63]

That polygamy carried with it certain problems for interpersonal relationships should go without saying. The English translations of the Talmud refer to "rival wives" in what was undoubtedly an apt choice of adjectives. It was reported in the Torah, after all, that the rival Hagar had run away from home because of the treatment she got from Sarai.(Gen 16:7) Nor does it seem necessary to demonstrate that polygamy was in many respects burdensome to women and, at the expense of women, quite beneficial to men. In a Talmudic discussion one

---

60   Ze'ev W. Falk, *op cit.*, p. 6.
61   cf. E. Schillebeeckx, *Marriage, Human Reality, and Saving Mystery*, New York: Sheed and Ward, 1966, pp. 89-90.
62   *Judaism in the First Centuries of the Christian Era: The Age of the Tannaim, Vol. II,* Cambridge, Mass: Harvard Univ. Press, 1932, p. 122.
63   Even some Jewish scholars wish the same against the overwhelming evidence to the contrary. For example, J. H. Hertz writes, "The Biblical ideal of human marriage is the monogamous one . . . Polygamy seems to have well-nigh disappeared in Israel after the Babylonian Exile." (p. XVII, Foreword to *The Babylonian Talmud,* Vol. 1, Seder Nashim, I. Epstein, ed., London: The Soncino Press, 1936.) And in a cavalier disregard for data, Paul Johnson (*A History of the Jews,* New York: Harper and Row, Publishers, 1987, p. 200) says "monogamy was the rule from post-exilic times." (6th century BCE) *The Universal Jewish Encyclopedia in Ten Volumes,* Isaac Landman, ed., New York: 1942, Vol. 7, p. 370, presents a more accurate picture based on available data. See also Ze'ev W. Falk, *op. cit.*

rabbi demonstrated an awareness of that burden. His wife had passed the years of procreation without children and he faced the prospect of taking an additional wife. Were he to marry another, as he put it, it would be said that "one was his wife and the other his mistress."[64] It may also have been an unwritten but widely felt notion that monogamy was somehow superior to polygamy. Many Jewish theologians think that monogamy was held to be the implied ideal from early history and was generally practiced for the sake of harmonious family relations.[65] And in the long course of Jewish history it is quite obvious that polygamy has gradually been eroded, with monogamy becoming the general practice as well as the ideal. Nevertheless, the stark and incontrovertible fact remains that in Biblical and Talmudic literature, polygamy continues to be tolerated and monogamy never commanded.

If rabbinic interpretation of the Torah accepted polygamy, this should not be construed as a cavalier attitude about sexual liaisons generally. Social and religious convention, in accord with rabbinic interpretation, was highly fearful of the temptress and the adulterous woman and highly restrictive of social contact between men and women. We see evidence of this in the New Testament, where Jesus appears to flout some of these restrictions. The conventions themselves were clearly part of an effort to keep sexual relations under some kind of control. But this does not add up to an endorsement of monogamy, and even less, of sexual asceticism.

Jewish law made almost no allowance for what other cultures refer to as "illegitimate sexual relationships." A natural relationship, that is, a sexual liaison of any kind, had virtually the force of marriage itself. Likewise, concubinage, a common practice in Israel, was regarded almost on the same level as marriage.[66] A child born to an unmarried woman was not illegitimate in rabbinic tradition.[67] Marriage itself added the dimension of sealing family ties and in this sense was, of course, superior to concubinage. It appears, then, that in Israel any sexual relationship a man developed with a woman, except for adulterous or incestuous ones, would take on the form of marriage or quasi-marriage.

---

64 TB Kethuboth 62b.
65 See esp. Feldman, *op. cit.*, p. 37.
66 Marcus Cohn, *Universal Jewish Encyclopedia*, Vol. 7, p. 370.
67 Robert Gordis, *op. cit.* (citing M. Kiddushin 4:1,2; B. Yebamot 100 b), p. 376.

Religious and Philosophical Origins

We see this idea illustrated in the Midrash:[68]

> Rabbi Jonah said in Samuel's name: If a harlot was standing in the street and two men had intercourse with her, the first is not culpable while the second is, on account of the verse, "Behold, thou shalt die . . . for she has been possessed by a man." (Gen 20:3)

Since the sex act is tantamount to marriage, the prostitute here became the de facto wife of the first man who had intercourse with her. The second man, therefore, was subject to the penalty for adultery. (Needless to say, prostitutes may not wish to exercise the right of marital obligation. The story is hypothetical, to illustrate a principle.) In other words, there is no such thing as a casual, obligation-free sexual encounter, in principle at least. This might be perceived as part of the view that women were property of males, on the order of domesticated animals. Undoubtedly such an abusive connotation is possible here. On the other hand, the contention that every sexual liaison carries with it the potential for obligation has a positive aspect. A man could never expect with certainty to be able to have sexual relations with a woman and simply walk away.

The same kind of thinking prevailed with regard to the fathering of children. It could almost be said that there were no bastards (Hebrew "*mamzer*") in Israel. Whoever in fact fathered a child was the child's legitimate father. The definition of bastardy was highly restrictive, especially compared with later Christian usage, limited only to cases of children born of proven incestuous or adulterous unions. The latter have been extremely rare, since Jewish law does not admit confession or self-incrimination. It would almost have to be limited to a case where a husband was absent for a long enough period for a woman to be obviously impregnated by another man in the interim. The rabbinical courts of the State of Israel faced such a case concerning a brother and sister who were born to a woman in a Nazi concentration camp.[69] Hebraic tradition makes the status of bastardy quite unusual

---

68 *Midrash Rabbah in Ten Volumes,* H. Friedman and M. Simon, trans., London: The Soncino Press, 1939, Vol. 1, p. 144. The Midrash is a Post-Talmudic Jewish commentary on the Biblical texts. The Genesis Midrash is dated early, in the 4th-6th centuries. Other books are dated later in the medieval period.
69 Gordis, *op. cit.,* pp. 184-186.

and difficult to achieve. Even in the rare cases where a bastard is identified, a rabbinic ruling holds that a bastard who is a scholar of the Torah takes social precedence over an ignorant high priest.[70]

Therefore, while the monogamy of Greco-Roman culture was prima facie more humane than the polygamy of Israel, closer examination reveals a quite different picture. The one wife of a Roman citizen held a stronger position than any one of the two or more wives of a Jew. But the mistresses or casual liaisons of a Roman were in a far more vulnerable position, and especially so were any "illegitimate" children who issued from such liaisons.

The unique character of Hebrew anthropology was to a large extent lost to the later church simply because Christians in subsequent centuries began reading the Old Testament increasingly through the lens of Hellenism. As the developing church gradually adapted itself to Greco-Roman philosophy and the values of syncretistic religion, its ability to read accurately the Old Testament texts was lost. By the 4th century, when a platonic body/soul construct was adopted by the church, concupiscence was identified with sin, and sexual asceticism was elevated to the highest value. The Hebraic valorization of sex was eclipsed.

The Jews themselves had struggled against the incursions of Hellenistic philosophy, but, unlike the later church, the Jews for the most part prevailed. From the time of the rise of Greek imperial power under Alexander III the Great in the fourth century BCE, Jews were increasingly influenced by Greek thought. Those most affected spawned what has come to be known as Hellenistic Judaism. In a sense, all Jews of the period were Hellenistic, since all were affected, but some more than others.[71] In general, the more Hellenistic Jews attempted a synthesis of Greek philosophy and Jewish religious tradition. The Old Testament was translated into Greek during the early years of this period, i.e. the third and second centuries BCE. The Hellenists tended to treat the stories of the Old Testament allegorically, no

---

70 See David Novak, "Some Aspects of the Relationship of Sex, Society and God in Judaism", in *Contemporary Ethical Issues in Jewish and Christian Tradition,* Frederick E. Greenspahn, ed., Hoboken, New Jersey: KTAV Publishing House, Inc., 1986, p. 143.
71 Martin Hengel (*Judaism and Hellenism,* John Bowden trans., Phil.: Fortress Press, 1974, pp. 104-5) argues that all Judaism is Hellenistic from mid-third century on. But Geza Vermes disputes this in *Jesus and the World of Judaism,* p. 26.

Religious and Philosophical Origins

doubt in order to ameliorate their earthy offensiveness. Hellenism flourished and reached the zenith of its power and influence more or less at the beginning of the Christian era. By this time Stoicism was the dominant philosophy of Hellenism and it was through Stoicism that a platonist anthropology was promoted.[72] Philo, an Alexandrian contemporary of Jesus, was perhaps the preeminent Hellenizing Jew. His monumental and futile attempt at synthesis was rejected by subsequent rabbinic tradition.[73]

VII

In contradistinction to rabbinic tradition, the developing church did achieve a gradual synthesis with platonism, a synthesis that provided the religious and philosophical basis for medieval Christendom. The result was that the Old Testament texts began to be read in the church through the lens of platonism.

The popular modern understanding of the Torah's commandment against adultery represents one of those platonically biased misreadings of ancient tradition. The law proscribing adultery applied only to women, requiring them to limit their sexual activity to one man. There was no such requirement for men. Since a woman was regarded normally as attached to a particular man, adultery was essentially a prohibition of the invasion of a man's sphere. Adultery did not apply to married men and their liaisons with unattached women, such as widows, concubines or maidservants.

The Old Testament, as a whole, contains an abundance of sexual allusions and sexually explicit stories. But its concern about sexual issues is a concern about covenant and interpersonal responsibility within it, not a concern about sexual purity as in the Greco-Roman tradition.

The prophets repeatedly use the metaphor of the unfaithful wife, the adulteress or whoring woman, in their condemnation of Israel's faithlessness. Hosea even dares to characterize Israel as the woman who has broken her vows to Yahweh, her husband. The unfaithful woman is a poignant and powerful metaphor in the Jewish world; but it is a metaphor that does not posit sexual purity or even monogamy as an ideal. God

---

72 Martin Hengel, *Jews, Greeks and Barbarians: Aspects of the Hellenization of Judaism in Pre-Christian Period,* Philadelphia: Fortress Press, 1980, p. 68.
73 *Ibid.,* p. 99.

himself is even described by Ezekiel as polygamous. Israel and Samaria are his unfaithful wives who rival each other in adultery and whoredom (Ez 23). Jeremiah similarly describes God as the husband of both Israel and Judah. (Jer 31:32)

The David and Bathsheba story, that modern synonym for illicit sex, is another popularly misunderstood biblical text. The story is more about the abuse of power than it is about sex. David becomes enamored with Bathsheba and directs that Uriah, her husband, be left in an exposed position in battle, which results in his death. David is then free to add Bathsheba to his collection of wives. It is typical of Old Testament tradition that Nathan, the prophet, in confronting David with his crime ("You are the man!") accuses David not of lechery or concupiscence, but of using his power to take from someone less wealthy than he. "A rich man had many flocks and herds, and a poor man had one little ewe lamb." (II Sam 12:7). Nathan does not focus at all on the sexual impulses of David, nor on the sexual dimension of his relationship with Bathsheba (II Sam 12), whom he subsequently marries and who, with the succession of Solomon, becomes the Queen Mother.

In the case of the law of the levirate, the Old Testament even requires what in modern English would be defined as adultery. The rule was that a childless widow was to be impregnated by her late husband's brother (Latin *levir*), so that the family lineage would be continued. The crime of Onan was his refusal to conform to the levirate rule (Deut 25:5-10). He elected to have intercourse with his widowed sister-in-law as required but, for reasons that are not known, practiced coitus interruptus. Perhaps he was jealous of his brother's lineage, or, as some rabbis suggest, she may have been especially attractive, tempting Onan to keep her that way. Whatever his motivation, he was struck dead for his disobedience. The severity of his punishment no doubt relates to the fact that a sister-in-law is a forbidden sexual relationship except for the levirate situation.[74] Jewish tradition has not viewed this story as a lesson about the improper emission of seed. Coitus interruptus is actually recommended in the Talmud in certain situations, such as its use to protect lactating mothers for whom pregnancy would endanger the infant.[75] It is typical of later ecclesiastical distortion that Onan is memorialized in onanism, masturbation, remembered for having spilt his semen on the ground. The later

---

74   Lev 18:16; see also Feldman, *op. cit.*, p. 151.
75   *Ibid.* (Feldman)

Religious and Philosophical Origins

Christian focus shifted from Onan's abrogation of social contract, his obligation to his deceased brother and his widow, to the peripheral matter of wasted semen and autoeroticism. The shift is a fruit of the later un-Jewish concern for sexual purity.

If onanism is tangential to the story of Onan, so also is sodomy to the story of the Sodomites (Gen 19).[76] The sin of the Sodomites was inhospitality to strangers, a very serious offense in Israel. "The stranger who sojourns with you . . . you shall love as yourself; for you were strangers in the land of Egypt" (Lev 19:34). Lot welcomed the strangers in Sodom. As the story goes, he did not know they were angels of God in disguise. The xenophobic men of Sodom surrounded Lot's house and threateningly demanded "to know" who the strangers were. In the altercation Lot offered his daughters as a peace offering. The Sodomites tried to break in the house anyway, but God intervened, striking the Sodomites blind, rescuing Lot and his family and raining brimstone and fire on the city.

The shift of interpretation from inhospitality to sexual sin, specifically homosexual, probably occurred in part because the Hebrew verb "to know" in some contexts means sexual intercourse. Out of the 943 times the verb is used in the Old Testament, it refers to sexual intercourse 10 times.[77] The fact that Lot offers his daughters without success lends further credence to a perverse sexual motivation in the story. Recent scholarship proposes, however, that sexuality is not the intended issue in this story, but a later Christian revisionist interpretation. That the men of Sodom intended to assault sexually the visitors, however, cannot be ruled out. (Edwards holds the minority opinion at present that sexual assault was implied in the story, that the guests were to be buggered just as the Athenians buggered the Persians after their defeat as a token of submission and humiliation. But even so, Edwards too agrees that sex is tangential to the story.[78]) Even if sexual assault were their intent, sex is a secondary theme. In fact, the intent of the story, as Raphael Patai points out, is to show how important the duty of hospitality was, more important even than protecting women

---

76 For a thorough discussion of this see John Boswell, *Christianity, Social Tolerance, and Homosexuality*, Chicago: University of Chicago Press, 1980, p. 92 ff., and George R. Edwards, *Gay/Lesbian Liberation: A Biblical Perspective*. New York: The Pilgrim Press, 1984.
77 Derrick Sherwin Bailey, *Homosexuality and the Western Christian Tradition*, London: Longmans, Green, 1955, pp. 2-3.
78 Edwards, *op. cit.*, p. 32 ff.

from potential sexual abuse.[79] There is not even a vestige of conflict in the decision to sacrifice the daughters, rather than the guests, to the mob. Though the story doesn't say so, the daughters may even have been part of the planned hospitality for the guests, a not uncommon practice in the ancient Middle East. Certainly the ancient hearers of the story would have made that connection.

Jesus understands the sin of Sodom to be inhospitality, (Mt 10:14-15) and there is no suggestion of sexual sin in any of the other Old Testament allusions to Sodom. Nor does the Septuagint, the LXX, (the Greek translation of the Old Testament, 3rd century, BCE) translate any implication of carnal knowledge between the men of Sodom and the visitors.[80] In the five New Testament references to Sodom only one, Jude 7, lends itself to a possible sexual interpretation. This interpretation of the text, however, is called into question by scholars.[81] Irenaeus, the preeminent Christian theologian of the second century, understands inhospitality to be the sin of Sodom, as does I Clement 11:1. John Boswell points out that "the increasing emphasis of Hellenistic Jewish and Christian moralists on sexual purity gave rise in late Jewish apocrypha and early Christian writings to associations of Sodom with sexual excesses of various sorts."[82] In the early church the shift of interpretation was a gradual process which gained momentum as the Greco-Roman influences made themselves felt and as the church sought mythological and textual support for its emerging standard of sexual purity.

Augustine and some of the other church fathers attempted to explain the polygamy and concubinage of the Old Testament patriarchs as entirely motivated by a desire for progeny rather than by concupiscence. The category "concupiscence" itself is, of course, a later Christian pejorative for sensuous, erotic human impulse. Certainly procreation was high on the scale of values for the people of Israel, as the levirate law itself illustrates. There is no question, however, but that erotic and sensuous impulse played a part as well. The stories of Jacob and Rachel, Shechem and Dinah, Michal and David, and even David and Bathsheba demonstrate clearly the Old Testament affirmation of the human sexual drive.

---

79 Raphael Patai, *Family, Love and the Bible,* London: MacGibbon and Kee, 1960, p. 124.
80 But see Edwards, *op. cit.,* p. 33.
81 Bo Reicke, *The General Epistles of James, Peter and Jude, The Anchor Bible,* New York: Doubleday and Co., 1964, p. 199.
82 John Boswell, *op. cit.,* p. 97.

The preeminent biblical affirmation of the erotic and sensuous is, of course, the Song of Solomon. Throughout much of Christian history the poem has been interpreted as an allegory for the love of Christ for his church, an obvious evasion of the explicit sensuality of the poem and a victory for the platonist and Gnostic interpretation. Not only is the Song a collection of erotic love poems, but, astonishingly, the relationship between the two lovers even appears to be illicit (Song of Songs 5:7). One of the lovers is seized in the night and beaten by the authorities. Perhaps it was a matter of violating some curfew, but whatever it was there is a clear element of subterfuge, and perhaps illegality, on the part of the lovers in the story. In the 20th century Karl Barth applauded the Song as an indication of divine blessing of the erotic.[83] Rabbi Akiba Ben Joseph (40/50-135 CE) in the midst of the debate on whether to include the Song in the Hebrew Bible, declared it to be the holiest part of scripture.[84]

VIII

The roots of Western sexual values are set in the problematical dialectic between Judaic and platonic anthropology. The Jewish tradition is clear in its support of an integrated anthropology affirming sexuality. But subsequent ecclesiastical tradition is a story of the gradual victory of a dualistic anthropology, in one way or another rooted in platonism. This story is one of the most significant and fateful developments in the history of the West. This anthropological tilt toward Athens and Rome has resulted in Christianity's evolution into a "sex negative religion."[85]

David Feldman illustrates this drift of Christendom from Jerusalem in his juxtaposition of the medieval contemporaries Nahmanides and Peter Lombard.[86] The "Epistle of Holiness" of Nahmanides

---

83 Karl Barth, *Church Dogmatics III/4*, Bromiley and Torrance, Eds., Edinburgh: T. & T. Clark, 1960, p. 216.
84 Simon Cohen, *The Universal Jewish Encyclopedia* Vol. 1, p. 148. Marvin Pope thinks the *Song* has its origins in ancient Near Eastern funeral rites. In such rites food and drink were brought to the dead and a celebration took place that featured excessive eating, drinking, and orgiastic sexual acts. This celebration was meant to symbolize, according to Pope, the faith that "love is stronger than death," which was the climactic message of the *Song* itself. Pope's interpretation here is very persuasive even though he acknowledges that his conclusions are tentative. (See Marvin Pope, *The Anchor Bible: Song of Songs,* Garden City, NY: Doubleday and Company, Inc., 1977, pp. 217-227.)
85 Vern L. Bullough, *op. cit.*, p. 175.
86 David Feldman, *op. cit.*, p. 100.

maintains that pious Jews prefer the Sabbath for their marital love because it is "holy unto the Lord." Lombard, however, argues that the Holy Spirit absents himself even from the room of married folk performing the act only for purposes of generation. The more rigorous Christian moralists in the era encouraged sexual abstinence on Thursday in memory of Jesus' arrest, on Friday for his death, on Saturday in honor of the Virgin Mary, on Sunday for the resurrection, and on Monday in commemoration of departed souls. Abstinence was also called for during fasts and even certain festivals, forty days prior to Easter, Pentecost, and Christmas, from conception until birth, and seven, five or three days before receiving the Eucharist. A highly devout or scrupulous married Christian was condemned virtually to perpetual continence.[87] The medieval era is over, but negative sexual valorization continues.

The 20th century American Jewish novelist, Herman Wouk, eloquently describes Judaism's continuing valuation of sexuality:

> What in other cultures has been a deed of shame, or of comedy, or of orgy, or of physical necessity, or of high romance, has been in Judaism one of the main things God wants man to do. If it turns out to be the keenest pleasure in life, that is no surprise to a people eternally sure God is good.[88]

The first Christians were all Jews, and the church's sacred documents are Jewish. For the first 1500 years of its history, the church increasingly repudiated its Jewish roots and looked to Athens and Rome, so to speak, for its valorization of sexuality. With Luther, the tide turned and, here at the end of the 20th century, we may be witnessing a substantial recovery of the Jewish roots in the arena of sexual valorization. If so, Christianity may yet shed its presently deserved but unfortunate characterization as a sex-negative religion.

---

87 D. S. Bailey, *Sexual Relations in Christian Thought*, New York: Harper and Brothers, 1959, p. 133.
88 Herman Wouk, *This is My God*, Garden City, NY: Doubleday & Co., 1959, p. 155.

Chapter Two
Sexual Valorization in the Jesus Movement

One has either got to be a Jew or stop reading the Bible. The Bible cannot make sense to anyone who is not spiritually a Semite.
-- *Thomas Merton**

The sexual attitudes and values of the very earliest Christian communities are for the most part shrouded in a mystery that will very likely remain forever impenetrable. There is no way, therefore, to establish definitively and conclusively the sexual values or practices of Jesus, Paul or the earliest church. The data is simply too fragmentary. However, what data is available has been consistently mistranslated and misinterpreted to a degree that is remarkable, in each case to support the values of celibacy or sexual self-denial in some form or another. The New Testament is read through the lens of Greco-Roman syncretism even in the twentieth century. When we examine the data piece by piece we will see that the likely meaning is not simply different, but often in direct contradiction to what is now commonly accepted interpretation. On the basis of available data, taken as a whole, we are compelled to conclude that the New Testament is critical of marriage but affirming of sex and that this position reflects not only the ideology but the practice of the early Jesus movement.

I

The letters of Paul probably represent the furthest reach back into Christian origins. New Testament scholarship agrees that the Pauline letters are the earliest documents as such, having been written in the sixth decade of the first century, and are therefore given corresponding weight as the earliest intact primary source. Any attempt to understand Paul is complicated by problems of language and context. Paul wrote his letters in Greek, as did all the other New Testament writers. He was thereby using the administrative and commercial language of imperial Rome. Only in the third century CE did Latin supplant Greek as the language of Roman political administration in the

---

* *Conjectures of a Guilty Bystander*, Garden City, New York: Image Books, 1968, p. 14.

empire.[1] Paul was born in Tarsus, a cosmopolitan Hellenistic trade center where Greek would have been widely used. In this respect Paul contrasts sharply with Jesus, who was born in a small semitic town where Aramaic, a cognate of Hebrew, would have been the more common tongue. Jesus' sayings come down to us already having been translated at some point from Aramaic to Greek. The idiosyncrasies of the Greek construction of Jesus' sayings testify to this. Aramaic was the language of the common people of rural Palestine. It had been the lingua franca of the Medes and Persians, adopted from the Assyrians and Babylonians before them. When Alexander III (the Great) conquered the Persian empire in the late 4th century BCE, he established koine Greek (the Greek of the New Testament) as the lingua franca of the Macedonian empire. When the Romans supplanted the Macedonians in the middle second century BCE, they continued the use of the Greek language of their vanquished foes as the language of international exchange. Hence it is said that Roman political power actually furthered Hellenism as a culture.[2] Not all Italians appreciated this continued use of Greek. Juvenal, the second century CE Roman poet, disapprovingly referred to Rome as "a Greek town." In this context, the differing language use of Jesus and Paul foreshadows the encounter between the Jewish and Greco-Roman cultures which was to become increasingly problematic later.

II

Paul's letters to a large extent represent a response to a particular situation, one which must be reconstructed almost entirely from the internal evidence of the particular letter itself. Assumptions about the situation Paul is addressing therefore necessarily shape any conclusion about Paul's intended meaning. We have evidence of a number of intense dialogues between Paul and various congregations, but only one side of the record is left. Nowhere is this problem more obvious than in the radically contradictory interpretations abroad today of 1 Corinthians 7:1b: "It is a good thing for a man to have nothing to do with women...," as The New English Bible translates it. This sentence, with several other seemingly anti-erotic statements, has quite unjustifiably given genera-

---

1 Jeremy Moiser, "A Reassessment of Paul's View of Marriage," *Journal for the Study of the New Testament*, 18, June 1983, p. 107.
2 Martin Hengel, *op cit.*, p. 76.

tions of readers, including some of the most reputable New Testament scholars, the impression that Paul was negative toward sexual relationships. The New English Bible in this instance is at least fair enough to give an alternative reading in a footnote with the opposite meaning: "You say, 'It is a good thing for a man to have nothing to do with a woman.'" Commentators are today divided on the question of whether Paul is sponsoring this proposition or in fact beginning his case against it. The increasingly accepted opinion is that the NEB footnote version is the intended meaning here and that the entire section is, among other things, a critique of the sexual asceticism of certain members of the community to whom Paul is writing. But the very fact that commentators debate the question demonstrates our tenuous grasp of the actual values and attitudes of Paul in particular, and the earliest Christian communities in general.

If we follow C. K. Barrett and other New Testament commentators who subscribe to the view that Paul was actually challenging the sexual asceticism in the Corinthian church, the footnote reading of the NEB will be adopted as giving the sense of the passage.[3] Parallel evidence supports as well an assumption that Paul could be expected to oppose sexual asceticism. He was, after all, by his own admission, a born and bred circumcised Jew of the tribe of Benjamin, in legal rectitude a faultless and pious Pharisee (Phil 3:5ff). Sexual asceticism was not practiced by Pharisees and other mainstream Jews, who considered it contrary to the Torah, though it was known among splinter groups such as the Essenes and among radically Hellenized Jews such as Philo of Alexandria.[4]

As a very serious Pharisee before his conversion, Paul would have been highly circumspect in all his behavior and rigorous in his effort to be obedient to every jot and tittle of the law. Improper sexual conduct would have been as abhorrent to him before his conversion as it was after. At the same time, Paul would almost certainly have been accepting of

---

[3] C. K. Barrett, *A Commentary on the First Epistle to the Corinthians,* New York: Harper and Row, 1968, p. 154. For a contrary opinion see Gunther Bornkamm, *Paul,* D. M. G. Stalker, Trans., Toronto: Hodder and Stoughton, 1971.

[4] When I refer to "mainstream Judaism" of first century Palestine, I should perphaps add "as the Mishna and rabbinic tradition later represented it." Furthermore, Jacob Neusner has cautioned that the Mishna was not "normative" but utopian and millenarian, "a vision of how things might have been and should once more be." See *Judaism: The Evidence of the Mishna,* University of Chicago Press, 1981, pp. ix-xi, 70-71; also E. P. Sanders, *op cit.,* pp. 62, 426.

polygamy. There is no evidence to support the view that his conversion might have changed that, except, of course, that Paul places marriage in any form under so-called eschatological judgment. George Foot Moore points out how circumspect pious Jews were in their relations with women.[5] In talking to, touching and even looking at women, they were anything but cavalier. Every gesture was subject to the demands of the Torah, and this was especially true for the Pharisees. Paradoxically for the modern mind, these same Jews were not in any respect sexually abstemious or attracted to celibacy. Sex with a slave or concubine was probably acceptable, and obviously was with additional wives. The modern consciousness simply does not readily grasp the workings of a mind intensely concerned about the moral quality of every sexual gesture and at the same time accepting of sexual relations unfettered by the constraints of monogamy.

III

Even more problematic to an understanding of Paul is the highly misleading translation of the Greek word Paul uses for "improper sexual conduct"---*porneia*. Almost every English version of the New Testament translates *porneia* as "fornication." In modern English, fornication means "sex outside the bounds of marriage." In Greek, *porneia* has the root meaning of prostitution. In Hellenistic times and particularly in early Christian Palestine, the word clearly developed a broader meaning than prostitution narrowly defined. As Bruce Malina points out, *porneia* probably had come to mean for Greek-speaking Jews "any unlawful sexual conduct," that is, anything prohibited by the Torah.[6] However, the Torah does not prohibit fornication. The modern English word "fornication" is simply not an identifiable Hebrew category. *Porneia* as used by Paul should be translated "sexual immorality as delineated by the Torah and its interpretation in Rabbinic tradition."

The New Testament use of Greek *porneia* essentially continues the

---
5 George Foot Moore, *op. cit.*, Vol. II, p. 267.
6 Bruce Malina, "Does *Pornea* Mean Fornication?" *Novum Testamentum*, Vol. XIV, 1972, pp. 10-17; also, Francis Firth, "Catholic Sexual Morality in the Patristic & Medieval Periods," *Human Sexuality and Personhood*, St. Louis: Pope John Center, 1981, pp. 36-52.

Hebrew *zanah*, meaning "illicit sexual behavior as defined by the Torah." *Zanah* has two main connotations: adultery and cultic sexual activity, referred to less precisely in modern times as "cultic prostitution." By metaphorical extension, *zanah* connotes also faithlessness in relation to God. It is interesting to note that Brown, Driver, and Briggs translate *zanah* as "fornication," whereas Holladay more correctly translates it as "illicit intercourse."[7]

New Testament references to *porneia* sometimes suggest the sexual immorality associated with various pagan religious rites. Thus, when Paul writes in 1 Cor. 10:8 that 23,000 were slain in one day for *porneia,* he is making reference to cultic sexual practice.

> Do not be idolaters, like some of them; as Scripture has it, 'the people sat down to feast and stood up to play.' Let us not commit *porneia,* as some of them did---and twenty-three thousand died in one day. (An allusion to Numbers 25:1,9 and Exodus 32:6. His numbers are a little off.)

Idolatry, or a competing religious cult, is the concern here, not sexuality as such. Similarly, in 1 Cor. 6:9-10, 15-18, Paul links *porneia* with idolatry. He compares linking oneself with a religious prostitute and uniting with Christ.

> Make no mistake: no *pornoi* or idolater, none who are guilty of adultery or of homosexual perversion, no thieves or grabbers or drunkards or slanderers or swindlers, will possess the Kingdom of God . . . Do you not know that your bodies are limbs and organs of Christ? Shall I then take from Christ his bodily parts and make them over to a harlot (*porno*i)? Never! You surely know that anyone who links himself with a harlot (*pornes*) becomes physically one with her (for Scripture says, "The pair become one flesh."); but he who links himself with Christ is one with him, spiritually. Shun *porneia*. Every other sin that a man can commit is outside the body; but the one who commits *porneia* sins against his own body.

This suggests Paul was thinking in this instance of porneia as a form of prostitution, or sexual immorality, associated with pagan cultic practices, as for example the cult of Venus.[8] By no stretch of the imagination

---

7 Brown, Driver, and Briggs, *A Hebrew Lexicon of the Old Testament,* Oxford at the Clarendon Press, 1907, corrected 1971; William L. Holladay, *A Concise Hebrew and Aramaic Lexicon of the Old Testament,* Grand Rapids, MI: William B. Eerdmans, 1971.
8 Frank Bottomley, *Attitudes To The Body in Western Christendom,* London: Lepus Books, 1979, p. 34.

could this be taken as any kind of comment about the question of sex outside of marriage.

So also Acts 15:19 and 21:25 would seem to support a connotation of *porneia* as cultic sexual activity. It is included in a list of ritual or cultic prohibitions required of Gentiles joining the predominantly Jewish early Christian communities. Converting Gentiles were excused from keeping the Jewish law except that they observe four prohibitions:

> eating meats sacrificed to idols
>
> *porneia*
>
> eating anything strangled
>
> eating blood

Porneia as strictly a social code here would make it out of place in this list.

The unmistakable linkage of *porneia* with pagan cultic practices is given further support and a slightly new slant by the biblical scholar, Marvin Pope. Pope notes that the threat of *porneia* in the New Testament is often associated with the early church's love feasts. (1Cor 10:7; 2 Pet 2:13 [Note the variant reading "reveling in their love feasts."]; Jude 12-13.) He suspects a relationship between the churches' love feasts and contemporaneous Near Eastern funeral love feasts. These mortuary love feasts included ritually excessive eating, drinking, and orgiastic sexual acts as part of a pagan affirmation that love is stronger than death (Song of Songs 8:6). Pope assumes that Christian love feasts, which were also celebrating the affirmation that "love is stronger than death," were both partially informed by as well as endangered by the pagan rites.[9]

The importance of *porneia* to Paul's theology can be measured in part by the fact that the word does not even appear in his letter to the Romans, which was his "greatest piece of sustained theological writing," written at the height of his powers as a theologian and preacher.[10]

Among Paul's several references to *porneia*, 1 Cor 5:1 ff. is unique in that Paul appears unusually vexed. In no other discussion of sexual issues does Paul exhibit the kind of intensity of feeling and

---

9 Marvin Pope, *The Anchor Bible: Song of Songs*, Garden City, NY: Doubleday and Company, Inc., 1977, pp. 226-8.
10 C. K. Barrett, *The Epistle to the Romans*, New York: Harper and Row, 1968, pp. 1,4.

unambiguous denunciation that he does in this reference. Paul is responding to a report that someone in the community "has the wife of his father."

> I actually hear reports of *porneia* among you, immorality such as even pagans do not tolerate: the union of a man with his father's wife. And you can still be proud of yourselves! You ought to have gone into mourning; a man who has done such a deed should have been rooted out of your company . . . this man is to be consigned to Satan for the destruction of the body, so that his spirit may be saved on the Day of the Lord.(NEB)

The vehemence and intensity of Paul's reaction here is understandable because, unlike most of the references to *porneia* in the Pauline literature, which are generalized, this one is a specific and unambiguous abrogation of the Torah, in fact a capital crime (Lev 18:8, 20:11).[11] Nowhere in Paul, or anyplace else in the New Testament, does *porneia* assume the boundaries of modern English "fornication", sex outside of marriage.

IV

Paul is often portrayed as a proponent of celibacy. However, when the texts presumed to support celibacy are examined closely, such an interpretation cannot be supported. The entire basis for representing Paul as an advocate of celibacy is his recommendation "against marriage," or what is commonly thought to be so. The problem of grasping where Paul stands on the subject of sex and marriage becomes at this juncture extremely complex. To understand Paul, a distinction must be made between sex and marriage. Paul confronts marriage, but not sex, with the so-called eschatological challenge, so that Paul's negativity toward marriage, such as it was, should not be taken blindly to be a negativity toward sex as well. Once again, Paul was a sex-affirming Jew and not an ascetic Greek philosopher. One of the most respected modern commentators on the early Christian movement misses the mark on this issue in quite a surprising way. Wayne A. Meeks first contends---erroneously, I believe---that Paul was a proponent of celibacy, monogamy and in general the sexual values of the Greco-Roman

---

11 C. K. Barrett, *A Commentary on the First Epistle to the Corinthians*, New York: Harper and Row, 1968.

world.¹² He then expresses puzzlement as to why Paul never links sex to procreation as the pagan philosophers did. Meeks does not seem to take into account the basic difference between the pagan and the Jewish world in the manner in which they valued sexuality. (Meeks does acknowledge that, in spite of Pauline suggestions to the contrary, there is no basis for assumptions of widespread sexual license in the pagan culture of the time.)

Contrary to popular notions, most scholars assume that Paul was at some point in his life married. In the absence of clear evidence either way, we have to assume that he was, simply because marriage was a clear religious obligation for a pious Jew. A Jewish male was expected to marry at about age 18 and those who had not married by age 20 were subject to criticism and perhaps penalties.¹³ The sages varied as to the appropriate marriage-age window for males, ranging from 16 to 24. Most seem to get concerned about a male unmarried at age 20. Hillel and Shammai had agreed in the same period that no one may abstain from fulfilling the first commandment of the Torah: "Be fruitful and multiply".¹⁴ In all the Old Testament, Jeremiah (16:1-4) is the only male thought to have refused marriage, having been so commanded by God because of the impending destruction of the nation. "You shall not marry a wife . . . you shall have neither son nor daughter in this place." (Jer 16:1-4) The catastophe is coming and all sons and daughters, husbands and wives will be food for birds and beasts. This is not a general commandment to Jeremiah, but a command distinctively specific to time and place. Marriage was not simply normative; it was required by divine commandment. The unmarried were considered to be without goodness because the Torah teaches that it is not good for man to be alone.

One late second century (CE) rabbi, ben Azzai, did refuse marriage in order to devote himself fully to the Torah but he is remembered as an extraordinary individual because of it. He was not considered exemplary. Quite the contrary, he is compared to a murderer deserving death in that he refused to obey the commandment to procreate.¹⁵ The Mishna regards unmarried men as suspect, clearly because sexual abstinence was not held in esteem. It was as if to say,

---

12 Wayne A. Meeks, *The First Urban Christians: The Social World of the Apostle Paul,* New Haven: Yale University Press, 1983, pp. 101 ff.
13 BT Kiddushin 29b.
14 BT Mishna, Yeb. 6.6.
15 BT Yebamoth 63b. Cf. Gen 1:28; 9:6-7.

"If a man wasn't married, what *was* he doing sexually?" Hence, an unmarried man was prohibited from teaching children, herding cattle, and from sleeping under the same cloak with another unmarried man.[16] That Paul could have evaded in silence this religious obligation to marry, well established in mainstream Judaism both before and after him, is at least unlikely. More likely he knew and observed the Talmudic proverb (written later, but reflecting a long oral tradition): "When is the fear of the Lord pure and enduring? When one marries first and studies the Torah afterward . . . He who reaches the age of 20 and has not married spends all his days in sin or thoughts of sin."[17] Or, he may well have known the Talmud's assertion that in the world to come the first three questions asked of a man are: Did you buy and sell in good faith? Did you have a set time for study? Did you procreate?[18]

The belief that Paul was married during his Christian period was widely held during the early centuries of the church. Clement of Alexandria (c.150-211/15) thought that Paul was married and that he did not take his wife with him on his journeys simply because of inconvenience.[19] Origen still later also assumed that Paul was married.[20] In his *Ecclesiatical History (3,3)*, Eusebius in the 4th century also reports that Paul, like the other apostles, was married. So too does the longer version of Ignatius' Letter to the Philadelphians (IV), which is thought to be an elaboration of the original.[21] These two latter works, as J. Massingberd Ford says, are even more credible in that they come from a period of history when virginity and sexual abstinence were already well established.[22] Jerome in the 4th century also advises not to "pay any attention to those who pretend that Paul had a wife."[23] We do not know who Jerome is referring to, but given Jerome's passionate contempt for sex in any form, his opinion on this matter is predictable.

Many modern scholars surmise that Paul was a widower or divorcee during his Christian years; some even suppose his wife may have left him because of his conversion.[24] The basis for such assumptions is

---

16 BT Kuddushin 4:13,14.
17 BT Kiddushin 29b.
18 BT Shabbat 31a.
19 *On Marriage* 3:3.
20 J. P. Migne, *Patrologiae Cursus Completus* (Latin), 14.839.
21 Migne, *op.cit.* (Greek), 5.825.
22 J. Massingberd Ford, "Levirate Marriage in St. Paul," *New Testament Studies*, Vol. X (63-4), p 361.
23 *Ep.* 22.20.
24 F. F. Bruce, *Paul: Apostle of the Heart Set Free,* Grand Rapids, Mich.: William B. Eerdman's Publishing Co.,1977, p. 269.

I Cor 7:7-9:

> I should like you all to be as I am myself; but everyone has the gift God granted him, one this gift and another that. To the no longer married and to widows I say this, it is a good thing if they stay as I am myself; but if they are not controlling themselves, they should marry. Better be married than burn with vain desire.

"Be as I am myself" and "Stay as I am myself" have been made to carry much more weight than the phrases allow. Some scholars even take the liberty of translating this as "remain single as I do."[25] Paul may mean that he is "no longer married" or a "widower." Clearly he is living a life in some way comparable to such, but he could mean simply that he is a married man living separately, temporarily perhaps, for the sake of his mission. He may be presenting himself as at once married and living as though not married (1 Cor 7:29), "not making any radical gestures . . ."[26] Furthermore, C. K. Barrett says that Paul is not advising here that the persons addressed should be like him, rather that they should stay as they are.[27]

Actually Paul may have been addressing his wife in his letter to the Philippians (4:3) requesting hospitality for certain women who assisted him in his work. As usual, Paul makes a few personal comments as he brings his letter to a close.

> I beg Euodia, and I beg Syntyche, to agree together in the Lord's fellowship. Yes, and you too, my loyal (*gnesie*) spouse (*syzyge*), I ask you to help these women, who shared my struggles in the cause of the Gospel, with Clement and my other fellow-workers, whose names are in the book of life.

The addressee is "*syzyge*" which means "spouse" in classical Greek, in the koine Greek Paul wrote, and in modern Greek as well. *Syzygos* (nominative case) means literally "yoke-partner," which provides the basis for most English translations ("true yokefellow" in the King James

---

25 For example: Eric Fuchs, *Sexual Desire and Love: Origins and History of the Christian Ethic of Sexuality and Marriage,* Marsha Daigle, Trans., New York: The Seabury Press, p. 75.
26 See the argument of Jeremy Moiser, *op. cit.,* p. 107.
27 Barrett, *op. cit. (Cor. Com.).*

Version and Revised Standard Version, and "loyal comrade" in NEB).[28] "Spouse" is the most natural and least complicated translation here, but translators have resisted it consistently. Obviously, if 1 Cor. 7:8 (discussed above) means that Paul was celibate, as Calvin and many others have thought, then he could not be addressing a wife here. However, with that passage open to question, we are no longer forced to assume Paul was celibate as we examine Philippians.[29]

If Philippians 4:3 is approached with an entirely open mind about whether Paul was married or not, "spouse" would have to be offered as the probable translation. "*Syzygos*" appears in Plato, Aeschylus, and several times in Euripides as "spouse." (It also appears as "comrade" in Euripides.) In post-New Testament usage the word is also used of one of a pair. Both Clement of Alexandria[30] and Origen[31] translated it as "spouse," which is perhaps the strongest evidence of all, since they were closer to the culture and Greek was their native language. Both Luther and Erasmus in the sixteenth century likewise translated the word "spouse."[32] So did Joseph-Ernest Renan, the renowned nineteenth century French theologian.[33] Furthermore, the "one addressed" here is asked to provide hospitality to certain visitors, a very natural request to make of a wife.

Further support for this argument is provided by the adjective "tested," "true," or "lawful" (*gnesie*), which precedes "*syzyge*" in Philippians 4:3. As Kittel says, the adjective and noun together "suggest the one addressed had a specific relationship with Paul which might have been limited in time and space but which was in some sense unique while it lasted."[34] Such a charac-

---

28 The same root word "yoke" appears in Mk 10:9, "What God has yoked together..."
29 John Calvin, *The Epistle of Paul the Apostle to the Galatians, Ephesians, Philippians and Colossians,* T.H.L. Parker, trans., D.W. Torrance and T.F. Torrance, eds., Edinburgh: St. Andrews Press, 1965, pp 285-6.
30 *On Marriage* 3:53: "Even Paul did not hesitate in one letter to address his consort," says Clement.
31 Migne, *op. cit.* (Latin), 14.839 (Ep ad Rom-Com 1:1).
32 *Luther's Works,* Vol. 28, Hilton C. Oswald, ed., St. Louis: Concordia Publishing Co., 1973, p. 22.
33 E. Haenchen, *The Acts of the Apostles*, Oxford: Oxford University Press, 1971, p. 494.
34 Gerhard Delling, *Theological Dictionary of the New Testament,* Vol. VII, (known commonly as "Kittel") Gerhard Friedrich, ed., Geofffrey W. Bromiley, trans./ed., Grand Rapids, Mich.: William B. Eerdman's Publishing Co., 1971, pp. 749-50. However, Delling does not think that Paul was married.

terization would fit perfectly Paul's own marriage, if he had one. "Let those who are married be as though they are not . . . " (1 Cor 7:29) was not a call to celibacy or divorce, but a paradoxical invitation to be married and "as though not married" at the same time.

The reluctance of modern scholarship to grant "spouse" as a possible, much less probable, reading of Philippians 4:3 has been universal and at times bordering on the hysterical. The Interpreter's Bible calls it a "wild conjecture" and an "absurdity." F. F. Bruce dismisses it as a "romantic fantasy," but on what grounds he thought it either romantic or unworthy of consideration he does not say.[35] F. W. Beare[36] says that "the wildest of all conjectures" is that the person addressed here is Lydia, Paul's wife. He does not specify exactly what would be "wild" about this. He argues that the addressee must be a male because of the masculine ending of the adjective, *gnesie*, an argument disputed by other Greek scholars,[37] who maintain that the gender of the addressee here cannot be determined conclusively. Beare's principle argument, however, is the common one, that a married man could not have written 1 Cor 7:7-9 & 32-4. Karl Barth recognized the problem here and proposed that "*syzygos*" might have been a proper name, which is the choice made by the Roman Catholic translators of The New Jerusalem Bible. Unfortunately for this argument, there is no other evidence for the use of such a name.[38] Furthermore, the adjective preceding makes it unlikely that it is a proper name. The fact is that it is not possible to determine with certainty what Paul meant by *syzygos* here, but the possibility that he was addressing his wife, whom he may have seen little of in the course of his work, is at least as plausible as any and clearly the most natural.

The conjecture that the "spouse" addressed in Philippians was actually Lydia is not so "wild" a suggestion as some scholars think. She is referred to as "a dealer in purple fabric" and was "a worshipper of God," i. e. a gentile convert or Jewish sympathizer. She "opened her heart" to Paul, responded to his teaching, and was baptized along with her household. "If you have judged me to be a believer in the Lord, I beg

---

35 F. F. Bruce, *op. cit.*, p. 209. Bruce also adds that Paul preferred celibacy, but thought monogamy the norm for Christians and declares it "reasonably clear that Paul was celibate throughout his apostolic career."
36 *A Commentary on The Epistle to the Philippians,* London: Adam & Charles Black, 1959, p. 144.
37 Specifically, Prof. Christopher Bryan, The School of Theology, University of the South.
38 William F. Arndt and F. Wilbur Gingrich, *A Greek English Lexicon of the New Testament,* Chicago: University of Chicago Press, 1957, p. 783.

you to come and stay in my house," she is quoted as saying to Paul. She not only invites Paul into her home; she insists. Paul was later arrested, beaten, and imprisoned in Philippi. When he was released he returned to Lydia's home. (Acts 16:14-15, 40.) It is not impossible that Paul took Lydia as a spouse in this context. "Taking a wife" was a quite different enterprise in that context than it is now.

Whether he was married or not, which is of little consequence in itself, Paul was not actually negative toward sex and only in a very qualified way negative toward marriage.

V

Much of the theorizing about Paul's views has tripped up on the anachronistic presupposition that sex is strictly limited to monogamy. Such an assumption is the cause of attributing to Paul such un-Jewish notions as celibacy. That Paul held to a view of sexual relations strictly limited to the boundaries of monogamy, the view held later by the church, is most unlikely. Paul seems to be quite affirming of sexuality in and of itself, as one would expect of a mainstream Jew. He is negative toward marriage only in the very restrictive sense that he confronts marriage---but not sex!---with the eschatological challenge. "Those who have wives be as though they had none" (1 Cor. 7:29) is not a call to celibacy or abstinence but simply a challenge to the claims of marriage as an institution in light of the eschaton.

The so-called "eschatological challenge" is the pivotal concept in the understanding of Paul, as well as Jesus and the entire early Christian community. Probably no other concept is more critical to an understanding of the New Testament. Eschatology derives from the Greek *eschatos* meaning "furthest, uttermost, extreme, or last." The eschatology of the early church promoted the belief that life is lived on the boundary of existence, on the edge of something new coming into being. This may have included but is not necessarily limited to the belief that history is literally about to end in some form of doomsday scenario. It is widely thought the early church generally subscribed to such a view. More likely, the early Christian communities were quite varied in their views, as some recent scholarship has emphasized.[39] It is apparent that some, if not most, of the earliest com-

---

[39] See especially Edward Schillebeeckx, *Jesus*, New York: Crossroad, 1979, and James M. Robinson and Helmut Koester, *Trajectories Through Early Christianity,* Philadelphia: Fortress Press, 1971.

munities of the Jesus movement held the view that in the person of Jesus an entirely new way of looking at life was inaugurated, that God was indeed on the side of this new way, and that it offered a challenge to all institutions, political, religious and otherwise. This kind of "eschatology" would not need to be literalistic and would not necessarily include a doomsday event. In fact, some of the early Christian communities may have known what Norman O. Brown later wrote, that to literalize the symbols is actually to rob them of their meaning.[40] With the texts we have, there is simply no way to form a definitive answer to the question.

It is astonishing that so many modern scholars reject New Testament eschatology as irrelevant to the modern world, after first having literalized it. So David Cartlidge asks: "What do we do with an eschatological ethic when we no longer expect the eschaton?"[41] Likewise, Gunther Bornkamm writes that "eschatology can mean nothing to us today."[42] By contrast, Jurgen Moltmann is one who in his various writings has emphasized and reemphasized that eschatology is the very heart of the New Testament faith. So Pheme Perkins similarly points out that, while the love command in the New Testament is not unique, the eschatological anticipation of final judgment is.[43] A literalized New Testament eschatology must, of course, be rejected. But it is we who suffer from what Schillebeeckx calls "the crude and naive realism . . . through our unfamiliarity with the distinctive character of the Jewish biblical way of speaking."[44] First having distorted eschatology from a literalistic bias, we then reject it as meaningless. However, God may be still today on the side of what is coming into being, just as the early church thought he was then. Eschatology that includes a literalized doomsday scenario may be nothing more than a vulgarization of the original eschatology of the Jesus movement.

For Paul, then, marriage was simply part of the scheme or "the whole frame of this world" which is in the process of being transformed, that is, subject to the eschatological challenge (1 Cor 7:31). Business and commerce were put under the same judgment.

What I mean, my friends, is this. The time we live in will not

---
40 Norman O. Brown, *op cit., passim.*
41 David Cartlidge, "I Corinthians 7 as a Foundation for a Christian Sex Ethic", *The Journal of Religion*, Ap 1975, Vol. 55, No. 2, pp. 220-34.
42 Gunther Bornkamm, *Paul,* D. M. G. Stalker, Trans., Toronto: Hodder and Stoughton, 1971, p. 208.
43 Pheme Perkins, *Love Commands in the New Testament,* New York: Paulist Press, 1982, p. 1ff.
44 Schillebeeckx, *Jesus,* p. 346.

last long. While it lasts, married men should be as if they had no wives; mourners should be as if they had nothing to grieve them, the joyful as if they did not rejoice; buyers must not count on keeping what they buy, nor those who use the world's wealth on using it to the full. For the whole frame of this world is passing away. (NEB)

All institutions were challenged as provisional, seen therefore as distractions from the central agenda at hand. At the same time he is not abolishing them. In a sense he is even strengthening them by acknowledging their rightful existence. As in the case of marriage, he authorizes those who need to to marry. But he relegates it to the realm of this world which is of little consequence when compared with what is coming into being. What is now coming into being transcends marriage even if it does not abolish it. This is the eschatological challenge.

It is possible, of course, that Paul was devaluing marriage specifically because of its patriarchal character, which may well have been precisely that feature of marriage that rendered it especially unfit either for the eschaton or the new communities that were preparing for that eschaton. More likely he saw marriage simply as one of the various institutions in the present order rendered irrelevant in light of what God was bringing into being.

The fact is that Paul seems to exhibit sexist attitudes at times, specifically in 1 Cor 11:2-15:
> ... while every man has Christ for his head, woman's head is man, as Christ's head is God ...

and 14:34-5:
> As in all congregations of God's people, women should not address the meeting. They have no license to speak, but should keep their place as the law directs. If there is something they want to know, they can ask their own husbands at home. It is a shocking thing that a woman should address the congregation.

It has been suggested by some that these reactionary statements on Paul's part may have been simply attempts on his part to cool the ferment created by his earlier proclamation of neither male nor female in the new community, as for example in Galatians 3:28:

> There is no such thing as Jew and Greek, slave and free, male and female; for you are all one person in Christ Jesus.[45]

Thus Paul's sexist reaction needs to be seen in the context of his (earlier?) proclamations of gender liberation. In other words, we may be seeing evidence of an internal conflict within Paul himself, as Fiorenza argues. Just as he counters the sexist circumcision rite with universal baptism, so he rejects the Judaic path of salvation for women---marriage and childbearing. In the new community sexual imperialism seems to have been abolished. Marriage, being intrinsically patriarchal, is consequently no longer necessary for Christians as it was for Jews. "Straw in the wind" though it may be, we also note that Paul, in a decidedly un-Jewish manner, addresses the woman first in his greeting to Prisca and Aquila (Rom 16:3).[46]

When Paul criticizes the churches at Thessalonica and Corinth for the apparent sexual excesses of libertinism or antinomian behavior, it is simplistic and misleading to interpret these sexual excesses as random aberrations or moral lapses. Rather they are more likely the direct consequences of the community's eschatological thrust into the new age, "the last age," the eschaton, where there is neither marriage nor giving in marriage. These excesses were likely the direct result of Paul's own preaching as he founded the new communities. The young churches probably considered themselves unencumbered by orders and institutions of the old and dying age, such as marriage, work, or established authority of any kind. As Werner Kelber puts it, "It is no accident that the fundamental norms of the human condition . . . were all subject to the eschatological challenge."[47]

The Christian community in Corinth probably attempted to establish new and idealistic patterns of social life rooted in their understanding of freedom in light of Paul's teaching that everything is permitted (1Cor 10:23) and all have knowledge (gnosis, 1Cor 8:1ff). The

---

45 For elaboration of this argument see Elizabeth Schussler Fiorenza, *In Memory of Her*, New York: Crossroad, 1984, pp. 205ff.
46 See Ben Witherington, "Rite and Rights for Women---Gal. 3:28," *New Testament Studies*, Vol. 27, No. 5, October 1981, pp. 593-604.
47 Werner Kelber, *The Oral and Written Gospel: The Hermeneutics of Speaking and Writing in the Synoptic Tradition, Mark, Paul and Q*, Philadelphia: Fortress Press, 1983, p. 171.

results, however, were chaos.[48] What Wayne Meeks calls the Corinthians' "cosmic audacity," their claim to a higher spirituality disassociated from the created world, produced the fruits of both asceticism and libertinism in the same community, each of which Paul attempted to counter. In the face of this cosmic audacity, Christians presuming themselves to be living *wholly* in the new age, the eschaton, Paul's burden is to bring them back down to earth and creatureliness.[49] In the process Paul may have set in motion, as Meeks suggests, a conservative reaction that resulted ultimately in the kind of misogyny manifested by the later Pastorals, Timothy and Titus.[50] The extraordinary power of the eschatological challenge may have been simply too dangerous and powerful for the young communities, who ultimately felt compelled to dilute the eschatological challenge into a pale metaphor of Christ literally coming *someday* to judge the world.

The basis on which Paul attempted to restrain the sexual behavior of the young church at Thessalonica is especially noteworthy.

> This is the will of God, that you should be holy: you must abstain from *porneia*; each of you must learn to gain mastery over his body, to hallow and honor it, not giving way to lust like the pagans who are ignorant of God; and no man must do his

---

48 David R. Cartlidge, "I Corinthians as a Foundation for a Sex Ethic,"*The Journal of Religion,* Vol. 55, No. 2 (April 1975), pp. 220-34.
49 Ben Witherington, *op. cit.,* p. 598.
50 Meeks, (*op. cit.,* p. 208), states that misogyny, not likely from Paul, manifests itself in the following: "A woman must be a learner, listening quietly and with due submission. I do not permit a woman to be a teacher, nor must woman domineer over man; she should be quiet. For Adam was created first, and Eve afterwards; and it was not Adam who was deceived; it was the woman, who, yielding to deception, fell into sin. Yet she will be saved through motherhood---if only women continue in faith, love and holiness, with a sober mind." (I Timothy 2:11-15) "Younger widows may not be placed on the roll. For when their passions draw them away from Christ, they hanker after marriage and stand condemned for breaking their troth with him. Moreover, in going round from house to house they learn to be idle, and worse than idle, gossips and busybodies, speaking of things better left unspoken. It is my wish, therefore, that young widows shall marry again, have children, and preside over a home; then they will give no opponent occasion for slander. For there have in fact been widows who have taken the wrong turning and gone to the devil." (I Timothy 5:11-15) [These men] "insinuate themselves into private houses and there get miserable women into their clutches, women burdened with a sinful past, and led on by all kinds of desires, who are always wanting to be taught, but are incapable of reaching a knowledge of the truth." (II Timothy 3:6- 7) "...the younger women [should] be loving wives and mothers, temperate, chaste, and kind, busy at home, respecting the authority of their own husbands." (Titus 2:4-5).

brother wrong in this matter, or invade his rights, because, as we told you before with all emphasis, the Lord punishes all such offences. For God called us to holiness, not to impurity." (NEB) 1 Thes 4:3-7.

This is an echo of the Torah's prohibition of adultery as well as an exhortation to sexual restraint. Paul is saying here essentially what he says in the Corinthian letter, "Do not go beyond what is written."[51] He is also establishing holiness as the basis for Christian sexual ethics, holiness juxtaposed to uncleanness (vs. 3 & 7). But this holiness does not in any way imply abstinence; rather for those nurtured on the Torah the opposite would be the case. Holiness would prohibit abstinence! Meeks calls this a key passage (1 Thes 4:1-8) for understanding the early church's sexual values because the section is part of a catechismal formula and therefore indicates an already established tradition.[52] Meeks rightly considers the accusation of lust directed against pagan society (vs. 5) "not objective" but hyperbolic.[53] Paul could well be thinking of cultic *porneia* here. In any case, it is obvious that he did not choose to simplify sexual ethics on a new basis by stating quite simply, as contemporary Greek and Roman philosophers had and as Athenagoras did a hundred years later within the church, that sex was for procreation in marriage and abstinence otherwise the rule. Paul was not creating a new law beyond what was already written in the Torah. Paul was a sex-affirming Jew and not a sex-negating platonist.

Paul in his own words makes it abundantly clear that he is not prescribing a new mode of ascetic life. He assures the reader that all these injunctions are by way of concession, not command (1 Cor 7:6), adding that these are his words and not the Lord's (vs. 12 & 25). He wishes that everyone would remain as he is, meaning, as Moiser says, "not making any radical gestures in view of the end."[54] The only "word of the Lord" that Paul reports on this subject is the "prohibition" of separation, divorce and remarriage.(1 Cor 7:10-11)

No new law, new institutions, or new patterns of human relationships are successfully created from the eschatological challenge itself; nor is that the intent of it. Whatever is newly created will itself be subject to the same challenge. That is why Paul can be quite revolutionary in one moment and in another quite supportive of existing patterns of the urban bourgeois, as in his directive for wives to be subject

---
51 Kelber translation of 1Cor 4:6, *op.cit.*, p. 177.
52 Meeks, *op.cit.*, p.100.
53 *Ibid.*, p. 101.
54 Moiser, *op. cit.*, p. 107.

to their husbands and instructions supporting traditional headwear in I Cor 11. The dialectic between the present order, even as it is in the process of change, and the eschatological challenge is quite subtle and is never finally resolved in human history.

VI

If marriage is marked for eschatological challenge and therefore in some profound sense robbed of any ultimate authority or permanence, sexuality itself seems to be treated differently. The "end" does not abolish sex or the body. We see this in Paul's argument against consorting with prostitutes in which he contends that in sexual intercourse the parties become one flesh in the way Christians become one body with Christ.

> You surely know that anyone who links himself with a harlot becomes physically one flesh with her (for Scripture says, "The pair shall become one flesh"); but he who links himself with Christ is one with him, spiritually. Shun *porneia*. Every other sin that a man can commit is outside the body; but the one who commits *porneia* sins against his own body. Do you not know that your body is a shrine of the indwelling Holy Spirit, and the Spirit is God's gift to you? You do not belong to yourselves; you were bought at a price. Then honour God in your body (I Cor 6:16-20).[55]

C. K. Barrett interprets this section to mean that "sexual intercourse, unlike eating, is an act of the whole person and therefore participates not in the transiency of material members but in the continuity of the resurrection life."[56] Sex and marriage are distinguished and separated from each other in a remarkably radical fashion. Sex belongs to the ultimate fulfillment of history; marriage does not.

Paul seems to equate the sexual union of bodies with the bodily union of the community with Christ, a remarkable equivalency. In striking contrast, Paul had just said (vs. 13) that food was for the belly and the belly for food and one day God will destroy both. Sex is therefore radically differentiated from eating. Furthermore, there is no good reason to see the metaphor as a limitation of this union to only two persons, much less to two persons for life. Polygamy is not ruled

---

[55] Note here that Paul could have saved himself a lot of argument had he subscribed to the Stoic view that sex was for procreation within monogamy and served no other good purpose.
[56] Barrett, *op. cit.*, (*Cor. Com.*), p. 148.

out by this section. The same could be said of the later, probably non-Pauline, comparison in Ephesians (5:23ff) of marriage with the relationship of Christ and his church.

> In loving his wife a man loves himself. For no one ever hated his own body . . . that is how Christ treats the church, because it is his body, of which we are living parts . . . a great truth is hidden here. I for my part refer it to Christ and to the church, but it applies also individually: each of you must love his wife as his very self; and the woman must see to it that she pays her husband all respect.

As Karl Rahner says of this metaphor, "With a little ingenuity, anything can be compared with anything else."[57] This metaphor of love, intimacy and commitment in no way requires monogamy. It is perhaps straining the metaphor a bit, but nonetheless true, that Christ is presumably non-monogamous with his bride, the church, since the church, though in some sense is one, is in fact many, and there are also persons outside the fold whom he presumably loves as well. Even though we see in Ephesians evidence of a rapprochement with Roman culture, specifically in its adoption of Stoic household codes ("Wives, be subject to your husbands, etc . . . ." 5:22 ff), we do not yet have in Ephesians the Stoic commitment to monogamy, much less its "sex for procreation" doctrine, both of which were adopted later in the history of the church.

I Corinthians 7:32-34 provides the strongest prima facie evidence in Paul that he favored celibacy:

> I want you to be free from anxious care. The unmarried man cares for the Lord's business; his aim is to please the Lord. But the married man cares for worldly things; his aim is to please his wife; and he has a divided mind. The unmarried or virgin (or the no longer married and widowed) woman cares for the Lord's business; her aim is to be dedicated to him in body as in spirit; but the married woman cares for worldly things; her aim is to please her husand.

The unmarried are in a better position, he says, to dedicate themselves to the Lord. But C. K. Barrett[58] argues that while Paul is not wholly consistent here, his teaching overall supports a holiness that glorifies God in the use of sexuality and that Paul here is not promoting sexual

---
57 Karl Rahner, *Inquiries,* New York: Herder and Herder, 1964, p. 289.
58 Barrett, *op. cit.*(Cor. Com.), p. 181.

denial. As Barrett points out, Paul in numerous other places contends that God commands persons to glorify him with their bodies (Rom 6:12; 12:1; I Cor 6:6,15,18,20; 15:44; 2 Cor 4:10; Gal 6:17; Phil 1:20; 3:21; 1 Thes 5:23). Once again, however, we must keep in mind that this section refers to marriage and not to sexuality as such. What we may be seeing here is a conflict in Paul himself who is both sex-affirming and yet critical of marriage from an eschatological perspective.

On certain sexual issues Paul seems actually rather permissive, as in 1 Cor 7:9. The English translations are misleading. Giving directives to the "no longer married and widows", Paul says: "But if they are not controlling themselves, let them marry." The English translations misrepresent Paul's Greek here by translating "but if they cannot control themselves they should marry." (NEB)[59] The subtle shift in translation of the verb here gives an entirely different picture of Paul's attitude and values. Paul, in fact, seems to be referring to persons who are already engaging in sex outside of marriage. The verb "control" here later came to mean "total sexual abstinence." It may mean that here, but it probably means something less absolute than total abstinence, that is, "If they are not presently managing their sex lives well . . . " Note also that in the next sentence we are reminded that it is Paul speaking here and not the Lord, the effect of which is to temper the degree of authority of this section.

Paul also appears quite permissive in Romans 7:23. Writing in the context of our obligation to the law only in this life, he says:

> For example, a married woman is by law bound to her husband while she lives; but if her husband dies, she is discharged from obligations of the marriage-law. If, therefore, in her husband's lifetime she consorts with another man, she will incur the charge of adultery; but if her husband dies she is free of the law, and she does not commit adultery by consorting with another man. (NEB)

It is difficult to read this any other way than that Paul is non-judgmental about sexual activity of a widow. And in this respect he would be quite consistent with Rabbinic teaching of his time.

Another curious suggestion of permissiveness appears in Paul's claim of the right to travel with a "sister" as a "wife/woman." The King James translation is quite literal: (1 Cor 9:5).

> Have we not power to lead about a sister, a wife, as well as the other apostles, and as the brethren of the Lord, and Cephas?

---
59   *Ibid.*, p. 161.

The NEB takes some liberties to translate:
Have I no right to take a Christian wife about with me . . . ?

The awkwardness of the King James translation reflects the awkwardness of the original Greek which has a peculiar double accusative in both "sister" and "wife/woman." (*Gyne* means "woman" but by extension can also mean "wife," depending on the context.) Commentators have differed over the meaning, but most ultimately settle on the opinion that, in spite of the peculiarity of the Greek, Paul meant simply that he had a right to take one of the believing women as a wife with him on his missionary journeys. Of course, he could have meant: "Have I no right to take a wife as a sister?" or, "Have I no right to take a 'sister' as a traveling companion?" The peculiar Greek here and the ambiguity of wife/woman may well reflect a situation in the early Christian community whereby some were simply cohabiting in light of the eschatological challenge to marriage. As horrifying as such a prospect might be to Stoics and the later Western middle class, that is a distinctly cogent reading of this passage. Given the Jewishness of the earliest Christian communities, Paul may have been alluding to such a practice here.

VII

It is known that a pattern developed in the earliest communities of sending out missionaries in pairs and that such pairs were at least sometimes of mixed gender. Were they celibate? Unlikely. Were these couples married? There is no way to be sure, particularly when the critique of marriage must have been stronger than it was later when most of the New Testament documents were finally written. Considering the Jewish affirmation of sexuality and the eschatological challenge to marriage, the earliest communities must have been of a peculiarly open ambience.

The missionary couple, Prisca (Priscilla) and Aquila, are referred to by Paul simply as a pair, without any reference to marriage or sexuality. He manifests a disinterest in their sexual/marital status that is typical of the New Testament generally. The author of Acts, perhaps a generation or more later, refers to Aquila and "Priscilla his gyne" ("woman", 18:2). Identifying a woman by way of her attachment with a man is typical of the culture of the time. That they were considered married is perhaps a reasonable conjecture. Furthermore, one would expect the later documents, and specifically the author of Luke and Acts, to tidy up the picture of the early church in a more conservative direction as he does in other issues.

Any discussion of the marriage of Prisca and Aquila, as well as the other paired missionaries, is always in danger of slipping into anachronism. We must be careful not to impose a certain framework on the early church that does not fit. Since polygamy was at least tolerated and marriage not a religious rite, the only significant moral question raised by the Torah would be whether the woman was married to or claimed by another man. If the pairs traveling together were sexual partners, that was enough in Jewish eyes to establish the man's claim over the woman, as well as to establish his responsibility for her welfare and the welfare of any children that might result. In the eyes of the syncretists, of course, a very pious couple would not be sexual partners whether they were married or not.

VIII

On the subject of sex and marriage, the section of Pauline material that has puzzled commentators more than any other is I Cor 7:25ff: "On the question of the virgins . . . " (RSV) or as the NEB with some liberty translates: "On the question of celibacy . . . " The Greek reads literally "virgins" (*parthenon*). (Paul here is responding to a query addressed to him, the substance of which we have to guess [cf. 7:25].) A credible explanation for who these virgins were has been hard to come by. Some have suggested they were wards or step-daughters, but the suggested marriages to such persons in verse 36 would appear to rule that out. Others have suggested that virgins here refers to spiritual or celibate marriages (hence NEB trans.), but such a practice is not known during this period in the church. The most plausible explanation has been made by J. Massingberd Ford[60] who proposes that "the virgins" were not virgins at all but young "once-married" widowed sisters-in-law. She claims support from Jewish sepulchral inscriptions during the

---

60 J. Massingberd Ford, "Levirate Marriage in St. Paul," *New Testament Studies,* Vol. X (63:4), p. 362.

first through the third centuries CE, which refer to the "once-married", both male and female, as virgins.[61] Ignatius of Antioch at the end of the first century also refers to "the virgins called widows," a statement which lends further support to Ford's argument.[62] I suggest that this is a curious example of the Jews transforming a Greek sexual purity category to suit their own sexual value system. In other words, a virgin among the Greeks is equivalent to the once-married among the Jews. In any case, Ford's reasoning is that these young once-married widowed sisters-in-law, if childless, would call forth the levirate obligation under Jewish law, an obligation that surely continued to be felt in the early Jewish-Christian communities. The levirate obligation on the brother-in-law would also result in polygamy (or fornication! by modern definitions) for those brothers-in-law who were already married. Note that Paul adds: "It is not wrong" for them to marry (vss. 28 & 36). Literally, he says: "They do not sin." Since polygamy was unacceptable in Greco-Roman society, unlike the Jewish community, the more Hellenistically oriented Jews may have been embarrassed by polygamy and the levirate obligation. Obviously, so would the Corinthian ascetics. Here Paul might be giving his blessing to the polygamy involved in fulfilling the levirate obligation, which Greco-Romans would have considered a "sin." The argument used against Ford's interpretation, that monogamy was so firmly established in the early Christian communities that polygamy was not an issue, is an argument that cannot be supported by data.[63] In fact, Mark 12:18ff, Matthew 22:24 and Luke 20:27ff seem to be direct references to ongoing levirate practice. Note also that Paul adds (vs. 39) that "a wife is bound to her husband as long as he lives." But if the husband dies she is free to marry whom she will, provided the marriage is within the Lord's fellowship. He does not say the same about a man being bound to his wife because that would have been absurd in a polygamous culture (also Rom 7:13).

Even the reliable C. K. Barrett argues against Ford's interpretation on the grounds that the levirate obligation was an obscure piece of Jewish law incomprehensible to the Corinthian church. However, the obligation was hardly obscure to Jews and was observed at least

---

61 See Harry J. Leon, *The Jews of Ancient Rome,* Philadelphia: The Jewish Publication Society of America, 1960, p. 130.
62 Epistle to the Smyrnaeans 13.
63 Nevertheless, for such an opinion see William E. Phipps, *Was Jesus Married?* New York: Harper and Row, Publishers, 1970, p. 103, and F. F. Bruce, *1 and 2 Corinthians,* London: Oliphants, 1971, p. 74.

into the Middle Ages in Europe and even into the present day by Sephardic Jews of the East. If Barrett means that the Torah would have been obscure to gentile Corinthian believers, he may be correct. However, the Corinthian church was at least partly Jewish. Crispus, who was one of the officers in the Corinthian synagogue, became a believer with all his household (Acts 18:8). Jewish believers, including Paul himself, continued to obey the Torah. Becoming a Christian resulted in a new perspective on the law, but it did not result in any cavalier abandonment of it. Therefore, some members of the Corinthian church would likely have taken the levirate obligation seriously, even as believers in the new way.

The following is a free translation of I Cor 7:25-28,36-38, drawing partly from C. K. Barrett and using Ford's translation of "virgin" as "widowed sister-in-law:"

> About the young widowed sisters-in-law I have no charge from the Lord, but I give my opinion, as one who by the Lord's mercy is trustworthy. I consider that on account of the present necessity this is a good thing, namely, that it is a good thing for a man to stay as he is. Are you bound to a wife? Do not seek release. Are you free from a wife? Do not seek one. But if you do marry, you have committed no sin; and if the widowed sister-in-law marries she has committed no sin . . .
>
> Whoever feels embarrassed by his obligation to his widowed sister-in-law, if she is passing the age of marriage, he has an obligation, let him go on doing what he wants. (Or, as C.K. Barrett prefers: "But if anyone considers that he is not behaving in a seemly way . . . if he is oversexed, and so it must be, then let him do what he wishes.") He commits no sin. Let them marry. On the other hand, he will do well who is already firmly committed in his affections, and is under no necessity, but has authority over his own will, and has determined in his own heart simply to take care of and watch over his sister-in-law without sexual involvement. He who marries his sister-in-law does well, but he who does not will do better.

None of the proposed translations of this section can be promoted with a high degree of confidence. It may be, for example, that the "virgins" in question referred both to widowed sisters-in-law and the yet unmarried. However, a Jewish perspective on this text results in quite a different meaning from the more traditional Greco-Roman perspective.

IX

If Paul seems impenetrable, Jesus is more so by geometric proportions. We have Paul's writings but we have no letters or documents of any kind written by Jesus. We have only the impressions of others written a generation or more after his death in a language Jesus did not speak, drawn probably from several decades of oral transmission. Further, the letters of Paul, the earliest written material, manifest little interest in biographical data about Jesus. Any sort of biography of Jesus based on all available data could at best reveal but the shadow of an historical figure. The actual person of Jesus undoubtedly left sharp and distinct impressions on many people, but the picture that is retrievable today is one that can be made only of broad strokes.

As to whether Jesus was married or not, the same argument would have to be made as in the case of Paul. That is to say, it would have been quite atypical for a male Jew of his time and place not to be, and no historical data suggests that he grew up in any way but the traditional one. That he was taken to the Temple at age 12 (Lk 2:41ff) or that he taught in synagogues regularly (Lk 4:15-16) and was called Rabbi (Jn 1:48 et alia) are indications, whatever their historical value, of a mainstream Jewish upbringing. A refusal to marry would have been extraordinary, and we have no data to support it. On the other hand, Geza Vermes seems to take for granted Jesus' celibacy and argues for a tradition of what he calls "prophetic continence."[64] At the same time he admits the weakness of the argument, granting that the Jews of Jesus' day had considered the age of prophecy to be past. But the more serious weakness to his argument is that the basis of his hypothesis of prophetic celibacy consists of a few comments in the Talmud and Philo, the latter the pre-eminent Hellenizing Jew, and hardly a reliable source for mainstream Jewish practice and belief. Finally, as if to undermine his entire argument, Vermes adds that Rabbinic obligation during the time of Jesus was "marriage for the purpose of procreating children." However, Vermes is partly wrong there, too. The purpose of marriage was for procreation *and* because it was not good for man to be alone!

---

64 Geza Vermes, *Jesus the Jew: A Historian's Reading of the Gospels*, London: Fontana/Collins, 1973, p. 100.

The Gnostic Gospel of Philip represents Jesus as intimately related (*koinonos* means "partner") to Mary Magdalene. Its portrayal of Jesus is unabashedly sensuous:

> ... But Christ loved her more than all the disciples, and used to kiss her often on her mouth. The rest of the disciples were offended ...[65]

The historical value of such material is difficult to assess. On the one hand the Gnostic literature was generally late, in this case estimated from the late third century, and the mainstream church accused the Gnostics of inventing stories about Jesus. Much of the Gnostic material has the distinct mark of invention. But that can be no basis for discounting the historicity of all Gnostic material out of hand. Helmut Koester suggests, for example, that the Gospel of Thomas, thought to have been composed c.140, may contain some tradition that is even earlier than the canonical gospels.[66] It is somewhat ironic that the flesh-denying Gnostics here present a picture of Jesus that is more sensuous than that of the mainstream church. However, it must be noted that Gnostic sensuousness was often a peculiar brand of sensuous abstemiousness, which the Shepherd of Hermas also exhibits to some extent. In fact, it is simply not known whether Jesus was married or not, or the nature of his sexual experience, and we probably never will know for lack of data.

The speculation that Jesus did marry is not novel. The most recent proponent of such a view is the monastic Episcopalian, Bonnell Spencer, who calls the idea of a married Jesus "a good guess" given the available data. Spencer thinks that Jesus lost his wife before the beginning of his public ministry, which is the period focused on by the four Gospels. Spencer assumes that if Jesus had a wife during his last years she would have been mentioned in the Gospels, which is, though plausible, an unwarranted assumption.[67] William E. Phipps presents a case favoring a married Jesus and concludes that Jesus actually promoted monogamy.[68] The fatal limitation of this otherwise interesting and thorough study is that the author considers only two possibilities for Jesus' life, celibacy or monogamy.

It is impossible to determine with certainty whether the New Testa-

---

65 *The Nag Hammadi Library*, James M. Robinson, ed., New York: Harper and Row, 1978, p. 138.
66 *Ibid.*, p. 117.
67 Bonnell Spencer, *God Who Dared to Be Man*, New York: Seabury Press, 1980, p. 87.
68 Phipps, *op. cit.*

ment authors thought of Jesus as married or as ever having been married. Their silence on the subject is ambiguous. In his culture, where virtually every male married between the ages of 18 and 22, silence could suggest conformity. However, if he were about 30 when he was crucified, silence about a young widow, and/or children, would seem odd. New Testament silence about a young crucified Jesus would tend, therefore, to support the argument that he never married. If he were middle aged, silence about a wife, and even children, becomes less significant. It also increases the possibility that he was a widower.

The mixture of legend and history about another rabbi a generation or so later, Akiba ben Joseph (40/50-150 CE), might be instructive on the subject. It is said that Akiba raised a family and at age 40 decided to study the Torah at the academy in Jabneh. After twelve years he returned home to see Rachel, his wife. On reaching his village he overheard her answering her neighbor's taunts about her absent husband. Rachel acquitted herself well, saying she would be happy for him to stay another twelve years if by so doing he would reach his goal. Thereupon Akiba left immediately for another twelve years of study. When he finally returned home one hundred disciples came with him. In the village welcoming crowd Akiba spotted his wife timidly lingering amongst the villagers. Pulling her out of the crowd Akiba hailed her as the true author of his success.[69]

In this piece of legend/history certain basic attitudes of Talmudic Judaism toward marriage present themselves. The sequence of marriage first, then study, was preferred. Rabbinic studies did not nullify the marital and sexual obligation. Rachel was exceptional in the generosity of her permission for Akiba to be absent and thereby to accept sexual deprivation. We see also that rabbinic studies were very much a male domain. The disciples of a middle-aged rabbi take precedence over his wife, at least in the eyes of the public. Akiba was generous to present his wife to the crowd and give her her due credit. While this story does not tell anything about Jesus, it does describe something of the public perception of a rabbi. In light of Akiba, silence about Jesus' wife does not appear significant, especially if he were at least in his middle years. On the contrary, silence about any presumed celibacy on Jesus' part must be considered strange.

The available data on Jesus' age at his crucifixion is quite fragmentary

---

69 Simon Cohn, *Universal Jewish Encyclopedia*, Vol. I, p. 148.

and hopelessly contradictory. Among established and reputable scholars George Ogg argues for an age of 44, with his birth in 11 BCE and death on April 3, 33 CE.[70] Ogg is not alone in his view, but the majority view at present seems to support an age of 37.

The traditional and popular view that Jesus was 30 or in his early 30 s at his death is supported by some of the Lucan data, but it was the Gnostics who really promoted the case for a young Jesus at his death, as Irenaeus tells us.[71] Gnostics thought that Jesus must have "left the earth" at some ideal or perfect age, which at least some of them took to be 30 plus one.

The numbering system of the Common Era, *Anno Domini* ("in the year of the Lord"), is based on the calculation that Jesus was born in the year "0." This form of dating history was introduced around 525 by a Scythian monk, Dionysius Exiguus, who objected to the practice during his time of dating from the reign of the Emperor Diocletian. Some have argued, though, that Dionysius merely popularized what had begun at least as early as Hippolytus in the third century.

By the very nature of the evidence, Jesus' death date is far more certain than his birth date. All four Gospels support the historicity of the crucifixion event at or before Passover when the Procurator was Pontius Pilate. The range of possible crucifixion dates runs from 27 to 33. Practically everyone supports either 30 or 33. There is no seriously contradictory data involved, but simply a matter of deciding the most likely date of an historical event that occurred sometime in the window of 27 to 33.[72]

Jesus' birth date is another problem altogether. The data available from early Christian sources is irreconcilable, as follows:

–Jesus was born during the reign of Herod the Great who died in 4 BCE after a 33-year reign. (Mt 2:1; Lk 1:5)

–Jesus was born when Quirinius was governor of Syria, 6-7 CE, at the time of the first census of its kind. (Lk 2:2) Quirinius did carry out a census in 6 CE, but whether it was the first is a matter of some speculation and debate. The first census in Egypt was carried out under the authority of Augustus in 23 BCE, the second in 9 BCE, the third in 6 CE, and at 14 year intervals thereafter.[73] Some think that general

---

70 George Ogg, *Peake's Commentary on the Bible,* Matthew Black and H. H. Rowley, eds., London: 1962, p. 728.
71 *Against Heresies,* 1.19.
72 See esp. Harold Hoehner, *Herod Antipas,* Cambridge: Cambridge University Press, 1972.
73 G. B. Caird, *Interpreters' Dictionary of the Bible,* Vol. I, p. 600.

pattern was followed throughout the empire. Some also think that Quirinius may have been governor of Syria more than once, at an earlier date.

—If Jesus were "about 30" when he began his ministry in the 15th year of Tiberias, as Luke indicates (Lk 3:1,23), then a birth date of "about 0" is indicated. Tiberias' 15th year is variously fixed at 25-29 CE, probably 28 or 29.

—Jesus' disputants tell him that he is "not yet 50" (Jn 8:57) which suggests he was close to 50, and therefore his birth date would be around 20 BCE, assuming the disputation occurred in his late years.

—Irenaeus (c120/140-c200/203) thought Jesus was about 50 and cites two pieces of supporting data. He took John 8:57 ("You are not yet 50.") at face value, but even more significantly, he had oral tradition that claimed Jesus lived about five decades.

As we see, Luke provides actually three possible dates, or windows, for Jesus' birth: 7 CE, "about 0-6 CE," and sometime before 4 BCE. Raymond Brown is among those who think it neither possible nor necessary to reconcile the conflicting data in Luke. Brown is willing to allow Luke's inconsistencies to demonstrate that he is simply not that interested in precision dating. Brown cites the glaring historical inaccuracies in Acts 5:36, also written by Luke, to support his argument.[74] Traditionally, scholarship on Christian origins has neglected Irenaeus in favor of Luke, no doubt because Luke is in the canon of Holy Scripture and also chronologically earlier. Irenaeus, however, should be given more weight than Luke on the matter of history. Irenaeus addressed explicitly the question of how old Jesus was at the end, whereas Luke only made allusions, and furthermore, allusions that are self-contradictory. It is not even apparent that Luke cared about Jesus' age at the end. The lack of internal consistency in Luke is really the most damaging evidence against Luke as a historical source on this matter. Irenaeus, on the other hand, is a very credible and reliable witness. According to Samuel Laeuchli, he is the most theologically sound churchman in the second century. He knew Polycarp, who in turn knew the disciple John in Ephesus. From that source he got the report that Jesus was no young man at his death. As he somewhat clumsily put it:

> . . . from the 40th and 50th year a man begins to decline towards old age, which our Lord possessed while he still ful-

---

74 Raymond E. Brown, *The Birth of the Messiah,* Garden City, New York: Doubleday, 1977, p. 554.

filled the office of a teacher, even as the Gospel and the elders testify; those who were conversant in Asia with John, the disciple of the Lord, affirming that John conveyed to them that information.[75]

He adds that John lived up to the age of Trajan, 98 CE. Thus we have good warrant for a view of Jesus as having reached about age 50. The only resistance to such a view is offered by the Gospel of Luke. Strangely enough, Irenaeus, who himself knew and accepted the Gospel of Luke, apparently had no difficulty meshing the reading of Luke with his own view that Jesus reached an age of about 50.

Finally, in the tantalizing exchange in John 2:19ff, Jesus is asked for a sign:

> He replied, "Destroy this temple and in three days I will raise it again." His opponents answer, "It has taken 46 years to build this temple. Are you going to raise it again in three days?" But the temple he was speaking of was his body.

Josephus reports that Herod undertook to build the temple in 20-19 BCE. The 46th year would have been 26-27 CE, if Herod "started" the year he "undertook" to build. The temple was still under construction during Jesus' life, completed finally in 64 CE. Since the passage is a double entendre of the temple and Jesus' body, it is tempting to think that Jesus and the temple may have been the same age, and that the coincidence had provided the platform for a discussion of mortality, of buildings on the one hand and persons on the other.

From the point of view of personality and character development, it seems unlikely that Jesus would have achieved the significant depth and wisdom capable of bringing on the reaction he got had he had only a brief ministry in his early 30 s. Some things are accomplished only through time and aging.

While no certainty can be reached about Jesus' age at his death, the preponderance of evidence points to his having at least passed his mid-thirty mark, and very substantial evidence supports the case for a Jesus crucified when he was about 50, especially if Irenaeus is given due credit. A 50-year-old Jesus does not prove that he was at any time married, but it makes it easier to incorporate the likelihood of his having married at one time or another.

---

75   *Against Heresies*, 2.22.5&6.

X

The remnants left to us of Jesus' life pertaining to sex and marriage are meager. Perhaps the most significant and radical aspect of Jesus' life in this respect is the consistent portrayal of his unconventional relationships with women, attested to by the canonical Gospels and some of the extra-canonical literature as well. He shocked even his disciples (Jn. 4:27) with the casual manner in which he flouted religious and social customs regarding women.[76] One can conjecture how this behavior was regarded by his detractors. Strict Jewish religious practice at that time did not permit a man to speak publicly even to his own wife, much less to a strange woman, a requirement rooted in Pharisaism, not in sexual asceticism.[77] The Gospels contain several episodes of Jesus relating to women in public places and in a manner that would have been considered brazen. The Samaritan woman of John 4:1ff and the woman in Luke 7:36ff are the most striking examples. The former is not only a woman, but a Samaritan of many husbands or lovers, so the urgency for a pious Jew, especially a Rabbi, to give her wide berth was great.

The unnamed woman in Luke 7:36 (with parallels in Mt 26:6ff, Mk 14:3-9, Jn 12:1ff) is identified as a sinner, a label attached to a variety of persons who did not keep the Torah, from prostitutes and tax collectors to fruit peddlers and seamen.[78] The woman looses her hair, itself a public gesture of intimacy. She wets Jesus' feet with her tears and then dries them with her hair. She then kisses his feet and anoints them with ointment. This was an act of extraordinary intimacy. If the episode occurred as Luke records it, it must have horrified pious Jews who heard of it. There are exegetical problems with the Lucan account. Matthew, Mark and John tell a similar story differently and less offensively. Jesus' head is anointed by an unnamed woman in Matthew and Mark. In John, Mary of Bethany anoints Jesus' feet and wipes them with her hair, all done with decorum, without tears or kissing his feet. Whether the various stories are variants of one original or different incidents that have become intertwined, it seems clear that Jesus was at least anointed by a woman, or women, in some manner

---

76 See esp. Leonard Swindler, *Biblical Affirmations of Women,* Philadelphia: The Westminster Press, 1979, p. 194.
77 See esp. Paul Ricoeur, *The Symbolism of Evil,* Boston: Beacon Press, 1967, p. 118 ff.
78 Fiorenza, *op cit.*, p.128.

and that objections were raised about it. However, Robert Holst argues that Luke's account is based on a very early source and more accurately reflects an actual occurrence than the other parallel accounts.[79]

Jesus appears to have had women disciples (Mt 27:55, Mk 15:40, Lk 8:1), women who even left home and openly traveled with him, for pious Jews an "unheard of breach of custom."[80] They are all given lesser status than the male twelve. This could mean that Jesus, though at some points outrageously unconventional, was on that issue following social custom. More likely, the Gospel accounts in one degree or another softened Jesus' assault on the patriarchal order by demoting the women in the written record. Similarly, women are further demoted in the even later misogynous letter to Timothy where women are saved not through discipleship but through childbirth (1Tim 2:15).

XI

Sparse as it is, Jesus' teaching about sex, marriage and women is as radical as his behavior. The commandment against adultery in the Torah and rabbinic interpretation was directed against women, not men. For a married man to have sex with an unattached woman was not adultery, but for a married woman to have sex with anyone other than her husband was adultery and made her subject to the death penalty. Jesus makes two radical interpretations of the Torah's adultery law. (Rabbis were continually interpreting the Torah.) He announces that men who divorce their wives and marry another commit adultery (Mt 19:9: ". . . if a man divorces his wife for any other cause than *porneia*, and marries another, he commits adultery." Mk 10:11-12: "Whoever divorces his wife and marries another commits adultery against her: so too, if she divorces her husband and marries another, she commits adultery." Lk 16:18: "A man who divorces his wife and marries another commits adultery; and anyone who marries a woman divorced from her husband commits adultery.") Though each is different, these sayings are directed toward men, especially the earliest (probably) of the three, Mark, with his pointed "against her." Since men were within their legal and religious rights to divorce their wives and marry another, this would have been received by men as an out-

---

[79] "The Anointing of Jesus", *Journal of Biblical Literature*, 1976, pp. 435-46. But see also Fiorenza, *op. cit.*
[80] Swindler, *op. cit.*, p. 194, and Schillebeeckx, *op. cit.* (1979), p. 344.

rageous inhibition of their options. Outrageous, too, in that Jesus turns the commandment against men in the same way it had been historically directed against women. Jesus confronted with judgment those who least expected it.

There is no evidence, however, to suggest that Jesus is espousing in this teaching a program of monogamy, which would have been a Jewish innovation. Rather he was undermining a legalistic ploy used by men to discard undesirable wives. Economics was no doubt the hidden agenda here, and perhaps the most compelling reason for a man to discard a wife. If he was sexually attracted to or in love with an available woman, he was presumably free to take an additional wife, provided he could afford her. Subsequent ecclesiastical tradition misunderstood and trivialized this teaching by turning it into a new and narrow rule, a categorical and legalistic prohibition of divorce, as if Jesus taught a new law, which he clearly disclaims. The Roman Catholic Church's recent policy of permitting escalating numbers of annulments is a cynical legalistic strategy which permits divorce by calling it something else. This maneuver is a way of both misunderstanding Jesus' teaching and at the same time subverting it.

Matthew 5:28 is another radical interpretation by Jesus of the Torah's adultery law: "If a man looks at a woman with desire, he has already committed adultery with her in his heart." The Greek word for "desire" *("epithumia")* can also mean "lust". It has both neutral and negative connotations. The context determines the meaning. If Jesus intended to bring men---all men, it seems---under the judgment of this law, "desire" is the likely meaning here. "Lust" is easier to evade. The manner in which he broadens and internalizes this law is similar to the way he deals with the law against murder (Mt 5:21-2). Anyone who nurses anger is under judgment as a murderer. Thus Mt 5:28 is a reminder that all men are adulterers. As Karl Barth put it in his own unique way:

> . . . it not only may but must be said that all are equally accused, each in his own and none in just the same way, but each in such sort that, especially affected at this point, he is unable to excuse, much less justify himself . . . [81]

The fact that subsequent tradition uses Jesus' teaching in an attempt to quash erotic impulses altogether is a travesty and distortion of it. The original thrust of the teaching is therefore turned upside down by sub-

---

[81] Karl Barth, *Church Dogmatics,* III/4, Bromiley and Torrance, Eds., Edinburgh: T. & T. Clark, 1960, p. 233.

sequent history as it is transformed into a means by which the sexually inactive, the sexually suppressed, or celibates may feel innocent.

Of Jesus' teaching on sexual issues, the one given the most weight in subsequent theology is his citation of Genesis (1:27 and 2:24 in Mt 19:4-6 and Mk 10:6-9):

> A man shall leave his father and mother . . . they shall become one flesh.

Jesus (or Matthew and Mark) adds to the Genesis,

> What God has joined together man must not separate.

Eric Fuchs calls this the most important New Testament text on sexuality.[82] What Fuchs means is that on this saying is built the entire case for monogamy in subsequent Christian theology, including his own. This is an astonishing inflation of this passage, particularly since Jesus' own Jewish tradition did not interpret Genesis to be an endorsement of monogamy.[83] It is clearly an affirmation of sexual union, possibly of marriage in some form, but not necessarily monogamy. The thrust of Jesus' own addition to the Genesis citation is likely no more than an assault on divorce and, for what it is worth, the New Testament context is a discussion of divorce. The rabbis of the time differed on the acceptable grounds for divorce. The school of Rabbi Shammai considered adultery and moral misconduct as the only grounds. Hillel accepted even the most trivial reason.[84] The purpose of the question was probably to force Jesus to side with one school or the other. Jesus responds with a blanket criticism of the practice of men divorcing their wives. The thrust here seems to be his concern for the abuse of women. This saying cannot be stretched to support an argument for monogamy. It is notable, furthermore, that for all Jesus' reinterpretation of the adultery commandment, there is no record of his criticizing polygamy which was practiced at least to some extent in his time.

This saying of Jesus has also been stretched to support the concept of androgyny, Plato's myth on the origin of sexuality. Much has been made of the change in wording from the Genesis, "They become one flesh," to the New Testament's "the *two* become one . . . they are no longer two

---

82   Eric Fuchs, *op cit.,* p. 41.
83   Gerhard von Rad, *Genesis*, Philadelphia: The Westminster Press, 1972, p. 85.
84   The Mishna, Gitten 9:10.

individuals."[85] This argument is established on the weakest sort of literalistic exegesis. If either Jesus or the authors of the New Testament narrative meant this to be an endorsement of androgyny, the theory of cosmic coupling, they do not well serve the theory by slipping it in unobstrusively between the lines of a discussion of divorce. Admittedly, we could have here the shards of a larger, lost teaching of Jesus in support of androgyny. But if this is the case, history has left only one obscure fragment to work with.

Indeed there were some rabbis who argued for a synthesis of Genesis and Plato. Eve taken from Adam's rib can be and was interpreted by some as a prototype of Plato's androgyny. The Talmud bears witness to this teaching at some points. However, the teaching never received wide acceptance in rabbinic tradition. Androgyny postulates a cosmic coupling, "a marriage made in heaven" of one man and one woman. The idea has ignited the imagination of many throughout history---not least of all, the modern romantics.[86] This ideology remains essentially alien to Hebrew theology and mainstream rabbinical tradition.

Each of the three synoptic Gospels records the dialogue between Jesus and the Sadducees on the question of whose wife a woman would be in the resurrection if she married successively seven brothers (Mt 22:23ff, Mk 12:18ff, Lk 20:27ff). Jewish hearers would understand the question as an attempt at entrapment. The fictional woman in question did not have seven husbands by choice but by the requirements of the Torah, specifically the law of the levirate. Each succeeding brother dies without issue and it therefore becomes the obligation of the next brother to marry the widow in order to continue the family line. Each of the seven successive brothers would likely have had other wives as well. The levirate law was set in the context of polygamy, and compliance with the law actually promoted polygamy. The Sadducees themselves did not believe in a resurrection, but for those who did, this story has a certain hook. Note that the dilemma is presented in androcentric, or patriarchal terms. A woman can belong only to one man. The attempt here is to force Jesus to deny either the resurrection or the

---

85 Arland J. Hultgren, *Jesus and His Adversaries,* Minneapolis: Augsburg Publishing House, 1979, pp. 120ff, and David Daube, *The New Testament and Rabbinic Judaism,* New York: Arno Press, 1973, pp. 72ff.

86 See Dennis deRougement, *Love in the Western World.*Montgomery Belgion, trans., Greenwich, Conn.: Fawcett Publications, Inc., 1956. For the best modern argument in support of androgyny, see Suzanne Lilar, *Aspects of Love in Western Society*, Jonathan Griffin, trans., London: Thomas and Hudson, 1965.

The Jesus Movement

Torah. Matthew and Mark represent Jesus responding:
> You are mistaken, you know neither the scriptures nor the power of God. At the resurrection, men and women do not marry, but are like angels in heaven.

Luke represents Jesus responding somewhat differently:
> The men and women of this world marry; but those who have been judged worthy of a place in the other world and of the resurrection from the dead, do not marry, for they are not subject to death any longer. They are like angels; they are the sons of God because they share in the resurrection.

Each of these responses challenges in some respect the institution of marriage and certainly undermines its cosmic significance, relegating it to "this world." The eschatological challenge to marriage manifests itself here. Matthew and Mark seem to place this challenge on the other side of death, whereas Luke is quite clear that the challenge is in effect in this life. "Those worthy of the resurrection do not marry," he says.

Luke's version could be construed to support celibacy or sexual asceticism. But such a reading is not persuasive. It must be kept in mind that Jesus in all three accounts is commenting on marriage, not sex. As even Barth argues, Jesus did not say there will be no male and female in the resurrection, rather simply no marriage.[87] We are perhaps seeing here the remnants of Jesus' radical criticism of patriarchal marriage and an invitation to his disciples not to marry under those terms. Such a radical teaching is consistent with his teaching as a whole. Such a critique of patriarchal marriage would not necessarily preclude some other form of heterosexual pairing or committed relationship.

Furthermore, we have evidence that the intimate followers of Jesus were heterosexually active in some manner, which itself would seem to rule out the celibacy interpretation here. Tertullian, 150 years later, in advocating sexual abstinence, argued that the Apostles lived with their wives "as sisters." But there is no evidence in the New Testament to support such an un-Jewish mode of life.

The participants in the early Jesus movement may very well have undertaken heterosexual commitments or quasi-marriages even though they rejected patriarchal marriage. They could subsequently have been perceived by the Gospel writers simply as married. "Peter's mother-in-

---
[87] *Church Dogmatics* III/4, p. 143.

law" could just as well have been the mother of Peter's "woman." We must always keep in mind the inevitable conservatizing trend in the Gospels, written one or more generations after Jesus' death.

Traditionally the best supporting text in the argument in support of celibacy is Matthew 19:9-12:

> I say to you: whoever divorces his wife, except for *porneia*, and marries another, commits adultery. The disciples said to him, If such is the case of a man with his wife, it is not expedient to marry. But he said to them, "Not all men can receive this teaching, but only those to whom it is given. For there are eunuchs who have been so from birth, and there are eunuchs who have been made eunuchs by men, and there are eunuchs who have made themselves eunuchs for the sake of the kingdom. He who is able to receive this, let him receive it.

It is not plausible that Jesus is promoting castration here, but many have been persuaded that this is a metaphorical call to celibacy. If it was a call to celibacy, it is peculiar that none of his disciples paid any heed to the teaching following Jesus' death. Paul points out that he and Barnabas are alone in traveling without female companions. (1Cor 9:5)

Some who think this is a call to celibacy believe it to be a point of similarity between Jesus and the Essenes who practiced a form of partial celibacy. Other commentators propose this saying as a poetic defense of monogamy, the argument being that men who renounce divorce make themselves eunuchs, in effect, if the marriage fails. This rather strained interpretation has received little support. If accepted it would be the only clear advocacy of monogamy in the Bible, and in this instance a rather severe form of monogamy.[88]

L. William Countryman offers the most persuasive reading of this text and he turns the traditional interpretation on its ear. He argues that this is not a sexual teaching at all, but rather an assault on the patriarchal family. He first notes that the context is one in which Jesus has deprived the male of his privileged patriarchal prerogative of divorcing his wife to marry another. Jesus equates such a move with adultery. His

---

[88] See W. F. Albright and C. S. Mann, *The Anchor Bible: Matthew,* Garden City, N.Y.: Doubleday and Company, Inc., 1982, pp. 1-10; William E. Phipps, "Did Jesus or Paul Marry?" *Journal of Ecumenical Studies*, Vol. 5, No. 4, Fall 1968, p. 741; Fuchs, *op. cit.*, p.240; Quentin Quesnell, "Made Themselves Eunuchs for the Kingdom of Heaven (Mat. 19:12)," *Catholic Biblical Quarterly,* 30 (1968), pp. 335-58.

disciples respond saying that if such is the case it is better not to marry. The cutting issue here is Jesus' encroachment on male authority in the family, and thus in fact an assault on the cornerstone of the family itself.

The eunuch is the one kind of male who is incapable of being a patriarch. Some eunuchs are indeed sexually competent, but none are reproductively competent. It is the patriarchal position in a family that eunuchs were universally deprived of rather than sexual gratification itself. As Countryman says, "Jesus was acknowledging, then, that his prohibition of divorce effectively dissolved the family and made eunuchs of all men, for it deprived them of the authority requisite to maintain their patriarchal position and keep their households in subjugation to themselves as the unique representatives of their families." Thus what appears on the face of it to be a teaching advocating an ascetic sex ethics actually appears to be a teaching which subverts the entire hierarchical institution called family.

The data on Jesus' life and teaching on sex and marriage is therefore inconclusive, but it suggests that of a rabbi[90] who was both well immersed in mainstream Judaism, and at the same time one who was at points critical of accepted religious opinion of his day, to a revolutionary degree.

XII

In Matthew and Luke Jesus is portrayed as tolerant of a pederastic relationship between a centurion and his "boy." Scholars believe the story is part of a common source document (Q), or oral source shared by Matthew and Luke.

> A centurion there had a slave (*doulos*) whom he valued highly (or who "was very precious"); this slave was ill and near to death. Hearing about Jesus, he sent some Jewish elders with the request that he would come and save his slave's life. They approached Jesus and pressed their petition earnestly: "He deserves this favor from you," they said, "for

---

89 L. William Countryman, *Dirt, Greed and Sex,* Philadelphia: Fortress Press, 1988, p. 176.
90 To refer to Jesus as a rabbi is somewhat anachronistic in that the office was not as clearly formed as it is today. See Geza Vermes, *Jesus and the World of Judaism,* Philadelphia: Fortress Press, 1983, pp. 30ff. However, as Peter Brown put it, "anachronism is an easy ghost with which to frighten historians." *Religion and Society in the Age of St. Augustine,* p. 250.

he is a friend of our nation and it is he who built us our synagogue." Jesus went with them; but when he was not far from the house, the centurion sent friends with this message: "Do not trouble further sir; it is not for me to have you under my roof, and that is why I did not presume to approach you in person. But say the word and my boy (*pais,* literally "male child") will be cured. I know, for in my position I am myself under orders, with soldiers under me. I say to one, 'Go,' and he goes; to another 'Come here,' and he comes; and to my slave, 'Do this,' and he does it." When Jesus heard this he marvelled at the man, and turning to the crowd that was following him, he said, "I tell you, nowhere, even in Israel, have I found faith like this." And the messengers returned to the house and found the slave in good health." (Lk 7:2-10)

The slightly different Matthean version (8:5ff) refers in each instance to the boy as "boy" (*pais*), not "slave" (*doulos*). "Boy" in Greek connotes a catamite or youth in a homosexual/pederastic relationship in the Greco-Roman world. These relationships were socially acceptable and not uncommon in that culture. At their best they were seen as mentor/protégé relationships which, in addition to being physically sexual, inducted the youth into the world of men. The boy would not be trained to become a lifelong or adult homosexual at his maturity, but would typically assume his place in the world as a heterosexual (or perhaps bi-sexual) male. This public acceptance of pederasty, an institution which the Romans inherited from the Greeks, was accompanied, however, by a measure of public anxiety. Effeminacy and submissiveness, for example, were viewed with contempt. Roman aristocratic families increasingly protected their young men by law from such assignations. Hence the pederastic relationship was increasingly assigned to slaves, who had no social reputation to lose.[91]

The practice of pederasty was, therefore, in decline early in the Christian era and was ultimately destroyed by Christendom, although it emerged curiously in another rather sublimated form in later monasticism. When the Gospels were written the practice was very much alive. Plutarch, the Greek biographer, who traveled widely and taught in Rome, was born about a decade after Jesus was executed. He discusses in his *Dialogue on Love* the question whether the love of boys is superior to the love of women, a critical question of the day. The tradition of

---

91 Michel Foucault, *op cit.,* Vol. III, p. 189.

the Greeks held the love of boys to be superior. The main argument deprecating the love of women was that such love was little more than a natural or animal inclination. The love of boys, on the other hand, was seen as the love of those who had a capacity for reason in their maturity. Pederasty was a part of the male world's denigration of women and an instrument for inducting young men into that mythology.

The meager data in the centurion's story does not permit us to conclude with certainty that his relationship with his boy/slave was a pederastic one. However, readers or hearers of the story in the first century would unquestionably conclude, given the language that is used, that the centurion was a pederast and his boy a catamite. Luke reinforces that impression by characterizing the boy as "very precious" to him.

The various English translations tend to obfuscate. The King James Version never translates "boy" at all, substituting the more benign "servant" for both "slave" and "boy" in each case. The Jerusalem Bible follows suit. The Revised Standard Version translates "boy" as "servant" in Matthew, but "slave" as "slave" in Luke, except at verse 7 where it translates "boy" as "servant." The New English Bible translates "servant" for both "slave" and "boy" in Luke, but in Matthew translates "boy" as "boy." None of the accepted English translations consistently follows the Greek text.

Thus a free translation of Luke should read: "A centurion there had a slave, a catamite who was very precious to him . . ." This supports a picture of Jesus as one who was tolerant of such relationships, a picture that is congruent with the rest of the New Testament. However, it is not enough to say that Jesus was merely tolerant of this apparent pederastic relationship. More then that, he was deeply impressed with the centurion's capacity for self-reflection on the ambiguity of his role as a soldier, as one under orders and who also gives orders. Jesus marvelled at him. "Nowhere, even in Israel, have I found such faith."

That such an interpretation of this text would surprise the modern reader simply demonstrates the gulf that separates the world of the early Jesus movement from the modern world, particularly in the arena of sexual values.

In Mark 14:50-52 we find another account that does not fit well into modern assumptions. Following the last supper, Jesus is arrested:

> Then the disciples all deserted him and ran away. Among those following was a young man with nothing on but a linen

cloth. They tried to seize him; but he slipped out of the linen cloth and ran away naked.

The account is enigmatic and troublesome to modern commentators. Most suggest the young man was the narrator himself, Mark, who was presumably rousted from his bed at home and dashed out half-dressed to see about the confusion surrounding Jesus' arrest. However, the sexual innuendo in the account cannot be so lightly dismissed. The hearer of this account is in fact more likely to associate the young man's dress, or lack thereof, with the last supper that took place earlier in the evening. After all, the last supper hardly resembled anything close to a modern formal sit-down dinner. Jesus himself was undressed at some point, according to the Gospel of John 13:4-5:

> [Jesus] rose from the table, laid aside his garments, and taking a towel, tied it round him. Then he poured water into a basin, and began to wash his disciples' feet and to wipe them with a towel.

If Jesus was undressed at some point in the evening, the half-naked young man becomes less surprising.

Jeremy Bentham, the 19th century moralist, proposes in the context of commenting on English sodomy laws, that this episode reflects a homosexual liaison, or boy prostitution.[92] Bentham speculates that the stripling may have been a rival to John, the disciple "whom Jesus loved," the implication being that Jesus and the beloved John were homosexual lovers. Bentham argues that the linen cloth over his otherwise naked body was a badge of his profession as a boy prostitute, but he does not give his source for this. Bentham's proposal is speculative, but cannot be lightly dismissed. The tradition holds that Jesus had some kind of special and affectionate relationship with John, but it would not need to be homosexual in the modern sense. That a boy prostitute would be drawn to Jesus, aside from any role John played, and might even have come offering his services, is certainly congruent with all the other marginalized persons who were drawn to Jesus.

Until Bentham's interpretation is better substantiated, that the linen cloth over a naked body was a homosexual prostitute's badge, we do not have to be limited to a homosexual interpretation of the story. There is good reason to doubt that the last supper itself was an all-male

---

92 For a discussion of Bentham, see Louis Crompton, *Byron and Greek Love: Homophobia in 19th Century England*, Berkeley: University of California Press, 1985, pp. 278ff.

gathering. Recent biblical scholarship has offered some compelling arguments to the effect that Jesus had women disciples who were expurgated from the written Gospels. The "Twelve" (male) disciples themselves may have been a retrospective creation for organizational purposes in a patriarchal culture. The lists themselves appear contrived. If women were present, the last supper would take a different tilt than it is normally given.

Just prior to the last supper, Matthew and Mark report that an unnamed woman anointed Jesus with oil, also at supper, though this one is placed in Bethany. (Mt 26:6-13; Mk 14:3-9) The (male) disciples object. Matthew and Mark have Jesus saying, obviously in retrospect, that the oil massage was "in preparation for burial."

All in all we have a very sensuous picture of Jesus whose body, in whole or in part, was rubbed with oil shortly before his execution. This picture is at least reminiscent of the woman who rubbed oil on Jesus' feet after washing them with her tears. (Lk 7:36ff) [93] Further, Jesus himself undressed to wash, and perhaps massage with oil his disciples feet, perhaps men and women. Footwashing carries overtones of sexual intimacy even in the most stylized and formal re enactments, and the last supper was hardly a liturgical event. Given this context, the half-dressed young man is no longer so incongruous.

All this sensuous attention to the body does not quite add up to a modern American orgy. But it assuredly does demonstrate at least an appreciation for and a loving care for each other's bodies in the circle of Jesus' intimates, a care that is quite alien to the modern Western middle class.

Subsequent ecclesial practice has so ritualized the washing of feet, the oil massage, and the last supper, that the sensual and possibly sexual aspects of those events in their original form are obscured from our awareness.

XIII

Any attempt to reconstruct a comprehensive picture of Jesus' attitudes, behavior and teaching about sex and marriage must deal with the fact that all the information available has been filtered through an

---

93 And may be another version of the same event.

androcentric screen. The consequences of such filtering are presented forcefully by Elizabeth Schussler Fiorenza in *In Memory of Her*.[94] She is not the first to observe that women seem to have been more important in the early Christian community than they appear to be in the texts. Women were apparently more significant in the Jesus movement and early Christian community than they were to become later. According to Fiorenza we have evidence in Paul and even more so in Luke and Acts and the later New Testament documents of the gradual reassertion of patriarchalism. Enough residual evidence exists for Fiorenza to suppose an original discipleship of equals and a picture of Jesus who placed himself squarely against the patriarchal structure of his culture.

We see in Mark, the earliest Gospel, that the women "disciples" were the only ones who remained nearby when Jesus was crucified. Mary Magdalene was the first to experience the resurrection and the one to deliver the message to the other disciples. Winsome Monro points out how remarkable it is that Mark leaves the women almost invisible until the very end of the Gospel (15:39). At Golgotha they suddenly achieve independent standing and are the ones who bring about the post-Golgotha recovery of the Jesus movement.[95] Her observations are entirely consistent with Werner Kelber's analysis of Mark as a Gospel of reversal of values, of insiders become outsiders, outsiders become insiders, the Gospel of disjuncture.[96] The outsider women became in the end the only faithful ones and, when the men had fled, they became the bearers of the word of the resurrection, which created the church. This crucial role of the women contrasts sharply with Paul's account of the resurrection in which not one woman appears in a recounting of all those who have witnessed the resurrection, numbering over 500. This is part of the so-called "pre-Pauline confession," in 1 Cor 15:5-7:

> . . . he appeared to Cephas, and afterwards to the Twelve. Then he appeared to over 500 of our brothers at once, most of whom are still alive, though some have died. Then he appeared to James, and afterwards to all the apostles. In the end he appeared even to me.

In the later Lucan accounts of the resurrection, males have similarly reassumed their place of importance, in accord with patriarchialism. (The dating of Luke is a matter of dispute, with arguments ranging from about

---

94 New York: Crossroad, 1984.
95 Winsome Monro, "Women Disciples in Mark?" *The Catholic Biblical Quarterly*, Vol. 44, No. 2 (Ap. 1982), pp. 225-41.
96 Kelber, *op. cit*, passim.

50 to 150. Most scholars seem to settle around 80-90. "Later" is actually in some sense a metaphor for "more patriarchal." It is probably safe to assume that the Jesus movement became less, rather than more radical as the decades passed. Any undermining of patriarchy would be seen as inflammatory in both Jewish and Greco-Roman environments. "Later" is therefore more a metaphor for documents that compromised with the culture in certain respects. However, actual dating as such is not an absolute indicator of authentic or original teaching. A chronologically "later" document may actually preserve "earlier" traditions.)

Finally, the still "later" documents of Ephesians, Colossians, and 1 Peter, whose authorship is disputed and probably unknown, include the virtually uncensored adoption of the patriarchal Stoic household code.[97] Colossians 3:18ff is typical:

> Wives, be subject to your husbands; that is your Christian duty. Husbands, love your wives and do not be harsh with them. Children, obey your parents . . .

In Ephesians, earthly patriarchal marriage becomes a metaphor for heavenly fulfillment. And in the Pastoral Epistles, 1 and 2 Timothy and Titus, we see the emergence of the bishop and his authority as the ecclesiastical counterpart to the *paterfamilias*, the patriarch of the typical upper-strata Greco-Roman household. The authority of the bishop is strengthened further in some of the early extra-canonical literature of the church, specifically 1 Clement and Ignatius.[98] Fiorenza surmises that this was not so much an attempt to exploit women as an attempt to lessen tension between the young Christian community and the Greco-Roman culture in which it found itself.

Jesus would not have been unique in his time in relating to women as equals. Something of a feminine revolution of sorts seems to have been

---

97 Fiorenza, *op cit.*, p. 254.
98 I Clement of Rome writes in his Epistle to the Corinthians 44:1: "Our apostles...knew there was going to be strife over the title of bishop." Ignatius is unceasing in his exhortations to submit to the bishop: "We should regard the bishop as the Lord Himself (Eph 6:1)...obey the bishop as if he were Jesus Christ (Tral 2:1)...let the bishop preside in God's place (Mag 6:1)." Both Clement and Ignatius are dated around the end of the first century.

taking place during this period of history. The Greek Olympics opened themselves to women for the first time in the first century BCE. Roman law of the imperial period greatly enhanced the political position of women.[99] During this time the Isis cult also flourished, and among other things, proclaimed the equality of women and men. This movement was significant enough to create at least some anxiety in the Roman world and led to the marshalling of the forces of reaction. The civil war of Mark Anthony and Cleopatra against Octavian, who defeated them, was at least partly shaped by that issue. Octavian is recorded as having made a speech to his soldiers urging them to defeat those who would destroy their traditions and allow "a woman to be made equal to a man."[100]

Furthermore, Jesus would not have been limited to Roman culture for signs of a yearning for sexual equality. J. B. Segal finds in the Old Testament prophet Elijah a precursor of that "special bonding" that is evidenced between Jesus and women.[101]

Fiorenza's thesis in support of a discipleship of equals is consistent with other aspects of Jesus' life and teaching. So is her conjecture that such radical teachings as are evidenced in the texts would seem to call for a critique of patriarchalism. That the texts contain so little teaching on the subject of marriage, and that what is there is hardly supportive of it, has been, after all, an ongoing problem for the church. Hence, the English Book of Common Prayer, in its prologue to the marriage rite, on the theory that weak documentation is better than none, resorts to the account of Jesus' presence at the wedding at Cana in Galilee (Jn 2:1-11) as a proof text for Jesus' blessing of marriage.

A reasonable conjecture would be that Jesus was as "negative" toward marriage as Paul was and on the same grounds---the eschatological challenge. The preserved teachings of Jesus seem to support this conjecture and so too does the fact of so little preserved teaching by Jesus about marriage. By the time the Gospels were written a

---

99 Wayne A. Meeks, "The Image of the Androgyne: Some Uses of a Symbol in Earliest Christianity", *History of Religions*, Vol. 13, No. 3 (Feb 1974), p. 168.
100 Dio Cassius, *Roman History,* 50.28.3. For discussion see esp. Fiorenza, *op. cit.*, p. 264; David L. Balch, *Let Wives be Submissive: The Domestic Code in 1 Peter,* Chico, CA: Scholars Press, 1981, p. 118; Kathleen O'Brian Wicker, "First Century Marriage Ethics: A Comparative Study of the Household Codes and Plutarch's Conjugal Precepts," *No Famine in the Land: Studies in Honor of John L. McKenzie,* Missoula, Mont: Scholars Press, 1975, pp. 141-53.
101 "Popular Religion in Israel", *Journal of Jewish Studies,* Vol. xxvii, No. 1, Sept. 1976, pp. 1-22.

generation or more after Jesus' death, the compilers were probably not eager to add to their tribulations by recording a frontal assault on the Greco-Roman world's second most precious institution, the backbone of the state itself, patriarchal marriage and family life. The significance of the family in Roman culture should not be underestimated. In early Roman culture (pre-7th century BCE) the *paterfamilias* was the priest, the household gods were passed from father to son, and the family was the religious community. Marriage, for a woman, meant the adoption of new gods.[102] That kind of religious family structure was to some extent still in place at the beginning of the Christian era.

Fiorenza, however, makes an unsubstantiated leap when she deduces that a rejection of patriarchal marriage in the young Christian community was a rejection of sexual relationships as well. She correctly argues that Paul's "neither male nor female" (Gal. 3:28) must certainly undermine patriarchy, just as the preceding phrases (neither Jew nor Greek, slave nor free) undermine ethnic imperialism and slavery. But there is no support for her conclusion that it also undermines or prohibits sexual relationships. Such a conclusion must be based on the modern assumption that sex is inextricably limited to the bounds of marriage. Fiorenza reveals the weakness of her argument at that point by substantiating it with the much later extra-canonical II Clement (12:16):

> When a brother sees a sister he should not think of her sex any more than she should think of his.

Sex-negative literature of this sort became quite common in the later church, and, in fact, became the rule rather than the exception. II Clement is an example of one of the earliest mainstream church documents that manifests significant sex-negativism, but its date is thought to be well into the second century and is therefore hardly a commentary on the life of the earliest Christian communities, as Fiorenza makes it. Suffice it to say that such negativism toward sexual relationships cannot be found in the New Testament.

XIV

The manner in which the New Testament makes use of the Greek word *psyche* (soul) is probably representative of the manner in which the New Testament as a whole deals with Greek values and concepts generally.

---

102 Edward Schillebeeckx, *Marriage,* New York: Sheed and Ward, 1966, p. 234.

It expropriates a Greek concept and refashions it within a Hebraic understanding of the human experience. Hence, "soul" (*psyche*) is used by the New Testament authors to mean virtually the same as the Hebrew *nephesh*, i.e. "life" or "person." "Soul" is also used in tandem with heart, strength and mind (Mk 12:30, Lk 10:27), in effect diluting its platonic character as the divine spark in human personality, making it one aspect among others in an anthropological construct. We should read "soul" in the New Testament with a heavily Hebraic rather than a syncretistic or platonic tilt.

XV

Three remaining references to sexual valorization in the New Testament deserve comment. Revelation 14:4 refers to the 144,000 who stood with the lamb on Mount Zion:

> These are the men who did not defile themselves with women, for they are virgins, and they follow the Lamb wherever he goes.

According to Caird, this is a military metaphor with allusions to Leviticus and to the identification of *porneia* and idolatry. Rome is cryptically identified (Rev 17.5) as "the mother of all prostitutes." To worship the gods of Rome was therefore to defile oneself with the religious rites (sexual or otherwise) of Rome. The "virgins" in 14:4 are those who have kept themselves from such defilement. "Virgin" is therefore a metaphor for those who have refused to worship false gods and in no way promotes sexual purity as such. John is not, according to Caird, asking his readers to believe that all victims of persecution would be male, still less that they would be celibate. "Nor is he even disclosing in an unguarded moment," says Caird, "his personal predilection for asceticism."[103]

The requirement in the Pastorals (1 Tim 3:4, 12 and Tit 1:6) that a deacon and a bishop be "the husband of one wife" is also open to quite different interpretations, depending on perspective. The simplest and most likely meaning is that this is a prohibition of polygamy for the leadership of the church. Such a reading would be impossible if

---

[103] G. B. Caird, *A Commentary on the Revelation of St. John the Divine*, 2nd Ed., London: A&C Black, 1984, p. 179. See also Robert H. Mounce, *The Book of Revelation*, Grand Rapids, William B. Eerdman's Publishing Co., 1977, p. 310; J. Massingberd Ford, *The Anchor Bible: Revelation*, Garden City, NY: Doubleday and Co., 1975, p. 234; Elizabeth Schussler Fiorenza, *Invitation to the Book of Revelation*, Garden City, NY: Doubleday and Co., 1981, p. 139.

polygamy were nonexistent in the early church. In a strictly monogamous context, such a prohibition would be superfluous. Another possible interpretation is that this is a requirement setting a limit of one wife in a lifetime. The Pontifex Maximus, the imperial high priest of Rome, was so limited theoretically. On the other hand, the Jewish high priest in Jerusalem was limited merely to monogamy. The early church would more likely mimic Jerusalem than Rome.

This requirement could also be translated "man of one woman," since the Greek words for "husband" and "man" are the same, as are "wife" and "woman". Phipps[104] has argued for this reading as a particular way to state the requirement for marital faithfulness. Phipps' interpretation here cannot be ruled out. The interpretation one settles on here ultimately depends on whether one reads this requirement from a Jewish or a syncretistic perspective. At the stage the Pastorals were written, late in the early church but when it was probably still largely Jewish, polygamy would likely have been the issue addressed. That these passages refer to polygamy is the simplest, least complicated interpretation.

The notion of the virgin birth of Jesus which was later inflated to a doctrine of penultimate importance has only the most shadowy sources in the New Testament. The idea is not mentioned except in the birth narratives of Matthew (1:18-25) and Luke (1:26-38;3:24), and even there it is not mentioned directly. A "virgin birth" is only one of the options that might be extrapolated from the text, and certainly not the most credible. For all its later importance, it is a curious phenomenon that the text never quite specifies a virgin birth but merely presents a mysterious pregnancy for which Joseph is not responsible and for which a virgin birth would be a possible explanation. The texts are very clear that Mary's conception with Jesus is both out of the ordinary and "of God," but they do not go beyond that.

In the Lucan account the angel tells Mary, who is referred to as a "virgin," that she will conceive and bear a son. She replies, "How can this be so since I have not known (sexually) a man?" The question is a very peculiar one, and so is the answer. She might have asked who her husband was going to be, the kind of question a typical young woman would have asked in such a situation. Her question suggests that she has not known a man and never intends to know one, not the kind of response we would expect from a Palestinian woman of the time. The

---

104 Phipps, *op. cit.*, p. 103.

angel answers that the Holy Spirit will come upon her, adding that her kinswoman Elizabeth, who was barren, has conceived in her old age. With God nothing is impossible, the angel adds. In the meantime Joseph enters the picture most unobstrusively as Mary's betrothed. Though the narrative is somewhat coy about the matter, the implication here is that Joseph's role is nullified in this pregnancy. Such a nullification is later supported at 3:23 where the text says "Jesus was the son *as was supposed* of Joseph." On the other hand, the role of Zechariah in impregnating Elizabeth does not seem to have been nullified. The stories of Mary and Elizabeth are set in a Jewish milieu with its numerous stories of God making barren women fruitful. In none is there any implication that the role of the male in conception is supplanted. God is at work in the sexual union, not in place of it. Sarah (Gen 17:17), Rebekah (Gen 25:21), Hannah (1Sam. 1:9ff), and the wife of Manoah (Jud 13:2ff) were all barren and by divine action gave birth to holy men. In none of these is the role of sexual intercourse supplanted. The story of Mary in Luke does suggest that Joseph's sexual role in the pregnancy was taken over by the Holy Spirit, but, strangely, it is never quite explicit on that point.[105]

The account in Matthew, on the other hand, is explicit about the fact that Mary was found by Joseph to be pregnant before he had sexual intercourse with her. She and Joseph were already betrothed when he found this out. Being a decent man he was determined to cancel the wedding and quietly release her. In this account the angel appeared to him in a dream and told him that that which was conceived in her was "of the Holy Spirit." Then the Matthean account refers back to Isaiah 7:14 where the Hebrew original reads simply that "a young woman shall conceive."[106] If Matthew intended to emphasize Mary's virginity as such, he does not strengthen his story much by referring to Isaiah. Matthew like Luke is very clear in the claim that God is working in this conception, and Matthew unlike Luke is explicit about the fact that Joseph had no part in it. But neither account follows up with a conclusion of a virgin birth. The narrator is quite oblique or coy about the precise origin of Mary's pregnancy, and that is puzzling.

In the world of the later church Mary's virginity was much more obviously written between the lines of the story because by then virginity itself had become a religious pearl of great price. In the semitic

---
105 For a discussion of this, see Geza Vermes, *op. cit.*, p. 222.
106 The Greek translation of the Old Testament, the LXX, does translate "young woman" as "virgin."

environment in which the Gospels were written virginity in a mature woman was not held in esteem and was more a curse than a blessing. The New Testament scholar G. B. Caird thinks the doctrine of the virgin birth arose out of a misunderstanding when the story was taken from its original Judaean environment into the Greco-Roman world.[107] As we have seen, the Greco-Roman world cherished virginity. That culture also encouraged the notion that gods impregnated mortals on occasion, a notion essentially repugnant to biblical theology.

Mary's virginity is never even mentioned in the rest of the New Testament, a very peculiar development if we are to consider the matter important. Paul seems even to refute it:

> On the human level [Jesus] was born of David's stock, but on the level of the spirit---the Holy Spirit---he was declared Son of God by a mighty act in that he rose from the dead. (Rom 1:3)

The various other references in the New Testament that mention Jesus' brothers and sisters suggest that Mary had other children in addition to Jesus. The later church doctrine of Mary's perpetual virginity had to postulate that these offspring were not really Jesus' brothers and sisters, at least not through Mary. One would think the New Testament texts would have wished not to leave the impression that Mary gave birth to other children if that were such an important piece of information.

Some commentators may be correct in their opinion that the story of Mary's pre-Joseph pregnancy has a kernel of historical truth.[108] Mary could have been the victim of an illicit pregnancy. Such a pregnancy would account for the peculiar obliqueness of the birth stories in Matthew and Luke. This suggestion has a very ancient history. The second century platonist critic of the church, Celsus, put forward the story (of uncertain origin) that a Roman soldier named "Panthera" was Jesus' biological father. The name was a common surname of Roman soldiers of the period and it is remarkably similar to "*parthenos*", "vir-

---

[107] G. B. Caird, *Saint Luke*, Philadelphia: Westminster Press, 1963, p. 53.
[108] See esp. Raymond E. Brown, "Luke's Method in the Annunciation Narrative of Chapter One," *No Famine in the Land,* pp. 179-94.

gin" in Greek.[109] The idea of Jesus' conception as illicit may seem irreverent in light of subsequent mariolatry, but theologically it is at least an apposite conjecture. If Jesus' birth was seen as a manifestation of God's power "exalting those of low degree," as Mary sings (Luke 1:52), and if he was for that reason born in a stable, his conception as an illicit pregnancy for a defenseless young woman within a patriarchal system would be perfectly fitting, even inspiring.

Several other shards of support for such an illicit pregnancy can be found in the texts. In a dialogue with his opponents in the gospel of John, Jesus is asked "Where is your father?" (8:19) Further on they say, "*We* (emphatic) were not born of fornication." (8:41)[110] This appears to be a fragment of a discussion about Jesus' paternity. We have other fragments as well. In the Gospel of Mark (6:3) Jesus' detractors ask, "Isn't this the carpenter, the son of Mary?" This is a curious epithet since men were identified by reference to their fathers. Of course this curious epithet could be used to support the argument for either a virgin birth or an illicit pregnancy. However, a persuasive virgin birth would likely have been boasted about by the promoters of Jesus in the New Testament. An illicit pregnancy we might expect would get short shrift.

The most astonishing piece of data suggesting an illicit pregnancy is Matthew's genealogical record in 1:1-6:

> The list of the genealogy of Jesus Christ, son of David, son of Abraham: Abraham was the father of Isaac, Isaac of Jacob, and Jacob was father of Judah and his brothers. Judah was the father of Perez and Zerah *by Tamar* and Perez fathered Hezron, who was the father of Ram. Ram was father of Amminadab, Amminadab of Nahshon, and Nahshon was father of Salmon. Salmon fathered Boaz *by Rahab*, Boaz was father of Obed *by Ruth*, Obed was father of Jesse, who was the father of King David. David was father of Solomon, *by the wife of Uriah* . . . (italics mine)

---

109 *Origen: Contra Celsum*, Henry Chadwick, trans./ed., Cambridge: Cambridge University Press, 1953, 1:32. Leslie Weatherhead (*The Christian Agnostic*, New York: Abingdon Press, 1965, p. 100.) thinks that Zechariah may have impregnated Mary in a cultic sexual act or sacral marriage that was known to have been practiced at that time. He cites Mary's haste to visit Zechariah and Elizabeth after her encounter with the angel, and the fact that she remained with them three months, precisely the length of time the Talmud uses to determine a pregnancy.

110 This may be one instance where "fornication" is an appropriate translation of "*porneia*". The crime here would not be sex or pregnancy prior to marriage as such but the abandonment of responsibility by the natural father which would make the sexual liaison illicit.

The insertion of women in this genealogical list is noteworthy in that no women appear in the Lucan list (3:23ff). Women generally were not important to genealogical lists in patriarchial biblical culture. In the genealogical list in Chronicles (1 Chron 1:34; 2:1,4,5,9-13; 3:5,10-15), which Luke seems to follow, several women do appear peripherally, but only Tamar and "Bathsheba (Bathshua), the daughter of Ammiel" are mentioned among the four women in Matthew's list. Thus the selection of these four women in Matthew's list seems to have a source or rationale different from the Chronicles list.

Matthew's four women undoubtedly have been selected either by Matthew or his sources as forerunners of Mary. Considering all the women available for this selection, such as Sarah, Rebekah, and Rachel, the choice of Tamar, Rahab, Ruth, and Bathsheba is nothing short of astonishing. Each of these women stands on the boundary of being a sexual outcast! Tamar played the prostitute role, deliberately seducing her father-in-law in order to get pregnant by him. Rahab was a professional prostitute. Ruth circumvented the levirate law and attempted to seduce Boaz in his sleep. Bathsheba was an adulteress. Bathsheba's adultery is even highlighted by Matthew who refers to her not as "the daughter of Ammiel," as Chronicles does, but as "the wife of Uriah," the husband against whom she and David committed adultery. Note also that each of these women found favor with God in spite of behavior that was not ordinarily acceptable, to put it mildly. We should even wonder what Mary was doing in such company unless she was indeed involved in something on the order of an illicit pregnancy.

In summary, the birth stories of Jesus may well be rooted in an oral tradition about Jesus' origins that included rumors of an illicit conception. The notion of a virgin birth as such is at the most a gossamer construct with only the thinnest thread of New Testament support. It has neither historical value nor any importance for New Testament theology. The extent to which virginity itself is important in these narratives is likely the influence of Greco-Roman syncretism at work, either in the texts themselves or on the early church's exegesis.

The New Testament as a whole is essentially a mainstream semitic Jewish document rather than a Hellenistic one, even though its language is Greek and a few of its categories, as in the Gospel of John, are drawn from Greek philosophy. While the New Testament reflects a wide range of sexual attitudes, it reflects essentially a Jewish rather than a syncretistic value system.

XVI

The early church's kiss of peace and its ultimate fate epitomize, perhaps, the sexual values of the New Testament and their subsequent transformation in history. The kiss of peace was an earthy, bodily act of fellowship and devotion between all the members of the community. It was congruent with the breaking of bread. Each betrays a religious materialism that was alien to syncretistic religion and its mental incorporeality. Paul closes four of his letters urging the "kiss of peace" (Rom 16:16, 1Cor 16:20, 2Cor 13:12, 1Thes 5:26). The author of 1 Peter closes his letter urging the "kiss of love" (5:14).

Stephen Benko believes the kiss was a powerful and important gesture in the early Jesus movement, and he believes that it was pointedly a mouth-to-mouth kiss.

> Through the holy kiss the holy spirit was transmitted and received . . . representing the life-giving breath of God . . . They saw the work of God in the world as the unification of the universe, and through the holy kiss the Christian, in a proleptic way tasted that unity.[111]

Benko suggests further that this intimate gesture might have been at least unconsciously evocative of memories of holy marriage and sacramental sexual intercourse that occur in other religions. Some of the Gnostic literature may be echoing this association when it proposes a sacrament of the bridal chamber, described in the Gospel of Philip as the highest of five sacraments.[112]

It was not long before the kiss became an embarrassment to the church because of obvious sexual overtones. Clement of Alexandria at the end of the second century reports:

> There are some who make the assembly resound with nothing but their kisses while there is no love in their heart. We should realize that the unrestrained use of the kiss has brought it under grave suspicion and slander. It should be thought of in a mystical sense . . . Let us . . . taste the kingdom with a mouth that is chaste and self-controlled . . . [113]

A contemporary of Clement, Athenagoras, refers to "our law," the record of

---
111 Stephen Benko, *Pagan Rome and the Early Christians,* Bloomington: Indiana University Press, 1984, p. 98.
112 *Nag Hammadi Library, op. cit.,* p. 142.
113 *Christ the Educator,* 3.11.81.

which is lost to history, which penalizes "any man who takes a second kiss for the motive of pleasure . . . " Anyone stirred by the kiss to passions in thought will be deprived by God of eternal life, he adds.[114] By the second decade of the third century Hippolytus reports that men and women are separated in church and that kisses are exchanged only by members of the same sex.[115]

Thus the kiss of peace/love became the "holy kiss," a highly stylized liturgical act in a setting where men were separated from women, and clergy from laity. For the Christian community the kiss finally became for the most part what it was in the religion of imperial Rome. There religious devotion required the liturgical kissing of statues and sacred objects, not people.[116] The twentieth century J. B. Phillips translation of the New Testament quite tellingly translates the "kiss" as a "handshake," attempting thereby to be relevant to the modern world.[117] That a handshake could replace a mouth-to-mouth kiss reveals much about the difference between the modern bourgeois church and the early Jesus movement. The recent charismatic movement has attempted to restore the kiss, an effort that has resulted in a nervously asexual, desultory cheek-to-cheek embrace. Observing them in action, it is not clear which is the main agenda, the embrace itself or pelvic avoidance. However, they deserve credit for demonstrating slightly more appreciation for the whole body, in their rituals at least, than those who content themselves with handshaking.

XVII

What then was the situation in the early Jesus movement with regard to sexual values and behavior? No definitive answer can be given to this question. That marriage was profoundly devalued in light of the eschatological challenge seems certain. Another way to say the same thing, perhaps, is that marriage, being inextricably tied to patriarchy, was subject to the radical critique of Jesus and the earliest Christian communities, as Fiorenza and others persuasively argue. That sexual desire and fulfillment were blessed and affirmed and considered one of the great gifts from the

---

114 *Embassy*, 32; see also Justin Martyr, *Apology* I,65.
115 *The Treatise on the Apostolic Tradition of St. Hippolytus of Rome,* Gregory Dix, ed., London: Society for Promoting Christian Knowledge, 1937.
116 Gustav Stählin in Kittel, *op. cit.*, "phileo".
117 *The New Testament in Modern English*, New York: The Macmillan Co., 1958.

Creator, intended for all human beings to participate in for sheer joy and delight, also seems certain. Jesus was a Jew and the earliest Christian communities consisted almost entirely of Torah-abiding Jews. We are left then with probability that the Jesus movement supported in the beginning sexual relationships that evaded, on terms that are no longer recoverable, the boundaries of marriage. Such a conjecture will of course elicit fantasies in many of unrestrained aggressive and narcissistic sexuality and the consequent horror of any such associations with Jesus or the early church. But such fantasies will be based on the assumption that the only sexual alternative to traditional patriarchal marriage is an unrestrained and unreflective pursuit of every sensual whim. It is not beyond the realm of human imagination to consider a pattern of non-marital---even anti-marital---sexual behavior that might be restrained, temperate, reflective, aware of unconscious processes, and rooted in a care for the other as well as the self. Given the radical nature of other teachings of Jesus, the supposition that his sexual teaching may have been equally as radical should surprise no one.

In summary, to read the New Testament as a thoroughly semitic document is to invite a radically different perspective on its sexual values than we have grown accustomed to in the Christian West. To read it as later tradition often has, from a sycretistic or Greco-Roman orientation, is to invite the misinterpretations of the texts to which we have become accustomed. The New Testament overreaches Judaism and the Old Testament in only one significant respect in the arena of sexual values. It confronts marriage with an eschatological challenge, leaving it henceforth subject to the judgment of "what is coming into being." The roots of that challenge, however, are not in Greco-Roman asceticism. They are firmly embedded in the Hebraic anticipation of a new creation, one that is like the old creation at least in this respect, that it too is a land flowing with milk and honey, those symbols of the goodness of physical creation.

Chapter Three
The First 400 Years: The Victory of Syncretism

To Christian disciples of the first century the conception of Jesus as a rabbi was self-evident, to the Christian disciples of the second century it was embarrassing, to the Christian disciples of the third century and beyond it was obscure. -- Jaroslav Pelikan*

I

The Christian Church, which began as a dynamic, spontaneous, ecstatic community, had to deal sooner or later with the institutionalizing process. It is one thing for a community to be shaped by ecstatic transforming energy, but it is another to provide for the kind of organization that will allow for an orderly continuity from one generation to the next. Boundaries of membership and belief as well as the lines and limits of authority very soon became preeminent concerns. If in the early years of the church marriage was subjected to the eschatological challenge, it was not long before the question of marital and sexual boundaries arose as thorny institutional issues to be faced. It is one thing to shed the necessity of marriage as Paul did in the newly organized Christian communities, but it is quite something else for an ongoing community to tolerate sexuality without boundaries. Therefore, the early church's confrontation of marriage with the eschatological challenge soon dissipated in the face of the necessity to give marriage a certain value and to control sexuality. In this valorization process the early church was presented with the two contrasting models which were deeply embedded in the surrounding culture, the Judaic and the syncretistic Greco-Roman. This predicament created considerable ambivalence for the young churches. They found themselves in the "no man's land" between sex-affirming Judaism and the sex-negating syncretistic imperial religion. The ecclesiastical documents of the first hundred years demonstrate that ambivalence.

In a quite comparable and related vein, the church was simultaneously forced to face the issue of authority. In the early years authority in the church was quite simple, malleable and fluid, itself under eschatological challenge. Authority was therefore dispersed and collegial. Boundaries were not entirely clear or fixed. There was no central ecclesiastical voice. Paul could claim authority on equal footing with the former disciples of Jesus on the basis of his own personal and

---

*   *Jesus Through the Centuries*, New York: Harper and Row, 1987, p. 17.

idiosyncratic vision. It is much too anachronistic to portray Peter as a first pope. Authority was scattered amongst the various apostles and various urban centers in apparently uneven degrees. Jerusalem certainly began as the principal center of authority. But its power soon began to wane, in part because it was synonymous with Judaism and, as Werner Kelber points out, identified also with the oral tradition and the apostolic "in group" which Jerusalem represented. The textual tradition beginning with the Gospel of Mark undermined both Jerusalem as the ecclesiastical center and supplanted the oral tradition of early ecclesiastical leadership.[1] The Jewish rebellion in the late 60's CE and the subsequent victorious Roman response further contributed to the eclipse of Jerusalem as a power center and the Jewish character of the church as well.

The church at Rome had not yet achieved political hegemony over the churches in the various other urban centers of the eastern Mediterranean. Therefore, what we see in the documents of the first 100 years is inconsistency, variety and the increasing influence of the values of imperial civil religion. The New Testament canon was not yet crystalized, though that process was underway, so there was no clear and well-established textual authority except for the law and the prophets of the Old Testament. As long as organizational and textual authority remained soft and malleable the young churches were vulnerable to the varieties of external influence. The strongest external influence was the syncretistic religion of the empire.

The syncretistic label that is attached to Roman civil religion comes from the fact that it was a mishmash of collected gods, rituals and philosophies. The salient features of this conglomeration were imperial nationalism, epitomized in emperor worship, and variations of the orphic and other mystery cults, principally Dionysian and Eleusinian, all this undergirded philosophically by platonism, mostly in the form of Stoicism. This civil religion was co-terminous with the empire and the emperor himself usually held supreme religious as well as secular authority. The best of the emperors were regularly deified, usually after their deaths, had temples built in their names, and were made objects of worship and sacrifices. The murdered Julius Caesar was the first to be made a god, in 42 BCE.

---

1 Werner Kelber, *op cit., passim.*

There were of course tensions within syncretistic imperial religion. Some of the Stoic philosophers were exiled or executed because their universalist and humanist teachings were seen to undermine the interests of Roman nationalism. Many Stoics opposed slavery, for example. Nero condemned to death the Stoic philosopher Seneca, his own tutor and advisor. However, in spite of these and other inner tensions and conflicts, syncretistic Roman imperial religion as a whole promoted a platonist dualism that was incongruent with Hebraic anthropology.

The popular juxtaposition of the sexual profligacy of Nero, for example, and the early Christians as illustrative of the situation of the early church within the empire is simplistic and highly misleading. Nero was of course notorious both for his extreme cruelty and his wanton sexual practices. He not only executed his mother, but is thought to have had an incestuous sexual relationship with her. He is also reported to have scapegoated early Christians for the burning of Rome, a conflagration thought to have been ignited by his own men. Both Peter and Paul are thought to have perished in this pogrom.

Nero represents the worst, not the best, of first century Rome. The fact that the young church in the third decade of its existence had to face 14 years (54-68) of the most depraved emperor in Roman history, as well as 4 years (37-41) of the less damaging Caligula in its first decade, was a concatenation of events that has forever maligned what was on balance a relatively humanistic political system. Nero as well as Caligula were in fact held in great contempt by literary and political figures of the century, such as Pliny, Suetonius, Seneca and Tacitus. The intelligentsia and ruling class of the period were hardly well represented by the characters of the two monsters of depravity. The men of letters in this era were humanistic and were eminently rational---too rational---and their sexual attitude might even be characterized as puritanical or effete. Nurtured as they were on Stoicism, they were sexually abstemious, or at least pretended to be. Furthermore, they disdained the personal lives of practically all the emperors of the century, especially the callousness and sexual excesses of Nero and Caligula.

However, Tacitus, for one, made clear his contempt for the sexual practices of the Jews as well, whose practices he also regarded as lascivious. The two charges he makes against the Jews are sexual immorality and lack of patriotism.[2]

> Among the Jews all things are profane that we hold sacred; on the other hand they regard as permissible what seems to us immoral. . . though a most lascivious people, the Jews avoid sexual intercourse with women of alien race. Among themselves nothing is barred. . . the very first lesson they [proselytes to Judaism] learn is to despise the gods, shed all feelings of patriotism. . . Their kings are not so flattered, the Roman emperor not so honored. . . the Jewish belief is paradoxical and degraded.[3]

Christians too, Tacitus felt, deserved to be punished for their degraded and shameful practices, but because of Nero's brutality in punishing them, he says, they were as a result pitied. It was felt they were sacrificed to one man's brutality rather than to the national interest.

Pliny, on the other hand, executed Christians without hesitation in his role as governor of Bithynia. And though he admits to having used torture to extract information from certain Christians, he presents himself not as a sadist who takes pleasure in another's pain, but as a decisive, gentlemanly, imperial functionary who unflinchingly and summarily sent those who challenged the authority of the Emperor to their deaths. He asked suspects three times if they were Christians, generously reminding them of their fate if answered affirmatively. Those who denied the accusation were given the opportunity then and there to repeat an invocation to the gods, to offer wine and incense to Caesar's statue, and to revile the name of Christ, after which the charges were dismissed. Pliny was engaged in no witch hunt. He pointedly disregarded anonymous pamphlets exposing covert Christians and was fully supported by the Emperor Trajan in this. Such anonymous accusations, Trajan wrote,

---

2 Even in 1985, Louis Farrakhan's reported attack on Judaism as "a dirty religion" seems to carry the same echo. *New York Times,* Oct 8, 1985, B-3.
3 Tacitus, *The Histories,* Kenneth Wellesley, Trans., New York: Penguin Books, 1964, pp. 273-4. The contemporary of Jesus, Strabo, also thought the Jews degenerate. "Such was Moses and his successors; their beginning was good, but they degenerated." (*Geography* 16.2.39, W. Falconer, trans.) He does not specify in what sense they were degenerate.

"create the worst sort of precedent and are quite out of keeping with the spirit of our age."[4] But neither Pliny nor Trajan was willing to tolerate an open adherence to what they considered "this degenerate sort of cult carried to extravagant lengths."[5]

It is not precisely clear what Pliny thought was degenerate about Christians. But it is at least possible that he held the same views as Tacitus, particularly since Tacitus was his friend and teacher and maintained an ongoing correspondence with him. We may reasonably assume that Tacitus viewed the "shameful and degraded" practices of Christians as being the same as those of the Jews, namely sexual immorality and disloyalty to the empire and its values. It would have been perfectly natural for Tacitus to view the Christians as simply a Jewish sect or splinter group, because in fact the church was hardly more than that during Tacitus' life. Tacitus was, after all, an astute politician, a senator who reached the penultimate office of consul. He was a survivor in a bloody and tumultuous era and no doubt kept himself well informed on political events in the empire. This Christian movement born in Judaism and adhering to the Jewish scriptures, owning only a few decades of history, would not be seen yet as any independent world religion.

The physician and philosopher Galen (129-199) several generations later does not distinguish between Christians and Jews when he criticizes them both for failure to attain a high philosophical standard. He mentions approvingly that some have refrained from cohabiting all through their lives, which is the earliest non-Christian witness to sexual abstinence in the church. Galen lived in the midst of the flowering of the church's Encratite movement, which promoted sexual continence.[6]

Celsus (second century) later also associated Jews and Christians, saying there was not "the shadow of an ass' difference" between them. Further evidence of the continuing weak boundary between Judaism and Christianity is the fact that as late as 160 there are still Christian-Jews

---

4 *The Letters of Younger Pliny,* Betty Radice, Trans., New York: Penguin Books, 1963, p. 295.
5 *Ibid.,* p. 294.
6 R. Walzer, *Galen on Jews and Christians,* London: Oxford University Press, 1969, pp. 37-65.

who keep the Mosaic law without any impediment to their Christian faith.[7]

So the nascent church apparently began its life under the suspicion of both treason and sexual immorality in the eyes of most respectable Romans. While the young church originally inherited both these stigmata from the Jews, the evidence on both charges escalated for Christians. While the Jews were allowed some leeway in their refusal to participate in what they considered idolatrous emperor worship, they at least had the advantage of being viewed behind a screen of a peculiar ethnic group or race. The Jews, for example, were exempt from emperor worship, required only to sacrifice twice daily in the Temple "for Caesar and the Roman people." In deference to the Jews, Roman troops in Jerusalem generally carried no image of the Emperor on their standards, and coins were minted without Caesar's image. Even the murderer of a Roman citizen within the temple precincts was exempt from Roman justice, an extraordinary concession.[8]

While Christians were tainted originally by supposed Jewish lasciviousness, certainly the Christian eschatological challenge to marriage heightened the fear among respectable citizens that they were witnessing the expansion of a debauched cult. This would be a particular concern for pious Romans for whom the family was seen as the backbone of the state, and both as essential to Roman religion.

Fuel was no doubt added to the fire by the reported sexual excesses of some of the heretical Gnostic groups in their zeal to demonstrate contempt for the flesh. Many if not most Gnostics considered themselves Christians and the Roman public was not likely to make subtle distinctions between orthodox and heretical Christians. It is quite simplistic, however, to attribute all the continuing charges of sexual immorality against the church to the behavior of the Gnostics, as some have done. The Gnostics only exacerbated the problem that originated for the church with its Jewish beginnings.

The charges of sexual immorality against the church were certainly

---

[7] Justin Martyr, *Dialogue with Trypho*, 47; see also Henry Chadwick, *The Early Church*, New York: Penguin Books, 1967, p. 22.
[8] Joseph B. Tyson, *A Study of Early Christianity*, New York: The Macmillan Co., 1973, p. 77.

The Victory of Syncretism

persistent and more intense than those made against the Jews, who, to the objections of Rome, were themselves still practicing polygamy during this time. These charges continued to be made for at least 200 years. We should take into account the argument made by Robert Haardt, who suggests that everyone was accusing everyone of sexual immorality in this era, thus discounting the significance of such charges.[9] Romans were especially fond of throwing around charges of sexual immorality, fixated as they were on sexual sins, and no doubt such charges were sometimes without basis in fact. However, this hardly provides a basis for universally discounting such charges.

Athenagoras in the late second century defends the church against three charges: atheism, Thyestean feasts (Thyestes sexually defiled his daughter in pursuit of an oracle), and Oedipal intercourse.[10] And Justin Martyr during the same period writes, "Do you believe of us. . . that. . . we meet together after our banquet, put out the lights, and wallow in promiscuous concubinage?"[11] But the most bizarre details come from Marcus Minucius Felix who defends the church sometime between 197 and 248 against the most lurid and detailed charges of sexual abandon. He paraphrases an anti-Christian speech of M. Cornelius Fronto, tutor and confidante to Marcus Aurelius, the philosopher-emperor who persecuted the church:

> Hardly have they met when they love each other. . . a veritable religion of lusts. Indiscriminately they call each other brother and sister, thus turning ordinary fornication into incest by the intervention of these hallowed names. . . It is also reported that they worship the genitals of their pontiff and priest. . . a suspicion that befits their clandestine and nocturnal ceremonies. . . On a special day they gather for a feast with all

---

9 Robert Haardt, *Gnosis: Character and Testimony,* J. F. Hendry, Trans., Leiden: E. J. Brill, 1971, p. 69.
10 Plea for Christians, ¶3, in *The Ante-Nicene Fathers,* Vol. II, Alexander Roberts & James Donaldson, Eds., The Christian Literature Publishing Co., 1885, p. 130.
11 *Dialogue Trypho,* paragraph 10.

their children, sisters, mothers---all sexes and ages. There, flushed with the banquet after such feasting and drinking, they begin to burn with incestuous passions. They provoke a dog tied to the lampstand to leap and bound towards a scrap of food which they have tossed outside the reach of his chain. By this means the light is overturned and extinguished, and with it common knowledge of their actions; in the shameless dark with unspeakable lust they copulate in random unions, all equally being guilty of incest, some by deed, but everyone by complicity.[12]

Fronto's opinion of Christians may reflect well-considered opinion in the imperial capital during the decade of 150-60.[13] As W. H. C. Frend points out, the eagerness of the church fathers to attribute the rumored sexual horrors to the Gnostic Christians, and to distinguish between them and orthodox Christians, tends to lend some credence to pagan accusations against them.[14]

The early church dealt with the two accusations, atheism and sexual immorality, in very different ways. Generally it faced the atheism issue head on and bore the consequences. Many of its leaders willingly gave their lives rather than deny the name of Christ in favor of that other religious authority, Caesar Imperator. They died accused of atheism rather than subscribe to what they considered idolatry. In fact, as the church understood itself, idolatry was the central moral issue of its life during the first three centuries. It was Jesus rather than the Caesar who deserved worship. We see this sharply portrayed in the *Martyrdom of Polycarp*, when the people shout, "Away with these atheists!"[15] Idolatry, or atheism in the eyes of Romans, was therefore the cohesive element in the Christian community. It was only when Caesar and Jesus were unified in the fourth century that idolatry ceased to be a real issue for the church. On the other hand, charges of sexual immorality

---

12   *The Octavius of Marcus Minucius Felix,* G. W. Clarke, Trans., New York: Newman Press, 1974, pp. 64-5.
13   W. H. C. Frend, *Martyrdom and Persecution in the Early Church: A Study of a Conflict from the Maccabees to Donatus,* New York: New York University Press, 1967, p. 167. One of the ironies of Christian history is that Marcus Aurelius, during whose reign Christians were so fiercely persecuted, himself came to be so highly esteemed later in the church for his "virtuous teaching." See Eusebius, *Ecclesiastical History,* Bk. 5, 1&2.
14   *Ibid.,* p. 188.
15   *The Martyrdom of Polycarp* 3:2.

The Victory of Syncretism

were simply denied. The leadership of the church gave the Romans the higher ground by conceding, implicitly, that Roman imperial sexual values were a standard by which even the church could be measured.

Much of the extant literature from the early church falls in the category of Christian Gnosticism, which ultimately was rejected and declared heretical by the mainstream church. The Gnostics were the syncretistic wing of the church. They promoted to one degree or another a spiritualistic dualism and interpreted the Christian faith as a special kind of knowledge (Gr. *gnosis*, knowledge, hence Gnostics) by means of which the soul/mind transcends the sphere of the earth and rises to the divine or heavenly (hence emanationism) sphere. In its contempt for the world and the flesh, Gnosticism usually promoted sexual asceticism, though sometimes a peculiar libertinism, rooted in the same contempt for the flesh. In contrast to the mainstream church which focused mainly on the issue of idolatry as the cohesive force in the life of the community, more typically the Gnostics placed sexual renunciation as the centerpiece of the Christian moral life.[16] In the *Acts of Paul and Thecla* the life of virginity comes before the life of prayer. In the *Acts of Thomas* sex is identified with sin. Typical of Gnostic literature is the *Act of Peter* which relates the story of Peter's beautiful but paralyzed daughter. Peter heals her to demonstrate his power, then paralyzes her again so that her suitors will be discouraged and her virginity left intact.[17] The Gnostics attempted to create a synthesis of the Judaeo-Christian religion and Greco-Roman spirituality. This synthesis generally meant that the names of the gods were changed to favor Judaeo-Christian tradition but the same Greco-Roman content was maintained. In the short term Gnosticism was defeated, but in the long term it continues to thrive in much of what is popularly known as Christian spirituality.

The body of surviving literature endorsed by the mainstream church during its first hundred years is small and, except for the *Epistle to Diognetus*, of little theological or literary value. Since this was the same period in which the New Testament was taking shape, obviously the young church placed its most highly valued literary works in the

---

16 Samuel Laeuchli, *The Language of Faith,* New York: Abingdon Press, 1962, p. 155.
17 *The Nag Hammadi Library*, James M. Robinson, ed., New York: Harper and Row, Publishers, 1978, pp. 475-77.

New Testament itself. This corpus of mainstream but extra-New Testament literature is referred to as the "Apostolic Fathers," an epithet invented much later, probably in the sixth century by Severus of Antioch. Most of the documents in this body of material are legalistic in tone and theologically shallow, but they probably reflect accurately much of the life of the church after the first generation had died. There is some evidence of syncretistic influence in this material, more so than in the New Testament, but there is no consensus in this material on sexual ethics. Exhortations about sexual behavior are generally conservative in nature and peripheral in context. Condemnations of adultery are frequent, not surprising in cautious literature, since adultery was equally anathematic to both Romans and Jews. In probable approximate chronological order this literature of the Apostolic Fathers consists of: the letters of I Clement of Rome, of Ignatius of Antioch, of Polycarp of Smyrna, the *Didache*, the *Shepherd of Hermas*, the letter of II Clement, *The Letter to Barnabas*, *The Account of Martyrdom of Polycarp*, and *The Letter to Diognetus*. I Clement, *Barnabas* and the *Shepherd of Hermas* appeared in some early versions of the New Testament canon but were eventually excluded.

How representative the collection of documents is of the whole church during its first century is not known. There was no apparent self-conscious preservation of these documents. In a sense they are the residue after the work of putting together the New Testament was complete. Nevertheless, these writings acquire a certain authority of their own in retrospect. For better or worse they are essentially all that remain of the early church, aside from the reporting of the New Testament.

Probably the earliest Christian document aside from those included in the New Testament is the long *Letter to the Corinthians* by Clement of Rome, so-called "I Clement" because another Clement also wrote a Corinthian letter later. I Clement flourished about 96 CE. He manifests no significant interest in sexual behavior except to mention "detestable adultery" twice (30:1, 35:8). He is in fact more concerned about political strife in the church, particularly the potential abuse of the office of bishop, which must have been fairly well established by this time. "Our Apostles were given to understand by our Lord Jesus Christ that the office of bishop would give rise to intrigue," he says (44:1). Clement also notes that some bishops have been unjustly deposed (44:4).

Ignatius, Bishop of Antioch, who was executed in Rome in 110 CE, has seven surviving letters. He is the church's first organization man;

in almost every letter he is reinforcing the authority of the bishop in one way or another. He seldom mentions matters of sexual behavior. But in his Epistle to Polycarp he reveals the presence of conflict in the church over the issue of sexual puritanism. "If anyone is able to remain sexually pure (Gr. *agneia*) . . . let him persistently avoid boasting. The moment he boasts he is undone, and if he is more highly esteemed than the bishop, he is undone" (5:2). "Sexually pure" here likely refers to sexual abstinence prior to receiving the eucharist rather than perpetual continence.[18] But either meaning would reveal some degree of syncretistic influence. Elsewhere he says, "Tell my sisters. . . to be content with their husbands in body and soul (5:1);. . . persevere in perfect purity (*agneia*) and sobriety (Eph 10:3); . . . those who ruin homes will not inherit the kingdom" (Eph 16:1). Ignatius refers to the eucharist as the "medicine of immortality," which (according to Laeuchli) is evidence of syncretistic influence on two counts: the focus on immortality and the view of the eucharist, i.e., bread and wine, as divine substance.[19]

The Greek words *encrateia* and *agneia* have the root meanings self-control and purity, respectively. They sometimes have specifically sexual connotations and therefore should be translated "continence" or "chastity." But they are also used less specifically to mean "self-control" in general and "moral sincerity." Neither *encrateia* nor *agneia* gets much use in the New Testament and never appears in the synoptics, but each word appears in both the general and specifically sexual sense. *Encrateia* means specifically "sexual self-control" in I Cor 7:9 (though not necessarily chastity as such) and more generally as "self-control" in Acts 24:25, I Cor 9:25, and Gal 5:23 (King James version correctly translates *encrateia* as "temperance").

Agneia has a specifically sexual connotation in 2 Cor 11:2 where Paul is creating a metaphor of "pure virgin" delivered to her bridegroom. So we know in this one instance that Paul knew how to

---

18 J. E. L. Oulton & Henry Chadwick, *Alexandrian Christianity*, London: SCM Press, 1954, p. 34.
19 Samuel Laeuchli, *op cit.*, p. 214.

say pure virgin![20] Otherwise, however, the word has either the more general meaning of "moral sincerity" or "moral purity" (I John 3:3, I Tim 5:22, Tit 2:5, I Pet 3:1, James 3:17, Phil 4:8 etc.) or, less often, "cultic" or "ritual purity" as of the Jews (John 11:55 or Acts 21:24,26).

If the New Testament had had an interest in promoting sexual purity as an ideal, *encrateia* or *agneia* would have been concepts the writers might well have used. In fact, these concepts did become important later in the church, so much so that Encratism became a splinter movement of those Christians promoting sexual purity, a movement that flowered about 170 CE.

The problem in translating *encrateia* and *agneia* is therefore one of context, both of the word in the sentence and the sentence in the cultural milieu. In a heavily syncretistic context they might mean chastity or continence in the strictest sense. As these words get used with increasingly greater emphasis later in the church, the translater's task is often difficult.[21] As time passes and the syncretistic influence is felt more heavily in the church, the use of *encrateia* and *agneia* becomes more specifically and narrowly sexual, meaning "continence" or "chastity".

Polycarp, Bishop of Smyrna, wrote his letter to the Philippians about 118 CE. He manifests no particular interest in matters of sexual behavior. In Chapter 4, after declaring that the beginning of all evils is the love of money, he exhorts his readers: ". . .teach our wives to remain in the faith given to them, and in love and sincerity/purity [*agneia*] tenderly loving their husbands in all truth, and loving all others equally in all temperance/self-control/chastity" (*encrateia*) (4:2). Whatever precisely Polycarp means here, sexual abstinence is not likely the agenda.

Then in 5:3 he writes, ". . . it is a noble thing to cut oneself off from the lusts that are rampant in the world . . . neither those who commit *porneia,* nor the effeminate [*malakoi*], nor male prostitutes [*arsenokoitoi*] will inherit the kingdom." Polycarp is simply repeating

---

20 If the early church had held virginity in high esteem one would think "pure virgin" would have been mentioned in other than this one metaphorical sense.

21 Robert M. Grant and Holt H. Graham, *The Apostolic Fathers*, Vol. II, New York: Thomas Nelson and Sons, 1965, p. 127.

Paul here and does not evidence syncretistic influence.

The date of the *Didache* is thought to be mid-second century but contains some material that originated much earlier. The author seems to give sexual sins a rather prominent place in his value system. The exhortation "Abstain from gratifying carnal impulses" appears at the beginning of the work (1:4). "Lust leads to *porneia*" (3:3), he says. Adultery, lustful desire and *porneia* are included in a list of 22 "ways of the wicked." Since the boundaries of *porneia* varied in the Jewish and Greco-Roman worlds, it remains an open question precisely what is meant by *porneia* here. This document manifests a concern about an unrestrained sexuality but it does not bear the distinct mark of syncretism.

The Shepherd of Hermas, written in Rome between 110 and 140, is a confused and confusing document. It opens with an erotic account of a certain Rhoda whom the author observed bathing in Rome. Noticing her beauty and manner, he led her by the hand from the river, fantasizing her as his wife. He then goes on to say he regarded her as a sister and goddess. This sort of ambiguous erotic abstemiousness is typical of syncretistic attitudes toward sex. The writer also applauds wives who live "as sisters" with their husbands (Vs. II 2,3). On the other hand, he explicitly approves widows' and widowers' remarrying, for which the puritanical Tertullian later labeled him the "lover of adulterers".[22] But widows and widowers who remain single gain greater honor, he says. Spouses who commit adultery and are unrepentant should be divorced. The offended party should not remarry, however, in case the offender decides to repent and return. And whoever does anything similar to what the heathen do commits adultery. The author's ultimate legalistic platitude is "keep your mind on your own wife and you'll never go wrong."

The author of *Shepherd* exhibits an ambivalence about sex, suggesting a tilt toward syncretism, and is bogged down in legalism as well. His ambivalence no doubt reflects something of the actual situation of some of the churches at that time. The work is so theologically shallow and literarily inept that B. H. Streeter calls it the "white rabbit of the Apostolic Age," to which Samuel Laeuchli counters that "blacksheep"

---

22 *De Pudicitia* 10.

would be more fitting.[23]

The unknown author of Clement's *Second Letter to the Corinthians* is referred to for clarity's sake as II Clement. That is, scholarship concludes the letter was written later and by someone other than I Clement. It is thought to be a product of Rome about 136-140. This letter seems to be the first piece of Christian literature, if the dating is accurate, that clearly and unambiguously promotes sexual abstinence as a great value. "Now I do not think that I have given any mean counsel requesting continence [*encrateia*], and whosoever performs it shall not repent thereof, but shall save both himself and me as his counselor" (15:1). "Whosoever performs it" also suggests that it was a rigorous ethical position taken only by some and not the general rule. However, he also writes, "When a brother sees a sister [of the Christian community] he is not to think of her sex, nor should she give any thought to his" (12:5). II Clement is clearly negative toward sex and therefore suggests the heavy influence of syncretism. The author's concern about his reputation as a counselor in these matters suggests that sexual behavior was something of a public relations problem for him.

The Epistle to Barnabas (c.125) inveighs in passing against adultery and *porneia,* but the author is mainly concerned about pederasty, sex change, and oral/genital sex. Popular belief at this time held that the hare grew a new anus every year, that the hyena changed its sex every year and that the weasel conceived through its mouth. Barnabas uses these popular notions, and the reputed uncleanness of these three animals, to condemn pederasty, sex change, and fellatio, "the forbidden act which debauched women do with their mouths." The author demonstrates that he is somewhat puritanical, legalistic and a misogynist, but hardly presents anything that resembles a clear philosophical or theological basis for sexual behavior.

The Martyrdom of St. Polycarp is thought to be an eyewitness account of the Bishop's trial and execution in 156 CE. The salient issue is his so-called atheism. He is called the Father of Christians, the destroyer of the gods, who teaches many neither to offer sacrifice nor to worship. There is no mention of matters of sexual behavior.

---

23 Laeuchli, *op. cit.,* p. 110.

The Epistle to Diognetus is of uncertain date, but thought to be a product of this period. It is something of a literary gem, considered one of the most brilliant things ever written by Christians in the Greek language.[24] Curiously, it is never quoted in other early literature, which further complicates attempts at dating the work. Its scant references to sexual behavior clearly manifest a Judaic bias rather than a syncretistic one. About Christians the epistle says, "they cultivate no eccentric mode of life."(5:2) "They marry like others and beget children (5:6) . . . their board they spread for all, but not their bed."(5:7) The latter is open to a variety of interpretations.

On balance, then, the documents of the Apostolic Fathers manifest no clear or well-defined sex ethics. Some of the documents to some extent suggest the influence of a syncretistic sex ethics which denigrated sexuality. Taken as a whole, the Apostolic Fathers depart little from the New Testament canon and its Hebraic orientation. All we can say for sure about these documents is that they call for temperance in the face of unrestrained sexuality. But as the church increasingly penetrated the gentile or pagan world, it was confronted more and more with the either/or of Stoic and syncretistic sexual denial on the one hand, and unrestrained sexual abandon, as epitomized by Nero, for example, on the other.

II

As the church increasingly penetrated Greco-Roman culture, marriage rites must have presented a complex and formidable problem. As long as the church remained in a Jewish milieu this was not the case. Among the Jews marriage was a secular event and had no cultic implications. It was a contract between individuals and families. Weddings were not in any way connected with religious observances, even though rabbinic interpretation of the Torah required all males to marry.

In Greco-Roman culture of this era marriage was a distinctly cultic ceremony. The family hearth was one of the major foci of religious rites, which in tandem with the public cults, sanctified family and em-

---

24 Joseph A. Kleist, *Ancient Christian Writers,* Westminster, MD: Newman Press. 1948, p. 211.

pire. The family hearth was the place where deceased ancestors were memorialized and the gods of each particular household worshipped. The *paterfamilias* was the priest and administrator of these rites. His wife was co-priest, which tended to sacralize the monogamy that was required in Greco-Roman culture. Marriage, then, meant a partial change of religion for the bride as she was taken into the new family. This is the origin of the tradition of carrying the bride over the threshold, and of the wedding cake, the sacramental food of the new family cult.

The first Christian bride marrying into a Greco-Roman family, whoever she was, faced a complex problem. There is no record of how this issue was negotiated. Idolatry and offering sacrifices to idols was, at least in the first generations of the church, a serious offense. This concern, perhaps, lay behind Bishop Ignatius' requirement that Christians should marry only with his approval. He could have monitored, thereby, any temptation presented to his people to adopt pagan family cults through marriage.

Tertullian and the Montanists late in the second century were the first known to have moved marriage itself into the church *in facie ecclesiasiae*. However, the mainstream church appears not to have taken up this practice of these dissident purists. The issue resolved itself naturally in the fourth century when Christianity became the religion of the empire. Marriage remained then, as it was, a family affair, sometimes with ecclesiastical blessing, but the problem with idols disappeared. Only at the end of the first millenium did the church finally assume administrative authority over marriage and bring the marriage ceremony proper into the church building.[25] The intriguing question remains, its answer now lost to history, how the early Christian communities which certainly began with a secular (Jewish) view of marriage meshed with Roman tradition and its practice of marriage as a religious rite.

III

After the church completed its first hundred years, from ap-

---

[25] Schillebeeckx, *Marriage,* pp. 234-237. See also Michael D. Place, "The History of Christian Marriage," *Chicago Studies,* Vol. 18, No. 3, Fall 1979, pp. 311-325.

The Victory of Syncretism

proximately mid-second century, profound changes began to take place. The church entered the so-called Age of the Apologists, a time in which dialogue with pagan philosophy and religion began in earnest. In the arena of sex ethics, we witness in this period the distinct, if gradual, adoption of the syncretistic standard of sexual purity by the fathers of the church. Supporting this trend was the simultaneous gradual adoption of a platonist anthropology by the theologians of the period. The transition was complete by the time the Empire adopted the church as the imperial religion in the fourth century. By that time the sexual ethics of the church were little more than a recasting of syncretistic sexual values. By then the church's original Judaic anthropology had been jettisoned.

A body of literature appeared at this time, related to if not synonymous with Gnosticism, which flourished for about a century, until mid-3rd century. It came to be known as Encratism, from the Greek word meaning "self-control." The movement promoted sexual abstinence. This movement virtually conquered the church in Syria, where celibacy became a requirement for baptism. Mani (or Manes or Manichaeus 216-276) was a product of this tradition in the Syrian Orient, which he reshaped in his own way.[26] Some local churches under encratic influence baptized only virgins. One particular literary form that represented this movement was the *Acts* of various apostles, a type of Hellenistic romance. What they all have in common is the view that sexual intercourse is prohibited in the Christian life. Of course, Encratism can be understood simply as part of the Gnostic adaptation and refinement of the sex-negative ideology of platonism within the church. However, Steven L. Davies points out, in a fascinating examination of these *Acts,* that sexual continence seems to be a device whereby women were able to assert themselves against their husbands in a patriarchal system.[27] He calls these *Acts* intrinsically hyperbolic. Davies argues quite persuasively that we are not witnessing here a simple ideological conflict, but the fragments of a complex political

---

26 Arthur Voobus, "Celibacy, A Requirement for Admission to Baptism in the Early Syrian Church," *Papers of the Estonian Theological Society in Exile,* Stockholm, 1951, p. 20.
27 Steven L. Davies, *The Revolt of the Widows: The Social World of the Apocryphal Acts,* Carbondale, Ill: Southern Illinois University Press, 1980.

struggle as women attempted to stave off the patriarchalization of the church. Asexuality was perhaps the only mechanism by which women could defend themselves against patriarchal exploitation. This may explain why Irenaeus seems to suggest that the Gnostics found in women an especially receptive audience.[28] Nothing is so powerful as religion against exploitative customs and laws. These *Acts* do not prohibit marriage. They do not propose a monastic life or celibacy. They do encourage women to refuse to submit to the desires of their husbands and to flee from home if they are unable to resist.

The leadership of the church, with the rise of the power of the bishops, was in the process of developing a strongly patriarchal character, forcing women into an increasingly submissive role. But there is no reason to assume that the bishops' power was established without a struggle. The writings of Ignatius and 1 Clement demonstrate that the assertion of authority by the bishops was a matter of significant and widespread controversy. It is noteworthy that Celsus in about 178 attacked the church in part because it was illegally subverting established institutions, not least of all the authority of the *paterfamilias* over his household.[29] Celsus would appear to be alluding not to the Apostolic Fathers of this period but rather to a movement on the order of the women in revolt. It must be wondered if a long simmering war of the sexes had not been taking place in the developing church from the very beginning. Certainly if Fiorenza is correct about the initial discipleship of gender equality in the early Jesus movement, the ultimate metamorphosis of the church into a typically Roman imperial patriarchal system could hardly have taken place without conflict. We may have the fragments of that conflct in some of these sex-negative Hellenistic romances that Davies analyzes.

The church ultimately came to reflect the Greco-Roman social order in its organizational character, and therefore gradually but ineluctably acquired a strongly sexist character. By the close of the second century, Clement of Alexandria appears only mildly sexist. But his contemporary, Tertullian, is the one who represents the future church:

It is not permitted for a woman to speak in the church, nor is it

---

28 For example, *Against Heresies*, 1.13.3.
29 See W.H.C. Frend, "Early Christianity and Society: A Jewish Legacy in the Pre-Constantinian Era," *Harvard Theological Review,* 76:1, Jan 1983, p. 53.

permitted for her to teach, nor to baptize, nor to offer the eucharist, nor to claim for herself a share in any masculine function---least of all, in priestly office.[30]

Addressing women in a sermon, Tertullian writes:

> The sentence of God on this sex of yours lives on even in our times and so it is necesary that the guilt should live on also. You are the one who opened the door to the Devil; you are the one who first plucked the fruit of the forbidden tree; you are the first who deserted the divine law; you are the one who persuaded him whom the Devil was not strong enough to attack. All too easily you destroyed the image of God, man. Because of your desert, that is, death, even the Son of God had to die. And you still think of putting adornments over the skins of animals that cover you?[31]

With patriarchy, if not misogyny, firmly established in the church, men had on their side both imperial and Christian law and custom.

One of the strangest ironies of Christian history is that this flesh-denying Gnostic/encratic movement became for women the instrument for the liberation of their flesh, and in turn that mainstream Christians who theoretically affirmed the body, in effect affirmed only the male body. Furthermore, it is doubly ironic that the sexual asceticism of the Gnostic/encratic movement ultimately achieved ascendancy in the mainstream church, whereas patriarchal exploitation continued unabated as well. The revolt of the women was in the long run to no avail. Only the weapon they used in their revolt, sexual abstinence, prevailed. Even it was ultimately used against them by the victorious males.

Theophilus, who became bishop of Antioch in 169, may or may not suggest a leaning toward encratism. "Among Christians," he says, "temperance is present, continence (*encratia*) is exercised, monogamy preserved, purity (*agneia*) guarded."[32]

Tatian, Justin, and Athenagoras were three contemporary philosophers who converted from Neoplatonism to Christianity during this period. Tatian ultimately abandoned his adopted faith and therefore

---

30 Tertullian, *Of the Veiling of Virgins* 9.
31 Tertullian, *The Apparel of Women,* 1.1, Deferrari, trans.
32 *Ad Autycum* 3:15.

perhaps should be taken less seriously as a spokesman for the mainstream church. In any case, sexual abstinence was for him almost the prime ingredient of the Christian life and he was said by several early church authorities to have been the founder of Encratism.[33]

Justin Martyr was born in Samaria (c100) and died a martyr for his faith (c165). In his conversion from Neoplatonism, he brought syncretistic sexual values with him into Christianity. He is explicit and unambiguous. Christians, he says, either marry in order to have children or declining marriage live in continence (*encrateia*).[34] Justin was defensive about charges that Christians practice promiscuous intercourse and had heard the story of the dog and the lampstand. Perhaps the Gnostics do those things, he suggests. Justin boasts of one of his fellow Christians who presented a petition to Felix, the governor of Alexandria, asking permission for a surgeon to make him a eunuch. Surgeons were not permitted to perform such operations on their own authority. The request was denied, but Justin made his point, that "promiscuous intercouse was not one of the mysteries" of the church.[35] There are many Christians now 60 and 70 years old, he reported, who have followed Christ since their youth and now remain spotless or undefiled (*aphthoroi*).[36] Reminiscent of II Clement, Justin is the first in mainstream ecclesiastical literature to relegate sex to procreation and unambiguously to promote sexual purity as a pious achievement. The tide has begun to turn.

Athenagoras, the Athenian philosopher who converted to Christianity in his mature years, similarly contends that sex is only for the purpose of procreation[37]. He uses the metaphor of the sower throwing seeds on the ground to await the harvest as a metaphor for proper sexual behavior. The sower does not continue to throw seeds upon seeds, he says. That would be an indulgence of the appetite. There are many among the Christians, he says, growing old unmarried in hope of living in closer communion with God. The virgin and the eunuch are brought close to God. Indulging in carnal thoughts and desires lead

---

33 *Tatian: Oratio and Fragments,* Molly Whittaker, ed./trans., Oxford: Clarendon Press, 1982.
34 *1st Apology* Section 29.
35 *Ibid.*
36 *Ibid.,* Section 15.
37 *A Plea for the Christioans,* Section 33.

away from God. Furthermore, he views a second marriage as specious adultery, because in the beginning God made one man and one woman. We are left to guess why Justin and Athenagoras jumped with such unambiguous clarity into the camp of sexual renunciation. Coming to Christianity from Greek philosophy as they did, they either brought it with them or reverted to it under social pressure. Paradoxically, they sided with biblical tradition against their own philosophical past in rejecting the notion of the immortality of the soul in favor of the resurrection of the body. However, on the sexual issue they were both Neoplatonists or Stoic throwbacks. It is clear that both Justin and Athenagoras were stung by pagan charges of Christian sexual immorality and were making every effort to neutralize these charges. But in doing so they gave all the ground to their opponents. They eventually adopted completely a syncretistic, specifically Stoic, sexual valorization.

Clement of Alexandria, who was born about 150 CE, represents as well as anyone could the ambivalence of the period. He is both attracted to and repelled by the dualism of popular syncretistic religion which regarded the flesh evil and the soul divine. On the one hand Clement writes like a man immersed in the Old Testament, giving a positive evaluation of marriage. He even goes so far as to contend that the unmarried man is inferior to the married.

> True manhood is shown, not in the choice of a celibate life, . . . but by him who has trained himself by the discharge of the duties of husband and father and by the supervision of a household . . . superior to every temptation which assails him through children and wife and servants and possessions . . . He who has no family is in most respects untried.[38]

Clement supports his argument by recalling that the apostles were themselves married, though he is quick to add that they lived together as brother and sister.[39] Further, he attacks as blasphemy the labeling of marriage as *porneia*, a popular syncretistic notion.[40] He also is willing to bless sexual intercourse for the married, though it must be done at

---
38 *Stromateis,* VII, XII, 70.
39 *On Marriage,* 6.53.
40 *On Marriage,* XII, Paragraph

night after dinner when it is time to retire, and all indecencies should be avoided in the intimate embrace. He doesn't spell out what they might be, but he does suggest it not be done in the daytime, or after returning from church or even from the market. He also objects to copulation at dawn, "like the rooster."[41]

On the other hand, Clement contends that the passionless life with one's wife as a sister is the resurrection state and that the only licit sex is that done for procreation. The best Christians may be married but they abstain from sex. This is Clement's interpretation of Jesus' teaching that in the resurrection there will be no marriage. This is not a rejection of marriage, he says, but merely a rejection of carnal desire. His interpretation is of course backwards. Clement tried his best to be faithful to the church's Hebraic origins, but on the critical issue of sex itself he threw it all away. He impugned sex in order to preserve marriage and therefore conceded to the syncretists their major argument.[42]

The second hundred years of the church's life could be epitomized as a transition from Irenaeus to Tertullian. Chronologically and geographically the distance between these two church Fathers was not that great, but theologically they were worlds apart. Irenaeus was Bishop of Lyon in what is now southern France. Tertullian was a priest in the North African city of Carthage. Irenaeus died in 202, Tertullian in c. 220.

Irenaeus stands virtually alone among theologians and church fathers of this period in resisting an ethics of sexual renunciation. This should not be a surprise, since, as Samuel Laeuchli demonstrates in *The Language of Faith*, Irenaeus is the one theologian of his century who is consistently faithful to biblical language and tradition. Irenaeus is the least swayed by syncretistic religious values of all the theologians of the early church after 150 CE whose works are left to us. Most of his extant written work is dedicated to counter the syncretistic or Gnostic cults on the edge of Christianity, but unlike other apologists who were often battling the same syncretists, he does not give away his Hebraic anthropology in the process. The closest he comes to a syncretistic theology is his defense of the Virgin

---

41 *Clement of Alexandria, Christ the Educator*, Simon P. Wood, trans., New York: Fathers of the Church, Inc. 1954, p. 174.
42 See *On Marriage* and "Introduction" in J. E. L. Oulton & Henry Chadwick, *Library of Christian Classics, Vol. II, Alexandrian Christianity*, London: SCM Press, 1954,, p. 34.

The Victory of Syncretism

Birth, itself an artifact of syncretism, but his motivation in this case was unquestionably his devotion to the canonical gospels. Irenaeus is in this sense a voice in the wilderness. The tide of history was running against him. During the century following his death a spiritualistic dualism, the heart of the syncretistic religion, will have been enthroned in the church.

The struggle for Irenaeus is not between soul and body, but between lost and recovered humanity, and in this he is faithful to biblical anthropology. He avoids metaphysical speculations about the nature of God and man that were the stock-in-trade of syncretistic religion. He avoids categories of deification that seeped into the church from the pagan world, such as Ignatius of Antioch's reference to the eucharist as "the medicine of immortality." In the faithfully biblical anthropology of Irenaeus man remains a creature of God and is never in any sense divinized. Irenaeus also avoids the (epidemic) legalism which transformed Christianity into a moral code.

On the other side of the Mediterranean, Tertullian represents the beginning of the end of Jewish anthropology in the church. He began in earnest what Augustine completed 200 years later, namely an unambiguously ascetic sexual ethics that was indistinguishable from the sexual ethics of syncretism. This decisive shift is one that dominates ecclesiastical ethics into the present era. In spite of the fact that he joined the heretical and puritanical Montanist party later in life and still later broke from them to organize the Tertullianists, he is considered alongside Augustine as the greatest theologian of the patristic period, a strange epithet for a man who finished his life as a heretic.[43] Certainly, Tertullian's historical importance is unquestionable and the substance of his contribution to Christian ethics is as unassailable as it is unfortunate. He was a major force in the uprooting of the Judeo-Christian anthropology on which biblical sexual ethics are based and in the construction of a sexual ethics of purity and continence.

More than any other early church theologian, Tertullian was unabashedly attracted to the sexual renunciation of the syncretistic religions of the empire. Tertullian sings the praises of the priestesses of Ceres who amicably separate from their husbands to live lives of

---

43 *The Oxford Dictionary of the Christian Church,* F. L. Cross, ed., London: Oxford University Press, 1957, p. 1334. The 1974 edition rewrote "Tertullian," dropping the epithet and substituting: "His language and thought was sufficient to justify the title of Father of Latin Theology," p. 1532.

celibacy. The virgins who attend the cult of Achaean Juno, Scythian Diana and Pythian Apollo draw his admiration. So do the priests who practice celibacy in their dedication to the Egyptian bull. Most of all he praises the obligations of the Pontifex Maximus, the supreme religious authority of the imperial religion, who was not permitted to marry again if widowed. This was a rule observed more by the abrogation than the keeping of it, especially when the emperors assumed the office of Pontifex Maximus, but Tertullian is lauding the original ideal. These pagan examples of sexual purity are a sentence of judgment on the infirmity of Christians, according to Tertullian.[44]

Tertullian was dismayed and outraged at the failure of the mainstream church up to this point to adopt an ethics of sexual purity. His outrage led him to reject the mainstream church and join the puritanical Montanists. He attacked the Catholics, accusing them of being "sensualists." His argument is strident. A second marriage is nothing more than a variety of fornication. What marriage and fornication have in common, he says, is sex, as if to use one to malign the other. The highest perfection in life is virginity from birth and the next is renunciation of sex in marriage. As children of the world to come, we kill concupiscence in order to prepare for paradise, he says. He also argues that the disciples and apostles kept wives as "sisters,"[45] a claim that has absolutely no basis in the New Testament. An ironic twist is that Tertullian defends monogamy against certain heretics who repudiate marriage altogether. But sex in Tertullian's monogamy is clearly for procreation and for nothing else. Like Clement of Alexandria, he is defending monogamy against its detractors but it is a monogamy bereft of sex.

However, if the theologians became increasingly negative toward sex, we do not have to assume that their theories reflect precisely the values and practices of the average believer. One of the few individuals remembered by name from the early church is Marcia, a certain concubine of Emperor Commodius (180-92). She was able to get relief for the Christian community in Rome because of her intimate position with the Emperor. While we should not make too much of her, the very memory of her in history is probably an appropriate antidote to the in-

---

44 "Monogamy", in *Tertullian: Treatises on Marriage and Remarriage,* William P. LeSaint, trans., Westminster, MD: The Newman Press, 1956, pp. 107-108.
45 *Ibid.,* p. 87.

creasingly rigorous views of theologians who were now beginning to express their contempt for sex in any form but procreative.[46]

We see the Tertullianizing process at work in Eusebius, Bishop of Caesarea (c. 260-340), the first church historian. There is in him still some ambivalence such as has been evidenced elsewhere. On the one hand he quotes Irenaeus condemning the views of Saturninus and Marcion, the so-called Encratites who advocated continence.[47]

On the other hand Eusebius lionizes Origen for having made himself a eunuch. Eusebius reports that Origen's bishop expressed contempt for Origen's act of self-inflicted castration, but Eusebius says the bishop was actually jealous of Origen's renown. In a similar vein, Eusebius also tells the martyr's tale of Domnina and her unmarried daughters "in the full flower of their girlish charm. . . seeing that her daughters and herself were in dire peril. . . of all dreadful things the most unbearable---the threat to their chastity. . . threw themselves in the river and drowned."[48] For Eusebius and Domnina suicide is a more righteous choice than to risk the involuntary loss of one's chastity. Later, Ambrose expressed his admiration for the fifteen-year-old Palagia, for the same deed. Augustine thought such action unwarranted.[49]

IV

The Constantinian adoption of the church in 312 as the favored imperial religion, and later in the century as the only imperial religion, was without doubt the singular political event in all of church history. From the status of a countercultural, sporadically persecuted institution constantly under suspicion of treason, the church was rather abruptly

---

46 Henry Chadwick, *op cit.,* p. 29.
47 Eusebius, *The History of the Church from Christ to Constantine,* G. A. Williamson, trans., New York: Penguin Books, 1965, p. 190.
48 *Ibid.,* p. 342.
49 *The City of God,* Henry Bettensen, trans., New York: Penguin Books, 1972, p. 37.

transformed into a new agency of the imperial bureaucracy funded by imperial taxes.[50] The rival religions and imperial cultic rites did not disappear at once. In fact, for the rest of the century the church co-existed in one degree or another with the so-called pagan religious practices of the empire.[51] By about 400 the Catholic Church was distinguished from all other religions by its privileged status and by the fact that all the others were suppressed in one degree or another.[52] In fact, the Catholic bishops themselves began to be experienced by heretics and non-Catholics as the primary source of persecutorial terror.[53] In the centuries after Constantine, according to Peter Brown, more Christians were persecuted as "heretics" than had earlier been persecuted as Christians by pagans.[54] Constantine himself retained his title of Pontifex Maximus, high priest of the empire, and did not object to the continuing practice of temples built and dedicated to his name and worship. Constantine was quite eclectic, though certainly not unique in this respect. The offices of the flamenes, the municipal priesthoods that served one or another Roman god, were sometimes held even by Christians.[55] The Council of Elvira inveighs against this laxity.

Constantine's religious sincerity is a subject of some debate even today. On the one side are scholars who support Constantine's personal piety, such as N. H. Baynes who argues that "it was not altogether unfitting that he should be laid to rest in the Church of the Twelve Apostles, himself the thirteenth apostle."[56] Eusebius, the contemporary historian, was perhaps in a position to know the truth of Constantine's sincerity, but he was a sycophantic devotee of the emperor and does not seem to

---

50 See esp. Jacob Burckhardt, *The Age of Constantine The Great,* Moses Hadas, trans., Los Angeles: University of California Press, 1949, p. 307.
51 And perhaps beyond. See especially Ramsay MacMullen, *Paganism in the Roman Empire,* New Haven: Yale University Press, 1981, pp. 131-7.
52 Peter Brown, *op. cit.,* 1972, p. 303.
53 *Ibid.,* p. 321.
54 *Ibid.,* p. 243.
55 Chadwick, *op. cit.,* p. 30, 121.
56 *Constantine the Great and the Christian Church,* Proceedings of the British Academy XV, 1929, p 28; see also *Constantine the Great,* Lloyd B. Holsapple, New York: Sheed & Ward, 1942, p 441; *The Conversion of Constantine and Pagan Rome,* Andrew Alfoldi, Harold Mattingly, trans., Oxford: Clarendon Press, 1948.

The Victory of Syncretism

have asked searching questions about the matter.[57]

On the other side are scholars like Jacob Burkhardt who argue that Constantine was a cynical and brutal politician who simply used the church for his own ends. The church had by that time created a politically useful, well organized network, which Joseph Brodsky has characterized as a system of mutual assistance that was "a combination of food stamps and the Red Cross."[58] Burckhardt points out that Constantine had considerable blood on his hands, including that of his wife Fausta and his sons Crispus and Licinianus, each of whom was murdered after Nicea.[59] His mother Eleni, a former concubine of Constantius, Constantine's father, is said to have found on a trip to Palestine the three crosses, nails, crown of thorns and sponge. In a somewhat narcissistic act of devotion, Constantine had the nails made into a bit for his horse and a helmet for himself. Ironically, he was baptized on his deathbed by a bishop of the condemned Arian party, the same party the Council of Nicea under his presidency had declared heretical.

Some argue in Constantine's defense that his guilt cannot be established with certainty in the murders of his relatives. Besides that, it is not quite fair to judge someone by the standard of another time. Constantine may have assessed some monumental threat to the stability of the empire. Henry Chadwick says his conversion was neither "an inward experience of grace" nor "a cynical act of Machiavellian cunning", but a military matter.[60] Peter Brown says, ". . . the peace and unanimity of both the Christian Church and his newly conquered Empire is so marked a feature of his public utterances that we are left to suspect that the craving for the unity of his own Empire under one God is the clue to his constant alliance with the Church."[61] In any case, the claims for Constantine's personal piety seem destined to remain, at the very least, under a cloud. Whatever Constantine's real motivation, however, the identity of the church was radically and permanently altered by him. The church as a result must have undergone a monumental identity

---

57 John Holland Smith, *Constantine the Great,* New York: Charles Scribner's Sons, 1971, pp 105-6.
58 Joseph Brodsky, "Reflections", *The New Yorker,* Oct 28, 1985, p 47.
59 Burckhardt, *op. cit.,* p. 283.
60 Chadwick *op. cit.,* p. 125.
61 Brown, *op. cit.,* (1972), p. 256.

crisis. No longer threatened with persecution, the clergy were now exempted from taxes and other burdensome public obligations. It is reported by Burkhardt that applicants for the priesthood increased to a dangerous level and had to be discouraged.[62] It is not surprising that Jerome a few decades later is appalled about clerical corruption in an institution in which membership might have meant execution only a few years earlier.

Samuel Laeuchli proposes in his brilliant and neglected *Power and Sexuality*[63] that the imperial adoption of the church eliminated idolatry as the central ethical issue of the Christian life, thereby creating a crisis in the church. No longer was it a choice between Christ and Caesar as lord of the world. Faced with an identity crisis, the church consequently seized upon sexual purity as the new central ethical issue of the Christian life. Sexual purity became therefore the new singular distinguishing mark for Christians, as well as the ecclesiastical instrument of control over the people. Laeuchli is unquestionably correct that idolatry was a dead issue from Constantine onwards. This is not to say that either the pagan cults or religious imperial nationalism disappeared. The former were harried until they were erased; the latter was absorbed by the church. The empire was essentially baptized, so that the boundary between church and empire disappeared. The church's distinctive identity surely must have been shaken as a consequence. In choosing sexual purity as its new and distinctive identifying mark, the church was choosing the same distinctive mark as that of syncretistic imperial religion. The names of the imperial gods were changed, but the basic ethical content remained the same.

Laeuchli bases his conclusions on his study of the canons of the Council of Elvira, a peculiarly neglected document in the church's history, perhaps because they stand as an embarrassment to the church. The lack of attention that Laeuchli's work on this council received is further evidence of the church's wish not to discuss Elvira. The reviews of *Power and Sexuality* in theological journals consistently missed the point of the book.

Several arguments are made to minimize the importance of Elvira. The council did not legislate for the international church. It was not an

---

62 *op. cit.*, p. 307.
63 Philadelphia: Temple University Press, 1972.

ecumenical council but a provincial one, taking place in "out of the way" Spain. However it was not far enough off the beaten track to prevent one of its leading actors, Bishop Hosius, from subsequently becoming Constantine's ecclesiastical advisor. There also is continuing uncertainty as to Elvira's exact date, which was probably 309. Finally, pronouncements at councils do not necessarily imply subsequent enforcement. Councils then, as councils now, have a certain propagandistic or public relations purpose.

Nevertheless, the canons of the Council of Elvira make a remarkable and shocking document, a fact ignored by many church historians who prefer to get bogged down in quarrels over the council's date. The canons are remarkable at any date because they reveal a church, or a part of it, obsessed with sexual purity. Almost half of its 81 canons legislate on sexual matters. Sexual purity in a rather extreme form was unambiguously proclaimed as normative for the Christian life.

The council proscribed sex in almost every imaginable form, premarital and extramarital sex of any kind, sex in youth and widowhood as well. For example, canon 30 prohibits ordination to those who have sinned sexually in their youth. The intensity of emphasis on this new morality of sexual purity manifests itself startlingly when one compares the variety of penalties in the various canons of Elvira. Canon 5, for example, reads: "If a woman overcome with rage whips her maidservant so badly that she dies within three days . . . she shall not be readmitted to communion for seven years." Canon 13 reads: "Virgins consecrated to God who break their vow shall not receive communion at the end. However, if they have intercourse only once and do penance for the rest of their lives, they may receive communion at the end."[64] For the laity the new rule of sexual purity meant coitus only within the bounds of marriage. But for the clergy the sexual purity standard meant total abstinence from sex. Married clergy---and presumably most were married---were to be defrocked if they fathered children, even by their wives (Canon 33). While Elvira may not have spoken for the whole church, its pronouncements were clearly an adumbration of things to come.

Sexual purity as a standard or norm is always in dialectic relation-

---

64   *Ibid.*, p. 128.

ship with a notion of sex as defilement. They are two sides of the same issue in positive and negative terms. This dialectic was a major driving force in syncretistic imperial religion and the driving force at Elvira as well. Nowhere else in the history of the church is there a more powerful illustration of the irrational sense of sex as contamination or defilement and of the manner in which this supersedes every other ethical issue, including even murder.

A similar prohibition of clerical sex also was proposed at the Council of Nicaea in 325, which was, unlike Elvira, an ecumenical council representing the entire international church, the first of its kind. Most of the bishops present were disposed to follow the rulings of Elvira prohibiting conjugal relations to bishops, priests, deacons and subdeacons. Ironically, Bishop Paphnutius, from Upper Thebaid, a lifelong celibate, dissuaded the council from such legislation. Paphnutius himself was one of the more colorful and likable characters in the church's early history. He had been condemned to the mines for his religion in the reign of Emperor Maximinus (308-13) after having his left leg mutilated and his right eye gouged out. He is said to have been a favorite of Constantine, who would send for the cleric and kiss the place where his eye was torn out. Paphnutius argued before the council that "none should be separated from her, to whom, while yet unordained, he had been united."[65] This suggests a humane quality in Paphnutius that took precedence over concerns for sexual purity. On the other hand, he also permits a tacit prohibition of marriage after ordination, a prohibition that is institutionalized in Eastern Orthodoxy. While this is a variant of the theme of sex as defilement, it is less rigorous than the requirements of Elvira. Paphnutius carried the council with him unanimously, due to the great veneration in which he was held and, not least of all, the fact that he himself was a lifelong celibate. However, the toleration of Paphnutius and Nicaea was to be short-lived.

In the spirit of Elvira rather than Nicaea, though with less severity, Pope Damasus (366-84), Pope Siricius (383-399), and the Synod of Carthage in 390 attempted to impose sexual continence on married bishops,

---

65 Socrates, *Ecclesiastical History*, I, 11.

priests, and deacons.[66] Celibacy was not the issue at this time, but rather purity at the altar. The pressure for total continence is thought to have originated with the rule that intercourse was to be avoided on nights prior to receiving the eucharist. This rule was undoubtedly following the example of the syncretistic religions which required that anyone approaching the altar must not have enjoyed the pleasures of Venus the night before.

For example, the Rules of Purity for Visitors to the Temple of Athena at Pergamom required one to refrain from intercourse with one's spouse that day, and from someone other than one's spouse for the preceding two days.[67] Later, certain Old Testament ritual purity requirements were called upon to justify this rule in retrospect (e.g., Ex 19:15; I Sam 21:5-7; Lev 15:16ff; 22:4).

The coincidental convergence in the Western church at this time of the practice of daily eucharist and the rule of sexual continence before the eucharist resulted, no doubt, in *de facto* celibacy for some. The failure to adopt the practice of daily eucharist in the Eastern church, rather than a more affirming attitude toward sex, probably determined in the long run Constantinople's and the Eastern church's toleration of married clergy.[68]

It is noteworthy that Pope Damasus' name is associated both with the beginnings of de facto celibacy and with the highest pinnacle yet reached in clerical opulence and corruption. His critics called him "the ladies' ear tickler." The pagan priest Praetextatus is reported to have said to Damasus, "Make me bishop of Rome and I will become a Christian."[69] The stridency of Jerome's criticism of clerical corruption and his own retreat to monastic life is in this context at least understandable. It is probably not coincidental that the monastic movement flourished during the century of the church's integration into the imperial bureaucracy.

---

66 Migne, *Patrologiae Cursus Completus, Latin*, Vol. 13, p. 1184. See also Karl Baus, *History of the Church,* Hubert Jedin and John Dolan, eds., Vol. 2, NY: Seabury Press, 1980, pp. 270-280.
67 Frederick C. Grant, *op. cit. p. 6*
68 R. Kottje, "Das Aufkommen der taglichen Eucharistiefeier in der Westkirke und die Zolbatsforderung", *Zeitschrift fur Kirchengeschichte,* 81, 1971, pp. 218-288.
69 Chadwick, *op. cit.*, p. 161.

V

While Ambrose (339-397), Jerome (331-419), and Augustine (354-430) hold title as the preeminent theologians of the fourth and early fifth centuries, it would be more precise to say that they were the victors in a fierce and bloody struggle waged among Christians of that period. The drift of history was toward uniformity; the forcible suppression of the Donatists and the Manichees was a sign of the times. In fact, the Manichees earned the distinction of being the first Christians in history to be executed by other Christians.[70] The fall of Rome and the collapse of the empire typically conjures up images today of disorder and chaos. For the central government that was in some sense true. On the local level, however, perhaps in compensation for what was happening to the empire, the times were marked by increasing tidiness and rigidity.[71] By the end of the sixth century, Western society would regard itself as totally Christian---Christendom was born.

Some of the victims of this progress toward uniformity are known only by the documents that condemn them. Jovinian, Helvidius, Julian of Eclanum, and Vigilantius form a ghostly collection of theologians, not known to belong to any particular school or splinter group, but are remnants of what Tertullian two centuries earlier would have called "Catholic sensualists." Whatever they may have written is lost to history, but we know something of them from the attacks of Jerome and Augustine. If it is an ironic and cruel fate to be remembered only in the attacks made by one's enemies, they might not be remembered at all had their enemies not attacked them so thoroughly.

Helvidius was condemned for declaring that the brothers and sisters of Jesus were the natural children of Mary and Joseph, thereby rendering impossible the notion of the perpetual virginity of Mary. Jerome said Helvidius had "fouled the sanctuary of the Holy Spirit by presuming to make issue therefrom a whole cartload of brothers and sisters."[72] Vigilantius

---

70 Brown (1972), p. 94.
71 *Ibid.*, p. 117.
72 St. Jerome, *Dogmatic and Polemical Works*, John N. Hritzu, trans., Washington: The Catholic University of America Press, 1965, p. 35. However, this is Pierre de Labriolle's translation from *History and Literature of Christianity from Tertullian to Boethius*, New York: Barnes & Noble, 1968, p. 351.

was accused by Jerome of rejecting celibacy and monasticism, as well as the cult of the saints and martyrs. Many bishops are said to have followed him. Jovinian, himself a monk, was condemned for denying that virginity is a higher calling than marriage. Augustine says Jovinian was so influential in the city of Rome that many nuns about whom there had been no suspicion were precipitated into marriage. He was teaching, according to Augustine, that Christian women need not attempt to surpass leading Old Testament women in their virtue.[73] Jerome says Jovinian commanded a large army, speaking metaphorically, with many officers.[74] The exact reach of the movement is lost to history, but it was large and influential enough to get the serious attention of the leadership of the church. They were dissenting voices, protesting the church's increasing vilification of sexuality. Though they remain pale figures in history, they seem to have been witnesses to a biblical anthropology as opposed to a baptized platonist one. The latter juggernaut overwhelmed both them and the church as well.

Somewhat better known were two others on the same side of this particular theological battle: Julian of Eclanum and Theodore of Mopsuestia. The latter's writings have survived his condemnation. A contemporary of Augustine like the others, Theodore escaped Augustine's polemics probably by an accident of geography. Mopsuestia, now called Mensis or Messis, is located 12 miles from the sea on the Pyramus river, 40 miles north of Tarsis,[75] and is therefore situated well into the Eastern region of the Christian world. Like the others, Theodore was condemned, but only much later. The Council of Constantinople in 553 under Justinian condemned him after he had been dead more than a century. Some of his writings were secretly preserved under the safe pseudonym of "Ambrose" and sheltered in sympathetic monasteries in the West.[76]

Theodore was not only relatively isolated from Western ecclestiastical politics centered in Rome, but he was situated in the orbit of Antioch, which was the focal point of anti-platonizing forces in the church. An intense battle was underway during the fourth century between the proponents of a "biblical" anthropology and those of a platonic one, the

---

73 *The Retractions*, II, 48.
74 *Against Jovinian*, II, 37.
75 William Smith and Henry Wace, A Dictionary of Christian Biography, 4 Vols, London, 1887, Vol 4, p. 936.
76 *Ibid.*, p. 938.

former centered at Antioch, the latter at Alexandria. The argument was focused on the subject of Christ's personhood. The Antiochenes in general stressed the fact of Jesus' humanity and stressed his role as a prophet in some special way related to God. The Alexandrians stressed Jesus as the incarnation of the Divine Logos, presenting him as the Divine Man. The Antiochenes were vulnerable to charges that they neglected Jesus' divinity; the Alexandrians, that they presented Jesus as a God in human disguise.

The early councils in their credal formulations attempted to strike a balance by affirming both Jesus' full humanity and full divinity. Obviously, no one has yet been able to explain the complexities of such a union. Furthermore, affirming Jesus' full humanity does not create the same kind of problems that affirming his full divinity does. Subsequent history, as one might expect, has given precedence to the Alexandrian view. Such is the context in which Edward Schillebeeckx begins his recent massive work on Jesus with the disclaimer that he is not dealing in history with gods in human disguise, only people.[77]

The outcome of the battle between Alexandria and Antioch was probably determined in advance by the fact that virtually the entire culture of the Mediterranean world was dominated by Plotinus and Porphyry, the patrons of what was subsequently labeled the Neo-Platonist movement. The pagan world was primed for a Logos theology of the Divine Man, God in human form. Of course, for a true platonist, any notion of the Logos appearing in human flesh would be a profoundly problematic, if not horrifying, proposition. Some think that the first Logos theology, especially the prologue to the gospel of John and its claim for the Word (Logos) becoming flesh, was an ironic assault on pagan Logos theology.[78] Since logos and flesh are antithetical, to unite the two is a basic contradiction in platonic terms. Nevertheless, the platonic categories were co-opted, transformed, and ultimately dog-

---

77 *Jesus*, Hubert Hoskins, trans., New York: The Seabury Press, 1979, pp. 33-34.
78 See John N. Wall, "Deconstruction and the Universe of Theological Discourse," *St. Luke's Journal of Theology*, Vol XXVIII, No 4, Sept 1985, pp. 251-65.

matized and literalized by the church in a way that tended to undermine the ground of the Antiochenes.

Theodore was the epitome of an Antiochene theologian. He rejected the assumptions of platonist anthropology that most other theologians in his day had come to take for granted.[79] He rejected the platonic construct of mortal body/immortal soul, asserting a biblical construct of man as in every respect creature.[80] He rejected the notion of redemption through "divinization," an essential component of platonist spirituality. Rowan A. Greer calls this his greatest insight.[81] He also declined to use the allegorical approach to the interpretation of the Bible, the trademark of the Alexandrians.[82] Further, he wrote a polemic, "Against the Defenders of Original Sin," which may have been an attack on Augustine.[83] Theodore, himself a monastic, is said nevertheless to have retained a "marked sympathy with those of his brothers who preferred the married state."[84] This sympathy was no doubt enhanced by his own experience. Theodore fell in love with a beautiful girl named Hermione after he had already resigned himself to celibate life. He was still in his teens at the time. He contemplated marriage, but after a soul-searching struggle decided to remain celibate.

There has been something of a revival of interest in Theodore in the twentieth century, signaled by the publication of two sympathetic studies on his life and work by Rowan A. Greer and R. A. Norris, Jr. As Norris puts it, he was not really a philosopher, but was more like what we in the twentieth century call "a biblical theologian."[85]

If Theodore avoided the direct attention of Augustine, Julian of Eclanum, who was within reaching distance, did not. He was harried out of Italy by Augustine, seeking refuge with the sympathetic Theodore.[86] The battle between Augustine and Julian has had a powerful and determinative effect on the subsequent history of the church. Though sex was the victim, the battle was fought over the nature of

---

79 Rowan A. Greer, *Theodore of Mopsuestia: Exegete and Theologian*, London: The Faith Press, 1961, p. 15.
80 *Ibid.*, p. 17.
81 *Ibid.*, p. 15.
82 *Ibid.*, p. 20.
83 Smith and Wace, *op. cit.*, p. 937.
84 Smith and Wace, *op. cit.*, p. 935.
85 R. A. Norris, jr., *Manhood and Christ*, Oxford: Clarendon Press, 1963, p. xii.
86 Peter Brown, *Augustine of Hippo*, Berkeley: University of California Press, 1967, p. 382.

evil. Julian was an optimist, a cultivated, leisured, married bishop with the best liberal education (unlike Augustine, he knew Greek), both the son and the son-in-law of bishops. He was a Christian humanist whose use of Aristotle actually anticipated Aquinas in many respects. He represented what Peter Brown calls "one peak of Roman civilization." He was sympathetic to Pelagius, another antagonist of Augustine who had emphasized the reality of human freedom to choose good and evil. In Julian's view Augustine had destroyed free will and made man a product of the devil. As for Jerome, Julian thought him so puerile that reading him one could "scarcely refrain from laughing."[87] From his perspective, Jerome was a kind of fourth century beatnik.

Augustine was, of course, correct that Julian's optimism about mankind is unfounded, that the human propensity for evil is both profound and complex and has roots that cannot be dug out, no matter how deep one digs. In this respect, Augustine was the spiritual ancestor of the twentieth century Freud, as Peter Brown repeatedly reminds us.[88] Julian, on the other hand, might be characterized as the precursor to those early twentieth century idealistic liberals who thought that World War I would make the world safe for democracy. Augustine saw more clearly than Julian the depth of the human propensity for evil. No one steeped in Augustine would have been surprised at the rise to power of Hitler. Unfortunately, Augustine identified the root of evil with sex.

With the defeat and condemnation of Jovinian, Helvidius, Vigilantius, Theodore, Julian, and nameless others, any vestige of sexual affirmation was expunged from the life of the Western church. Sexual desire was irrevocably tainted from that point on. Ambrose, Jerome and Augustine together established unambiguously the ideal of virginity or sexual purity as the highest forms of the Christian life and established a corresponding platonic anthropology of body/soul dualism. Tertullian would have been pleased to see the final defeat of what he scornfully called the "Catholic sensualist" tradition.

---

87 *Ibid.*, pp. 381-392.
88 See especially Peter Brown, (1972), p. 196, and (1967) pp. 261 & 366. But see also "Augustine and Sexuality," The Center for Hermeneutical Studies, Berkeley: University of California, 1983, p. 12.

VI

Of the fourth century's theological triumvirate, Jerome was the most strident. "All sex is impure" (*omnia coitus immundus*)[89] he says. "I praise the marriage bond but I do so because it produces virgins for me. I gather roses from the thorns . . ."[90] Jerome's shrill invective against the erotic even induces him to discourage feminine cleanliness:

> Speaking personally, I altogether disapprove of baths for a full grown virgin. She ought to blush at herself and be unable to behold her own nakedness. If she mortifies and enslaves her body by vigils and fasts, if she desires to quench the flames of lust and check the hot passions of youth by cold chastity, if she hastens to spoil her natural beauty by deliberate squalor, why should she rouse a slumbering fire by the incentive of baths?"[91]

While the fourth century ecclesiastical leadership quashed whatever sex affirmation might have been left in the church, there were extenuating circumstances. It was a peculiarly difficult time to be affirming of creation in any form. The church itself, now commingled with the empire, had grown corrupt, having lost the benefits of the purifying fires of persecution. Ambrose himself illustrates this blurring of boundaries between church and empire. He was a popular governor of Milan, elected Bishop before he was even baptized. To make matters worse, the very empire the church had wed was on the verge of disintegration. Some even blamed the Christians for fatally weakening its cohesiveness. Christian monasticism and idealization of sexual purity exacerbated the manpower shortage in Italy and in that respect contributed to the decline of the empire. Jerome's hometown, Vercellae in Dalmatia, was sacked by Goths in 377 and his parents likely slaughtered in the process.[92] It is not too surprising that he might have been inclined to reject the world and its joys and spend the last 33 years of his life in a monastery in Bethlehem with "beans in his belly" while Romans ate sturgeon, as he put it. His contempt for sex was no doubt reinforced by his contempt for a disintegrating world.

---

89 *Against Jovinian,* I.20.
90 *Epistle* 22.19.4.
91 *Epistle* 107,11.
92 Bottomley, *op. cit.*, p. 197.

The Poisoning of Eros

Augustine lived the last nine months of his life in a city besieged by the Vandals, to which it fell shortly after his death in 430. Twenty years earlier Rome had been captured and sacked by Alaric and the Goths. Ambrose, Jerome and Augustine each had something of a siege mentality, in part because of the disintegrating political climate in which they lived.

Jerome's stridency shocked even his friends when he attacked Jovinian with verbal violence and crudity. His purpose was to crush the Jovinian dissent in favor of the newly promulgated derogatory view of marriage and the hysterical exaltation of virginity that were emerging in the church. It was not a time of pluralism in church or empire. Jerome's relationship with the principal woman in his life is itself fascinating and revealing. The evidence suggests he was neurotically defended against his own sexuality. When they met, Paula was a Roman woman of illustrious descent and vast wealth, 35 years old and recently widowed, with five children. She herself had ceased sexual relations with her late husband after she provided him with a male offspring.

Jerome was quite enamored with Paula. He encouraged her to follow him to Palestine, which she did, finally to die there at age 56 in Jerome's company. The relationship between them was close, warm, and driven by intense sexual energy that the two of them defended against with dogged determination. It is not known whether they consummated their relationship. Paula no doubt made it somewhat easier on Jerome by her deliberate refusal to bathe except when she became dangerously ill. In spite of that help, Jerome still felt that sex was his "one crime" and that specifically and only in relation to Paula.[93] Presumably, but not necessarily, he meant the "crime" of fantasizing sex with Paula.

To place Augustine, Bishop of Hippo, in a list with Ambrose and Jerome as the fourth century triumvirate is somewhat misleading. Augustine, in fact, has no peers in the patristic period. In the post-canonical Christian literature he is in a class by himself. Both Thomas Aquinas and Martin Luther, the latter of whom opined that Augustine

---

93 *Epistle* 10.5.2; 45.2 "The only fault found in me is my sex, and that only when there is talk of Paula coming to Jerusalem." And see *Jerome: His Life, Writings and Controversies,* J.N.D. Kelly, New York: Harper & Row Publishers, 1975.

The Victory of Syncretism

was the only early church Father worth reading, treated him as the highest authority outside scripture itself. One might say of Augustine, as was said of one of the old rabbis, "One can disagree with him, but not without trembling." Augustine is the culmination of all post-New Testament thinking and the theoretician of Western Christendom. During the millennium that followed him no other name carried as much authority.

Despite Augustine's sagacity, sex was a casualty of his theology. Sex was the victim of the struggle against Julian's (and Pelagius') shallow optimism about humankind.

Augustine had been careful not to impugn the physical senses and thus to fall into the dualism that characterized the Manichees and, to some extent, even platonists. But willy-nilly he became trapped in his own construct which held that reason was superior to and by necessity controller of the appetites. As Peter Brown noted, Augustine came to the conclusion that one particular appetite, sexual desire, was the only one that "clashes inevitably and permanently with reason."[94] This led him to identify sex as the ultimate culprit, the root of evil, the means by which sin is passed on from one generation to another. "That's the place!" (*Ecce unde.*) he wrote.[95] No one sentence of Augustine better epitomizes the dark side of his theology and its consequences. It was a tragic conclusion from which Western culture has not yet recovered.

When Julian argued correctly that the sex instinct was a neutral energy, Augustine exhibited hysteria rather than insight:

> Really, really, is that your experience: So you would not have married couples restrain that evil . . . ? You would have them jump into bed whenever they like, whenever they feel tickled by desire. Far be it from them to postpone this itch till bedtime; let's have your 'legitimate union of bodies' whenever your 'natural good' is excited. If this is the sort of married life you led, don't drag up your experience in debate . . ."[96]

It was a tragic debate. Augustine was correct in his assessment of

---
94 Brown, *op. cit.* (1967), p. 389.
95 Sermon 151.5.
96 *Contra Julian* 3.14.28.

the complexity and intractability of human wickedness. He was wrong to tie that potential for evil intrinsically to sex.

It could be argued that Augustine, like Ambrose and Jerome, was virtually bound to endorse an ascetic sexual valuation, indebted as he was to Porphyry and Plotinus who were certain of the harmfulness of sex to the progress of the soul. As mentioned above, the Western church centered in Rome was deeply indebted to platonic spirituality. Porphyry and Plotinus were the spriritual fathers of that era. Abraham, Isaac and Jacob were incorporated into Ambrose's pantheon as part of the procession of authentic "philosophers."[97] Ambrose dealt with the biblical material allegorically, relieving him of embarrassment with the disgusting earthiness of the semitic narrative. He frequently cited the Song of Songs, but treated its sensuous material allegorically. Augustine rarely referred to the Song.[98]

Augustine's magnum opus, *The City of God,* reveals how deeply immersed he was in Greco-Roman religio-mythical tradition. The *City of God* is clearly juxtaposed to the cities of Rome and Athens. It is not really a new "Jerusalem." It is not a new semitic city, but a Greco-Roman one. The first pages make numerous references to Aeneus, the founder of Rome, and various figures in Greek myth and history. The second paragraph quotes Vergil's *Aeneid.* Augustine is drawing heavily from a sexually ascetic and woman-fearing tradition. The gods call upon Aeneus and Theseus, founders of Rome and Athens respectively, to abandon their lovers, Dido and Ariadne, in order to accomplish their heroic and patriotic work.[99]

Augustine may well have thought of himself as a kind of successor to Aeneus and Theseus, and in a real sense he was in that he laid the blueprint for Western Christendom in *The City of God.*

Augustine is unequivocal in his belief that the life of virginity and continence are the highest religious calling. He does concede that the faithful married are superior to faithless continents. But the fact that he engages in such a comparison reveals the intense power and prestige he and his contemporaries placed on sexual abstinence. As has been noted,

---
97 Brown, *op. cit.* (1967), p. 84.
98 *Ibid.,* p. 83.
99 Eva Keuls is especially helpful here, *The Reign of the Phallus,* New York: Harper and Row, 1985, p. 62.

he is careful not to condemn pleasure or the physical senses themselves, but only concupiscence. However, the sexual pleasure that Augustine affirms is both constrained within the intention to procreate and also rid of chaotic erotic excitement.

Procreation redeems sexual intercourse within marriage, so that "something good is made out of the evil of lust."[100] For the purpose of generation intercourse has no fault attached to it, but for the purpose of satisfying concupiscence it is a venial sin. Athenagoras and Justin had said essentially the same thing 200 years earlier, but they did not carry as much personal authority in subsequent history as Augustine.

The purpose of marriage was not limited solely to procreation in Augustine's view. It was to be valued also for the companionship it provided "between the two sexes." However, marriage is "better in proportion as they begin the earlier to refrain by mutual consent from sexual intercourse."[101] Furthermore, continence from all intercourse is better than marital intercourse itself which takes place for the sake of begetting children."[102]

In Augustine's version of the Garden of Eden, had there been no sin, sex would have been free of lust and its excitement. The genitals would have been aroused by the will for purposes of procreation. The libido would have been subject to the control of the will---neither orgasm nor impotency would have been experienced. The sperm could have been dispatched into the womb without even the loss of virginity, "a woman's integrity" as he puts it, just as menstrual flux comes from the womb without loss of maidenhead.[103] Similarly, the resurrection body is an idealized version devoid of sexual desire. There will be sexuality but no sexual intercourse in paradise. "The female organs will not excite the lust of the beholder. . . but will arouse the praises of God for his wisdom and compassion."[104] Far more human and appealing is

---

100 *St. Augustine: Treatises on Marriage and Other Subjects,* Roy J. Deferrari, ed., New York: Fathers of the Church, Inc., 1955, p. 13.
101 *Treatises on Marriage,* p. 12.
102 *Ibid.,* p. 17.
103 Augustine, *The City of God,* Henry Bettenson, trans., New York: Penguin Books, 1972, pp. 587-91, Bk. 14.16.24.
104 *Ibid.,* p. 1057, Bk. 22.17.

a saying in the Talmud that heaven consists of three things: Sabbath, sunshine and sex.[105] In Augustine we see how wide the gulf has grown between Judaism and the church.

VII

Augustine's personal life is also relevant to any discussion of his ideas. He was the first in Western history to write an autobiography, *The Confessions*. It is a narcissistic genre and in this instance narcissism served him well. Not only does he expose his ideas to the judgement of history, he makes himself quite vulnerable by exposing his personal life as well. If he is easy to criticize, he must be given credit for being the first person in history to reveal enough of his personal life to make it possible to attempt a psychoanalytic evaluation of him 1500 years later.[106]

Augustine's personal history manifests certain disturbing characteristics. His relationships with his mother, his mistress and women in general are at least problematic and have been the subject of considerable debate. Monica, his mother, was a willful woman who had her own plans for her son and pursued him relentlessly to that end. He had to deceive her in order to free himself from her enough to sail from his native North Africa to Italy. She followed him there two years later. Soon after her arrival in Milan where Augustine was teaching, he abandoned his mistress of 14 years, for whom he cared deeply and with whom he had a son. "She with whom I had lived so long was torn from my side as a hindrance to my forthcoming marriage. My heart which had held her ever dear was broken and wounded and bleeding," wrote Augustine. This unnamed woman, whom for the good of his soul or his

---

105 Berakoth, 57b, p. 356, *The Babylonian Talmud*, I. Epstein, ed., M. Simon, trans., London: The Soncino Press, 1948. There being no Hebrew word for sex, the text reads: " Three things are a reflex of the world to come: Sabbath, sunshine and service (*tashmish*). Service of what? Shall I say of the bed? This weakens. It must be then service of the orifices."

106 For recent discussion and bibliography on the subject of Augustine's psychopathology, see Paul Rigby, "Paul Ricoeur, Freudianism, and Augustine's *Confessions*," and Donald Capps "Augustine as Narcissist," in *Journal of the American Academy of Religion*, LIII/1, March 1985.

mother he had callously discarded, vowed to remain constant to him.[107] The plan was for him to improve his social standing by marrying an heiress selected by his mother. As Nicholas Berdayev said, this decision "shows how low was his conception of love."[108] In this decision Augustine had not only pressure from his mother, but moral support from ecclesiastical leadership. Both Ambrose and Pope Leo viewed the abandonment of a mistress to take a wife, not as functional bigamy or divorce, but as a demonstration of moral improvement.[109] When Augustine finally subscribed to his mother's brand of Ambrosian Catholic Christianity, her prayers were answered. She moved in to keep house for him and his son Adeodatus (meaning "Gift of God") and his mistress was sent packing back to North Africa.

Monica died in the company of her son a few months later, no longer concerned about being buried next to her husband in her native soil. Augustine's relationship with his mother and treatment of his mistress are troubling and suggest what psychoanalytic theory refers to as an Oedipal win. His subsequent decision for celibacy and his identification of sex with sin is similarly troubling and also congruent with the suggestion of an unresolved Oedipal problem.

Another piece of data that casts a shadow on Augustine personally is the record of his dealing with his enemies. In particular, his participation in the heartless and coercive suppression of the Donatists is troublesome, as are his quite ruthless attacks on Pelagius. So too his singleminded, vehement assaults on his fellow bishop, Julian, were unmitigated by any hint of graciousness. As Peter Brown puts it, Augustine was "a hard victor."[110] He was also the only writer who wrote at length in defense of religious coercion. To quote Donald Capps, "In a number of ways, Augustine seems preoccupied with himself, and relatively unconcerned with the welfare . . . of persons beyond himself, except as they affect him."[111]

The question of Augustine's psychological health cannot be laid aside, particularly in view of abundant indications of pathology. The

---

107 *Confessions* 6.15 (Sheed trans.).
108 Nicholas Berdayev, *The Destiny of Man*, New York: Harper and Row, 1960, p. 233.
109 Peter Brown, *op. cit.* (1967), p. 88.
110 *Ibid.*, pp. 387, 335.
111 Donald Capps, *op. cit.*, p. 117.

issue for Augustine, as for anyone, is to what extent he may have come to terms with his pathology, an issue still under lively debate. Psychoanalytic theory holds that an unresolved Oedipal process is essentially a disturbed individuation process, manifesting itself in inordinate narcissism. On balance, the process of self-disclosure of his pathology may be the best evidence that Augustine overcame his pathology. Self-disclosure of one's pathology is, after all, the basis of modern psychoanalysis as well as other varieties of psychotherapy. Capps suggests he was a "not unambiguously transformed narcissist."[112] However, regardless of whatever healing Augustine may have found, his continuing identification of sex with sin must be viewed as an alarming symptom in his personality as well as tragic for the subsequent development of the church.

It is said of Augustine, somewhat simplistically, that he converted from Manichaeism to Neoplatonism and finally to Christianity, at which time he was baptized. In fact, Augustine was a sort of nominal Christian all his life. In the christianized empire one had to be a Jew or quite committed to some form of paganism to avoid being a Christian. It could be said that Augustine progressed in his thinking through stages of Christian dualism, Manichaeism being the most extreme form. The Manichees were the spiritual descendants of the earlier and more extreme Gnostics. They viewed the flesh and the world as evil and practiced a rather austere asceticism. They rigidly distinguished between the Perfect, the Elect men and women, and the rank and file Hearers. Augustine, with his mistress, was only a Hearer, not one of their most devout followers. Mani, the founder of the sect, who considered himself "The Apostle of Jesus Christ", had been executed in 276.

Augustine's conversion to a less rigorous dualism in the form of platonism was simultaneous with his movement into the orbit of Ambrose, Bishop of Milan, himself a Christian platonist who often quoted Plotinus verbatim in his sermons. Monica had become a devotee of Ambrose after her arrival in Milan. The platonists offered a more transcendent God than the Manichees, who identified their souls with God unambiguously. In one respect, then, this departure from Manicheeism represented for Augustine a lessening narcissism, a lessen-

---

112 *Ibid.*, p. 125.

ing of notions of human divinization. However, in spite of this less austere body/soul dualism, the platonists also advocated sexual abstinence. (In a curious development, Porphyry suddenly at age seventy married a widow with eight children. He was the leading Neoplatonist who had written a treatise promoting sexual abstinence as well as one attacking Christians, and confessed to a hatred of the human body.)[113] Augustine was not without his criticism of the platonists. He attempted to refute their neglect of the body in their promoting the notion of the immortality of the soul. But on the specific issue of sexuality Augustine and the platonists remained in agreement. Even as Augustine affirms the body against the platonists he affirms a body devoid of the erotic both in this life and the next. His teaching is congruent with his personal life.

The early church's preeminent theologian thus categorically impugned sex, allowing only the most meager approval, with second class status, for marital sex whose intended purpose is procreation. Augustine with his antisexual dualism was to dominate both Christian ethics and the intellectual life of the Western world for the subsequent millennium. Only Luther, 1100 years later, was strong and aware enough to challenge the Augustinian-platonist theological juggernaut with partial success.

VIII

One can never quite dispose of Augustine. A final postscript is called for. For the sake of the redemption of eros, the malevolent aspects of Augustine's influence on Western Christendom cannot be minimized or sloughed off. Nevertheless, one is daunted by the task of evaluating Augustine. Sexual renunciation in Augustine was both very real and very problematic, and its curse still permeates Western culture, for which Augustine is summoned before the bar of history. What makes the task a daunting one is that Augustine's profundity, complexity, and greatness ultimately surpass even the malevolence of the curse he has bequeathed us, a greatness that Peter Brown has so brilliantly illumined in his life's work on Augustine.

---

113 Brown, *op. cit.* (1967), pp. 92-100.

Sexual renunciation in Augustine was actually something of an accident of his history, the result of a coincidental convergence of a variety of factors and events that were somewhat tangential to the core of Augustine himself. If we make allowances for his neurotic relationship with his mother, the weighty and pervasive influence of sex-negative Neoplatonism in the empire, and the "sour wine"[114] of his last eighteen years, we see something much more profound at work in Augustine than a simple renunciation of sex. His renunciation of sex was simply a tangential part of his renunciation of a proud, self-confident church that had elevated itself to imperial and divine status even as it became more aristocratic. Popes and bishops walked the red carpets with emperors and kings and believed themselves worthy. Against this proud inflation of the self Augustine proclaimed: "Build up yourself and you build a ruin."[115] He believed he had found in the concupiscence of the flesh an "incurable eddy" of wickedness in the soul itself.[116] If he had nailed sex to this "incurable eddy" of wickedness, he had intended to nail pride, optimism, and the kind of self-confidence that elevates the inflated self to a status it ought not to have.

So when Augustine in 385-6 came to the critical turning point of his life, having sent his beloved mistress of fourteen years away, who was herself almost certainly a baptized Christian, he prepared himself for the grand life of a good Catholic prelate. He was betrothed to a young socialite woman approved by his mother and was now ready for the aura of religious and social respectability in a privileged class. In the two-year interval he felt driven to take a temporary mistress. At that point the fabric of his life unraveled. He renounced his engagement and left Italy. If he gave up forever any further genital gratification, he was more especially giving up forever Roman Catholic society and its inflated, self-serving, liberal and optimistic theology.

In comparison Jerome, his contemporary, was a shallow soul. He saw the corruption of the Italian church and fled to the barren hills of Palestine to save himself in monastic isolation. Augustine reacted not so much to the obvious material corruption as the theological banality, the self-serving optimism of the Catholic ruling class who, while they accepted the teachings of the church, really believed mostly in themselves. Perhaps the only effective way Augustine had of assaulting the

---

114 Brown, *op. cit.* (1983), p. 28.
115 Sermon 169.11.
116 Brown *op. cit.* (1983), p.4.

entrenched social and religious elite was to renounce not only his impending socialite marriage but sexual gratification itself. However, Augustine's central vision was not one of salvation through sexual purity. That came later in the church's history. His primary vision was that of a loving community of men and women in which private purposes, individual wills and joys, were surrendered for the sake of a loving kindness that reaches out to the other, especially the excluded other. In the context of an elite, established, exclusivist and imperial church, Augustine was thus more profoundly counter-cultural than the ascetic Jerome.

Augustine was deeply ambiguous and complex, a mixture of wisdom and neurosis. Nevertheless, he is remembered in the West not for the depth of his understanding of the disjunctive character of human personality, an understanding that foreshadowed Luther and Freud in its scent of the root of human corruptibility that never can be dug out. Nor is he remembered for his vision of the human community as a great partnership of warm and lasting friendships based on service to others, which, as Peter Brown says, prefigured the idealistic yearnings of Rousseau, Hegel, and Marx. Rather, he is remembered mainly---and tragically---for his excoriation of sex, the obliteration of the remaining Catholic sensualists, the final erasure of the biblical/Hebraic affirmation of the flesh and the world. Because of him, as Peter Brown puts it, "The loving cleaving of Israel to God would never be re-enacted in the marriage beds of Western Christendom---only the sad shadow of Adam's estrangement from the will of God."[117]

---

117 *Ibid.*, p. 12.

Chapter Four
The Medieval Synthesis

The Middle Ages wobbled between the excesses of hot sensuality and cramped virginity.

-- Richard Marius*

I

The thousand year period between Augustine and Luther, the Middle Ages, was a time of the implementation and solidification of the Augustinian valorization of sexuality. This was accomplished principally by an aggressive program of monasticization of the clergy, a process that was completed by the 13th century, by which time all the clergy lived either the monastic life or as celibates in a quasi-monastic rectory. Simultaneously a lively resurgence of Gnosticism emerged in a new form in the 11th and 12th centuries mostly under the names of Catharism and Albigensianism. At the same time there also appeared an unabashed flowering of clerical homosexuality, the spiritualization of marriage and women in the invention of the sacrament of matrimony, and the cult of the Virgin Mary. Such were the fruits of a victorious Augustinian/platonist anthropology in the church. The so-called medieval synthesis was in a real sense the implementation of a dualism not unlike that against which the very early church attempted to defend itself.

The first significant ecclesiastical figure subsequent to Augustine was Gregory I, "the Great", who became pope in 590. He was a monk and reportedly an invalid who suffered incessant pain.[1] From Gregory to the so-called "Gregorians" of the 11th century, those organization men who radically centralized Western ecclesiastical power in Rome, the extant literature is sparse. It was the Dark Ages of the early medieval period, a relative judgment of course, and a time that may not have appeared any darker to those who lived it than our own does to us. It is dark to us because of its opacity and because of the fragmentation of political power in the demise of the Roman empire in the West. The Eastern half of the empire centered in Constantinople remained more or less intact, though weakened and increasingly hemmed in by advancing Islam, which finally overran it much later, in 1453.

The collapse of Imperial Rome was a gradual process rather than a single event. Political power simply became more and more fragmented, and Rome became less and less powerful as the center. The Huns,

---

*   *Thomas More*, New York: Vintage Books, 1984, p. 15.
1   Bottomley, *op. cit.*, p. 103.

The Medieval Synthesis

Goths, Slavs, Hungarians, Vikings, and other tribes that devoured the empire were only in part invaders from the outside. The failure of the Empire's population to grow required that some of these tribal people be brought in to cultivate the land in Italy and North Africa in the 3rd century.[2] The imperial army had also made increasing use of manpower from the further provinces, so that cousins of the same barbarians defending the empire from within were attacking the empire from without, and both eventually came to rule what was left of it. The political power of Rome was not erased when the Goths overran and sacked it in 410. Its power was simply reduced and its character became less Italian. The skin-clad kings of the Goths gradually replaced the purple robed Roman princes.[3]

Rome continued to have some, though ever diminishing, political power as the Western center for another century or so. It was only in the 7th century that the international political power centered in Rome was laid to rest entirely. Or so the historians say.[4] Roman imperial power was in actuality metamorphosed into papal "spiritual" power.

By that time the eastern Mediterranean was lost to the Saracens. Jerusalem, Antioch, and Alexandria, all major urban centers of early Christianity, were overrun by the Moslem advance. By the 7th century, only Rome and Constantinople survived as Christian cities from the geography of earliest Christianity. The Christian orbit shifted westward.

The rivalry between Rome and Constantinople was set in motion by Constantine himself. The eclipse of Rome as an international political center had begun in earnest in 330 when Constantine transferred the seat of the empire to Byzantium, renamed Constantinople. That move began the historic division of the church between Western Roman Catholicism and Eastern Orthodoxy. While the church in the 4th century was becoming first "an imperial religion" and later "the imperial religion" the empire itself was becoming two-headed, with Constantinople nominally supreme. Rome continued to be a political power center, particularly when the empire was divided up among Constantine's sons at his death. But Rome was relegated to secondary

---
2 Noonan, *op. cit.*, p. 24.
3 Charles Bigg, *Wayside Studies in Ecclesiastical History,* New York: Longman's Green and Co., 1906, p. 75.
4 R. W. Southern, *Western Society and the Church in the Middle Ages,* Harmondsworth: Penguin, 1970, p. 24.

status. Even as late as 663 the Greek emperor visited Rome as the legitimate ruler.[5]

All the first ecumenical church councils were held in the East in what is now Turkey, in or near Constantinople:

325	Nicaea
381	Constantinople I
431	Ephesus
451	Chalcedon
553	Constantinople II
680	Constantinople III
787	Nicaea
869	Constantinople IV

Only much later in 1123 (Lateran I) was there any pretense of the international church's finally convening in the Western region of the empire, and by that time the division between East and West was set in stone.[6] Therefore, the Lateran Council was in fact only the Western church in council. All the truly ecumenical councils in the history of the church have been convened in the East.

From Constantine until the 11th century the Bishop of Rome was something of a poor relation to the Bishop of Constantinople.[7] However, Rome obviously retained a certain aura of authority from having been the seat of the empire for centuries. It was into this vacuum that the Bishop of Rome moved. In that sense, the Pope became something of a successor to the Roman emperors, even though the explanation of his power and authority was based on the supposed tradition of Peter's transferring the locus of authority in the church from Jerusalem to Rome. Fourth century documents refer to this Petrine tradition that was used by Rome in an effort to establish hegemony. It is not without significance that the Pope adopted the same title (Pontiff) as the imperial Pontifex Maximus, the supreme high priest of the imperial cult. Political rivalry between the clergy of old Rome and New Rome (Constantinople) appears in church documents. The 28th Canon of the Council of Chalcedon (451) gave equal privileges to "the most holy throne of New Rome" with that of old Rome. This canon was denounced by Pope Leo and never accepted in the West.[8]

---

5   *Ibid.*, p. 54.
6   *Ibid.*, p. 107.
7   *Ibid.*, p. 27.
8   *Documents of the Christian Church,* Henry Bettenson, ed., New York: Oxford University Press, 1963, p. 116.

The Medieval Synthesis

The further progress of sexual valorization was significantly shaped by the writings of Gregory the Great (c. 540-604). His *Pastoral Care* established itself as something of a classic in Christian literature. In this work Gregory further tightened the Augustinian identification of sin and sexuality. Concupiscence, now understood as "sexual desire," and sin are used interchangeably and in that respect he both goes beyond Augustine and trivializes him.[9] It is perhaps superfluous to add that Gregory viewed the purpose of sex as procreation and, as he puts it, when a couple "transfer the occasion of procreation to the service of pleasure . . . though they do not then pass beyond the bounds of wedlock, yet in wedlock they exceed its rights."[10] As for the unmarried, "they must not think that they may have intercourse with unmarried women, without incurring the sentence of damnation."[11]

Not only was sin equated with concupiscence, but sexual pleasure itself came under a cloud, a position Augustine would have objected to in principle. Sex may have been for Augustine the root of sin, but he strove to save sexual pleasure from condemnation when procreation was intended. The Venerable Bede (672/3-735CE) in England, commonly regarded as the most influential writer between Gregory the Great and the coronation of Charlemagne (800 CE), follows the Gregorian line. He points out that "the pleasure is in the bodily union, and the pain is in the birth" and that "the fault lies in the bodily pleasure, not in the pain." He adds that even "lawful intercourse must be accompanied by bodily desire . . . the desire itself is not blameless."[12] Bede also notes that a man who has approached his wife should not enter church before he has washed, "nor enter at once even though washed."[13] As to how soon a woman can enter church after childbirth, he authorizes 33 days for a son and 66 for a daughter.[14]

---

9   The etymology of the word "concupiscence" demonstrates the shift here. Its root meaning in Latin is "strong desire," with suggestions of covetousness. However, "sexual desire" has evolved as its principal connotation.
10 St. Gregory the Great, *Pastoral Care*, Part III, Chap. 27, Henry Davis, trans., Westminster, Md.: The Newman Press.
11 *Ibid.*; For a different view see Thomas C. Oden's *Care of Souls in The Classic Tradition, Theology and Pastoral Care,* Don S. Browning, ed., Philadelphia: Fortress Press, 1984. Oden's effort to rehabilitate Gregory according to 20th century standards is not only unconvincing; it is astonishing. He makes no mention of Gregory's deprecation of sex, and even goes so far as to say that Gregory "does not deprecate marriage." p. 99.
12 Bede, *A History of the English Church and People,* Leo Shirley-Price, trans., New York: Penguin Books, 1955, p 80.
13 *Ibid.*, p 79.
14 *Ibid.*, p 77.

In all this focus on sex as sin, women continued to be scapegoated by the men who controlled the church and wrote the documents. Thus it was quite logical for the Council of Auxerre in 578 (Canon 26) to decree that women should not receive the eucharist into their naked hands on account of the impurity of their sex.[15]

In the spirit of Gregory, an ecclesiastical "art form" developed between the mid-6th and mid-12th centuries known as "the penitentials." The penitentials were manuals for clergy that provided guidance in directing the behavior of parishioners, particularly in relation to their confessions. The penitentials focused heavily on sexual behavior. Pierre J. Payer examined the many penitentials and found that 25% to 45% of the material in each of the penitentials was concerned with sexual behavior. This concern was invariably sex-negative. Each penitential had its own particular proposed schedule of required sexual abstinence. The Vinnian Penitential, a fairly typical one, proposed three 40-day periods (Lents) of sexual abstinence annually, along with all Saturday and Sunday nights, and the period from conception to childbirth. The penitentials typically condemned any form of non-reproductive sex, and specifically oral and anal intercourse. Frequently condemned also was retroposition (rear entry), and the dorsal position (woman on top). Unquestionably, the penitentials were universally fascinated with the subject of sexual behavior.

The penitentials developed a life and authority of their own and probably for that reason were ultimately suppressed by the ecclesiastical hierarchy. A major effort to suppress them in 813 was unsuccessful. They were finally abolished only in the 12th century. The newly developing system of canon law actually absorbed by then the content of the penitentials without acknowledging its source. Unlike the penitentials, canon law had no independent life of its own, but was entirely under the auspices and control of the church hierarchy.[16]

Of major significance for the course of sexual valorization was the nature of the political revolution taking place within the church between Gregory the Great of the 6th century and the Gregorians of the

---

15 J. D. Mansi, *Conciliorum*, Vol. 9, 1763, p. 915; see also comment by Bottomley, *op. cit.*, p 109.
16 Pierre J. Payer, *Sex and the Penitentials*, Toronto: University of Toronto Press, 1984.

11th century. The fact that Gregory himself was a monk and a protégé of Benedict, the founder of the Benedictine order, was itself a harbinger of that revolution. What was taking place in the church was essentially a monastic coup. For while the monastics initially represented simply one option for those dedicated to religious work, the celibate life they chose was required ultimately of the entire body of clergy in the Western church. The process took time and was not complete until the early 13th century, a process we call the monasticization of the clergy.

The monastic movement was introduced to Rome by Athanasius around 342 and rapidly flourished, probably as a negative reaction to the church's political and material prosperity after Constantine, coupled with the awareness that the empire was in steep decline. In the early stages monastic life was fluid in form and barely removed from the traditions of the solitary religious hermits that occupied the North African desert.

In subsequent centuries, as the Western Empire disintegrated, monasticism waxed in seeming inverse proportion to the declining health of the empire. If the Pope in a sense occupied the empty imperial throne, the monastic movement like a hermit crab occupied and revivified the empty shell of the international empire. Ultimately these monastic communities were the instruments by which the Pope was able to exercise autocratic international power in the West. As such, they were to become the basic fabric of medieval Christendom.

Benedict (circa 480-543), who renounced the world at age 14 and who founded his monastery at Monte Cassino, was the individual who impressed his stamp on the monastic or cenobite movement that emerged from the North African desert. He apparently did not imagine himself actually founding the first monastic order. He was simply inventing an organizational structure for his own community which in turn was adopted by the burgeoning monastic movement. His *Rule of Benedict* spread rapidly as an idea whose time had come. It gave the monastic movement a uniformity that transformed this originally diffuse movement into an army marching to the sound of a single drum, the "Benedictine Rule." As such, the Benedictines, or the "black monks" as they were commonly called, were the foundation of Christendom in the Western world.[17]

---

17   Bottomley, *op. cit.*, p. 111.

As anyone should expect looking back in history from a psychoanalytically informed perspective, a tightly organized intimate community restricted to one gender would necessarily foster homosexuality and no doubt would attract persons whose libidinal drives tended in that direction. Benedict's Rule both fostered homosexuality organizationally (though unconsciously perhaps) and at the same time energetically defended itself against it. The *Rule* contains bizarre and elaborate safeguards against homosexual activity. Monks were required to have separate beds and to sleep together in one room. A light was required in the dormitory all night where the monks slept with their clothes on, girdled with belts or cords, but without knives lest they hurt themselves. In the bed arrangements young men were required to be interspersed among older men. What the monastic system itself created was a profound double bind in which enormous energy was spent attempting to thwart the very thing it created. This double bind continues into modern times where in monastic life considerable energy continues to be spent to discourage homosexuality. One of the prohibitions that is common to modern monastic life, though somewhat diluted since Vatican II, is the injunction against cultivating "special friendships" because of their homosexual potential.

On the positive side, the Benedictines fostered the value of community in a politically fragmented era. They preserved culture and literature as well as art and science, and created an international network at a time of political and cultural disintegration. On the negative side, the Benedictine system was authoritarian and male chauvinist, sexually repressive and fostered homosexuality.[18] In time the monastic movement effectively overran and eliminated the regular married clergy.

II

At the millenium mark the Western church was beginning to come out from under the shadow of the East politically. Rome was beginning to exercise its muscle vis-a-vis Constantinople. She finally claimed supremacy in 1053, demanding the submission of Constantinople,

---

18 Some may object to labeling this a negative value. I am inclined to agree with Karl Barth that single sex communities are a form of disobedience. This should not be read as homophobia or any sort of condemnation of individuals who choose to express their sexuality homosexually.

The Medieval Synthesis

proclaiming that "Rome is the mother and her spouse is God."[19] Thus began officially the rupture between East and West which continues into the present. Economics played a significant part. Prosperity was flowing westward and the East was increasingly hemmed in and harassed by Islam, which ultimately reduced the Eastern Church to a mere shadow of its former self and the Patriarch of Constantinople to a political beggar in a Moslem world. Furthermore, the Pope, as both a secular power in the papal state and head of an international network of clergy, was a political figure to be contended with and something of a kingmaker. Unlike the Patriarch of Constantinople, the Pope did not have to play supporting roles for the Imperial Court. The Roman stage was entirely his and in the West he had what even the so-called "secular" rulers envied, an international organization at his command.

When Pope Leo III, on Christmas Day in 800, placed the imperial crown on the head of the surprised King of the Franks, Charlemagne, proclaiming him Emperor of the new "Holy Roman Empire", he was in that one act seizing as much power for himself as he was bestowing upon Charlemagne. From thenceforth successive popes could and did claim the authority to name Charlemagne's successors.[20]

As the Dark Ages gave way to the later Middle Ages, the Western church increasingly asserted itself as an ingredient in the political order. One of the significant manifestations of this increasingly political coloration of the church was its assumption of administration over the institution of marriage. Previously marriage had been a civil contract made around the family hearth, sometimes but not necessarily supplemented by a priestly blessing. Early bishops had sometimes functioned as marriage brokers,[21] a chore Augustine refused to undertake. As early as the 4th century there is evidence of priestly blessings of marriage contracted civilly. In 432 there is first evidence of a nuptial mass, not marriage itself. In the 10th century a marriage liturgy is found in service books, but still not marriage itself.[22] Only in the 11th century was the marriage ceremony brought into the church as a liturgical event presided over by the clergy and administratively governed by diocesan authorities. For the first time the church had complete jurisdiction in matrimonial affairs. It

---

19 Southern, *op. cit.*, p. 61.
20 William Ragsdale Cannon, *History of Christianity in the Middle Ages: From the Fall of Rome to the Fall of Constantinople,* New York: Abingdon Press, 1960, p. 81.
21 Cf. Ignatius of Antioch.
22 Edward Schillebeeckx, *Marriage,* New York: Sheed and Ward, 1966, p. 255.

was a gradual but radical move, one which provided the church a burden many think should never have been assumed. The vestiges of this remain today in the United States and some other Western countries where the clergy function as *ad hoc* officers of the state in that one task of presiding over marriages. Of necessity this means that the clergy explicitly or implicitly rule administratively over divorce as well.[23]

Both Luther and Barth later expressed regret that the church had ever gotten in the marriage business. Luther especially felt this way because in separating his churches from Roman administration he himself inherited the customary task of ruling on marriages and divorces, a task that he regarded inappropriate to pastoral functioning. Like many ventures, the marriage business was easier to take up than to put down. Neither Protestants nor Catholics have found a way to put down this civil burden which was taken up in the 11th century.

The 11th and 12th centuries are characterized as the period of the "Gregorian Reform," a period coinciding with Western economic prosperity. The reform was in actuality the intensification of papal power and the radical centralization of ecclesiastical power in Rome. Targeted as culprits in this reform were simony (the buying and selling of spiritual favors) and clerical marriage, mostly the latter. Pope Leo IX, elected in 1049, was the first of the so-called Gregorians. The story of the Gregorian campaign against clerical marriage, one of the better kept secrets of church history, is explored in great detail in an obscure and fascinating academic work by Anne Barstow.[24]

Marriage in the West was, of course, already under a cloud. The Eastern church at Constantinople was accusing the Latins of disparaging marriage. The impact of the Benedictine movement, the Augustinian-Gregorian identification of sex with sin, the requirement to abstain from intercourse the evening before eucharist, and the daily eucharist itself conspired to encourage de facto celibacy for many clergy. It is assumed that most of the regular clergy continued to marry, but that the leadership generally did not. Even so, at least one pope, Adrian II (867-72), was married before his election. And a certain

---

23 "The History of Christian Marriage", Michael D. Place, *Chicago Studies*, Vol. 18, No. 3, Fall 1979, p. 316.
24 Anne Llewellyn Barstow, *Married Priests and the Reforming Papacy: The Eleventh Century Debates,* New York: The Edwin Mellen Press, 1982. Barstow follows up on the work a century earlier by Henry C. Lea, *History of Sacerdotal Celibacy*, Philadelphia: 1867.

The Medieval Synthesis

Bishop Clemens in 745 argued that fathering two children after his elevation to the episcopacy was no impediment to his role as bishop.[25]

Clerical marriage fell victim to the program of centralizing ecclesiastical power partly by an accident of history. In spite of continuing depreciation of sex by the church, no prohibition to clerical marriage had yet been instituted. The priesthood of married clerics had come to be treated generally as a matter of inheritance and therefore often handed down from father to son. Economically and politically, married clerics were generally tied to an established and tightly controlled order. The barely emerging artisan and bourgeois class, therefore, saw Rome as a force for freedom and progress, breaking the back of privileged families who owned and jealously guarded for themselves the office of priesthood. Rome was successful in this struggle, though the victory took more than a century to achieve. Ultimately, virtually every priest in the Western church was separated from the economic and political ties of family inheritance and local politics and incorporated into a powerful international bureaucracy centered in Rome.[26] One of the peculiar ambiguities of history is that marriage and sexuality had to suffer a further defeat in the West in order to make way for a more egalitarian clerical order.

The Gregorian popes, however, were more likely driven by the quest for papal power than by egalitarian ideals. One of the first moves made to consolidate power was to shift the election of popes into the elite House of Cardinals, made by decree of Pope Nicholas II in 1059.

As the Gregorian "reform" progressed the popes found themselves fighting a war on two fronts. They had to contend with the resistance of married clergy on the one hand and the prerogatives of secular rulers on the other. The centralization of ecclesiastical power was a challenge to secular rulers who were accustomed to having their own favorites appointed to episcopal offices. Thus began the so-called Investiture struggle. Henry IV, the Holy Roman Emperor, joined a number of ranking ecclesiastics to denounce Gregory VII in 1076 for his attempt to abolish royal prerogatives over ecclesiastical appointments. Pope Gregory in turn deposed Emperor Henry and "released" all his subjects from obedience to him. At first a fairly even match, Rome finally had her way. With the Concordat of Worms in 1122,

---
25 *Ibid.*, p. 35.
26 *Ibid.*, p. 157.

Emperor Henry V agreed to relinquish to Rome final authority over all ecclesiastical appointments and the Investiture struggle was over. The sequel was Pope Innocent III's "Moon and Sun" proclamation in 1198 in which he declared that royal power derives its dignity from pontifical authority just as the moon derives its light from the sun. Political power was never before or since so firmly held by a pope.

The campaign against clerical marriage and the subsequent celibacy rule were simply part and parcel of the campaign for papal power. It is significant that the particular Gregorians who were the most insistent on the celibacy issue were also those who were the most absolutist in their use of power: Gregory VII, Calixtus II, Alexander III, and Innocent III.[27] Celibacy was the instrument of control, the tool by which the bureaucracy exercised its power over the whole body and finally the arcane mark of the clerical class whereby it distinguished itself from the laity.

Pope Hildebrand (c.1021-85), who took the name of Gregory VII, continued what Leo IX had begun, branding married clergy "nicolaitist heretics." He tightened sexual discipline by requiring priests to live in a clerical household with a communal dorm and refectory, supporting each other's moral purity and reporting on each other if necessary.[28] This was the origin of the modern Roman Catholic rectory.

The campaign against married clergy was an ecclesiastical bloodbath. The resistance was fierce and continuing. Siegfried, the Archbishop of Mainz, was excommunicated in 1076 for defending clerical marriage.[29] Bishop Ulric of Imola in Italy composed the first defense of clerical marriage since Jovinian in the 4th century. A group of schismatic bishops in North Italy convened at Pavia to denounce Gregory VII. A rival pope, Honarius II, became the rallying point for those favoring clerical marriage, but most of his "reign" was spent in prison. Street riots are known to have taken place in at least Rouen and Milan over the issue. The Norman clergy were the most resistant to the abolition of clerical marriage.[30] But the pope's power was formidable. He was able to release secular rulers from obedience to dissenting bishops and thereby leave the undercut clerics powerless in the face of greedy and ruthless princes. Count Robert of Flanders was an example of just that kind of prince. With the local

---

27 *Ibid.*, p. 180.
28 *Ibid.*, p. 57.
29 *Ibid.*, p. 69.
30 Christopher Brooke, *Medieval Church and Society*, New York: New York University Press,1971, p 84.

The Medieval Synthesis

bishop undercut by Rome, Robert moved against married priests, seizing their property, and choosing not to recognize the rights of inheritance of the "illegitimate children" of priests and their "concubines." Some of the wives who were victims of these attacks are reported to have committed suicide.[31]

A chronicler of the period, referred to as "Norman Anonymous," was a shadowy, prophetic figure who wrote sometime between 1075-1120. He was a clerical dissenter from the Gregorian juggernaut. He made an effort to defend the rights of clergy wives and their children.[32] He also called for the abolition of the priesthood and all other legal distinctions between Christians. He was in the end fatalistically resigned to the cruelties of life as he witnessed this tragic transformation of the church. The actual identity of Norman Anonymous remains unknown. "We do not know his fate, but we can imagine", as Barstow puts it.[33]

Another chronicler of the period, Archdeacon Henry of Huntingdon, reports in his *Historia Anglorum* that Anselm (1033-1109), Archbishop of Canterbury, in forbidding wives to clergy was imposing a discipline not formerly known. Being far from Rome and protected geographically by the waters of the English Channel, the Britons were facing the new regimen later than their continental brothers. At the turn of the 12th century at least 25% of British priests were still married, but their numbers were declining. William of Ely (d. 1222) was, officially at least, the last known English cleric to marry until 300 years later when the Reformation restored clerical marriage. Boniface, Archbishop of Canterbury, was accused of matrimony in 1250, but even the accusation itself illustrates the status of clerical marriage by then.

The consequences of the Gregorian juggernaut were no doubt as complex as they were momentous. The salient features of the Gregorian contribution to Western history fall into two categories: power and sexuality. The Roman Pontiff reached an unprecedented level of autocratic power in the Western Church and the Benedictine monastic ideal was imposed upon the entire clerical body in the institution of celibacy. The 2nd Lateran Council in 1139 produced the first ecclesiastical legislation imposing the celibacy rule for priests and deacons. The vow of ordination was given precedence over the marriage vow. Married

---
31 Barstow, *op. cit.*, p.81.
32 *Ibid.*, p. 159.
33 *Ibid.*, p. 173.

men expecting ordination were required to separate from their wives. Barstow surmises that the strong hand of Bernard of Clairvaux had pressured the pope to endorse this legislative action.[34] The legislation formalized a requirement that the Gregorian popes had been gradually and successfully imposing on the Western Church for the previous century. The Gregorian victory meant that sexuality was in effect expunged from the life of the Western Church by virtue of its being entirely disallowed to the leadership.

Bishop Ulric had earlier expressed the fear that the celibacy rule would result in an increase in homosexuality among clerics. His anxiety was prophetic. According to John Boswell, the century from 1050 to 1150 witnessed the most intense flowering of Christian homosexuality in the church's history. The proportion of gay literature from this period he calls astonishing.[35] Twelfth century Moslems in Spain support this view in their observations that Christian clergy appeared particularly prone to homosexuality.[36] It is of course not clear whether enforced celibacy actually created the apparent increase in homosexuality, whether more homosexuals were simply drawn into celibate clerical ranks, or whether homosexuals in larger numbers simply felt free to express themselves in the literature. Very likely all these processes to some extent were at work simultaneously and synergistically. In any case a gay, or as contemporaries called it, a "Ganymede" subculture came into its own simultaneously with the erasure of clerical marriage in the 11th and 12th centuries, a period which Boswell labels "The Triumph of Ganymede."[37]

This gay efflorescence died down and the number of practicing gays either disappeared or took cover in the 13th and 14th centuries, for reasons which have not yet been deciphered. Boswell characterizes these latter centuries as repressive and authoritarian, a time of more absolute government and strictures against Jews and women and a period of xenophobia and crusades. In any case, Lateran III in 1179 was the first ecumenical council to rule against homosexuality.[38] Though Boswell does not say so, the most likely explanation for the suppression of homosexuality was the same as the suppression of heterosexuality, namely that church and culture had built its life and symbols on the presuppositions of a philosophical spiritualist dualism which held the

---

34 *Ibid.*, p. 103.
35 Boswell, *op. cit.*, p. 209.
36 *Ibid.*, p. 233.
37 *Ibid.*, p. 253.
38 *Ibid.*, p. 277.

flesh and its pleasures in contempt. So the brief homosexual flowering, Ganymede's brief moment in the sun, was likely a short-lived by-product of the vicious annihilation of clerical marriage. It was as if the church rewarded itself for a brief homosexual moment after abolishing heterosexuality and before sexuality in any visible form was shut down or driven underground.

III

The historical development in the West from Augustine into the high Middle Ages can be seen as a deepening institutionalization of a spiritualistic dualism. Rooted in the Neoplatonism to which Augustine was so deeply indebted, nurtured by centuries of Benedictine monastic tradition and hardened by the Gregorian political reform which made celibacy a clerical requirement, this spiritualistic dualism with its contempt for the flesh and sexuality prepared the way for the emergence of the Cathars. The Cathars, and cognate groups such as Albigensians and Bogomils, were the unwelcomed fruit of the ineluctable drift into dualism. They were to some extent the spiritual heirs of all the dualist traditions: platonism, gnosticism and Manicheism. With the Cathars, Jewish anthropology is left far behind.

The Cathars took their name from the Greek word, "katharo", meaning "clean" or "pure".[39] They despised the world, the body, and especially sex, which they held to have a corrupting influence on the soul. The attention of the Cathars was focused on that other world, the world of imagination, wish and dream---and in that sense Catharism is the ultimate narcissism in its negative aspect. They promoted an ascetic discipline of self-redemption which delivered humanity from this world of darkness and led to "a state of final and fortunate detachment in which an individual can undergo the deliberate death of the Perfect."[40] They promoted a mystical union with God and a kind of romantic idealization of love and of women which was as intense as it was platonic. The idealized eternal woman

---

[39] Emmanuel LeRoy Ladurie (in *Montaillou: The Promised Land of Error*, Barbara Bray, trans., New York, George Braziller, Inc., 1978, p. VIII.), disputes this etymology, claiming "Cathar" comes from a Germanic word having nothing to do with purity. He does not cite his source. Even if he is correct and *Webster's Ninth New Collegiate* wrong, the Cathars *ought* to have been called by a name that meant "clean or pure."
[40] Denis deRougement, *op cit.*, p. 145.

leads the way and the goal is death. The created world is the devil's domain and death saves humankind from both.

The Catharist movement swept through the medieval church and set off alarms in the leadership of the church because of the excessiveness of its dualism. When the Cathars replaced water baptism in favor of a baptism with the spirit and replaced the eucharist with their own *Consolamentum,* in which the candidate was given back his own holy spirit which he had left behind in Paradise, they went too far for the institutional church.[41] Ultimately they condemned the church as *ecclesia carnalis,* reminiscent of Tertullian's condemnation of Catholic sensualism.[42] In its turn the church condemned them as heretics at the Lateran Councils II (1179) and III (1215), and in 1209 Pope Innocent III mounted against them what deRougement calls the first act of genocide in Western Christian history, though whether it was really the "first" is a matter for debate. It is ironic that the same church which was itself promoting a rather extreme form of dualism was engaged in a political campaign to crush a slightly more extreme manifestation of that same dualism. But of course the Cathars had challenged the central practices of the church, the sacraments, a challenge which could not be ignored.

The religion of the Cathars took secular shape in the form of the romance, according to deRougement's brilliant and persuasive analysis. Romantic love, this Catharist offspring, promotes a love too pure to live on this earth, a love consummated only by death. Hindrance, physical or political, is an inevitable dimension in romantic love. The lover is either married or restricted in some other way so that love cannot fully flower on this corrupt earth. Tristan, Romeo and Juliet (placed in Verona, a center of the Catharist movement) and, more recently, *Love Story* inherit this secularized Catharist motif. As deRougemont puts it, "The melodies in their distressing morbidity disclose a world in which carnal desire has become no more than an ultimate and impure apathy of souls in the process of curing themselves of life."[43] This passion leading to death has, of course, superficial resemblances to the Christian passion story, but it in fact is a radical perversion of it. Romantic passion seeks the unattainable or faraway princess; Christian passion seeks the neighbor. Christian passion loves

---

41 Bottomley, *op. cit.,* p. 125.
42 *Ibid.*
43 deRougement, *op. cit.,* p. 243.

the earth and the flesh; romantic passion longs to be delivered from life. One seeks more and more fullness of life; the other death.

The Cathars represent a romantic rebellion against creation and follow faithfully the dualist tradition in that regard. It is fascinating to note the revival of so many Catharist themes in the 20th-century National Socialist movement of Adolph Hitler. Naziism was a kind of romantic nationalism. Purity was a central driving force for Hitler as it was for the Cathars. He was intent on purifying the nation. His extermination camps made gypsies and retardates as well as Jews and political opponents the first object of a program to purify the nation. The antithesis to Catharist anthropology was Jewish earthiness, which may be the real reason Hitler focused principally on the Jews. In place of a priesthood, the Cathars created the office of guides ("Fuhrer" in German) who were said to have taught the secrets of initiation with their divinizing voices. Hitler, who ordained himself "Fuhrer," initiated millions of Germans with his hypnotic voice at huge rallies in Nuremberg and elsewhere. Initiates grasped the Nazi banner and swore allegiance to this new religion. Physical sexual expression was apparently as anathematic to Hitler as to the Cathars, for whom marriage was *uirato fornicato*, "lawful fornication".[44] Hitler was sexually puritanical, countenancing no obvious evidence of sexual acting out among his associates, either homosexual or heterosexual. It is not known for certain whether Hitler ever actually consummated his relationship with Eva Braun, his long time mistress, though circumstantial evidence suggests he did. He declined to marry Eva on the grounds that marriage would weaken his image as Fuhrer. His relationship with her had the marks of a Catharist original. Among the Cathars a mistress was considered spiritually superior to a wife, preferably a platonic mistress. The marital vows of the Cathars were not exchanged for this world, but for the next.[45] Hitler married Eva in his underground bunker only hours before they jointly committed suicide.

Popular opinion at the time held that the Cathars commonly practiced anal intercourse, probably because the wives and/or lovers of devout Cathars were not getting pregnant. To what extent they may have practiced exotic forms of sex to avoid pregnancy or in fact practiced sexual abstinence is not known. Only the content of popular opinion is known. Much of the Catharist movement was centered in

---

44 *Ibid.*, p. 142.
45 *Ibid.*, p. 323.

The Poisoning of Eros

Bulgaria, hence the word "bugger" as a synonym for anal intercourse and other noncoital sexual acts.

The institutional church crushed the Cathars institutionally. On the other hand, the church responded ideologically to the Cathars with the cult of the Virgin Mary and by making marriage a sacrament.[46] Peter Lombard was the first to name marriage as one of seven sacraments, in the early 12th century.[47] Thus the church put an end to the Cathar movement and to a significant degree absorbed Catharism. The Virgin Mary became its imaginary eternal woman, sexually untainted, the beloved woman waiting beyond death. By sacralizing marriage, sex was controlled more than blessed. Fixed within the boundaries of matrimony, and even there only within the narrow purposes of procreation, sexual expression was all but eliminated for faithful Christians.

IV

One of the strangest and most poignant love stories in all Western history is that of Peter Abelard and Heloise. No other story so well epitomizes the peculiar shape of sexual valorization in the life of the medieval period. Abelard and Heloise dramatized clearly the deprecation into which sexuality had fallen and the forced antithesis between the life of the body and the life of the mind. Peter Abelard was a 12th century intellectual, a brilliant cleric, who was perhaps more than any other one person the father of the modern university. He was an innovative and daring individual, both in thought and deed.

In the 12th century the monasteries and the cathedral schools were polarized in a competitive battle for their respective claims as intellectual centers of Western life. Abelard was a product of and promoter of the cathedral school, the precursor to the modern university. Abelard's life and work deepened the polarization between the respective philosophical positions of the monasteries and cathedral schools. The cathedral schools were centers of questioning and innovative thinking. As such, they pointed to the future. The monasteries were centers of pious devo-

---
46 Schillebeeckx (1966), p. 313.
47 Marriage as a sacrament originated with the gnostics. The central concern of the late 3rd century gnostic Gospel of Philip is the "sacrament of the bridal chamber." See *The Nag Hammadi Library*, James M. Robinson, ed., San Francisco: Harper & Row, Publishers, 1972, p. 131ff.

tion and obedience, supporting traditional and conservative values and ways of thinking. They looked to the immediate past. Bernard of Clairvaux, the champion of celibacy, was Abelard's counterpart and adversary in monastic life. The conflict between the two men was the *cause célèbre* of the 12th century.[48]

Bernard defended a faith that transcended human knowledge, a faith achieved through mystic contemplation. He was offended by Abelard's exploration of even the deepest matters "without reverence." Bernard successfully appealed to the Pope for a judgment. The Pope declared Abelard a heretic, ordered his books burned and ordered him confined to perpetual silence in a monastery. Shortly before his death, the papal rescript against Abelard was lifted, but his writings continued to be both suspect in traditional quarters and honored in free-thinking quarters. So Abelard stands as a 12th century symbol of freedom of thought and investigation who emerged within a heavily authoritarian and repressive system which threatened to annihilate him and his writings. The personal price Abelard paid for pointing to the future was quite high. In death, as in life, Abelard was not allowed to rest. His remains were interred seven times before they were finally left in peace.

In the long term Abelard has been remembered more for his love affair with Heloise than for his creative intellect, but the two aspects of Abelard are a parallel process. Many of Abelard's contemporaries were even more chagrined by his love affair than his progressive and innovative thinking. In both respects he became a symbol for personal freedom against repressive authoritarianism. Bernard disdainfully said of him that he "argues with boys and associates with women."[49] He may have been, as Mary Martin McLaughlin contends, alone among his contemporaries

---

48 *The Letters of Abelard and Heloise*, Betty Radice, trans., New York: Penguin Books, 1974, p. 35.
49 *The Letters of St. Bernard of Clairvaux*, Bruno Scott James, trans., London: Burns Oates, 1953, Letter 244. Bernard added that Abelard "corrupts the integrity of the faith and chastity of the church . . . Lord, do I not hate the men who hate thee, and am I not sick at heart over their rebellion...?" Letter 241.

in promoting the dignity of women, even a kind of 12th-century feminist. He set a parity of women with men in the religious life. At Paraclete convent the male clergy entered the sanctuary with nuns, rather than the sexes being separated by walls and screens.[50]

Abelard's daring relationship with Heloise was congruent with his philosophy. He challenged the church's established view that sexual pleasure was to be avoided. He wrote in *Ethics 3*: "If to lie with a wife or even to eat delicious food has been allowed us since the first day of our creation which was lived in paradise without sin, who will accuse us of sin in this if we do not exceed the limit of the concession?"[51] He brilliantly mocks the accepted teaching of his day: ". . . they say . . . marital intercourse . . . should be performed wholly without pleasure. But assuredly, if this is so, they are allowed to be done in a way in which they cannot be done at all and it was an unreasonable permission which allowed them to be done in a way in which it is certain that they cannot be done."[52]

They met when Heloise was about 17 and Abelard in his mid- 30 s. Heloise's uncle and guardian (it was speculated that he was her natural father), Fulbert, was a colleague of Abelard's and canon at the Cathedral of Notre Dame in Paris. Abelard was a teacher, a *magister scholarum*, and a cleric, but it is not known to what major or minor order of the clergy he had risen at this point in his career. Abelard became her tutor. Their love affair blossomed and was consummated in secret. As they fell deeper in love they became more and more bold, or careless, and were eventually caught *in flagrante delicto* by Fulbert. Shortly thereafter Heloise found herself pregnant. Abelard sent her to his family in rural Brittany where a son was born whom they named Astralabe.

The dilemma for the two lovers was by now quite complex. Neither really wanted marriage which, being children of their times, they both held in low esteem. Furthermore, marriage would inhibit if not terminate Abelard's career as a cleric. Abelard was born in 1079,

---

50 Mary Martin McLaughlin, "Peter Abelard and the Dignity of Women: Twelfth Century 'Feminism' in Theory and Practice", p 287-333; and John F. Benton, "Fraud, Fiction and Borrowing in The Correspondence of Abelard and Heloise", p. 469-511, in *Pierre Abelard; Pierre Le Venerable, Les Courants Philosophiques, Litteraires et Artistiques En Occident au Milieu de XII Siecle, 1972*, Paris: Editions du Centre National de le Recherche Scientifique, 1975.
51 *Peter Abelard's Ethics,* D. E. Luscombe, trans., Oxford: Clarendon Press, 1971, p. 21.
52 *Ibid.*

The Medieval Synthesis

about 40 years after the commencement of the Gregorian "reforms." Fulbert, however, was a force to reckon with as Heloise's guardian and perhaps father. Abelard proposed a secret marriage as an attempt to protect both Heloise and himself at the same time. After the marriage he sent Heloise to a convent, apparently giving Fulbert the impression that he was attempting to rid himself of her. Abelard's real motivation is not known, but he did visit Heloise at her convent at least once where, in his own later description, they made love in a corner of the refectory for lack of any other private space. Fulbert, enraged at what appeared to be cavalier exploitation and disposal of Heloise, sent his servants to Abelard's quarters under cover of night and, catching him asleep, they castrated him. Abelard then retreated to monastic life. The two lovers continued to maintain some kind of correspondence subsequently.

At this point in the story we are confronted with a complex problem.[53] A collection of eight letters between Abelard and Heloise after his castration survives in nine manuscript copies. Since the late 18th century a persistent suspicion has circulated that the letters, though basically original, have been doctored. Abelard portrays himself in these letters as a traditional monk who has sinned sexually and is doing penance with the rest of his life. The documents in the form we now have them reveal a penitent Abelard who comes to subscribe to the official Roman view of sexuality, and who regrets his relationship with Heloise, denigrating it as a result of "lust." John F. Benton is the major exponent today of the view that the letters are a doctored version of original documents. He conjectures, further, that Abelard and Heloise continued to be mutually supportive, personally and spiritually. The scholarly world has not reached a consensus on the matter. It boils down to a question of whether Abelard reverts to the established sex values of his day or continues in his later years the radical values he had espoused in his prime.[54]

If we ignore doubts about the integrity of the letters and take them at face value, Heloise ultimately acquitted herself more admirably than Abelard. First of all, she remained stalwart and constant in her devotion to her lover and was clearly willing to endure any hardship in order to nurture their relationship. She was unconcerned about her

---

53 For an excellent review of the debate see Peter Dronke, *Abelard and Heloise in Medieval Testimonies,* University of Glasgow Press, 1976.
54 *Ibid.,* p. 491-501.

reputation or her public image. She did not want anything from Abelard except his love. About marriage, she later wrote from her convent: "The name of wife may seem more sacred or more binding, but sweeter for me will always be the word mistress, or, if you will permit me, that of concubine or whore."[55] She preferred "love to wedlock and freedom to chains. God is my witness that if Augustus, Emperor of the whole world, thought fit to honor me with marriage and conferred all the earth on me to possess forever, it would be dearer and more honorable to me to be called not his Empress but your whore."[56] She also makes it clear that she had entered into the secret marriage only because Abelard insisted on it.

While Abelard seems increasingly to separate himself affectively from Heloise, thereby intensifying her grief, Heloise reveals in her letters her continuing devotion and deepening pain.

> Why, after our entry into religion which was your decision alone, have I been so neglected and forgotten by you. . . I wish I could think of some explanation which would excuse you and somehow cover up the way you hold me cheap.

She in no way repented of her sexual liaison with him and clearly would continue it if she had the opportunity.

> I can expect no reward for this from God, for it is certain that I have done nothing as yet for love of him. . . I would have had no hesitation, God knows, in following you or going ahead at your bidding to the flames of Hell.

> I should be groaning over the sins I have committed but I can only sigh for what I have lost. Everything we did and also the times and places are stamped on my heart along with your image, so that I live through it all again with you. Even in sleep I know no respite. . .[57] Now particularly you should fear, now when I no longer have in you an outlet for my incontinence.[58]

In dealing with her sexuality, the later Heloise appears the better theologian of the two, even a better exponent of Abelard's own dialectical theology. She understood the paradox of her supposed guilt in her relationship with Abelard:

---

55 *The Letters of Abelard and Heloise,* p. 113.
56 *Ibid.,* p. 114.
57 *Ibid.,* p. 133.
58 *Ibid.,* p. 116-7, 133-5.

Wholly guilty though I am, I am also, as you know, wholly innocent. It is not the deed but the intention of the doer which makes the crime, and justice should weigh not what was done but the spirit in which it is done.

In sharp contrast to Heloise, Abelard appears to repent and renounce their love affair. Further, he sounds in his letters to her more and more like a traditional monk, successfully sublimating his sexual energy:

You were previously the wife of a poor mortal and now raised to the bed of the King of Kings.[59]

He also reverted to the established Augustinian-Gregorian excoriation of sex itself:[60]

My love, which brought us both to sin, should be called lust, not love. I took my fill of my wretched pleasures in you, and this was the sum total of my love.

And finally, in a farewell letter to Heloise, he composed a prayer for her addressed to God on their behalf, a prayer that must have ended (if authentic) any hope Heloise may have had for reuniting with her lover:

Punish the guilty now, I beseech thee, that thou mayest spare them hereafter. Punish now, lest thou punish in eternity. . . Afflict their flesh that thou mayest preserve their souls. . . Farewell in Christ, bride of Christ, in Christ farewell and live in Christ.

Joseph Campbell's judgment of Abelard is quite severe.[61] He assumes, of course, that the letters are authentic in their present form. He labels him Nietzsche's "pale criminal:" "Adequate was he to the deed when he did it: but the idea of it he could not bear when it was done." Campbell may be correct, but he may also be simply adding one more in a long series of insults against a man whose daring could not be tolerated. Condemned by Rome, harassed by local authorities, forced to burn his own books by his own hand, and castrated, Abelard may have suffered the final indignity of having his letters amended to conform to the medieval Roman Catholic ideology he was opposing.

Abelard had rocked the theological world both by his sexual behavior and his audacity in using human reason to measure the value of scripture and tradition. He and Heloise together represented the emerg-

---
59 *Ibid.*, p. 138.
60 *Ibid.*, p. 115.
61 Joseph Campbell, *Creative Mythology*, p. 59; Campbell quotes from Nietzsche's *Also Sprach Zarathustra* 1,6.

ing myth of self-discovery and self-reliance that was coming into being in this century, as Campbell himself asserts.[62] Heloise simply followed in her personal life the path Abelard had cleared theologically and intellectually. She learned her lessons well. It is not so rare that a student surpasses her teacher, that is, assuming the documents have not been tampered with.

Though she remained in the convent, Heloise refused the life of the supernatural beatific vision that the monastic ideal offered, just as she had also rejected marriage. She was as audacious and as innovative in her personal life as Abelard was in his theology. Rejecting both marriage and celibacy, she followed, in Campbell's words, the "womanly, purely human experience of love for a specific living being" and demonstrated the courage to suffer for that love.[63]

If we accept the letters as genuine in their present form, Heloise ultimately earns more of our admiration and sympathy. It was difficult enough to challenge the basic assumptions of the culture, but it must have been unspeakably painful to be rejected finally by her teacher and lover, Abelard himself.

If we permit ourselves the luxury of bypassing the detailed complexity of scholarly debate over the integrity of the letters, one salient aspect of the debate presents itself. Abelard's renunciation of his affair with Heloise would have been a dramatic reversal in values and philosophy. After castration, he may well have changed his mind. Indeed, he could have changed his mind without it. His reversal looks suspicious if for no other reason than that it well serves the established medieval Catholic theology. However, Abelard's reversal appears even more suspicious in light of parallel data. For example, a poem composed by Abelard in his last years for his son Peter Astralabe does not reflect the same hardened monastic that the letters portray:

... Yet there are those whose past sins still so allure them
    that they can never feel truly penitent.
Rather, the sweetness of that bliss remains so great that
    no sense of atoning for it has force.
This is the burden of complaint of our Heloise, whereby
    she often says to me, as to herself,
"If I cannot be saved without repenting of what I used to
    commit, there is no hope for me.

---

62 *Ibid.*, p. 64.
63 *Ibid.*, p. 59.

The Medieval Synthesis

The joys of what we did are still so sweet that, after delight
   beyond measure, even remembering brings relief."
For one who tells the truth there is no strain in telling---it is
   feigning that's the effort, before one speaks.[64]

Peter Dronke also points to several epitaphs for Abelard and Heloise which praise the unity of human and divine love and which neither condemn nor slough aside the sexual union between them. One reads: "One flesh, one tomb, one spirit, one bed of earth . . . the oneness of lovers in Christ."[65]

Then there is the letter which Peter the Venerable wrote to Heloise to console her after Abelard's death. Peter the Venerable, abbot of Cluny, was a prince of the church and had given shelter and protection to the fugitive Abelard in his final years. The letter reveals no hint of a transformation on Abelard's part. In fact, the letter ends with the assurance that the two lovers will be united in paradise:

> My illustrious and dearest sister in God: this man to whom you cleaved, after the sexual oneness, with the stronger and finer bond of divine love, he with whom and under whom you have long served God---I tell you, God is now cherishing him in his lap, in place of you, or like a replica of you. And at the second coming, at the sound of the archangel and the trumpet heralding God descending from the heavens, God will restore him to you through his grace, having preserved him for you.[66]

The tragedy of Abelard and Heloise is not only the story of their personal anguish. It is also the tragedy of a culture which required persons to choose between a sensual and an intellectual/spiritual life. Though they challenged the assumptions of this false dichotomy, Heloise (perhaps) more persistently than Abelard, they were both ultimately defeated by it. The forms of medieval life in the West simply demanded that one choose between a life of the body and a life of the soul and mind. Such a hateful choice was the philosophical bedrock of established Augustinian medieval Christendom.

---

64 From Peter Dronke, *op. cit.*, p. 15.
65 *Ibid.*, p. 22.
66 *The Letters of Peter the Venerable in Two Volumes,* (G. Constable, ed.) Cambridge, Mass.: 1969, Vol. 1, pp. 307-8, Letter 115.

V

Thomas Aquinas (1225-74) was the preeminent theologian of the medieval period as a whole in the eyes of subsequent ecclesiastical tradition, and his *Summa Theologica* was the preeminent theological document of the period. He attempted a synthesis of Aristotelian philosophy and Christian theology. Aquinas was a lifelong celibate as a Dominican monk and probably without sexual experience himself, since he was acclaimed in his own lifetime for his sexual purity.[67] He generally followed Augustine on sexual matters, because he looked on Augustine as a man whose evaluation of sexual behavior carried with it the testimony of experience, an attribute Aquinas himself probably lacked. Thomas apparently attempted to ameliorate the harshness of the identification of sexual pleasure with concupiscence that had come to be accepted as the Augustinian/Gregorian position. In this respect Thomas was following his teacher, Albertus Magnus, who argued that pleasure is God's will for mankind and is not in itself evil. But he was not successful, nor is it likely he could have been, in modifying the long-established Augustinian-Gregorian position. His reasoning follows the same line as Augustine's. He intends clearly to affirm sexual pleasure itself, a kind of theoretical starting point. When experienced by a married couple desiring to procreate, the pleasure should not be condemned, he argues. But neither should the pleasure be sought for its own sake. Furthermore, the pleasure itself is not sinful, but rather the violent, destructive, animal-like qualities of it which are "untempered by reason." As if to give weight to his affirmation of pleasure, he says that in the Garden of Eden the pleasurable sensation of sex would have been even more intense, ruled as it was by reason. Furthermore, it would not have damaged the woman's integrity, which is to say that her virginity would have been preserved. He follows Augustine's reasoning, that the semen would impregnate in the same way menstruation flows. Like Augustine, he abolishes *intercourse* in Paradise, but he does not abolish sex itself. Sobriety and reason would govern the sex act, not "impetuous lust and disturbance of mind."[68]

---

67 Michael F. Valente, *Sex: The Radical View of a Catholic Theologian,* New York: The Bruce Publishing Co., 1970, p. 48.
68 St. Thomas Aquinas, *Summa Theologica,* London: Blackfriars, Vol 13, I.a, 98.

The Medieval Synthesis

The argument is frequently made that Thomas is basically sex affirming, since he clearly intended to affirm sex in the Garden. The argument is insupportable in view of the highly peculiar and restrictive limitations he places on his idealized sex, a sex without vaginal penetration or orgasmic ecstasy. Thomas' paradisiacal sex would scarcely resemble the ecstatic, orgasmic experience of entering and being entered that makes sex what it is in the human experience. Thomas, in fact, promotes the continuation of the typically Stoic and Augustinian fear of the disordered mind which attends the ecstasy of sex. As Dennis Doherty puts it, Thomas is not helpful in the present context, except for his basic wish to affirm sexual pleasure in theory.[69] Thomas' affirmation of sex does not reach beyond the theoretical. He writes: "The use of sex keeps the soul back from that perfect intention to tending toward God. . . [and] there is nothing which perverts a man's mind more than the caresses of a woman and that bodily contact without which a wife cannot be had."[70]

Other lesser-known theologians in the late medieval period proposed a more radical affirmation of sexual pleasure, moderated by temperance, and regarded such pleasure as a legitimate goal in the marital relationship.[71] Cardinal Cajetan (1469-1524), for one, thought it stupid that sexual pleasure should be abhorred.[72] But he and others of a similar view are all but lost in the history of theology, overshadowed by Thomas and his interpretation of Augustine. Subsequently, the joint authority of Augustine and Aquinas more or less in unison sealed even more effectively the separation of sex and religion. As John Noonan writes, "If the most independent of medieval theologians could not escape Augustine, how much less could most of his successors confronted with both Augustine and Thomas?"[73]

---

69 Dennis J. Doherty, *Dimensions of 'Human Sexuality'*, Garden City, NY: Doubleday & Co., 1979, pp. 39-78. This collection of essays engages the heated debate going on as to who accurately understands Thomas, a debate that flared up with the publication of *Human Sexuality*.
70 *Summa Theologica*, II,II,186,4.
71 See especially Michael Valente, *op. cit.*, pp. 52-5; John T. Noonan, *Contraception*, Cambridge, Mass: Harvard University Press, 1965, p. 355; and Eric Fuchs, *Sexual Desire and Love*, New York: The Seabury Press, 1983, pp. 127-8.
72 See Dennis J. Doherty, *Sexual Doctrine of Cardinal Cajetan*, Regensburg: Verlag Friedrich Pustet, 1966.
73 Noonan, *op. cit.*, p. 254.

The Poisoning of Eros

Perhaps even more important than his contribution to theological thought, and certainly more intriguing, is the fact that, at age 49, Thomas put down his pen in the midst of his work on penance and apparently decided to die. On December 6, 1273, Thomas became strangely disturbed in the course of celebrating mass. Though he was in full possession of his faculties and in good health, he ceased from that moment the composition of his theological masterpiece. There is nothing comparable to it in history.[74] Thomas then visited his sister, who subsequently queried his colleagues: "What has happened? Thomas seems to be in a stupor; he will not talk to me." Thomas confided to a colleague: "Everything I have written seems to me like so much straw compared to the truths which I have seen, and which have been revealed to me." On March 7, 1274, exactly three months after his disturbing experience, he died of "mental exhaustion. . . extreme lassitude and weakness, and lack of appetite, but no fever."[75] In his last days he had celebrated mass with flowing tears.

The traditional interpretation given to this strange sequence of events is that Thomas experienced a vision of God who called him home. Petitot even wonders why he lingered for three months. "Why did St. Thomas' soul remain in his body even after his constant ecstasies?" he asks.[76] Whether one accepts the validity of such an interpretation or not, the interpretation itself has powerful implications in Christian anthropology. Thomas' final act is a monumental expression of disdain for creaturely existence, the ultimate renunciation of the world as the place God made for mankind. In Thomas' dying, the syncretistic vision supplants the Hebraic. Thomas, comfortable and overweight in his monastery, revered as a great teacher in his own lifetime, can be juxtaposed to the miserable Jews at Treblinka and other 20th century extermination camps. Thomas' God bids him in the prime of his life to lie down and die, but the Jews, some of them at any rate, driven by abuse to the threshold of death, make their evening prayer, "Next year in Jerusalem!" In the Hebraic vision, the world and human life are God's work and are to be affirmed with unflagging zeal to the very edge of human existence. In the syncretistic vision creaturely existence is characterized by mud and filth, to be shunned for the sake of a higher life of mental incorporeality

---

74 L. H. Petitot, *The Life and Spirit of Thomas Aquinas,* Cyprian Burke, trans., Chicago: The Priory Press, 1966, p. 154.
75 *Ibid.,* p. 160.
76 *Ibid.,* p. 166.

and life in another world. The implications for sexual valorization here are obvious.

VI

Joan of Arc (1412/1431) was another of the celebrated figures of the late medieval period and in some ways she was a harbinger of things to come.[77] The passion of her life was to drive the English out of France and consequently she has become perhaps the most important symbol of French nationalism. In heeding the voices that she heard calling her to her vocation she became a symbol of the claims of individual conscience against the authority of the international church which had withheld permission for her to trust those voices. In that respect she challenged the church's authority as powerfully as her contemporary, Jan Huss, the early Protestant reformer of Bohemia. In fact, Joan was suspected of Hussite influence. The Inquisition, that ecclesiastical court founded in the 13th century to deal with Cathar heretics, found her guilty of refusing to yield to the church's authority and ordered her burned at the stake. The Cardinal of Winchester, Henry Beaufort, who was the pope's special representative in his crusade against the Hussites, was appointed one of the witnesses to Joan's burning.

Joan was posthumously acquitted of heresy and rather much later sainted by Rome, in 1920. Having been refused burial in consecrated ground, her ashes long since had been cast into the Seine at Rouen. By semantic gymnastics, the 20th century church simply declared the church court that had sentenced her illegitimate. In the calendar of saints she is identified as "virgin" rather than martyr, which is convenient since the latter reference would raise the question of who martyred her.

Joan's faithfulness to her conscience over ecclesiastical authority and her fervent nationalism suggest her as a precursor to the Reformation, but her sexual values identify her as thoroughly medieval. She vowed not to marry when she first heard the voices at age thirteen. She dressed as a male and took to the field with her soldiers. Much was made of her chastity and virginity. She was examined in prison by friend and foe alike before her execution and found to be a virgin. Her

---

77 For a comprehensive study of her life and the myth, see: Marina Warner, *Joan of Arc: The Image of Female Heroism,* New York: Vintage Books, 1981.

virginity was a kind of talisman of her divine commission. Soldiers who fought beside her reported later that it was impossible to desire her sexually. Her squire, Jean d'Aulon, opined later that she never even menstruated. Joan seems to have presented herself as a prepubescent virginal androgyne. Certain artists subsequently portrayed her without breasts or buttocks. How much all of this might have been projection rather than Joan's own experience of herself cannot be known for certain. Being unlettered, she left no documents of her own. The 15th century certainly experienced her as an asexual, virginal androgyne and viewed her sexual purity and innocence as the source of her power. In that sense she was unambiguously medieval in her sexual values.

VII

Largely because of Thomas Aquinas, the medieval period is seen in retrospect as a time of synthesis and harmony. However, the so-called synthesis was in reality a defensive apologetic for the rather rigidly dualistic quality of medieval life. The gulf between those who lived by the flesh and those who lived by the soul/mind was a deep one. The "religious" were separated from the laity. Rather than an age of synthesis, it was an age of extremes---of renunciation on the one hand and worldliness on the other. Barbara Tuchman[78] supports this view, pointing out that in the 14th century the extremely rigorous Celestin monastic order was one of the favorite orders of a nobility who were themselves steeped in worldliness.

Frank Bottomley is one of those who espouse the view of the medieval world as a period of laudable synthesis. He published in 1979 a monumental and generally perspicacious contribution to the subject of sexual valorization in the West called *Attitudes to the Body in Western Christendom*. In support of his argument that the medieval synthesis promoted an integrated anthropology that blessed the flesh as well as the spirit Bottomley points to a variety of data. He points to the epic erotic poem of the early 13th century, *Carmina Burana*, which was preserved hidden in a Benedictine monastery at Beuern in Bavaria. (It was not entered in the library catalogue of the monastery.) Bottomley also points to the frequency with which erotic and scatalogical material

---

78 ﹨ Barbara Tuchman, *A Distant Mirror: The Calamitous 14th Century*, New York: Ballantine Books, 1978, p. 468.

appear in stone carvings and gargoyles in various medieval churches. For example, St. Martin de l'Isle at Adam-sur-Oise has a stone carving explicitly illustrating cunnilingus. Evreux Cathedral has a depiction of coprophagy. Harlots with their identifying sugar-loaf hats are common in ecclesiastical stone work. Likewise, popular plays and tales of the period abound with elaborate accounts of adultery and promiscuity. As James Cleugh says, they ride these themes to death.[79] Bottomley argues further that mixed bathing was common and that there was none of the prudish concern about nakedness that developed subsequently. He points also to the medieval marriage rite in which the concluding words of the bridegroom were "with my body I thee worship," words which were always uttered in the vernacular while the rest of the rite was in Latin. Bottomley argues too that the medieval Venus had a double aspect, that of divine love and that of lechery, and that medieval life fully embraced the bawdy and the scatalogical, an embrace that demonstrates the health of the times.

The synthesis that Bottomley and others argue for is probably a synthesis only when viewed from a distance. It is doubtful that a perspective from within medieval life would have supported a case for an integrated anthropology that embraces flesh and spirit. For the medieval person it was one or the other. The peasant and the ruling class on the one hand embraced the flesh and the religious on the other embraced the spirit and mind. The so-called synthesis was more like a stand-off between the religious and the non-religious. The latter embraced sexuality in some fashion; the former were celibate. At the beginning of the 13th century an estimated 10% of the adult male population were celibate clergy.[80] Furthermore, this group was the bearer of the intellectual and cultural life of the times. What synthesis could have meant for this celibate class is difficult to imagine. *Carmina Burana* may have been preserved by anonymous Benedictines, to whom we owe gratitude, but the document was saved like a Jew in the attic of Nazi Germany. Such a gesture does not qualify as a representative occurrence but as an exceptional one. *Carmina Burana* and erotic and scatalogical sculpture and literature illustrate the revolutionary energy of a suppressed sexuality. It was a rebellious response to a repressive regime, which does not add up

---

79   James Cleugh, *Love Locked Out: An Examination of the Irrepressible Sexuality of the Middle Ages*, New York: Crown Publishing Co. Inc., 1963, p. 295.
80   Derrick Sherwin Bailey, *op cit.*, p. 152.

to synthesis. If the rebellion was seemingly obsessed with sex, so too was the religious class in its determination to devalue it.

Serious challenges arose from time to time to the established sexual valorization of the medieval church. The earliest significant challenge to medieval ecclesiastical authority in general was made by the Waldenses, who appeared in Italy in the 12th century. They were an obscure proto-protestant group and were severely persecuted by established authority. Two centuries later, John Wycliffe (1324-84) in England and the Lollard movement that followed him revived the dissident challenge. *The Lollard Conclusions*, a document produced in 1394, explicitly condemned "the law of continence enjoined on priests, which was first ordained to the prejudice of women, (and) brings sodomy into all the Holy Church." The document similarly condemns monastic life for women, wishing "they were given in marriage."[81]

In Bohemia, similar unrest was developing under the leadership of Jan Huss (1369-1415), who was influenced by Wycliffe. Both Wycliffe and Huss seem to have focused more on the issue of authority than sexuality, but in both men the two issues are related as they were in the later Protestant movement. These two early Protestants were condemned by the Council of Constance which met in 1414-18 and Huss himself was burned at the stake there in 1415.

An even more radical challenge came from the Brethren of the Free Spirit, who flourished for over a century, mainly during the 14th century in Germany, France and the Low Countries. They unequivocally rejected the authority of the church and eschewed both private property and marriage. They practiced free love, nudity and group sex, and dressed deliberately in ragged monk's robes. They preached, begged and interrupted church services. They treated men and women equally. Some of the movement's leaders were women, including Schwester (Sister) Katrei, Marguerita Porete and Jeanne Dolenton. The latter two were burned at the stake by the Inquisition along with their books. Tied to the stake with Jeanne Dolenton was the corpse of a male associate who had died in prison.[82]

Even in Russia in 1311 a church council felt called upon to condemn a certain Novgorodian priest who had denounced monasticism.[83]

---

81 *Documents of the Christian Church,* 2nd Ed., Henry Bettensen, ed., New York: Oxford University Press, 1963, p. 175.
82 Barbara Tuchman, *op. cit.,* pp. 316-17.
83 Nicholas V. Riasanovsky, *A History of Russia,* New York: Oxford University Press, 1963, p. 135.

Another group emerged in the same city in 1470 labeled "Judaizers" because of their emphasis on the humanity of Jesus and their regard for the Old Testament. They were suppressed and their leaders burned at the stake.[84] These recusant precursors of the Reformation to come were each crushed by the joint action of ecclesiastical and political authority which was committed to the suppression of sexual expression among the religious. The ecclesiastical juggernaut which had been fashioned by the Gregorian popes continued intact until Martin Luther who in the early 16th century finally sparked a rebellion that could not be quashed, and the walls that separated the religious from the contamination of sex were irreparably breached.

---

84 *Ibid.*

Chapter Five
The Tide Turns: Luther and the Reformation

Perhaps Luther's greatest merit was to have had the courage of his sensuality (in those days one spoke, delicately enough, of "evangelical freedom").

-- Friedrich Nietzsche*

I

Voices like those of Abelard and Heloise continued to be heard in one corner of the world or another throughout the medieval period, affirming the sensuous and erotic and rejecting the antithesis of eros and religion that had become the warp and woof of Christendom. By the beginning of the sixteenth century, however, these voices were no longer scattered and obscure voices of contrariness. They increased in volume and authority until by the middle of the sixteenth century they had shattered Rome's universal and autocratic grip on the Western world. The Protestant Reformation was by then fully under way, a movement that would result in the formation of several independent churches that would eventually displace Roman ecclesiastical power throughout most of northern Europe and Britain.

The early sixteenth century was hardly a puritanical time. In Luther's Europe priests who kept mistresses were required to pay the bishop an annual tax of one guilder, resulting in the proverb, "Chaste priests are the bishop's enemies."[1] Cardinal Albrecht, with whom Luther had some dealings, kept a mistress.[2] As a rule the popes were sexually active, as well as in other respects duplicitous. Innocent VIII (1484-92) fathered three illegitimate children before he became a priest. Even worse in the eyes of Vatican historians, he "openly avowed his illegitimate children," one of whom he married to the daughter of Lorenzo di Medici to seal an alliance with Florence. Vatican historians

---

*   *Genealogy of Morals*, 3.2, Frances Golffing, trans., Garden City, NY: Doubleday & Co., Inc. 1956.
1   John M. Todd, *Luther*, New York: Crossroad, 1982, p. 244.
2   *Ibid.*, p. 305.

add further that he lacked a sense of the dignity of the papal office because he "even entertained women at his table."[3] Alexander VI (1492-1503) sired six natural children, sumptuously marrying one of his daughters to a Medici.[4] Paul III (1534-49) kept a mistress and fathered three illegitimate sons and a daughter while he was Cardinal.[5] Cardinal Wolsey, the highest ranking cleric in England, and one who tried unsuccessfully to stem the Lutheran tide and keep the English church loyal to Rome, had at least one bastard son, whom he dearly loved, named Thomas Winter.[6] The Swiss Bishop of Constance, Hugo von Hohenlandenberg, is said to have fined his priests in 1522 four guilders for every child they fathered, and to have received a large income from such fines. In a pastoral letter he complained about priests who openly kept concubines.[7] Zwingli, the Protestant reformer of Zurich, who married in 1522 when the Reformation was under way, had had a sexual liaison in his early days as a Roman priest.

Though it was an age of laxity, a fascination with sexual sins also prevailed. Martin Luther as a young monastic suffered from the repercussions of his failure to confess sexual sins. Being an intense and willful young man, he succeeded at great personal cost in suppressing his sexual drive. He confessed other, what he considered more significant sins, which led to puzzlement and suspicion on the part of his mentors. As Luther himself put it,

> I was very pious in the monastery, yet I was sad because I thought God was not gracious to me. I said mass and prayed and hardly saw or heard a woman as long as I was in the order. I often made confession to Staupitz, not about women but about really serious sins. He said, 'I don't understand you.' This was real consolation. Afterwards when I went to another confessor I had the same experience. In short, no confessor wanted to have anything to do with me.[8]

---

3 *The Popes: A Concise Biographical History*, Eric John, ed., London: Burns & Coats, Publisher to the Holy See, 1964, pp. 302-3.
4 J. Rilliet, *Zwingli,* Harold Kight, trans., Philadelphia: The Westminster Press, p. 32.
5 *The Popes, op. cit.,* p. 335.
6 Richard Marius, *op cit.,* p. 366.
7 Philip Schaff, *History of the Christian Church,* Vol. VIII, Grand Rapids, Michigan: William B. Eerdmans Publishing Co., 1958, p. 6.
8 *Luther's Works, Vol. 54, Table Talk,* Helmut T. Lehmann, ed., Philadelphia: Fortress Press, 1967, pp.94-5.

The Poisoning of Eros

Luther discovered early on that the deepest and most decisive theological issues were not sexual.

The widespread clerical concubinage, as it is sometimes called, can be understood in different ways. Obviously it can be seen simply as corruption, which indeed in some sense it was. It can also be seen as part and parcel of an age that was groping toward an affirmation of the sensual life and no longer believed in the antithetical relationship between the erotic and the religious. In that sense, this so-called corruption might be labeled a sort of sixteenth century "sexual revolution."

The lines of this revolution can be traced both from the radical, persecuted underground groups that appeared throughout the medieval period and from several low profile and mostly forgotten Roman Catholic theologians like Martin Le Maistre (1432-81) and Cardinal Cajetan. (See p. 159) Le Maistre separated sex from procreation, arguing that there were other legitimate purposes for marital intercourse. Le Maistre has never been taken very seriously because his was a suppressed minority opinion. He was overruled by the party of Aquinas before he could get established.[9]

The art of the fifteenth and sixteenth centuries supports the view that something of a sexual revolution was taking place in that period. Hieronymous Bosch was productive from 1480 to 1516, right up to the cusp of the Reformation. His work is notable for its polymorphous and humorous sensuality and earthiness. Some think he belonged to the radical Brethern of the Free Spirit, but, whatever his religious connections, his artistic statement is a powerful affirmation of sex and the body.[10] Though he preceded Luther by a generation, he and Luther speak the same language.

Bosch may have been unique, but he was not an aberration. Congruent with Bosch, but in a different genre, are the great number of paintings and sculpture in this period from a variety of artists which even depict Jesus in

---

9 For further elaboration of Le Maistre and his colleagues, see Michael F. Valente, *Sex: The Radical View of a Catholic Theologian,* New York: The Bruce Publishing Company, 1970, p. 52.
10 Norman Cohn, *The Pursuit of the Millennium,* Fairlawn, New Jersey: Essential Books, 1957, p. 174.

sexually suggestive poses. Leo Steinberg's extraordinary work in 1983, *The Sexuality of Christ in Renaissance Art and In Modern Oblivion,* documents the evidence.[11]

As Steinberg demonstrates, Christ is frequently portrayed having his penis fondled by the Virgin Mary, a practice not unknown in modern times whereby mothers stimulate the sexual development of their infant sons. Similarly, he himself is portrayed in mastubatory positions as an infant. Even more striking, however, are the numbers of portrayals of the adult Jesus with erections or suggestions of erection. An unknown artist of Cracow, circa 1480-90, said to be a pupil of Veit Stoss, produced a linden wood bas-relief, the "Baptism of Christ," which portrays Jesus stepping out of the water wrapped in a loincloth with a large, ostentatious and erect pubic bow.[12] Veit Stoss himself produced a wooden sculpture, "Crucifix," which has a peculiarly erect pubic bow.[13] Lucas Cranach, Albrecht Durer, Maaerten van Heemskerck, and numerous others portray both the crucified and the risen Jesus in which his sexual member is roused.[14] Steinberg thinks there is an inherent connection between resurrection and erection, the latter being "the body's best show of power."[15]

In Steinberg's view such art affirms the full humanity of Jesus, an affirmation which has subsequently been cast into oblivion. He thinks this forgetfulness was "profound, willed, and sophisticated," and a decision for which the modern world has paid dearly. He calls it a "retreat from the mythical grounds of Christianity."[16] More precisely, he might have said it was an obfuscation of Jesus' Hebraic origins.

The artistic portrayal of Jesus' sexuality was a process that developed over two centuries. The first wholly nude artistic renditions of Christ appeared around 1350.[17] Not everyone was of the same mind about the rendering of Jesus' penis in these portraits. The humanist educator, Luis Vives (1492-1540), declared the male member "improper in art because of

---

11 Leo Steinberg, *The Sexuality of Christ in Renaissance Art and in Modern Oblivion,* New York: Pantheon, 1983.
12 Reproduced in *Gothic and Renaissance Art in Nuremberg 1300-1500,* New York: Metropolitan Museum of Art, 1986, p. 247.
13 *Ibid.,* p. 246, located in Heilig-Geist-Spital, Nuremberg.
14 Steinberg, *op. cit.,* p. 87.
15 *Ibid.,* p.91.
16 *Ibid.,* p. 108.
17 *Ibid.,* p. 28.

lechery and dishonor."[18] Such opinions were countered, as Steinberg documents, by others who apparently felt that an affirmation of Christ's sexuality was appropriate. The fig leaf was a later invention.

Steinberg's work raises some difficult questions for theologians. Boniface Ramsey, a monastic who wrote a review of the work in a theological journal, candidly admits the work to be "surprising and sometimes even consternating," and that he was "taken aback" by some of the 246 reproductions.[19] As Ramsey correctly notes, neither Augustine nor Thomas Aquinas would have allowed Christ either masturbation or an erection, on theological grounds. These artists are, therefore, defying the directives of Augustinian/Thomist orthodoxy which theologically ruled the medieval period. Martin Luther, who was also to affirm the erotic in defiance of Augustine and Aquinas, might well have thought as Freud did centuries later, that in all his discoveries the artists had been there first.

II

A significant dimension of the sixteenth century Reformation, perhaps even its driving force, was its rediscovery of Christianity's Jewish roots, manifesting itself in a renewed appreciation for that Jewish document, the Bible. The reformers appealed to the Bible as an authority over against the authority of a corrupt ecclesiastical hierarchy. The motivation for this polarization of Bible and church was not simply the wish for moral purity, though that wish was present. The assertion of biblical authority was the assertion of that distinctively Jewish anthropology which had been gradually lost through the centuries by the increasing Hellenization of ecclesiastical thought, culminating in Thomas Aquinas' synthesis of Aristotle and Christian theology. The Reformation was a defeat for salvation through sublimation or suppression of the sensuous and the sexual, and a victory for the body and sex and for a religion that affirms both.

More significant than anything any reformer said about sex was the fact that the various reform movements in Western Europe universally restored marriage to the clergy and abolished monastic life. In these two ges-

---

18 *Ibid.*, p. 45.
19 *Theological Studies,* Vol. 46, No. 1, March 85, p. 164.

Luther and the Reformation

tures the entire Reformation movement turned its face from Athens to Jerusalem, restoring, in principle at least, a more Jewish valorization of sexuality. The rationale for religious celibacy was swiftly and unambiguously dismantled in the burgeoning Reformation churches.

Of the many characters of the Reformation whose works have survived the expurgations of history, Martin Luther (1483-1546) is preeminent. In terms of political power and influence he is matched by John Calvin, the Geneva reformer. In terms of profundity of thought and a capacity to present himself in his writings as a vibrant, living human being, he has no peer. Luther was outrageously earthy. Who else in the history of religion would have had the audacity and candor to locate his experience of enlightenment, or conversion, at the time and place of tending to the needs of his bowels?[20] In the Wittenberg monastery toilet Luther was reflecting on the justice of God and the words of Paul, "the just live by faith," particularly in the context of his own inner urgency to be "right." Luther was a conscientious, if not obsessive, monastic. What came to him in the Wittenberg toilet, his so-called "tower experience" (*Turmerlebnis*), where the toilet was located, was the awareness that human existence is not really justified by any amount of righteous living, but rather simply by a faith that is given. He saw that the pursuit of righteousness or justification for one's existence through pious works or beliefs of any sort was a vain and hopeless pursuit. In a real sense Luther rediscovered the theological idea of creatureliness, in which not only life but also its justification is a given, that human beings are recipients both of life and of its validation. This awareness was an intellectual and emotional breakthrough for Luther and marked the beginning of his new life, as well as of the Reformation itself. Luther's own personal drive for perfection was dismantled and reordered. He, in turn, launched an attack on the system that had supported his obsessive striving for purity, attacking in particular the church's practice of marketing certificates called "indulgences" which provided the purchaser or his nominee special access to

---

20 Some scholars have challenged the accuracy of reading Luther's intent here but the arguments are not persuasive. See Erik Erikson, *Young Man Luther*, New York: Norton, 1958, Norman O. Brown, *Life Against Death*; Middletown, CT: Wesleyan University Press, 1959, and the challenge in Roger A. Johnson, ed., *Psychohistory and Religion: the Case of Young Man Luther*, Philadelphia: Fortress Press, 1977.

the merits earned by Jesus' sacrifice. Needless to say, these certificates were sometimes purchased in advance as a hedge against future sins. Even more significantly, Luther attacked the church's system of salvation through the denial of sex.

Luther's religious experience related to his bowels has continued to embarrass generations of effete theologians for almost five hundred years. One theologian, Lewis Spitz, still awaits a work on "a wholesome Luther."[21] Certain partisan Roman Catholic theologians gleefully have continued to hurl "*Turmerlebnis*" in the faces of embarrassed Lutherans. Heinrich Denifle at the beginning of this century was heir to a tradition that originated in the sixteenth century when he argued that Luther's attack on the church was a projection of "his own diseased, oversexed soul."[22] Some take the position that God is, of course, everywhere, even in the toilet, and that Luther simply revealed more about himself than he needed to. Others, epecially Erik Erikson and Norman O. Brown, interpret Luther's particular enlightenment as integral to the nature of his faith. They contend that the context of his illumination was not an unhappy embarrassing coincidence, but was congruent with the nature of his healing experience. What Erikson and Brown explicate is a view of Luther's experience from a psychoanalytically-informed perspective.

This psychoanalytic perspective proposes that anality is both the bodily locus and the psychological issue raised by Luther's salvation-by-faith experience. Anality is the issue of order, organization, and creativity. Primitively it is the question, beginning at about age two, of what to do with one's feces. Developmentally, it is the question of how to order one's life, the nature of one's lifework, and beyond that the justification of one's existence. A sublimated anality operates as an inner force, continuing its work separated from its bodily locus. A coin collector might exemplify a creatively sublimated anality with tendencies toward orderliness. A pathological, or unresolved anality is separated from awareness of its bodily locus and origins, even struggling to deny them. Norman O. Brown proposes that a pathological anality was the driving force in Luther's call to monastic life. He

---

21 Roger A. Johnson, *op. cit.,* p. 84.
22 Kenneth G. Hagen, "Changes in the Understanding of Luther: The Development of the Young Luther," *Theological Studies,* Vol. 29, No. 3, Sept. 1968, pp. 472-96.

strove mightily to clean up his life and achieve purity, a pathological manifestation of his wish to separate himself from his excrement. His enlightenment in the monastery toilet takes the shape of a sudden recognition of his passionately denied anality. Luther discovered not only that such denial is in vain and impossible to accomplish, but that the goal itself was simply an illusory rearrangement of one's own excrement. Even more significant, he discovered it to be a denial of human creatureliness.

From his enlightenment on, Luther proclaimed that all human efforts to justify existence by deeds are merely spiritual arrogance. Luther presages Freud's observation that all art, religion, culture, even civilization itself, are intrinsically rooted in the primitive experience of ordering excrement. Only the pretense that it is not is dangerous. Luther's illumination, then, is a profound return to the reality of the body and the cessation of his extraordinary effort to rid himself once and for all of the filth of the body. Excrement is now an intrinsic part of the human experience. The devil, who in Luther's symbolism is associated with excrement, in fact rules the world until the kingdom comes at the "eschaton." In vain persons harbor expectations of finally purifying themselves or any human institution. Luther achieves in his conversion another (higher/lower) level of integration in the recognition that he is irrevocably "full of shit" and that any shred of pretense not to be is the most corrupting illusion of all. In this dark view of human personality Luther makes a cultural link between Augustine and Freud, and thus becomes like them one of the purveyors of a hermeneutics of suspicion about all human motivation.

For Luther neither the devil nor excrement is projected "out there." The devil is a constant companion and tempter, offering to deceive by illusions of purity. The most attractive of these illusions is the one created by the church. Hence the pope is the primary agent of the devil. The devil is the invisible agent of corruption and filth, and the pope is a visible, sublimated agent of that same filth, pretending not to be.

This psychoanalytic interpretation of Luther's religious experience does not diminish but rather enhances the theological significance of it. It clarifies by adding another perspective. It reinforces the theological notion of justification by faith with the psychological notion of health through deepening awareness of the irremediably conflicted nature of human development. Furthermore, this interpretation appears firmly supported in Luther's subsequent writing. No one in all ecclesiastical history consistently reveals himself to be more body affirming and more human. Throughout his life he continues to reveal himself in scatological and erotic images, his feet planted firmly on the earth under heaven. Luther's candor about the context of his enlightenment in the monastery toilet is only the beginning.

Conveniently for subsequent Lutheran institutionalism, which was not altogether comfortable with Luther's scatological and erotic revelations, Luther was not a systematizer. Theoretically he could not have been since systems themselves are a sublimated form of anality and therefore carry the constant potential for self-deception. So Werner and Lotte Pelz follow Luther when they say that "the system is of the devil."[23] So also does Karl Barth in his refusal to write a "systematic" theology, electing instead to call his life work *Church Dogmatics*. A Vatican document printed in 1964 says correctly that Luther "never achieved a coherent [theological] system."[24] The same charge could be hurled at Paul and biblical literature as a whole. The same Vatican document overstated the case, however, when it claimed that "he always despised logic."[25]

Much of Luther's theological teaching has an *ad hoc* quality, and therefore any given part can be deliberately ignored, as it often is. Some of his teaching is contradictory as well. He changed his mind about some things in the course of his development. With skillful screening one could construct quite varied pictures of Luther's thinking. Furthermore, Luther was not free of certain presuppositions of his time. Male chauvinism, anti-semitism, elements of platonism, and biblical fundamentalism are found to some extent in Luther's writings. Much in Luther is ordinary and dated by the times he lived in, but the main thrust of Luther's work is extraordinary and deserves attention. Principally, what was extraordinary about Luther was that he almost singlehandedly restored to Christendom its original and forgotten Jewish anthropology.

Luther rejected the established ecclesiastical doctrine of his day that marriage was a lesser vocation, available to those who could not give themselves to the higher, "religious" life of monasticism. In Catholic Christendom marriage was subservient to monasticism, a concession to the

---

23 Werner and Lotte Pelz, *God Is No More,* London: Victor Gollancz, 1963.
24 *The Popes*, p. 329.
25 *Ibid.*

Luther and the Reformation

flesh and the devil. Even before his own marriage Luther came around to the Old Testament view, or very close to it, that everyone should marry. Long after he had begun assisting others to leave monastic life to marry, and shortly before his own marriage he wrote:

> Whoever is ashamed of marriage is also ashamed of being a man or being thought a man, or else thinks that he can make himself better than God made him. Adam's children are and must remain men, and hence they should and must let men be begotten by them.[26]

He ultimately saw marriage as a welcome opportunity to give expression to bodily and sensual drives in which he personally delighted.

In his monastic years Luther had no mistress and obediently kept his distance from younger women. He was a serious monastic. When his ideas about monastic life changed he at first helped others leave and marry. He operated a kind of underground railroad and marriage mating service for fleeing monastics. He thought himself too busy and in too precarious a position to marry. The Emperor, Charles V, had personally declared him a heretic in 1522, so he was living under a death sentence. Furthermore, to liberate nuns from monastic life was itself punishable by death under both civil and canon law. He wrote to Spalatin in 1521, "They will never force a wife on me."[27] In 1523 Luther assisted nine nuns who escaped the cloister at Marienthron in Nimbschen. One was the sister of John Staupitz, who had been Luther's confessor. Another was Katharine von Bora, who fell into a romantic encounter with Jerome Baumgaertner. They planned to marry, but Baumgaertner failed to return from a journey and Luther failed to find Katharine a replacement. On June 13, 1525, Luther married Katharine himself. He wrote later that he was not in love with her at the time.[28] The decision was apparently rather sudden and without much courtship. He surely was writing about himself when he wrote to Wolfgang Reissenbusch, who was himself vacillating about his plans to set aside his own celibacy vows and marry:

---

[26] *The Library of Christian Classics: Luther: Letters of Christian Counsel*, T. G. Tappert, ed. & trans., Philadelphia: Westminster Press, 1960, p. 275.
[27] E. G. Schwiebert, *Luther and His Times: The Reformation from a New Perspective*, St. Louis: Concordia Publishing House, 1950, p. 588.
[28] *Ibid.*

> Why should you delay? . . . It must, should, and will happen in any case. Stop thinking about it and go to it right merrily. Your body demands it. God wills it and drives you to it. There is nothing you can do about it.[29]

Luther not only affirmed sexual self-actualization; he came to be contemptuous of chastity vows:

> There is never less chastity than in those who vow to be chaste. Almost everything about it is befouled, if not by unclean seminal emissions, then by the continual searing of lust which never dies out . . . if anything fictitious has to be vowed in the monastery, it should be fictitious chastity.[30]

Chastity, according to Luther, is a godless vow because it boasts of a special faith over and above the common general faith. Chastity is therefore a disservice to Christ.[31] "Nature does not cease to do its work when there is voluntary chastity . . . To put it bluntly, seed . . . if it does not flow into the flesh will flow into the nightshirt."[32]

Luther drew heavily from the Jewish biblical valuation of marriage. He was not, therefore, entirely constrained by the monogamous ideal. He did understand marriage as a covenant between persons. Hence it is not surprising that, while he deplored divorce, he also showed himself to be tolerant of bigamy in certain circumstances. He sided with the Pope in the latter's refusal to grant Henry VIII a divorce from Catharine of Aragon, but, unlike the Pope, Luther was merely opposing divorce. He recommended that Henry take on Anne Boleyn as a second wife if he had to have her. Closer to home, Luther responded in a similar fashion to his own protector, Philip of Hesse. He later regretted that decision, not on religious, ethical, or theological grounds, but because his support of Philip's bigamy became an unpleasant public relations problem for him.[33]

Luther rejected the ecclesiastical dogma of his day which held marriage to be a sacrament. The precise nature of the marriage ceremony in his marriage to Katharine is not known. It was a private event with a

---

29 *Letters of Spiritual Counsel,* Tappert, ed., p. 275.
30 *Luther's Works,* Vol. 44, James Atkinson & Helmut T. Lehman, eds., Philadelphia: Fortress Press, 1966 p. 369.
31 *Ibid.,* p. 372.
32 Cited by Todd, "Against the Spiritual Estate of Pope and Bishops Falsely So-called," 1522, p. 244.
33 *Letters of Spiritual Counsel,* ed. Tappert, p. 288.

few friends and there is no transcript, but apparently they did not celebrate the Sacrament of Holy Matrimony, no longer considered a sacrament. A fortnight later they gave a party which included a service of rejoicing in church. This event coincided with Katharine's moving into the friary to set up housekeeping.[34]

Repeatedly Luther also deplored the church's inherited tradition of administrative authority over marriage and divorce. As spiritual head of the German Reformation movement it fell to him to respond in one way or another to numerous requests for judgments about marriage and divorce. People simply expected from him what they were used to getting from the Roman clergy, so he was drawn willy-nilly into marital judgments. Luther wished the church out of the marriage business altogether, but either did not know how or did not want to pay the price for another radical change. He expressed his chagrin about the matter:

> As soon as we begin to act as judges in marriage matters the teeth of the mill wheel will have snatched us by the sleeve and will carry us away to the point where we must decide the penalty. Once we have to decide the penalty, then we must also render judgment about the body and goods, and by this time we are down under the wheel and drowned in the water of worldly affairs.[35]

If Luther sometimes speaks in a traditional manner of marriage as an instrument for the control and inhibition of a polymorphous sexuality, there is also ample evidence to demonstrate him at variance with such a view. Luther was ambivalent on the matter. In at least two complex pastoral counseling cases Luther further demonstrated his lack of commitment to strict monogamy. In one case a woman presented herself as married to a

---

34 Todd, *op. cit.*, p. 263.
35 *Luther's Works,* Vol. 46, Robert C. Schultz & Helmut T. Lehmann, eds., Philadelphia: Fortress Press, 1967, p. 266.

man who was impotent. She wanted to have children and felt herself personally unable to remain sexually continent. Her husband had refused his consent to a divorce. Luther recommended that the woman seek her husband's consent for her to take a lover, preferably her husband's brother. Luther was undoubtedly thinking of the Jewish levirate law here. He further advised that any such liaison be kept secret so as not to cause scandal, and that any children issuing from such a liaison be ascribed to her husband. Should her husband refuse his consent, Luther suggested she consider marrying another and fleeing to a distant place.[36] Such pastoral counsel demonstrates just how seriously Luther regarded a person's sexual fulfillment.[37]

Luther's pastoral direction in this case would not have been understood to be as radical in his day as it would be today, since both Westphalian and Saxon common law prescribed that a man who could not perform his conjugal duty was required to seek satisfaction for his wife through a neighbor.[38] What is astonishing, however, is to hear such a prescription from a Christian theologian in any era after Augustine.

In a similar case Luther was consulted by a man whose wife exhibited symptoms of syphilis and was unable to fulfill her marital obligation. The man felt himself unable to sustain the burden of chastity, and asked for Luther's advice. Luther replied that one of two things must happen, either he commit adultery or take a second wife. Luther favored the latter option, exhorting him to provide sufficiently for his first wife and not abandon her. Once again we see Luther's antipathy toward divorce, at least toward men divorcing their wives. A divorced woman

---

36 *Luther's Works,* Vol 36, Abdel Ross Wentz & Halmut T. Lehmann, eds., Philadelphia: Fortress Press, 1959, p. 103.
37 For a very different reading of Luther see the conservative Paul Althaus, *The Ethics of Martin Luther,* Robert C. Schultz, trans., Philadelphia: Fortress Press, 1972. In his chapter "Love, Marriage, and Parenthood" he makes no mention of the quotes used here. The author presents Luther as one who was totally congruent with 20th century middle-class sexual values prior to the upheaval of the sexual revolution. Althaus' interpretation of Luther demonstrates how Luther can be enlisted by almost any point of view. However, Althaus screens out the most vibrant parts of Luther's teachings and leaves him bloodless.
38 *Luther's Works, Vol. 36, Word and Sacrament II,* Wentz & Lehmann, eds., Philadelphia: Fortress Press, 1967, p. 103.

was then, as now, usually put in an economically disadvantaged position. We also see in this pastoral incident Luther's unambiguous conviction that no one should be placed in a position of enforced celibacy, that sexual needs are necessities. By this time too, he understood that his recommendations were being used by others as excuses for unbridled licentiousness, and he advised his counselee to keep his actions secret or bear the negative consequences.[39]

Luther was an energetic and spontaneous character and was obviously very little concerned that everything he said be consistent. He was never very far removed from a joyful, playful, and even mischievous attitude toward his own sexuality. This playful and joyful approach to things sexual was congruent with his attitude toward life generally. The devil is the one, according to Luther, who fills the world with a "sour spirit," making our "days stretch out and appear saltless." To counter the devil we must "get up, seek company, start to dance and sing, to play cards and make music. For the devil cannot stand joy."[40] Luther was often playfully erotic and scatological in his conversation. He was almost embarrassingly fond of associating the Pope and the Roman Catholic clergy with things excremental. When a cardinal lets wind, he said, we Germans are supposed to believe a new article of faith is born.[41] Of course, Luther was more than just playful, since the Roman system of salvation was in his vision a work of rationalization and self-justification, and therefore profoundly excremental.

Much of Luther's playfulness was phallic, too. When a visiting Waldensian minister named Lawrence shared with Luther his regret at having castrated himself as a youth, Luther replied, "For my part I'd rather have two pair added than one pair cut off."[42] In a letter to his friend Justice Jonas, Luther reveals a similar playfulness with sexual innuendo, "My Katie cordially and reverently greets you and all your family. But hold a minute, if my wife greets you, I in turn greet your wife. What is sauce for the goose is sauce for the gander."[43] Luther's

---

39 *Luther's Works* Vol. 54, Theodore G. Tappert & Helmut T. Lehmann eds., Philadelphia: The Fortress Press, 1967, p. 65.
40 Heiko A. Oberman, "Luther and the Devil," *Lutheran Theological Seminary Bulletin*, Winter 1989, p. 10.
41 Todd, *op. cit.*, p. 320.
42 *Luther's Works,* Vol. 54, p. 177.
43 Todd, *op. cit.*, pp. 342-3.

phallic playfulness even tested the boundaries of reverence in ways that no doubt horrified the pious then as it still does today. When he was met by a man whose wife had suddenly died without any warning or illness, he said, "Our Lord God is the worst adulterer. This morning she slept with her husband and tonight she sleeps with our Lord God."[44]

Six months after his marriage, Luther wrote to his dear friend Georg Spalatin, who was about to marry a woman, also named Katie. Luther expressed his regrets at not being able to travel to his friend's wedding, the hazards of the route being too great. So he wrote:

> I will calculate how long it will take my courier to reach you. The very night you receive this letter, you penetrate your lovely Katie, and I will penetrate mine. Thus we will be united in love.

Heiko A. Oberman, one of those few theologians who is unembarrassed by Luther's radical affirmation of sex, has recently called attention to this passage which has long been deleted even from the authoritative German publications of Luther's writings.[45]

Luther's conversations at mealtime with his family and friends were recorded for posterity by some of his followers and published as *Table Talk*. On one occasion Luther ventured the opinion at supper that the time would come again when a man will take more than one wife, as he had in patriarchal times. The conversation between Luther and his wife sounds like one that might have occurred in the twentieth rather than the sixteenth century:[46]

> *Katie:* Let the devil believe that.
> *Martin:* The reason, Katie, is that woman can bear a child only once a year while her husband can beget many.
> *Katie:* Paul said that each man should have his own wife. (1Cor. 7:2)

---

44 "Table Talk," July 15 or 16, 1539, no. 4709, WA.TR 4:441.14-16; cited by Eric W. Gritsch, *Martin --- God's Court Jester,* Philadelphia: Fortress Press, 1983, p. 162.
45 Oberman, *op. cit.,* Letter of Dec. 6, 1525, *Luthers Werke, Weimar Edition,* 40/1:314.14-15.
46 *Luther's Works,* Vol. 54, p. 153.

Martin: Yes, his own wife, and not "only one wife," for the latter isn't what Paul wrote.

Katie: Before I put up with this, I'd rather go back to the convent and leave you and all our children.

Even at death's door Luther remained playfully perverse and affirming of his sexuality. As a very sick man, perhaps with congestive heart failure, he traveled to Eisleben to settle a political dispute between the Counts of Mansfield, a journey from which he was to return in a coffin. On the outgoing leg of the trip he wrote his beloved Katie that he had recovered from his illness and "now suffer merely from the resistance of the beautiful ladies, which prevents me from wrong or fear about my virtue."[47] Luther is unique in Christian history as a theologian who was both aware of and candid about his own polymorphous sexual energy. There may have been others like him, but they have not left a public record. Luther was so unambiguously affirming of sex and so personally comfortable in that affirmation that intellectual and theological development in the West has not found a way yet to integrate him. Luther has remained too radical in his sexual values even for most of his own followers in the Reformed tradition.[48]

III

The upheaval of the early sixteenth century produced far more radical individuals than Luther and his colleagues. A spate of radicals appeared who rebelled not only against Rome but against the mainstream Protestant Reformers as well. They presented themselves under a variety of banners: Anabaptists, Spiritualists, Evangelical Rationalists, Melchiorites, Batenburgers,

---

47 *The Last Days of Luther,* Justice Jones, Michael Coelius, & Others, Martin Ebon, trans. & ed., Garden City, New York: Doubleday & Co., Inc., 1970, p. 21; the translation here is debated, since the German leaves itself open to several possiblities: e.g., ". . . I am well, except for the fact beautiful women tempt me so much that I neither care for nor worry about becoming unchaste" or " . . . except for the fact that beautiful women do not bother me so that I neither care for nor am I afraid of any kind of unchastity." See Vol. 50 of *Luther's Works,* Gottfried G. Krodel & Helmut T. Lehmann, eds., Philadelphia: Fortress Press, 1975, p. 291.

48 Richard Marius is one of the exceptions. He writes: "Some of Luther's thoughts on marriage sound radical to many even today. Certainly one is not likely to hear them proclaimed from the bashful Protestant pulpit, where sound and fury generally signify nothing very much. But all of them arise from Luther's desire to make marriage a humane institution." (*Luther,* New York: J.B. Lippincott Company, 1974, p. 132.

Blood Friends, and so forth. What they shared in common was a radical challenge to the existing order. They seized upon the eschatological challenge of the New Testament and took it to its limits. In the context of these groups, Luther seemed quite conservative. They challenged marriage, private property, the state, the courts, royalty, the church, and every other structure in the existing order. Each group had its own particular agenda and vision. In their attack on marriage, they varied in their tactics. Some promoted polygamy, some free sex, and some sacramental sex. Some gave their allegiance to monogamy, choosing to fight the established order on other issues.

Typical of these groups were the Lithuanian Brethren in Vilnius, who were anti-trinitarian Anabaptists. They shared dreams and visions, introduced a plurality of wives, a community of goods, contempt of the magistrates, of courts, and of every hierarchy in whatever form.[49]

The Anabaptists, precursors to modern Baptists (so named because they rebaptized their followers), were preeminent among these varied radical groups. Many Anabaptist groups established polygamous communes in various parts of Germany. One John of Leyden took sixteen wives and seized control of Munster in 1534. He was defeated by the combined action of Protestant and Roman Catholic princes and executed. One recent scholar, Jack Goody, argues that the driving force behind this revived polygamy was the fact that women outnumbered men four to one. Population problems may have given a motivation and impetus for polygamy, but the radical challenge to the existing order was typical of these groups, irrespective of gender imbalance in the population.[50]

IV

Only a couple of hundred miles separate Wittenberg and Geneva, but it is a long way from Martin Luther to John Calvin (1509-1564). Calvin, twenty-six years younger than Luther, was of the next generation, but the two of them essentially share the Reformation stage in the view of later history. Luther spoke no French and Calvin no German, and to say they

---

49 George Huntston Williams, *The Radical Reformation,* Philadelphia: The Westminister Press, 1952, p. 692.
50 Jack Goody, *The Development of the Family and Marriage in Europe,* New York: Cambridge University Press, 1983, p. 163.

spoke a different language is true in more ways than one. Luther understood himself as breathing the spirit of truth into the corrupt and contorted shell of Christendom. He did not think of himself as the founder of a new church. He was in fact suspicious of the increasing pressures on him to assume a more authoritative role as an institutional religious patriarch. He warned associates that he was being tempted to become a new pope as various and sundry persons appealed to him for judgments and spiritual advice.

Calvin, on the other hand, designed and built a theocracy in Geneva where he became the willing *de facto* ruler of both church and state. He built a new civil and ecclesiastical order to replace the old. He was a systematizer. His *Institutes of the Christian Religion*, something Luther could never have written, defined his theological system.

The separation of church and state was not one of Calvin's operating principles. Separation and theocracy are, of course, two different political visions in polar relationship. Each presents monumental philosophical and political problems. Neither is achievable in any absolute fashion without undesirable consequences. Church and state are two contiguous institutions with the same clientele and concerned about many of the same issues, not least of which is justice. Luther leaned strongly toward separation and Calvin toward theocracy.

Calvin's position has considerable appeal. From his perspective the state is commanded to be obedient to the word of God just as the church is. As a consequence, Calvin's Geneva was hardly a pluralistic, permissive city. The moral life of all Genevans fell under the supervision of the governing Consistory---a combination of clergy and lay political appointees. No one in Geneva could exclude himself from periodic "home-visitation" by local clergy concerned about the religious and moral life of the citizenry. Thought and behavior control were implemented further by "City Servants," a kind of semi-police that observed citizens and enforced regulations.[51] Public and private discipline was a very serious concern. A man was banished from the city for three months because, on hearing an ass bray, he said in jest, "He prays a beautiful Psalm." A girl was beheaded for striking her parents.

---

51 David Little, *Religion, Order, and Law,* Chicago: University of Chicago Press, 1969, p. 77.

In four years between 1542 and 1546 fifty-eight death sentences and seventy-six banishments were handed down in a population of 20,000. We must be careful, however, not to judge such evidence by the standards of 20th century liberalism. There was hardly a Protestant leader in Europe who was not under continual sentence of death, and many paid the penalty when they fell into the hands of Catholic authorities. The religious battle in Europe was being played for keeps.[52]

In popular thinking Calvin is made something of a whipping boy for all that was austere and restrictive in subsequent Calvinism and puritanism. However, many scholars have defended, correctly so, the profound humanism of Calvin and his programs. He was attempting to create a just political order. Usury was brought under control; interest was limited to five percent. Women were granted increased rights in marriage.[53] Perhaps more important than anything else was the fact that Calvin was taking the civil order quite seriously. David Little, following Troeltsch, points out that the Renaissance was generally unproductive in the social realm in spite of the fact that it had challenged the basic assumptions of Medieval Christendom.[54] Calvin intended to be socially productive, and in the context of the time he was. Freedom of speech and religious toleration simply did not exist anywhere in Europe at the time.

By virtue of the new order he created, Calvin moved inevitably to a position of ordering and controlling sexual behavior. On issues of sexual behavior his humanism is apparent but limited. Like Luther, he restored marriage to clergy, and he taught that God wants married couples spontaneously to enjoy themselves sexually. He also contributed significantly to the developing notion of marriage as a companionate undertaking. However, we observe none of Luther's exuberant affirmation of sex. Calvin's position on the valorization of sex falls somewhere between Rome and Luther. As William J. Bouwsma points out in his perhaps definitive biography, there are really "two Calvins coexisting uncomfortably within the same historical personage." One was the Renaissance humanist who

---

52 See Philip Schaff, *op. cit.*, pp. 491-2.
53 W. Fred Graham, *The Constructive Revolutionary,* Richmond: John Knox Press, 1971, p. 152. See also Bieler, *The Social Humanism of Calvin.*
54 Little, *op. cit.*, p. 36.

promoted marriage for clergy and who celebrated sexuality as a delightful divine gift. The other Calvin was the medieval Catholic, ever anxious to control any sexual impulse lest it get out of hand, who was, for example, scandalized to hear of a 70-year-old woman who sought sexual gratification for herself.[55]

Calvin was not one to attend to his own personal feelings, and this disposition no doubt informed his theology, and especially his sexual valuations. When he decided to marry at age thirty-two he assigned several of his closest friends the task of selecting a candidate. They first brought him an unacceptable young woman who spoke no French, only German. A second candidate was found, but rumor had it that she would not be content with Calvin's austere life, and she was rejected before Calvin met her. Finally the widow of an Anabaptist who had died of the plague was suggested to him.[56] Thus Idelette de Bure became his wife and brought her two fatherless children into Calvin's home.

They must have been a curious pair. Idelette was respectful and compliant, impressed with Calvin's status as a cleric and political leader. Calvin was in need of a nurse as much as a wife. Only thirty-two, he was prematurely aged, with graying hair, hollow face, and bent back. Colds, headaches, and indigestion plagued him. She bore him three children, all of whom died at childbirth. She herself died after ten years of marriage. However, neither the death of child nor wife caused Calvin to skip a beat in his work schedule. He consoled her on her deathbed, but her body was hardly cold before he left his house to resume his civic and religious duties. Personal feelings were not high on Calvin's list of priorities. If he could be dropped into twentieth century American life he would undoubtedly be most astonished at the level of self-indulgence he would observe.

In the twentieth century Karl Barth criticized Calvin for the manner in which he chose his wife. Barth felt one should pay attention to one's feelings of attraction, and that this "mutual recognition of man and woman" was part of divine guidance. Barth thought it wrong to enter a marriage with the detachment of a gambler, and he thought

---

55 See William J. Bouwsma, *John Calvin*, New York: Oxford University Press, 1988, especially pp. 136-8, 230.
56 Bouwsma questions this, suggesting Calvin may have met her on his own when she attended his church.

Calvin had not set a good example to follow.[57]

Calvin not only affirmed clerical marriage, but he assaulted the orders of "monks, nuns, and the whole scum of Papistical clergy, than whose celibacy nothing can be imagined that is more obscene."[58] He attacked Jerome for petulantly demeaning marriage. God ordains marriage, says Calvin, not for our destruction, but for our salvation.[59]

It must be noted that the blessing Calvin gave to marital sex was only to the restrained and temperate exercise of sexual expression. Thus he attacked those "adulterers of their own wives [who] have no regard to modesty or decorum."[60] Calvin manifests here the considerable influence of Stoicism and its identification of God with the universal order of things and who sensed in the ecstasy of sex a threat to that order.[61]

In seeming contradiction of himself, Calvin continues to hold virginity and chastity in high esteem. He even goes so far as to say that "celibacy is better than marriage because it has more liberty, so that persons can serve God with greater freedom." He argues that his objection to Roman Catholic celibacy was that it was imposed. When given to a few, but not required of all, celibacy is a special and excellent gift.[62] Calvin came very close to the Roman Catholic position here, but, in spite of that, neither he nor subsequent Calvinism accepted monasticism even for the few. One has to suspect that the driving force in his affirmation of virginity and celibacy was his wish to control non-marital sex.

Calvin goes beyond Luther in claiming that monogamy was divinely instituted. The conjugal bond subsists between two persons only, he says, and "nothing is less accordant with the divine institution than polygamy".[63] Thus quite unlike Luther, he condemns the polygamy of the Hebrew patriarchs.

Historically, institutionalized Protestantism has generally ignored the sexual teachings of the polymorphously *perverse* Luther in favor of those of the more tightly controlled, almost ascetic Calvin. The only aspect of

---

57 *Church Dogmatics*, III/4, p. 215.
58 *Corinth Com.*, p. 262.
59 *Gen. Com.*, p. 128-9.
60 *Institutes*, Book II, VIII, 44.
61 Little, *op. cit.*, p. 35.
62 *Corinth. Com.* pp 232, 268-9; *Com. on Four Books*, p. 324.
63 *Gen. Com.*, p. 136.

the Reformation that provided an ongoing victory for sexual expression was the abolition of monastic life and the restoration of clerical marriage, matters on which Protestants universally agreed. Sexual expression was therefore partially redeemed while at the same time tightly confined within the boundaries of monogamy. Among Protestants sexual expression has been freed both from the virginal ideal and the limited purposes of procreation within marriage. Outside the bounds of monogamy Protestants and Roman Catholics historically have spoken with one repressive voice.

V

Luther was the protagonist of the Reformation, but Thomas More of England perhaps best epitomized those who opposed both Luther and the Reformation in all its manifestations. It is not without significance that the sexual aspect of Luther's life and teaching fired More's antipathy the most.

More was a royal Councillor to Henry VIII, a part of his ruling inner circle, and in 1529 became Henry's chief deputy, the Lord Chancellor. His tenure was short-lived. From this pinnacle of power his skid down the slopes of royal disfavor was rapid. He resigned in 1532 and was beheaded in 1533 for opposing, or seeming to oppose, Henry's plan to dissolve his marriage to Catharine of Aragon, and for appearing to raise a flag of rebellion against his plans to marry Anne Boleyn. In fact, More simply refused on grounds of conscience to sign an oath of allegiance, but in those days to oppose publicly royal policy on any important matter was tantamount to treason.[64]

For both Luther and More the issue of sexuality was central to their respective stories, though the manner in which each engaged the issue was very different. Luther had for the first half of his life suppressed his sexual desires in monastic life. In the latter half he enthusiastically reversed himself to affirm his polymorphous sexual desires as gifts of God. More, though not a cleric, tested for four years the monastic voca-

---

64 Jasper Ridley, *Statesman and Saint: Cardinal Wolsey, Sir Thomas More and the Politics of Henry VIII*, New York: Viking Press, 1982, p. 291.

tion in the strictest order of the day, the Charterhouse. He appears never to have reconciled himself to his decision to leave, continued to wear a hair shirt, and though twice-married, longed all his life for the priesthood and the monastic life.[65]

More's marriages were joyless. Unlike Luther, he did not like women. He first married seventeen year-old Jane Colt, though he had actually preferred her younger sister. It seems to have been a typical More decision in that it was based on principle, in this case the principle that the elder daughter ought to marry first. He may also have deliberately chosen the less attractive woman in order to make sexual abstinence in marriage easier for him. In marriage he was highly paternalistic, domineering, and abusive. He may or may not have actually beaten Jane, but she at least took an emotional beating from him and died at age twenty-three after bearing him four children. On her tombstone More referred to her as his "dear little wife."[66]

Recent historians critical of More think that his marriage caused him deep inner conflict and guilt because he felt he had bowed to the demands of the flesh. Sex was "the ruling drama of his life," says Richard Marius, More's most persuasive and perhaps definitive biographer.[67] The worst sign of depravity, according to More, is our propensity to sexual sins---"the filthy pleasures of the flesh."[68]

Within a month of Jane's death More married his second wife, Alice Middleton. The alacrity of this act has embarrassed his admirers and puzzled his biographers ever since. The shape of Alice's character, as well as the timing of the marriage, contribute to the puzzle. Nothing suggests Alice possessed significant redeeming features. She is described as quarrelsome, petty, ignorant, stupid, aged, blunt, and rude. Even More himself made her the target of many unkind jokes. More's longtime friend, Erasmus, who visited their London home, found her inhospitable and made unflattering mention of her to others, referring to her in such vivid metaphors as "the hooked beak of the harpy." Richard Marius doubts that

---

65 G. R. Elton, "The Real Thomas More?" in *Reformation Principles and Practices: Essays in Honour of Arthur Geoffrey Dickens,* Peter Newman Brooks, ed., London: Scholar Press, 1980, p. 29; and Alistair Fox, *Thomas More,* New Haven: Yale University Press, 1983, p. 254.
66 Marius, *op. cit.* (1984), p. 41.
67 *Ibid.*, p. xxiii.
68 *Ibid.*, p. 298.

More and his second wife even consummated their relationship, which may in turn have exacerbated her well-known quarrelsomeness. More himself had complained during his first marriage that it was harder to remain chaste in the married state than single.[69] Alice was no doubt adequate medicine for such an ailment.

Marius does not say so, but More may well have been struggling against homosexual impulses. His marriages would have been some protection against such forbidden feelings. Marius does suggest that his quick second marriage was deliberately to disqualify himself from the priesthood, since the twice-widowed were proscribed by canon law from the priesthood.[70] More certainly knew from his own monastic experience that an all-male community in the monastery or rectory would present florid temptations to one with homosexual urges. Erasmus, who is thought to have been homosexual, and if so certainly a less than conflicted one, was More's intimate friend for all their adult lives. Ideologically they were a most unlikely pair. Except that each was a Renaissance man of the new learning, their convictions were quite different. Though an Augustinian monk, Erasmus was anything but devoted to Roman Catholic traditions and doctrines. He never indicated he ever felt guilty about anything, and assiduously avoided all conflict in a conflict-ridden age. Erasmus thought More too violent in his reaction against Protestants.[71] In spite of More's constant pleading, for example, that he join in the verbal assault on Luther, Erasmus remained aloof from the fray. William Tyndale, one of the fiery English reformers of this period may have been privy to information lost to history when he referred to Erasmus as "More's darling."[72]

More shared with Luther as well as Erasmus a concern about the level of corruption in the church, though it was no worse than it had been in the generations preceding them.[73] There the similarities between More and Luther cease. The issues that separated them were profound, mainly the respective esteem, or lack thereof, in which they held ecclesiastical tradition and especially their valuations of sexuality. More held a view of the church as infallible whereas Luther was radically critical of the church. More was sexually repressive and viewed genital sexual abstinence as a

---

69 *Ibid.*, p. 37.
70 *Ibid.*, p. 42.
71 Elton, *op.cit.*, p. 26.
72 Marius, *op. cit.* (1984), p. 289.
73 *Ibid.*, p. 268.

mark of the higher life. Luther thought everyone deserved a sexual partner.

More became aware of Luther soon after he nailed his Ninety-Five Theses to the Wittenberg church door in 1517. Erasmus sent him a copy. Luther was even more conspicuous after publication of his *Babylonian Captivity of the Church* in 1520. King Henry VIII felt called upon to answer Luther, which he did in his *Assertion of the Seven Sacraments* in the same year. More was Henry's closest theological advisor and probably assisted in the writing. Its publication in London was accompanied by a public display of Lutheran book-burning. Henry probably regretted later some of the "purple passages," as William Lazareth calls them, with which he defended Roman ecclesiastical authority and the doctrine of the indissolubility of marriage.[74]

Henry wrote,
> What serpent so venomously crept in as he who calls the Most Holy See of Rome 'Babylon,' and the Pope's authority 'Tyranny,' and turns the name of the Most Holy Bishop of Rome into that of 'Anti-Christ'?

In championing the indissolubility of marriage, Henry charged Luther with teaching that a woman should run off with another man if her husband could not satisfy her. Henry's attack had an element of truth though he exaggerated and made Luther appear quite trivial. The Pope expressed his appreciation to Henry for his assault on Luther and in a papal bull of 1521 bestowed on Henry and his successors the coveted title, "Defender of the Faith" (*Fidei Defensor*), an epithet every British monarch since has claimed. Henry in fact remained all his life a defender of the faith, but his opinion about the substance of that faith eventually changed significantly, much to Rome's chagrin. Particularly changed were Henry's opinions on the authority of Rome and the indissolubility of marriage.[75]

What was at stake in Lutheran teaching, as More knew full well, was not just Roman ecclesiastical authority, but rather the infallibility of ecclesiastical tradition itself, a doctrine dear to More's heart. More believed

---

74 William H. Lazareth, *Luther and the Christian Home,* Philadelphia: Muhlenberg Press, p. 192.
75 Neville Williams, *Henry VIII and His Court,* London: Weidenfeld & Nicolson, 1971, pp. 87-8.

Luther and the Reformation

in ecclesiastical infallibility, but with qualification.[76] He did not believe that every act or teaching of the church was God's will, but simply that the general trends and traditions were. Simply put, More believed that God would not permit the church to be wrong for very long before he would correct it. Such is the substance of what is called ecclesiastical positivism. It affirms that what we see generally in ecclesiastical tradition is God's will. Luther held such a view to be nonsense. The entire ecclesiastical tradition is to be judged by scripture and reason in his view. More answered that the scriptures are to be believed only because the church endorses them.

Luther, for example, dismissed most of the literature of the early church fathers, the so-called "Patristics" of the first four centuries. Among them only Augustine he held in some esteem. The early church fathers, he said, had wished to avoid a drop of voluptuousness and fell into an ocean of sensual pleasure.[77]

More was no doubt disturbed by Luther's writing in 1520 when he certainly assisted Henry with his anti-Luther *Assertion etc.* However, when Luther married a nun in 1522, More was undoubtedly aghast. From then on his antipathy for Luther and his teachings was fueled with hot indignation. Canon and civil law characterized the marriage of a priest and a nun as incest, punishable by death. To the bitter end More expressed his contempt for this "incestuous" relationship in the most vitriolic terms. The relish with which More burned so many Protestants at the stake, often personally mocking their anguished dying cries, was perhaps in part displaced rage he felt toward Luther whom he could not reach.

Luther's marriage to Katie, the sexual union of the priest/monk and nun, inspired many with its clear affirmation of sex. However, it horrified many others in ways that his challenge to the authority of the church might never have done. Not only had Luther married a nun, but he had done so with zest. He relished the thought that the pope and his stalwarts were so much more thoroughly horrified by this marriage than they would have been had he married a laywoman. Pope Adrian VI warned rulers in the West to beware "the filthy German Mohammed"

---

[76] This matter is the subject of some debate at the present time and I follow here the position taken by Marius.
[77] *Luther's Works*, Vol. 54, p. 177.

who is loose in their midst, and who grants men permission to have many wives.[78]

If More did not have enough trouble with Lutheran theology spreading through Henry's kingdom like a virus, it was increasingly apparent that his king was scheming to dispose of his very Catholic queen, Catharine of Aragon, in favor of the Lutheran, Anne Boleyn. Henry was driven in this direction by more than simple lust. He was eager, even anxious, to sire a male heir to the throne in order to insure a peaceful transition of power to the next generation. Catharine had had a number of stillbirths and one viable daughter, but no sons.[79] Henry requested of the Pope a dissolution of his marriage, not an unusual request from someone with the political standing of a king, and one normally granted. Unfortunately, the Pope was at that moment a virtual prisoner of the Holy Roman Emperor, Charles V, who fortuitously happened to be Catharine's own nephew. The Pope therefore faced a no-win decision. He was not about to bring disaster on his own head by dissolving that marriage. So he did nothing. Henry's request went unanswered. Luther, hearing of Henry's dilemma, ever faithful to biblical values, suggested Henry simply take on Anne as an additional wife, being sure to maintain Catharine in the manner to which she was accustomed. The suggestion came to nought. Meanwhile Henry became more and more enamoured of the Lutheran manner of dealing with papal authority in general. Lutheran teaching was spreading rapidly all over Europe. When one English Lutheran preacher was arrested in 1531 and appealed personally to the king, Henry read the first charge against him, that he had preached that the pope was not the true sovereign over the Christian Church. Charles V's ambassador to England reported hearing Henry say, "This proposition cannot be counted as heretical, for it is both true and certain."[80] Thus Lutheran renunciation of papal authority coincided with Henry's own personal and political needs. An autonomous national church answerable to the king rather than the pope was the result, and the floodgates were opened to Lutheran and other Reformation "heresies."

---

78 Lazareth, *op. cit.,* p. 200.
79 Goody, *op. cit.,* p. 185. Fitzsimons Allison was making the same point several decades earlier in his lectures at The School of Theology, University of the South.
80 Marius, *op. cit.,* (1984), p. 380.

More was chagrined by these developments in two respects. The ultimate authority of the church was now given over to a man who handled female genitalia, and the sanctity and indissolubility of marriage was violated.[81] More raised a flag of protest against this sacrilege, which Henry took to be a threat to his rule, and thus More soon found himself in the Tower and later on the scaffold.[82]

More's execution was in itself unremarkable except for the humor and cheerfulness with which he went to his death. Many on all sides died heroically for their ideas and beliefs in that era, though perhaps few so cheerfully. Luther himself would surely have been executed had he been apprehended by the Emperor or any other of the Roman Catholic authorities. What was remarkable about More was, as Richard Marius puts it, his "habitual waging of such hard, inner warfare." His life was in that respect "a lesson for our season," as Marius puts it in his oblique rebuttal of Robert Bolt's admiring interpretation of More, *A Man for All Seasons*.[83] Bolt presents More as a highly principled man of great integrity who stands against the power of the state, a misrepresentation of More by oversimplification. As Jasper Ridley says, "There is only one criticism that can be made of *A Man for All Seasons*---that the spendidly upright hero of the play should not have been named Thomas More."[84]

While dedication to principle in itself is an admirable trait, it will hardly suffice as the measure of a particular life. The nature of the prin-

---

81 *Ibid.*, p. 459.
82 *Ibid.*, p. 442.
83 *Ibid.*, p. 520. Compare Robert Bolt, *A Man for all Seasons: New English Dramatists,* Harmondsworth, Middlesex: Penguin Books.
84 Ridley, *op. cit.*, p. 290.

ciples themselves is subject to examination, as well as the principled person's rigidity. More, for example, was the kind of person who is a menace to the human community in any era.[85] He cared so intensely about his own personal purity, especially his sexual purity, and believed so strongly in the infallibility of the Roman Catholic Church, that he was willing to destroy anyone and sacrifice the public peace in defense of those principles. The irony, as Jasper Ridley points out, is that More stood for almost the opposite of everything for which his admirers today sing his praise. There was nothing he more strongly disapproved of than freedom of individual conscience or religious toleration.[86] Nor does More's widely acclaimed virtue show well next to the relish with which he burned at the stake as many heretics as he could lay hands on. Even in that cruel age his cruelty was notable. Marius thinks he could have been an English Torquemada, the notorious fifteenth century Spanish Inquisitor, had he been able to remain in power.[87]

Both Luther and More are poignantly transparent in their respective struggles with their own sexuality. The great difference between them was the same as the difference between Bernard of Clairvaux and Peter Abelard. More used all his inner resources in an effort to obliterate his sexual energy, and all his political power to destroy those who threatened to relax the social controls on sexual expression. He was a stalwart soldier for the ideals of virginity and chastity. Luther, on the other hand, found in the Hebrew religion and its symbols a blessing for all his libidinal energies, and thus joyfully affirmed sex for himself and for

---

85 Ridley says: "One can also imagine Thomas More in the twentieth century and it is sad that this is a far more frightening picture. It is a picture of a sincere and well-meaning idealist and a brilliant intellectual, whose principles and flawless logic, combined with a repressed but deeply engrained emotionalism, have turned him into a fanatic determined to crush what he considers to be the forces of evil. One can imagine him, after writing books about socialism and planning, becoming more and more obsessed with the menace of the enemy who was assaulting civilization, and reaching the point where he justified, by specious arguments, the liquidation of millions of human beings as a regrettable but necessary measure in the fight against Jewish bolshevism or Trotskyist deviationism, or the extermination of three quaraters of the world's population by nuclear weapons in order to protect his way of life. In the midst of the unparallelled dangers which confront mankind in the last quarter of the twentieth century, our greatest hope is that our fate will lie in the hands of a modern Wolsey (a pragmatist) and not of a modern Thomas More." (*op. cit.,* p. 293.)
86 *Ibid.,* p. 291.
87 Marius, *op. cit.* (1984), p. 406.

others. More died on the scaffold, confident he had been obedient to his principles, and relieved to be unburdened of living. Luther died in bed grateful for a full life and for the psychic healing that had been granted him, by which he was able to affirm the whole human experience, especially the sexual dimension of it. Of both life and its healing he was a grateful and creaturely recipient, dying reluctantly but with grace. Among Luther's very last papers was found the aptly put note, "We are all beggars."[88]

---

88 Todd, *op. cit.*, p. 370.

Chapter Six
From Luther To The Twentieth Century's Sexual Revolution

For when we have Christ we shall easily issue laws, and judge all things aright, and even make new decalogues.
-- *Martin Luther**

I

Between the 16th century Reformation and the sexual revolution of the mid-20th century, sexual values were in no significant way altered in mainstream Western thought and practice. Out of the mainstream, in the wilderness and on the lunatic fringe a variety of radical individuals and groups offered their challenges, but the stability of the center was never seriously threatened until after the mid-20th century. The center was held together by the common ideology of the Roman Catholic Church, Protestant orthodoxy, and the growing middle class, each of which from its own perspective supported a view of sexual pleasure limited to the bounds of monogamy.

With the passing of the yeasty 16th century each principality or state of the Western world settled into a Protestant or Roman Catholic identity. From 1618 to 1648 these polarized identities on the European continent engaged each other in a massive and prolonged bloodletting known as the Thirty Years War. Subsequently Protestants and Roman Catholics settled down to a permanent cold war peace. Protestants, who themselves began as a prophetic response to Catholicism, chose or were forced to create their own alternate religious culture, generally referred to as Protestant orthodoxy. Thus there came about two rival religious cultures in Western Europe.

The difference in the respective sexual attitudes of the two religious cultures was perhaps more in theory than in practice. In Roman Catholic culture the supposed models of highest virtue, especially clerics and monastics, were virginal and/or sexually abstinent. In Protestant culture the models of virtue were married. Unmarried clerics were often viewed even with a certain suspicion. Thus Protestantism adopted, implicitly and in muted form, the Jewish injunction that everyone should participate in a sexual relationship. Unlike Catholicism, Protestantism also promoted,

---

*   Cited by Jurgen Moltmann, *Theology of Hope,* New York: Harper and Row, Publishers, 1967, p. 335, [WS39, I, 47.]

From Luther to the Twentieth Century's Sexual Revolution

theoretically, the idea that the purpose of sex was pleasure as well as procreation. Therefore birth control never emerged as an issue of ethical concern. Though Protestants were generally more affirming of the pleasure of sex, demonstrated especially through clerical marriage, it never achieved the exuberant Jewish affirmation of the pleasure of sex for its own sake. In spite of being Luther's progeny, Protestant clerics were not heard proclaiming, as the Talmudic rabbis were, and as Luther might, that sex on the Sabbath carried with it an extra blessing.

One of the ironies of the two polarized religious cultures is that, while the Protestants were originally and theologically more affirming of sex, in actual practice there was ultimately very little to show for it. Catholic culture, paradoxically, in certain respects seemed more affirming of the sensuous and sexuality. We can see this irony played out in the respective attitudes of the two cultures toward art.

Protestants taken as a whole were iconoclastic toward art, Lutherans generally much less so than Calvinists and other traditions. Veneration of relics, icons, statues, and paintings were seen as part of the idolatry of medieval tradition. As a consequence, many Protestant churches and their liturgies were austere and plain, relying almost entirely on the spoken word. Zwingli, for example, who was himself an accomplished musician, opposed both music and art in church.

Roman Catholic tradition, on the other hand, was strongly pro-art. Baroque became the accepted art form of the Catholic Counter-Reformation. This sensuous art form developed in spite of the urgings of the Council of Trent, that gathering called to face the threat of Protestantism, which called both for continuing the art forms of the medieval tradition and for chaste art as well. In Baroque it got neither. The bishops nevertheless continued their efforts to keep art under their control and were often zealous in censoring anything they considered vulgar or sexual. Veronese was summoned to the Holy Tribunal of the Inquisition on the grounds that the figures in his "Last Supper" were vulgar. He merely changed the name of the painting to "The Feast of the House of Levi." The Vatican ordered the nudes in Michelangelo's "Last Judgment" to be draped.[1]

In spite of the supervision of bishops, the sensuous, erotic character of Roman Catholic art in the Counter-Reformation period was not quashed, as evidenced by the works of Rubens, El Greco, and Bernini, to

---

1 John Dillenberger, *A Theology of Artistic Sensibilities,* London: SCM Press, 1987, p. 77.

name a few. Bernini's sculpture "The Transverberation of St. Teresa" (1647-52) portrays the mystic ecstasy that Teresa herself described the moment the angel penetrated her entrails with his spear, and on pulling it out, leaving her on fire with the love of God. Here we have a sensuous, even orgasmic, portrayal of a religious experience in the Roman Catholic tradition. Thus we have the irony of sexual celibates in a sex-negative tradition portrayed in the most erotic imagery, while the sex-affirming Protestants limited themselves to the most austere religious symbols, the affective impact of which is a negation of feelings and the physical senses.

In a similar vein, Protestant-sponsored civil statutes about pre-marital and extra-marital sex, prostitution, and even some of the minutiae of sexual behavior, such as sodomy, were often more rigorous than statutes in Catholic cultures. Among Catholics only "the religious," the priests, nuns, and monks, were expected to be obedient to the highest standards of sexual behavior. The rest, "the non-religious," were granted a certain latitude, at least implicitly. On the other hand, among Protestants, who had abolished celibacy and monasticism and restored clerical marriage, there was no virginal class and no distinctive sexual ethics for a religious elite. In turn, the same standards of behavior were expected of all. We see this difference reflected in the generally more tolerant attitudes toward prostitution in Catholic cultures. A modern vestige of that difference can be observed in the way Roman Catholic Mexico tolerates and governmentally regulates prostitution, as compared with the more Protestant United States with its statutory penalties for prostitution.

The Roman Catholic Church made a strong and largely successful attempt, beginning with its defensive Counter-Reformation, firmly to establish most aspects of religious theory and practice that had held sway prior to the disruption of the 16th century. Thus most of the trappings as well as the substance of pre-16th century Western Christianity were defensively held in place: the scholastic theology of Thomas Aquinas, the seven sacraments, celibacy and monasticism, the Latin liturgical language and medieval liturgical garments, clerical retention of the Bible as a document lay people were not competent to understand, autocratic administrative processes inherited from the Gregorian popes, religious censorship of literature, and the aforementioned use and control of religious art. Rome acted as if the disruptive Reformation had never taken place. Indeed, for Rome it had not. A significant milestone in this continuing medievalization of the Roman

From Luther to the Twentieth Century's Sexual Revolution

Catholic Church was the "Encyclical Letter" of Leo XIII in 1879 that made Thomas Aquinas the official theologian of the Church. Pope Benedict XV followed up in 1917 with a canon requiring that "the study of philosophy and theology must be carried out . . . according to the arguments, doctrines, and principles of St. Thomas, which they are inviolately to hold."[2]

For 400 years the wagons remained circled around Thomas Aquinas and all things medieval until 1962 when Pope John XXIII convened an international council of the Church, known as Vatican II. That council began uncircling the wagons, adopted some of the principles of the Reformation and Enlightenment, such as the liturgy in the language of the people, promotion of lay study of the Bible, the application of reason and historical criticism to the study of scripture, and lessening of religious censorship. In the arena of the autocratic exercise of ecclesiastical authority and the negative valorization of sex no important concessions were made. Certain seemingly unimportant concessions that were made had powerful symbolic and actual consequences, as for example, permission for nuns and sisters to unveil themselves. Taking off the veil, itself a symbol of sexual suppression, removed a powerful inhibition to sexual experimentation. Not surprisingly, the present Pope John Paul II has made a futile attempt to put veils back on the nuns and sisters. Great numbers of Roman Catholics, inspired by John XXIII, boldly have challenged Thomist sex ethics by calling for such further changes as clerical marriage and the decriminalization of birth control. Those who openly have challenged Thomist principles of sex ethics have either been silenced, ignored, pushed to the outer fringes of ecclesia, or have left the Church.

II

After the Thirty Years War Protestant thought was next shaped by a cultural and philosophical movement known as the Enlightenment. Just as the Thirty Years War was fought mainly on German soil, so the Enlightenment, or *Aufklarung* (literally, "clarification") as it was called in German, found in a German, Immanuel Kant (1724-1804), its consummate theoretician. His central theme was the advocacy of human reason,

---

2   Canon 1366.2.

though he identified also its limitations. As Kant put it, "Have the courage of your own reason!" an injunction that was far more radical then than it seems now.[3] The Enlightenment, according to Kant, represents man's emergence from a self-inflicted state of minority. A minor is dependent on someone else for parental guidance. Hence Enlightenment ideas ultimately undermined, or at very least challenged, all authority in any form. The American and French Revolutions of the late 18th century were the fruits of Enlightenment ideas in the political arena. The Enlightenment concluded that neither kings nor autocrats in any form were needed in a society where the people can depend on the dictates of their own reason. One of the most persistent intentions behind the development of the United States Constitution was the determination that the president as the highest political authority should be thwarted in advance from assuming royal or absolute power.

In the religious arena Enlightenment ideas similarly challenged and weakened the receptacles of authority in Protestant orthodoxy. This led directly to the new discipline of historical criticism of the biblical texts. The Bible was no longer treated as a sacrosanct or protected object of devotion, but was made subject to the same kind of scrutiny as other literature. Thus the Enlightenment did to Protestant orthodoxy what Luther and Calvin had done to Roman Catholic authority. The Enlightenment was, of course, the logical and inevitable flowering of the Reformation itself, merely extending to full length the principal tool---reason---that the Reformers had employed. As the Reformers appealed to reason and scripture, so the Enlightenment appealed simply to reason. It was a flowering that could only have occurred under the auspices of a Protestant spirit with its willingness fully to accredit reason itself.

Thus Protestant theological thought was a continuing conversation, dialogue, and sometimes imbroglio, with the various and quite varied directions of Enlightenment thought. One of the earliest Enlightenment figures, Jean-Jacques Rousseau (1712-1778), who passionately proclaimed that everyone was capable of finding the truth of God in his own heart, found himself harried out of his own Protestant Geneva as well as other cities, both Protestant and Roman Catholic. He converted from the Protestantism of his birth to Catholicism, but later gave that up

---

3 Immanuel Kant, *Critique of Practical Reason and Other Writings in Moral Philsophy*, L. W. Beck, ed./trans., University of Chicago Press, 1949, p. 286.

From Luther to the Twentieth Century's Sexual Revolution

too. Orthodox theologians of both religious cultures detected in Rousseau a threat to their theological systems, as well they might.

It could be said that with the coming of the Enlightenment in the Protestant world, theology, philosophy, and ethics departed the confines of the churches and their orthodoxies. Until the Enlightenment those who shaped theology, philosophy, and ethics were invariably clerics. Not only were Luther, Calvin, and Zwingli clerics, but even such a 16th century rationalist as Erasmus was a monk, an Augustinian. Virtually all serious thinking that was attended to was done from within and with at least the tacit approval of the church, whether Catholic or Protestant. With the Enlightenment, to follow the Kantian metaphor, philosophy, ethics, and even theology reached their majority and went out into the world without a guardian. At various times the public at large reached the limits of its toleration for questioning, however. So it was that Johann Gottlieb Fichte (1762-1814) lost his university teaching post in early 19th century Berlin for the presumption of atheism. But that was a temporary setback in the increasing permission granted to reason to reach its own conclusions freely.

III

The distinctive contribution to the sexual values of Protestant culture subsequent to the Reformation was what could be called "the privatization of sex." Privatization did not challenge the orthodox Protestant contention that fully affirmed sex only within the bounds of marriage, but it did add the implicit proposition that sex was otherwise a private matter between two persons and of no ethical or religious concern. Privatization was a long way, of course, from both Talmudic and Medieval Christian assumptions that any and every detail of one's sexual behavior was subject to theological reflection. Talmudic discussions suggesting the Sabbath as the best day for sex and suggesting that God bids man to help a woman reach orgasm first so as to ensure her satisfaction, are not the kind of discussions one can expect from the lips of Enlightenment theologians and philosophers. (In the 20th century *The New Yorker* magazine, until the mid-80's reputed never to discuss sex, sits in the mainstream of the Enlightenment's privatization of sex.) By contrast, 18th and 19th century Roman Catholic moralists continued the fascination they inherited from the medieval church with its vivid details of all aspects of sexual behavior, especially including the so-called "solitary sins." So, for example, the Jesuits went so far as to invent a stick to be used in dressing that would permit a cleric to tuck in his shirt while guarding against inadvertent touching of his genitals. The Jesuit saint, Aloyisha Gonzaga (1568-1591), is said never to have looked even his mother in the face so as to avoid sexual temptation. Protestant sex ethics restricted sexual pleasure to marriage and otherwise limited it only by the principle implied in the humorous Victorian saying that it was of no social concern "unless it frightened the horses." Steeped in the tradition of privatization, the Episcopal Bishop of Texas in the early 1970 s appointed an ad hoc committee to study what might be done by the church in response to the sexual revolution. To the satisfaction of the Bishop, the committee's conclusion was that the less said on the subject the better.

Following the Thirty Years War a religious revival of a pietistic bent appeared and ran a parallel track with the Enlightenment, a movement known in Germany as Pietism, in England as the Evangelical movement, and in the United States as the Great Awakening. Philip Jacob Spener (1635-1705) in Germany, John Wesley (1703-1791) in England, and Jonathan Edwards (1703-1758) in the United States, were the three major figures associated with this pietistic revival. On the face of it the pietists had little in common with the Enlightenment's devotees of reason. But in fact this revival was allied with the Enlightenment against the authoritarian, impersonal, and doctrinal character of Protestant orthodoxy. Pietism appealed strongly to human feeling as well as reason. Its vocation was to recover religion as an experience, a feeling, a passionate commitment of one's life, and as a radical alternative to the dry, cold, intellectual assent to dogma that characterized orthodox Protestantism. As the orthodox Protestants appealed to a distillation of Luther's doctrines, so Spener appealed to Luther's deeply felt personal experience of justification.[4]

Wesley, an Anglican priest who was radicalized by an experience of personal conversion that left his heart "strangely warmed," found himself increasingly alienated from the church as he went about the task of organizing small bands of persons who would take upon themselves the burden and liberation of the Christian life. In spite of his own intentions, he ultimately founded a new denomination---the Methodist Church. In an approach reminiscent of the Talmudic rabbis, Wesley gave strict attention to the minute details of everyday life, subjecting every form of human activity to rigorous theological reflection. Thus it was that dancing, card-

---

4   See Paul Tillich, *A History of Christian Thought,* Peter H. John, ed., 1956, p. 235.

From Luther to the Twentieth Century's Sexual Revolution

playing, fancy clothes and food, consumption of alcohol and coffee, smoking, and shallow talk became prohibited activities in Wesley's Societies of Methodists. Today such prohibitions are recalled by Methodists as largely irrelevant and negativistic echoes of the past. Actually, Wesley's original emphasis was considerably more positive than negative. His direction was toward maximum investment of energy toward faithful obedience to God in every aspect of life, a commitment that might well be revived in the late 20th century. One of his frequent themes was the injunction against wasting time in idleness or on empty or self-indulgent enterprises.

One would expect, therefore, that Wesley would have subjected sexual activity to the same rigorous scrutiny to which he subjected other spheres of human activity. But that was not the case. He, too, was infected with assumptions about the privatization of sex. While he does have something to say about sexual behavior, what he leaves unsaid is more significant. He appears to have been somewhat conflicted on the subject, perhaps as a result of his own unsatisfactory marriage. On the one hand he seems to view sex as a distraction to the agenda at hand, as it no doubt was in his own experience. In that sense he has a medieval aspect to him. Thus he segregated by gender and marital status his early Methodist bands. Married men and women met separately on certain days, and the singles met, also separated by gender, on other days.[5] In his pamphlet, "Thoughts on the Single Life," he declared it expedient to avoid all needless conversation, much more all intimacy, with those of the opposite sex.

> . . . check the first rising of desire. Watch against every sally of imagination, particularly if it be pleasing. If it is darted in, whether you will or no . . . cry out, 'My God and my all, I am thine, thine alone!'. . . Avoid the sin of Onan . . . all softness and effeminacy . . . all delicacy, first in spirit, then in apparel, food, lodging . . . all needless self-indulgence . . . Be never idle.

On the other hand, Wesley seems to recoil at hearing himself sound like a monastic. So he hastens to assert that it is not possible to avoid all pleasure without destroying the body, which he assuredly does not intend to do. Further, he is not unwilling to take a Protestant shot at the "Romish Church" which despises and condemns marriage, adding that persons can be as holy in the married state as the single.[6]

---
5 Minutes of the Methodist Conference, 1744, p. 11.
6 *The Works of John Wesley*, Vol. XI, London: 1892, p. 457.

Wesley was therefore solidly Prostestant in theoretically affirming that marital sex was in no way religiously or morally inferior to a single life without sex. However, in practical terms he seems troubled by the dangers of erupting sexual drives. One must wonder how an unmarried member of one of his societies who was eager for a spouse might have undertaken to find one. For all his careful attention to the minutiae of daily life, Wesley did not offer guidance in this arena. What guidance he did offer is tilted toward a suppression of sexual desire. In the sexual arena he abandoned his otherwise Talmudic approach to human behavior and becomes quite privatistic and somewhat sex-negative.

IV

Subsequent to the 16th century those who contributed most to the reshaping, or, depending on perspective, the corruption of sexual values were those who had left or had never been in the confines of Roman Catholic or Protestant orthodoxy. The sexual revolution of the 20th century was the fruit of the labors of such lonely religious outsiders. Jean-Jacques Rousseau (1712-1778) was one of the earliest. As one who was a kind of conflicted roué with a severe conscience, he mightily affirmed the value of sexual feelings and the importance of their gratification, though it is doubtful he achieved much in the way of personal satisfaction for himself in his miserable life. Nevertheless, he is quite self-disclosing rather than privatistic in presenting unashamedly the details of his own sexual struggles, even the extraordinary account of his pleasure from a tame form of masochism. His experience with his guardian, Miss Lambercier, became something of a sexual watershed experience for him. She was altogether loving and just with him, but found an occasion to give him a deserved whipping. Rousseau says, "I discovered in the shame and pain of the punishment an admixture of sensuality which had left me rather eager . . . for a repetition by the same hand."[7] Rousseau is the harbinger of the Romantics. He and they generally affirmed their sexual needs, but they were relegated by the Protestants, Roman Catholics, and the middle class to the lunatic fringe. The center held firm. Rousseau became something of a permanent refugee. As Karl

---

7   *The Confessions*, J. M. Cohen, trans., New York: Penguin Books, 1953, pp. 25ff.

From Luther to the Twentieth Century's Sexual Revolution

Barth said of the tormented Rousseau, "The time he lived in was his disease."[8]

James Boswell is another who in his *Journals* candidly shared with the world his sexual adventures, the details of his numerous lonely encounters with debauched street women who infected him repeatedly with gonorrhea and who-knows-what other venereal diseases. With his mentor and dear friend, Samuel Johnson, he walked arm-in-arm the streets of London discussing every subject under the sun, but sex is a curiously neglected subject. Johnson's few comments on the subject suggest he was something of a prude, a matter of curiosity in light of Boswell's personal behavior and the intimacy between the two men. This dyssynchroneity demonstrates the privatization of sex.

The leaders of the American Revolution were very much men of the Enlightenment. They were generally private about their sexual behavior and values. Benjamin Franklin was the notable exception. Critics and biographers have long disagreed about Franklin's precise attitude toward sex, particularly whether he might be a prude or libertine. He was probably neither in any precise sense, but certainly more the latter than the former. He was in so many respects abstemious, highly practical, and unromantic. He often writes of sex as a physical necessity. In his autobiography he calls it the "use of venery," to which D. H. Lawrence later sardonically commented that he thought Franklin was referring to deer hunting.[9] Franklin is also cautious about the risks to health that indiscriminate sexual relations may bring.[10] However, he is unique in his candor about his occasional sexual adventures. At least they appear occasional in his autobiography. However, his autobiography, though candid, leaves much unsaid and only covers his early life. Whether he was a prude, libertine, neither, or a peculiar mixture of each, he made it unambiguously clear that he dissented from the venerable claims that sex belonged only to the institution of marriage. Franklin, in fact, never married. His common-law wife, Deborah, simply moved in and began using his name. She helped raise his illegitimate son, William, thought to have been Franklin's child by a woman in "inconvenient"

---
8 Karl Barth, *Protestant Thought,* Freeport, NY: Books for Libraries Press, 1959, p. 101.
9 Benjamin Franklin, *The Autobiography and Other Writings,* Kenneth Siverman, ed., New York: Penguin, 1980, pp. 92, 206.
10 *Ibid.*, p. 75.

circumstances. William became the governor of New Jersey, and sired an illegitimate grandson, William Temple, who followed suit with illegitimate great-grandchildren.[11] During Franklin's long stays in Europe, both while Deborah was living and afterwards, he gave the appearance of having numerous sexual liaisons, though none can be documented.[12] The Franklin Court Museum, Independence National Historical Park, Philadelphia, gives tourists the erroneous impression that Franklin "married." Since common-law marriage is also marriage, the distinction can be easily sloughed over. The same museum also tones down John Adams' opinion of Franklin, stating merely that Adams thought Franklin's reputation as "a moralist and philosopher questionable." Adams' opinion of Franklin was in fact almost unprintable, as we see below.

Franklin, however, did not represent the religious tradition and its values. He separated himself from the orthodox Protestantism of his Presbyterian upbringing. He continued to keep himself aloof from religious authority, even if he was not aloof from religious organizations. He greatly admired and financially supported the preaching of George Whitefield, and helped manage a lottery for the raising of funds to build the Church of England's Christ Church in Philadelphia. He even had his daughter baptized in that church. In his non-marital sexual adventures, however many he actually had, Franklin felt under "no religious restraint," as he put it.[13]

Franklin's distance from orthodox Protestantism did not protect him from the vituperation of John Adams, who held him in highest contempt for his sexual behavior. Adams considered Franklin an indolent old roué, a liar, intriguer, and hypocrite. His morals, said Adams, were "like those of Sir Walter Raleigh . . . not sufficiently exact for a great man . . . his whole life has been one continual insult to good manners and decency." Conjuring up the polygamous associations of the Moslem world, Adams added that Franklin was a man whose reputation for philosophy and statesmanship was "one of the grossest impostures . . . practiced upon mankind since the days of Mahomet."[14] It has to be suspected that Adams reacted as much to Franklin's candor about his sexual behavior as to the behavior itself. He had violated the prin-

---

11 *Ibid.*, p. 206.
12 Claude-Anne Lopez & Eugenia W. Herbert, *The Private Franklin*, New York: W. W. Norton & Co., 1975, pp. 26-7, 83-5, 273-5.
13 *Autobiography*, pp. 49, 116.
14 *The Warren-Adams Letters*, Vol. II, The Massachusetts Historical Society, 1925, pp. 209-210.

From Luther to the Twentieth Century's Sexual Revolution

ciple of Protestant orthodoxy and the middle class, that sex was first and foremost a private matter. Franklin had, so to speak, frightened the horses. Both Franklin and Adams represented the American revolutionary government in Paris, and the difference between the reactions of the two men toward the open sexuality of pre-revolutionary Parisian society is dramatic. Adams was never comfortable, but Franklin delighted in it unabashedly.

The moral indignation that Adams directed at Franklin might also have been directed toward George Washington and Thomas Jefferson had Adams known what we know today. The difference was that Washington and Jefferson kept to themselves insofar as they were able the facts about their private sexual lives. Washington nurtured for years a love affair with Sally Fairfax, his neighbor's wife, an affair which was the most passionate romantic relationship of his life. Whether it was physically consummated is not historically recoverable and is in some sense irrelevant to us, if not to them. The important fact which is not disputed is that his sexual energy for many years was directed toward another man's wife. We might know more about the nature of that relationship if his widow, Martha, had not burned all their personal correspondence after his death.[15]

V

The story of Thomas Jefferson's sexual values and behavior invites closer and more extensive scrutiny. The manner in which most Jefferson scholars have treated his sexual life is nothing short of astonishing. Otherwise sober and reputable historians seem seized by hysteria and irrationality on the subject. The accepted treatment of Jefferson by most historians is a stark example of a basic assumption about the ugliness of sex---a poisoned eros. The treatment of Jefferson bears the same marks of distortion and manipulation of data that are seen in scholarly treatments of the lives of Jesus and Paul. In Jefferson's case the sexual issue is, of course, mixed with a racial issue, which no doubt exacerbates the problem for some.

A mountain of circumstantial data suggests that Jefferson spent the last four decades of his life with a shadow wife almost thirty years his junior who also happened to be one of his slaves. Fawn Brodie (d. 1981)

---

15 James Thomas Flexner, *George Washington and the New Nation,* Boston: Little Brown & Co., 1969, pp. 30-1.

The Poisoning of Eros

is almost alone (and the only woman among the top echelon of Jefferson scholars) in treating this covert relationship as probably factual. She treats it as very probable.[16] The vitriol and venom which she experienced from other scholars in response to her scholarly work is symptomatic of how much is at stake here. It is intense and mean-spirited academic warfare in which no prisoners are taken.[17]

Like Washington, Jefferson kept his own counsel on the subject of his sexual liaisons. Nevertheless, a good deal more is known about Jefferson's sexual history through personal letters, third parties, and because political developments forced Jefferson to disclose information about his private life that he would not have chosen to disclose under normal circumstances. The *cause célèbre* of Jefferson's personal life is, of course, the story of his relationship with his slave and chambermaid, Sally Hemings, who served him for the latter 38 years of his life. Hemings has been the subject of intensely heated controversy for almost 200 years and conclusions about her significance to Jefferson are as varied as night and day.

The events in Jefferson's life which impinge upon the story, and which are not generally in dispute, are as follows: Jefferson was widowed in 1782 at age 39.[18] Two years later he was on his way to Paris to join and assist Adams and Franklin who were negotiating treaties of commerce for the new nation. He took his eleven year-old daughter Martha (Patsy) with him. He was not long in Paris before he received

---

16 Fawn M. Brodie, *Thomas Jefferson,* New York: W. W. Norton & Co., Inc., 1974; also William K. Buttorff, *Thomas Jefferson,* Twayne Publishers, 1979; for a contrary opinion, see Dumas Malone, *Jefferson and His Time,* Vol. 3 (1962), & Vol. 4 (1970), Boston: Little Brown & Co.; Merrill D. Peterson, *Thomas Jefferson and the New Nation,* New York: Oxford University Press, 1970, and *Adams and Jefferson,* New York: Oxford University Press, 1976; Virginius Dabney, *The Jefferson Scandals,* New York: Dodd, Mead, and Co., 1981; *Virginius Dabney's Virginia,* Algonquin Books of Chapel Hill, 1986; Douglas Adair, *Fame and the Founding Fathers,* Trevor Colbourn, ed., New York: W. W. Norton & Co. Inc., 1974.

17 Even the tourist guides at Jefferson's home, Monticello, are trained to dismiss Brodie as "not reputable" or "not dealing in historical data." Her book in the Monticello and Jefferson Exhibitions in Charlottesville seems to be perpetually "on order." On one occasion when I asked for the book at the Jefferson Exhibition, the clerk said as I expected that it was "on order" and suggested I read Virginius Dabney's rebuttal of Brodie instead!

18 The deathbed scene was preserved in oral tradition by the slaves and told by overseer Edmund Bacon in his recollections when he was an old man. Jefferson is said to have promised his wife never to marry again. Sally Hemings, nine years old at the time, was one of six slaves of the most trusted, inner circle, at the bedside. They included Sally's three sisters and her mother, Betty, as well as Great George's wife, Ursula. Jack McLaughlin describes the scene in memorable fashion in *Jefferson and Monticello,* New York: Henry Holt & Company, 1988, p. 198. See also Brodie, *op.cit.,* p. 209.

word that his two and one-half year-old, Lucy, had died of the whooping cough. When it became clear that he would be in Paris for longer than he initially anticipated, he resolved to have sent over his only remaining child, Maria (Mary or Polly). She was nine when she finally made the transatlantic voyage, arriving in July, 1787. She was accompanied by one of Jefferson's slave girls, Sally Hemings, who was 14 or 15 at the time. Sally was actually Jefferson's late wife's half-sister.

In the summer and autumn of 1786, prior to the arrival of Maria and Sally, Jefferson had encountered through mutual friends an English woman named Maria Cosway, the wife of the famous miniaturist and member of the Royal Academy who was in Paris doing commissions. Jefferson was infatuated with her at first sight. He contrived to spend time with her almost daily for many weeks, even canceling previous engagements to do so. They toured the Paris environs while her husband, Richard Cosway, worked. It is not known whether they consummated their romantic liaison, but even some conservative historians presume that they did. As Dumas Malone put it, "If as a widower he ever engaged in it [sex], this was the time."[19] Virginius Dabney implicitly justifies the liaison on the grounds that Richard himself was a fool and a womanizer and therefore deserved to be cuckolded. During Maria Cosway's visit, in what may have been a symptomatic accident, Jefferson fell and dislocated his right wrist with very painful and persistent consequences. He subsequently learned to write with his left hand. After her departure on October 5, Jefferson wrote his essay "My Head and My Heart" on his experience with Maria. The essay is a love letter to Maria, one of the many exchanged between the two lovers in the following months. When Maria made her next eagerly awaited trip to Paris at the end of August the following year, the affair took on a very different tone, and the difference seems to have been mainly with Jefferson. He confided later to his friend Trumbull that he had not seen as much of Maria as he expected. "From the mere effect of chance, she has happened to be from home several times when I have called upon her, and I, when she called upon me."[20] This was not the same Jefferson who previously canceled other engagements in order to make time for Maria on an almost daily basis. She, on the other hand, wrote to Jefferson, "If my inclination had been your law I should have had the pleasure of seeing you more than I have."[21] For whatever reason, Jefferson did not continue to pur-

---
19 Malone, *op. cit.*, vol. 2, p. 72.
20 Brodie, *op.cit.*, p. 287.
21 *Ibid.*, p. 289.

sue Maria Cosway in the manner he had the year before. The question is whether he was already infatuated with Sally Hemings. Some think it ludicrous that Jefferson might have chosen his young slave over the cosmopolitan, sophisticated Maria Cosway. However, Jefferson did like his women to keep their place around hearth and home. Maria was no doubt exciting, but she had also abandoned home, husband, and children, a fact that Jefferson could hardly have failed to notice.[22] Maria left for London in December and the two lovers never saw each other again, though they maintained a lifelong correspondence. She invited him to visit her in London on his return voyage to America in 1789, but he declined. When she later wrote suggesting a trip to America, he discouraged it. When she wrote him in 1795 telling him she had ended her marriage, he delayed responding for six months.

Sally Hemings, reportedly almost full-term pregnant, was with Jefferson on his return voyage to Monticello.[23] She subsequently gave birth to probably seven children, five of whom reached maturity and at least some of whom resembled Jefferson. In later years some of the visitors to Monticello were reportedly shocked to be served at table by slaves who strikingly resembled Jefferson himself. Even Thomas J. Randolph, Jefferson's grandson, who was himself attempting to discredit the Sally Hemings stories, verifies the resemblances. The 19th century biographer, Henry S. Randall, quotes him saying, ". . . in one instance, a gentleman dining with Mr. Jefferson looked so startled as he raised his eyes from the latter to the servant behind him, that his discovery of the resemblance was so perfectly obvious to all." Randolph also "revealed" that the reason for the resemblance was that Sally had had a sexual liaison with Peter Carr, Jefferson's nephew, and that she bore his children. Jefferson's overseer, Edmund Bacon, attempts to support the family's denial of the Hemings stories. He claims to have seen the father of Sally's daughter Harriet leave Sally's room in the very early morning, and adds that the man was not Jefferson. Harriet was born in 1801 and Bacon did not come to Monticello until 1806. The only conception he could have observed would have been that of Eston who was Sally's last child, born in 1808. Randolph also disclosed that another nephew, Samuel Carr, had a similar liaison with Sally's half-sister Betsey. Randolph further maintained that his grandfather was in sexual matters

---

22 *Ibid.*, p. 36.
23 As reported by Madison Hemings, who was born later.

From Luther to the Twentieth Century's Sexual Revolution

"chaste and pure," indeed "as immaculate a man as God ever created."[24] He revealed this information, as he said, because Sally's children obviously had Jefferson blood in their veins. If Randolph is correct, his grandfather underwent some kind of conversion to chastity late in life that is not otherwise documented. However, Randolph's account here serves much too neatly the family's ongoing attempt to quash the Sally Hemings stories.

Problems surround Randolph's revelations about the nephews, Peter and Samuel Carr. It is not typical that the offspring of a nephew will strikingly resemble an uncle. Peter married Hettie Smith in 1797, the daughter of a distinguished and politically powerful Baltimore family. The wedding fell in the middle of Sally's childbearing years. Carr would have had to get himself to Monticello quite a lot before and after his marriage in order to father all Sally's children, certainly not an impossible task. However, Brodie shows that Peter was elsewhere during the various impregnation periods of Sally. After his marriage he had his own plantation and cadre of slaves. So too was Samuel occupied elsewhere for much of the time in question. On the other hand, Jefferson was with Sally during each of her various impregnation periods.

Stretching the evidence rather thin, one historian, Alf J. Mapp, jr., even claims that we have a confession of guilt by Peter and Samuel Carr. What we do have is Randolph's later account as reported by Randall, that the two Carr nephews were sitting under a tree at Monticello with "tears coursing down their cheeks" after having seen the newspaper attacks on Jefferson for keeping a slave concubine. "Aren't you and I a couple of____pretty fellows to bring disgrace on poor old uncle who has always fed us! We ought to be ____!" Randolph has them saying. This is hardly a credible account. "Poor old uncle" was by this time President and the weeping nephews were rich and distinguished men of repute with plantations of their own. Samuel became a Virginia state senator. Of course, this would not rule out a liaison with Hemings, but it makes Randolph's account of their confession unbelievable. And as even Virginius Dabney points out, the basic flaw in the Carr stories is that Jefferson is hardly relieved of responsibility if his nephew is repeatedly impregnating his principal housekeeper.

Jefferson's *Farm Book,* in which he recorded meticulously the minutest details of daily life on his plantation, neglects to record the

---
24 *Ibid.,* p. 672.

paternity of Sally's children. Normally the paternity of slave children was known and recorded. It would seem that Jefferson either did not know or wished to conceal the information. The story of Sally's liaison with Peter Carr thus serves two functions. It deals with the reported Jefferson resemblance of Sally's children, and it provides a rationale for Jefferson's silence about their paternity. Jefferson would probably not have recorded his own nephew as the father of slave children. It is on this basis that the distinguished historian, Douglas Adair, postulated a covert "conjugal" relationship between Peter Carr and Sally. As Adair argues, no evidence exists that Sally was promiscuous. Thus he argues for a Sally who was faithful to Peter, and a Peter who was busy traveling to Monticello to impregnate Sally four times during the same period in which he was fathering four legitimate children by his lawful wife. Adair borders on the gothic when he argues that Sally herself repudiated Peter's paternity of her children out of jealousy toward Peter's wife.[25]

One of Sally's sons, Madison Hemings (b. 1805), wrote an account published in the *Pike County (Ohio) Republican* in 1873, which was part of a series by former slaves called "Life Among the Lowly." He revealed that his mother had disclosed to him that she and Jefferson were lovers and that their relationship had begun in Paris, and that she was pregnant during the return voyage, giving birth shortly after their arrival home. The child, supposedly named Tom, seems to have vanished from the record at age 10-12, at the time of the first public airing of Jefferson's supposed slave liaison. Madison further revealed that his mother had been happy in Paris, became fluent in French, and at first refused to return with Jefferson, preferring to remain a free woman in France. Jefferson persuaded her to return, agreeing to free all her children at their maturity. In the same newspaper the account of another Monticello slave, Israel Jefferson (not one of the Hemings clan) supports Madison's claim that Sally was Jefferson's concubine. These small town newspaper accounts seem to have gone unnoticed by historians for 75 years. Both these accounts have been treated with contempt by most Jefferson historians, cavalierly discarded as "not evidence."

For the last 38 years of Jefferson's life, Sally seems to have been the de facto "first lady" of Monticello, if such an epithet could be applied to a slave. Of course, whenever they were around, particularly

---

25 Douglas Adair, *op.cit.*, p. 188.

From Luther to the Twentieth Century's Sexual Revolution

after 1809, one or the other of Jefferson's daughters played that role in the formal sense. No other significant women made an appearance in Jefferson's life. Sally's children were permitted to live in the "big house" until they were 14 and appear to have been given preferential treatment. For that matter, the Hemings clan consistently received preferential treatment. Sally's son Beverly is reported by Edmund Bacon to have "sent off a balloon," not a hobby one would expect of a run-of-the-mill slave. Jefferson himself had acquired some knowledge of balloons during his Paris tour. The first manned ascent was made in Paris the year before Jefferson arrived there. All Sally's children were either freed at maturity or permitted or assisted in running away and passing for white. She herself was freed a year after Jefferson's death by Jefferson's only living "white" child, Martha.

In 1802, during Jefferson's first term as President, James Callender published several accusations against Jefferson in a Richmond paper. One was that he had attempted to seduce a friend's wife, Betsey (Mrs. John) Walker, and another was that he kept as a concubine at Monticello a "slave wench" named Sally. Other papers throughout the country among Jefferson's Federalist opposition picked up the charge and spread it, eager to prove Jefferson a Jacobin enemy of public morals. Jefferson admitted his guilt to the first charge, but he refused to respond directly to the Hemings charge, and held his silence for the rest of his life.

Exactly what Jefferson may have been guilty of in the Betsey Walker affair is not recoverable. His admission was a very general one. He and John Walker had been friends from childhood and he was one of the groomsmen at Walker's wedding. In the summer of 1768 Walker was commissioned by the State of Virginia to travel west and make a peace treaty with certain Indians. He left his wife and child in Jefferson's care during this four-month absence, and even made the handsome bachelor the executor of his will. By Walker's later account, Betsey was subjected to sexual overtures that summer and for the next eleven years, including many episodes of nightshirt encounters when the Walkers and Jeffersons were visiting each other, even after Jefferson was married. Betsey is said to have disclosed this information to her husband in 1785 when Jefferson was in France. The friendship between Walker and Jefferson was first disrupted when Jefferson opposed Walker's bid for a senate seat in 1792. Whatever the truth of this eleven-year dalliance, the story remained private until Callender's exposé. At that point Walker threatened Jefferson with a duel, which Jefferson avoided by admitting his guilt in a nonspecific form and gallantly attesting to Betsey's virtue. With that gesture the matter was laid to rest. The Walkers had the multiple benefits of a Presidential assurance of Betsey's virtue, that John had not been cuckolded, and the glamorous innuendo that she had perhaps been the President's mistress. Walker, on his deathbed in 1809, sent word that a visit from Jefferson would be received kindly. Jefferson sent a basket of figs instead, which as Fawn Brodie points out is an ancient symbol of love and sin.[26] Whatever the truth in all this theater, Jefferson at very least attempted an adulterous relationship with his close friend's wife.

Callender, who exposed all this, was something of a scalawag. He had been jailed during the rather more authoritarian presidency of John Adams for violating the Sedition Act, that is, slandering a public official. Jefferson restored First Amendment rights when he took office and the handful of people in jail under the Sedition Act were released, including Callender. But when Jefferson refused to appoint him Postmaster of Richmond as he somehow thought he should have been, he turned his vitriol on the President. Scalawag or not, Callender did not always have his facts wrong, as we see from the Walker story. He accurately exposed Alexander Hamilton for adultery. He may also have been correct about Sally Hemings.

Biographers and historical accounts in their various references to Sally almost invariably give a distorted picture of her. Epithets of the 19th century such as "Black Sal," "Dusky Sally," or "The African Venus" similarly misrepresent her. Reputable historians are often more subtle, misrepresenting her by innuendo. First of all, she was no Aunt Jemima, nor was she some pitiful illiterate African recently disembarked from a slave ship, nor was she lured in from the turnip patch to meet Jefferson's sexual needs. She was certainly not to be counted among what Virginians used to call "field niggers" as opposed to the higher class "house niggers." (Such derogatory language would likely not have been used by Jefferson who referred to them all somewhat euphemistically as "servants" or "my people.") Among Jefferson's hundred-odd slaves in 1810 there were some 25 whom Jefferson himself referred to as "house servants." Among the house servants was an elite inner circle of favorites consisting of Sally and her sisters and their children.

---

26 *Ibid.*, p. 84. See also Gertrude Jobes, *Dictionary of Mythology, Folklore and Symbols,* New York: Scarecrow Press, 1961, p. 567.

From Luther to the Twentieth Century's Sexual Revolution

To refer to Sally as a "Negro" at all is somewhat misleading, true only in the political sense. She was technically a quadroon, with 25% Negro ancestry. Her grandfather was an English sea captain from whom the name Hemings was taken, and her father was Jefferson's own father-in-law. John Wayles had taken Betty Hemings, Sally's mother, as his slave mistress during his own widowhood and fathered six children by her. Betty must have been a healthy specimen of womanhood. She bore 14 children, six by a black slave first, then one each by a black and white respectively after Wayles had died. All but three reached maturity and she herself lived to age 73. Jefferson inherited the whole Hemings clan at the death of his father-in-law. They were the light-skinned elite among the 135 he inherited from the Wayles estate. Sally and her sisters were, therefore, Jefferson's wife's half-sisters. Sally herself is said to have been very light-skinned, beautiful, intelligent, and had long, straight (i.e. Caucasian) hair. During her Paris sojourn Sally had the services of a private French tutor. She was apparently so light-skinned that after Jefferson's death she and her two youngest children passed for white in the 1830 census. She was 56 at the time and living with her sons Madison and Eston in Charlottesville.

Jefferson's daughters, Martha and Maria, were at least first cousins of Sally's children, even if they were not half-sisters as well. Sally was, of course, an aunt to Martha and Maria. From this distance we can only wonder what the effects on everyday family relationships such a conflicted pattern of relationships might have been. The same blood ran in the veins of slave and master. Since Sally's children presumably had only one-eighth Negro ancestry, there must have been little or no skin color differential to distinguish master from slave.

Up to this point in the account the information is generally well substantiated and historians do not dispute it. Needless to say, a sexual liaison between Jefferson and Hemings is not proven. Circumstantial evidence, however, strongly points in that direction.

The late Fawn Brodie created quite a stir when she published in 1974 what was the very first scholarly examination of the Jefferson-Hemings relationship done by one who suspected that the stories of a sexual liaison were true. Brodie's purpose was to flesh out and give further credence to her belief that the liaison was an intimate one. She examines Jefferson's behavior and writings seaching for data that might in some fashion indirectly comment on his relationship with Sally. For example, she suspects she finds Jefferson's unconscious wish to reveal his relationship with Sally when, in a letter to Maria Cosway, he refers to himself as an orangutan who dislikes the unusually cold Parisian winter. Just a few months before he had written in his *Notes on the State of Virginia* that the orangutan preferred black women to those of his own species. Obviously one such comment does not carry much weight, but Brodie's accumulation of data does. Her conclusion is that Jefferson was deeply conflicted over his relationship with his slave, but that on balance it was a rewarding, caring, and ultimately a long-term relationship---indeed even a poignant and tragic love story. Brodie, of course, does not really "prove" that the relationship was sexual. The matter is in fact unprovable short of an unlikely authenticated written admission by one of the parties in question, or a credible eyewitness account, in flagrante delicto. But Brodie's account is persuasive. The accumulated evidence has the ring of truth.

Brodie seems to have acquired few allies in the high places of Jefferson scholarship. Virginius Dabney, himself a Jefferson scholar, offers his opinion that the three preeminent Jefferson scholars are Dumas Malone, Merrill Peterson, and Julian Boyd. None of these four give Brodie's conclusions even the blessing of a remote possibility. The two biographies by Noble E. Cunningham[27] and Alf J. Mapp jr.[28] which were published in 1987 also debunk Brodie's conclusions. Jack McLaughlin in 1988 is more judicious.[29] He treats the matter as a distinct possibility but remains noncommittal himself. On the basis of numbers it would seem that Brodie supporters should throw in the towel. However, when the reasons are examined which these scholars give for rejecting Brodie's conclusions, they are not very persuasive.

Cunningham writes naively that "it is impossible to find in Jefferson's voluminous writings any indication that the arrival of Sally Hemings made any difference in his life."[30] But to whom would Jefferson have written about what would surely have been seen as his foolish dalliance with a slave girl? If there was such a sexual relationship, the point is that it would certainly have been deeply problematic for him and would have been kept covert. He would have been a very lonely man with this kind of secret. Public admission of it would have been political suicide.

---

27 *The Pursuit of Reason: The Life of Thomas Jefferson*, Baton Rouge: Louisiana State University Press, 1987.
28 *Thomas Jefferson: A Strange Case of Mistaken Identity,* New York: Madison Books, 1987.
29 J. McLaughlin, *passim.*
30 Cunningham, *op.cit.*, p. 116.

From Luther to the Twentieth Century's Sexual Revolution

Cunningham rejects Brodie's exploration of the possible significance of unconscious associations. In response to Brodie's pointing out that soon after Sally's arrival Jefferson began making a surprising number of references to the "mulatto" color of the soil, Cunningham argues that if Brodie is correct, references to red soil color must have some conflicted unconscious association with his redhead daughter. Cunningham takes a wooden, misinformed stance regarding possible unconscious associations. Precisely the character of unconscious associations, as psychoanalytic theory has identified them, is that they are sometimes persuasive and sometimes not, and impossible to prove in either case. Like the orangutan reference, they are certainly not hard historical data, but merely small individual shingles that might help build a roof if there are enough of them and a credible framework to which to attach them. Brodie has both a credible framework and very many shingles with which to build her roof.

Alf J. Mapp, jr. similarly debunks the Hemings stories, bowing to Dabney who, he says, has settled the dispute. On the occasion of the publication of his biography, a Washington reception was given for Mapp. Then Secretary of Defense, Caspar Weinberger, attended the reception and is reported to have asked one question, "Did Jefferson have a sexual liaison with any of his slaves?" Mapp is reported to have responded, "While no one can prove a man never did something, there is absolutely no evidence this man did anything in that regard at all."[31] Mapp's answer is congruent with his handling of the Jefferson-Hemings story in the biography. On that issue he proves himself a propagandist, not a historian.

The debunkers of the Jefferson-Hemings liaison dig themselves into a hole by the manner of their attack which, in spite of their credentials as historians, is laced with hysteria. The dean of Jefferson scholars, Dumas Malone, says quite candidly that he wishes he did not have to discuss the subject.[32] He also notes that Callender had never visited Monticello, as if through a visit he might have found out the truth. (More to the point, Callender did visit the neighborhood of Monticello and there presumably got the data to support his charges.) Finally, Malone concludes that such behavior was "virtually unthinkable in a man of Jefferson's moral standards and habitual conduct." Malone outdoes himself when he writes:

---

31 Quoted by William Ruehlmann, "A Map of History,' *The Virginian-Pilot/The Ledger-Star*, Ap. 19, 1987, p. J1.
32 Malone, *op.cit.*, Vol. 3, p. 497.

> [It is] inconceivable that this fastidious gentleman whose devotion to his dead wife's memory . . . bordered on the excessive could have carried on through a period of years a vulgar liaison . . . as absurd as charging him with being a secret drunkard.[33]

Finally, racist overtones infiltrate Malone's argument when he reports that Thomas J. Randolph said his mother, hearing the rumor, "would have liked to have sent the whole brood away," but that Jefferson would not have considered such a suggestion. Malone opines that such a move by Jefferson would have looked too much like a confession.[34] Malone does not say that such a response would have been an act of brutality against a whole clan of persons who, though slaves, were Jefferson's relatives. These were not just ordinary relatives either. They were all born at the family plantation and spent their entire lives serving the family. Nor does he consider the possibility that Jefferson may have valued his long-standing relationship with the woman who was at very least his principal housekeeper for 38 years. And why would the relationship be vulgar in Malone's view?

The appeal to Jefferson's "moral standards and habitual conduct" by Malone is not persuasive. Quite the contrary, Jefferson was a cosmopolitan, Renaissance man of the Enlightenment, a man generally of the mold of Benjamin Franklin, his mentor. Franklin felt "under no religious constraints" in the matter of his sexual behavior, and it seems that Jefferson felt the same way. Like Franklin he delighted in late 18th century Paris, in contrast to the prudish John Adams, who was appalled by its sensuality. Jefferson considered his five years in Paris the happiest of his life. He also had had two adulterous relationships, with Betsey Walker and Maria Cosway. He was no prude on this issue, and no sexual ascetic. One of his favorite derogatory adjectives was "monkish." After Sally entered his life, no other woman who might have been a sexual liaison appears on the scene for the rest of his life. That fact by itself should lead to suspicion of an intimate relationship with Sally. Furthermore, a sexual liaison with a slave, particularly if it were a caring relationship, would seem to be less morally questionable than adultery. Were Jefferson in love with Sally, and wanting her to remain with him in Virginia, he acted in the only responsible way left for him to act. He could not have married a slave or an ex-slave without expecting to be ruined. He could not even free her and keep her in his household

---
33 *Ibid.*, Vol. IV, p. 214.
34 *Ibid.*, Vol. III, p. 498.

without scandal. Freed slaves were perceived to be a threat to society. A law was passed in Virginia in 1806 requiring all newly freed slaves to be banished from the state, except by legislative exemption.

Similarly, Merrill Peterson discredits the Hemings story, arguing that Jefferson would have had to slip badly out of character if he were caught up in such a miscegenous relationship, and in particular, "such a ruthless exploitation of the master-slave relationship."[35] Peterson, reputable scholar though he is, overreached himself on this. Miscegenation was epidemic in slavery and Jefferson was hardly innocent regardless of which member of his family or community might have been impregnating Sally. Since she was a quadroon, there would seem to be less miscegenation involved in her mating with a white than in mating with a black. As regards the "ruthless exploitation" of the master-slave relationship, such a relationship would seem by definition "ruthless exploitation." Sally had been a free woman in France, and Jefferson brought her back to slavery. The only humane reason he might have done so was that he loved her and was unwilling to part with her. If Hemings were Jefferson's functional wife for 38 years, one is compelled to conjecture that she would have experienced such a role as a happy softening of her slavery. Short of emancipation, what better life could she have had? Had she been dark, dull-witted or homely, or for whatever reason been of little interest to Jefferson, she might have been sold off to other owners for economic considerations, as most of Jefferson's other slaves were. As it was she perhaps had a closet marriage for 38 years to one of the most interesting men in history and was assured of freedom for all her children.

The historians who debunk the Jefferson-Hemings liaison, of course, dismiss Madison Heming's and Israel Jefferson's accounts as mere self-serving fabrications. Such a criticism cannot be ignored. However, the cavalier manner in which these persuasive documents are dismissed as "not evidence" is nothing short of astonishing. Dabney charges that the accounts were too well written to have been produced by ex-slaves. Perhaps. And perhaps they did get help writing what was essentially a truthful account. Dabney points out that a slave would not have used the French word "enciente" ("pregnant", properly spelled "enceinte") as Madison does, and that furthermore it is misspelled! Dabney wants it both ways. Since his mother and the Jeffersons were fluent in French, it would seem quite plausible that

---

35 Peterson, *op.cit.* (1970), p. 707.

Madison might both know some French and be poor at spelling it. Madison's account does contain some errors of dating and of fact concerning events prior to his birth, information passed down to him by his mother. That oral tradition should be precisely dated and free of factual error is to expect too much. Dabney also repeats Malone's argument that Madison's and Israel's accounts are simply abolitionist propaganda, written to make slavery look bad. He also says that many blacks claimed parentage by distinguished whites. Then he proposes that Sally was in fact attempting to protect another white man by passing down the story of Jefferson's paternity. Through it all one hears a note of hysteria motivated by the determination to separate Jefferson from this "scandal" at all cost.

What gives it all away is that the liaison is seen as a devastating threat to Jefferson's greatness. Why this should be so is puzzling. Other venerated giants in history, like Rousseau, have loved women beneath their station without suffering the vilification of posterity. Yet for Jefferson, the Hemings story is said to "drag him like a dead cat through the pages of history."[36]

Dabney says that Jefferson's children and grandchildren likely would not have remained loyal and affectionate to him had he fathered Sally's children. The fact that they remained loyal and affectionate is evidence, he says, that the story was false---a strange argument indeed.[37] Dabney also claims that Brodie wishes to "judge a man by the frequency of his sex life," a charge that grossly distorts the character of Brodie's work.[38] Douglas Adair, another Jefferson scholar, says Jefferson would have had to be a hypocrite, grossly insensitive, and callously selfish to have had a sexual liaison with Sally.[39] The possibility that Hemings and Jefferson might have been happy to have each other seems to have eluded most Jefferson scholars.

The debunkers of the liaison curiously see it as a threat to Jefferson's status as author of the American dream of the rule of reason. Julian Boyd writes: "The great passion of Jefferson's life was directed toward the preservation of 'the last best hope of earth,' not toward a

---

36 Sidney P. & Carolyn Moss, "The Jefferson Miscegenation Legend in British Travel Books," *Journal of the Early Republic,* Vol. 7, No. 3, Fall 1987, p. 274.
37 Dabney, *op.cit.* (1981), p. 85.
38 Dabney, *op.cit.* (1986), p. 90.
39 Adair, *op.cit.,* p. 182.

From Luther to the Twentieth Century's Sexual Revolution

quadroon slave."[40] On what basis does such a scholar decide to set the issue in such either/or terms? Must Jefferson have passion for either democracy or a woman but not both? Brodie's adoring portrait makes him not one whit less the lover of democracy for being the lover of Sally.

The possibility, indeed, high probability, that this giant of a man paired himself intimately with a beautiful and intelligent, mostly Caucasian woman who was trapped in slavery because one of her four grandparents happened to be Negro takes nothing at all from his greatness. Brodie's account makes Jefferson seem all the more human because of the tragic character of his relationship with Hemings, and certainly more human than portraits that depict him as an abruptly transformed sexual celibate in the last half of his life.

Whatever his relationship with Hemings, Jefferson kept his own counsel on the matter as far as we can tell at this point in history. Whatever this giant of the Enlightenment may have been doing sexually is mostly obscured behind the screen of the privatization of sexual behavior. Even the question of how he reflected upon his two significant adulterous relationships from the first half of his life is hidden from us. In his many references to virtue, he studiously avoids references to chastity. In a letter to James Fishback in 1809 on the subject of the Ten Commandments he avoided mentioning adultery.[41]

The treatment of Jefferson by Malone, Peterson, Boyd and others is very instructive in that it reveals much about the covert values of modern historians themselves. They are quite vexed by the possibility of an assignation with a slave woman, but not one whit concerned about the abrupt disappearance of any sign of sexual activity in the prime of a man's life. This bias betrays a profound and covert allegiance to an ideal of sexual purity in the historians themselves.

VI

The mid-19th century saw the waters of sexual valorization begin to stir. The stability of the center was weakening. Karl Marx (1818-1883) and Friedrich Engels (1820-1895) in political and economic theory were the harbingers of significant changes to come, changes of which the

---

40 Quoted by Page Smith, "A Revealing Biography," *American Heritage,* Vol. 26, No. 6, Oct. 1976, pp. 28-33.
41 *The Writings of Thomas Jefferson,* 20 Vols., Andrew A. Lipscomb and Albert E. Bergh, eds., Washington: 1903, Vol. 12, p. 315.

sexual revolution would be only a part. These theoreticians of communism saw monogamy, along with private property and the state, as an inextricably related triumvirate, the foundation of industrial capitalist society and of male chauvinism as well, and the source of the dehumanizing bondage of modern industrial life. On the other hand, 20th century political attempts to institutionalize communist theory have paid little attention to the critique of monogamy made by their spiritual fathers. Engels' teaching on marriage and sex has reached fruition thus far only in the West, in the sexual revolution itself.

Later in the century Friedrich Nietzsche (1844-1900) in philosophy made a parallel contribution. He brought forward in secular garb all the power of the biblical affirmation of sex, and roundly condemned the church for its sex negativism.

In his own way Sigmund Freud (1856-1939) further fueled the fires of change, demonstrating that sex is considerably more than genital intercourse, but rather a whole galaxy of complex bodily gratifications around which all human personality is shaped and without which human personality cannot exist. The full weight of the challenge of these 19th century prophets was eventually to undermine the orthodox Protestant doctrine that what had been thought of as sex belonged exclusively within marriage.

Marx, Engels, Nietzsche, and Freud were at first, in their own times, more or less relegated to the radical or lunatic fringe. Freud more than the others lived to receive certain modest honors. For awhile history marched on mostly as if they never existed. But their influence increasingly permeated Western culture at large until their theories ultimately disturbed the center itself. The sexual revolution in the late 20th century was the fruition of their combined challenge to the established forms of sexual valorization in the Western middle class, both Protestant and Roman Catholic.

The victory of the sexual revolution was undoubtedly assisted by the powerful influence of these prophets on the two most influential theologians of the 20th century, Karl Barth and Paul Tillich. Tillich and Barth were influenced not only by Marx and Engels directly, but by their disciples and quasi-disciples. A certain Edward Carpenter (1844-1929), for example, became quite popular at the turn of the century. He was an English cleric and socialist visionary who, among other things, promoted sexual freedom in rather bold terms. The prime object of sex, he argued, was not procreation at all, but physical union which he called an allegory for the union of all. He denigrated marriage as an archaic and unnecessary "life sentence, not even reducible as in the case of ordinary convicts to the maximum term of 20 years."[42] He even deprecated the ideal of a sexually exclusive commitment, arguing that it ran the "fatal risk of lapsing into a mere stagnant double selfishness."[43] Though Barth and Tillich do not mention the influence of Carpenter, he was quite popular as they were entering the adult world. Carpenter's German translation of *Love's Coming of Age* was printed in 1902 and had "phenomenal" success, even better than it had in Carpenter's native England.[44]

Thus both Barth and Tillich began their long lives as theologians with strong ideological support for rejection of the orthodox Protestant tenet that sexual gratification should be limited to the boundaries of marriage. As the theologian James Luther Adams put it, Marx, Nietzsche, and Freud together had undercut bourgeois conventions in every respect, "laying open the realities of class structure and the depths of the human inner experience."[45] Both Tillich and Barth, each in his own way, saw himself as heir to that revolution, of which the sexual revolution was only a part. At the same time each exemplified, paradoxically, a privatistic attitude toward the sexual dimension of his own life. Thus when Tillich wrote his theologically interpretive autobiographical sketch, "On the Boundary," he described various aspects of his personal life experience that had been boundary situations. One was, for example, the boundary between his native Germany where he lived his first fifty years and alien America where he spent the rest of his life. However, he omitted the boundary of sexual values, in retrospect perhaps the most significant boundary that he challenged, the one with the most far-reaching consequences.[46] After Tillich had listened to a lecture in the 1950s by Seward Hiltner on sexual ethics, he thanked Hiltner afterwards especially for what he "did not say." Similarly, it has been said of the late Scottish

---

42 Edward Carpenter, *Love's Coming of Age,* London: Swan Sonnenshein & Co. Ltd., 1909, p. 74.
43 *Ibid.,* p. 103.
44 Edward Carpenter, *The Story of My Books,* London, George Allen & Unwin Ltd., 1916. p. 7.
45 James Luther Adams, *The Thought of Paul Tillich,* James Luther Adams, Wilhelm Pauck, & Roger Lincoln Shinn, eds., San Francisco: Harper & Row, 1985, p. 13.
46 Paul Tillich, *The Interpretation of History,* New York: Charles Scribner's Sons, 1936.

theologian, D. M. Baillie, that he lectured all year on the meaning of God's incarnation in the flesh of Jesus and not once mentioned sexuality. Even later, the popular and liberal Roman Catholic theologian, Hans Kung, in his massive tome, *On Being a Christian,* made only one passing derogatory comment about sex in the context of the illusory benefits of recreation with drugs.[47] Only a commitment to the privatization of sexuality can permit one to write hundreds of pages on the nature of religious life and never seriously discuss sexuality.

VII

By almost any assessment, the most influential shapers of religious thought and ethical practice in the Western world in the 20th century have been Barth and Tillich. The mark these two men have made on theological and ethical thinking crosses generational, national and religious boundaries. Pope Pius XII characterized Barth as "the greatest theologian since Thomas Aquinas."[48] He should probably have added that if Barth was the greatest, Tillich was the most influential, not only among Protestants, but among Roman Catholics, Jews and even the non-religious. Both these powerfully influential theologians demonstrated by their behavior especially, and to some extent by their teaching, their rejection of the basic assumptions of Western middle class sexual ethics. In the case of each man his personal life speaks louder than his words. Barth and Tillich reached their prime in the 1920s and 30s, well before the public availability of the birth control pill and its presumed effect on Western behavior.

To state the facts simply, Tillich was a philanderer, or "womanizer," as one of his fellow theologians, Norman Pittenger, put it.[49] And Barth was a functional bigamist, having lived the entire second half of his 80-year life in a household with two women, each of whom he was sexually involved with.

Unfortunately, Barth left no self-reflection in the public record on the subject of his own variant sexual history. Tillich shared his thoughts and feelings on the matter privately with several close colleagues. In that respect, the challenge of each to normative sexual ethics remains a muted one, one made sotto voce, demonstrated almost entirely by the facts of

---

47 Edward Quinn, trans., Garden City, New York: Doubleday and Co., Inc., 1976.
48 John Bowden, *Karl Barth,* London: SCM Press Ltd., 1971, p. 11.
49 Personal communication.

From Luther to the Twentieth Century's Sexual Revolution

their respective biographies. While the challenge to normative sexual values is a muted one, in each case it is clear and unmistakable in its content.

The parallels in the biographies of these two men are striking. Each was born in 1886, Barth May 10 and Tillich August 20. Tillich was a Brandenberger German, and Barth a German-speaking Swiss. Each was sympathetic to the socialist movement early in the century. Barth came to be known as "the red pastor" in his first parish, in part because of his support of unions over the objections of the factory owners who were members of his parish. Both were teaching in German universities in the 30s, Barth at Bonn and Tillich at Frankfurt. Barth had taken German citizenship. Each was targeted for dismissal very early in the Nazi era. Tillich was dismissed immediately when the Nazis came to power, in 1933, and Barth two years later.

In response to the Nazis Barth initially declared that the church should continue doing "theology and only theology . . . as though nothing had happened."[50] He thought he could continue working under the new regime. He even filled in some of the university lectures that were to be given by Karl Ludwig whom the Nazis suspended. However, he was under suspicion from the beginning for, among other things, his adamant refusal to open his lectures with the recommended Hitler salute. Barth did not demonstrate any particular sensitivity at first to the Nazi assault on the Jews which began within the first month of Nazi rule. Later he expressed regret that he had not done more to protest the treatment of the Jews.[51] Only when Hitler moved to Nazify the Protestant churches did Barth come into direct conflict with the government. When the Nazis attempted to install "Reich Bishop" Ludwig Muller as a pro-Nazi authority over Protestants, Barth assumed leadership of a pan-Protestant anti-government movement that formalized itself as "The Confessing Church." The Confessing Church was a shadow church which developed first out of Martin Niemoller's Pastors' Emergency League, founded in November, 1933, to oppose Hitlerite authority in the Protestant churches. In May 1934 The Confessing Church organized itself around the Barmen Declaration, a document drafted by Barth himself. The Barmen Declaration provided the theological rationale for renouncing the pro-Nazi "German Christian" movement among Protestants. In November 1934, Barth refused to sign the Nazi loyalty oath and the next month was dismissed. Just prior to his dismissal, Barth preached a sermon entitled, "Jesus Christ was a Jew," in a

---

50 Eberhard Busch, *Karl Barth*, John Bowden, trans., Philadelphia: Fortress Press, 1976, p. 226.
51 *Ibid.*, pp. 225-48.

service in which some the members of his congregation walked out in protest.

The Vatican had in the first months of the Nazi regime ingratiated itself by signing a peace treaty with Hitler known as the Concordat. Photographs show the Roman Catholic bishops and clergy giving the Nazi salute on Catholic Youth Day in Berlin in August 1933.[52]

Tillich emigrated for the United States and Barth for Basel, Switzerland. In the postwar period the two were the unchallenged patriarchs of Western theology. Tillich died in 1965; Barth in 1968.

Unlike Barth, Tillich has very little to say about sexual behavior in his published works. Nothing of what he wrote could be taken as supportive of traditional monogamy. What he does say is congruent with what we now know about his private life. For example, Tillich uses human sexual development as illustrative of the journey from "dreaming innocence," symbolized by the Garden of Eden, to personal self-actualization. The actualization of one's potential, he wrote, results in "experience, responsibility, and guilt." The human predicament, like that of the adolescent, is one of being caught between the desire to actualize oneself and the wish to preserve a dreaming innocence. No one wants to lose either innocence or the potential for actualization. Anxiety, therefore, is experienced in either direction.[53] The loss of innocence was for Tillich a mark of "the fall," the exile from the Garden, as he correlates platonic and biblical metaphors. The fall, however, was "a fall upward," as he put it. Tillich also registers his critique of Augustine, and even Luther, who "never overcame the Hellenistic and especially the Neo-platonic devaluation of sex." He writes that each, but especially Augustine, tended to identify sexual desire with sin, even though each knew that spiritual pride, not sex, was the basic human sin.[54]

Tillich was deeply concerned, however, about the countercultural character of his personal life in two respects. He was afraid his personal life would become a public relations or political problem and thereby discredit him as a theologian. Given the public mood and mores in the 1940s and 1950s in the United States such a concern was probably appropriate. Seward Hiltner, who personally shared Tillich's dilemma to some extent, has also suggested that knowledge about Tillich's private life was the cause for "a stoney silence" that followed proposals to ap-

---
52 See Roland Kleming, ed., *Jews in Germany under Prussian Rule,* Berlin: Bildarchiv Preussischer Kulturbesitz, 1984.
53 Paul Tillich, *Systematic Theology,* Vol.II, University of Chicago Press, 1957, p. 41.
54 *Ibid.,* p. 59.

point him to teaching positions at the University of Chicago in the 1930s and 1940s. (In 1962 he did win a Chicago appointment, after several years of a distinguished appointment as "University Professor" at Harvard.) Undoubtedly, many of the ministers, priests, and nuns who flocked to hear him would have been shocked, perhaps outraged, to have known of his private life.

Tillich was also concerned about his personal sexual life from a moral perspective. He was fully aware that he was treading dangerous and uncharted ground and that such trangressing of the social code carried profound psychic risks. He was also fully aware that the inevitable human journey from innocence to guilt was more than theoretical. He experienced genuine guilt. Rollo May reports him to have asked: "Was my erotic life a failure, or was it a daring way of opening up new human possibilities?"[55] The question was not an academic or rhetorical one, but a deeply felt expression of existential anguish and uncertainty.

The facts of Tillich's sexual life remained safely below the surface, at the level of gossip, during his life and until 1973 when the matter appeared for the first time in print. His widow, Hannah, published a kind of biography, or story of their life together, called *From Time to Time*.[56] Simultaneously, one of Tillich's students, the widely respected theologian and psychotherapist, Rollo May, published a brief biography entitled *Paulus*, Tillich's actual given name in German. May's work was essentially a rebuttal to Hannah's account.

In that publishing event and the subsequent reaction, we see the theological community's great wish to deny the troublesome facts of Tillich's personal life. Hannah disclosed a lifelong pattern of countless sexual adventures on her husband's part as well as details about her own adventures, including some experimenting with bisexuality. She and her husband had also participated in "swinging" (spouse swapping) with another couple. Hannah circulated her manuscript privately for some time prior to publication, and most of her friends advised her against publication. Rollo May, a longtime family friend of the Tillichs, very likely saw the manuscript or at least knew of it. Hiltner and others assume that May's book was an attempt to mollify the impact of Hannah's book on her late husband's reputation.

---

55 Rollo May, *Paulus,* New York: Harper & Row, 1973, p. 65.
56 New York: Stein and Day, 1973.

The Poisoning of Eros

May's alternate account of Tillich's sexual life was embarrassingly naive, especially from an individual who has in other ways demonstrated such good sense. Although he never argued explicitly that Tillich was entirely innocent of the stories about him, he suggested as much by going to great lengths to distinguish between the "sensual" and the "sexual" in Tillich. He writes: "His letters to his women friends were filled with such words as touch, light, warmth, glow, and other terms which express sensuality rather than sexuality."[57] May also tells how Tillich spent an afternoon in the park with May's fiancée, an afternoon in which he enchanted the young woman with erotic fantasies. May felt some pangs of jealousy, but he "knew" the encounter was an innocent one. "Another man might easily have turned the spiritual seduction into a physical one. Not Paulus . . . He was genuinely devoted to the sensual in life by contrast to the sexual."[58] May then procedes to explain Tillich's behavior on the grounds that he was continually seeking his lost mother, and that his sexual mores were inherited from German intellectual society between the wars which was in rebellion against middle class values. Finally, May discusses Tillich's own guilt feelings about his sexual life. May seemed to want it both ways, but the overall impression he presents of Tillich is of a man whose bohemian sexual life was mostly if not entirely in the realm of fantasy and imagination. In the theological community *Paulus* was generally accepted with a sigh of relief. *The Expository Times,* a British theological journal, thought May's account a welcomed correction to Hannah's distorted image, in which she "lays bare in the most distressing fashion, details of his private life damaging to his good reputation . . . How much do we need to know?"[59] *The Expository Times* seemed to be saying it had no interest here in the question of ethics but was concerned about public relations.

Hannah's book, however, had the advantage of specific biographical data and with that data she totally destroyed May's thesis. Like *The Expository Times,* many in the religious community reacted as though Hannah had calumniated her late husband. Some even thought she was revealing fantasies rather than facts. The word went out in theological circles that the book was a bitter widow's act of personal revenge and spitefulness. The

---

57 May, *op.cit.*, p. 55.
58 *Ibid.*, p. 51.
59 F. Pratt Green, *The Expository Times,* 86.352 (Aug 1975). See also "Editorial," 86.161 (March 1975). A couple of notable exceptions to the preference for May's bowdlerized version of Tillich's life can be seen in two reviews by women: Jani Sherrard, *The Drew Gateway,* Vol. 44, p. 142, 1973-74, and Ina Kau, *Radical Religion,* Vol. 1, No. 2, Spring 1974.

From Luther to the Twentieth Century's Sexual Revolution

question of its accuracy, whether it was fact or fantasy, was for some time left unresolved.

In spite of characterizations to the contrary, Hannah's account in no way communicates ill feelings toward her late husband. The story itself in its extreme unconventionality simply derailed many conventional readers. The information was plainly indigestible to some. Rather than an assault on her husband, the book is in fact a poignant testament to their devotion to each other, a love which grew deeper in their last years. No one can read the chapter on their last years in Chicago, and especially their time together when he was dying, without being deeply moved by their devotion to each other. Their relationship had been shaped by plenty of difficulties and, at times, unspeakable suffering, betrayal, and intense emotional turmoil. No doubt many people would just as soon not have heard of the negative aspects of that relationship, particularly its bohemian sexuality.

Three years later the couple Tillich had appointed to be his authorized biographers, Wilhelm and Marion Pauck,[60] supported the accuracy of Hannah's account and thus vindicated her. Since the facts are now well documented, Tillich is often now simply forgiven this particular "sickness," thereby discredited by innuendo. As one seminary dean used to put it, "Tillich was simply defenseless in the face of seductive women." To relieve individuals of moral responsibility for their actions on the grounds of sickness or weak defenses is a fashionable gambit in American life, but it is just a more socially acceptable form of character assassination. Such an explanation entirely ignores the fact that Tillich chose to live the way he did for his entire adult life, and presumably was a relatively free agent. The picture of a defenseless Tillich in this regard is not persuasive and is, as well, an egregious assault both on him in particular and women in general.

Seward Hiltner, on the other hand, is one of the few theologians who took Tillich's challenge to conventional sex ethics seriously. His assessment was that Tillich's challenge, though serious, was not serious enough. He wrote, "I am a little less sure that a fresh flower, even in a crannied wall, every day, is an effective way to break the unduly prurient and legalistic bonds of our own theological past."[61] Hiltner is suggesting that Tillich's sexual adventures were too frivolous and that

---

60 *Paul Tillich: His Life and Thought,* Vol. I, New York: Harper & Row, Publishers, 1976, pp. 86-90.
61 "Tillich, The Person: A Review Article," *Theology Today,* 30, Jan. 1974, p. 387.

therefore he became less effective than he might have been in commenting theologically on sexual ethics. Hiltner's critique is persuasive.

Frivolous or not, the Tillichs' sexual lives now stand as a serious critique of conventional religious sexual morality. The Paucks confirm that Hannah spoke also for her husband when she characterized her sexual experience as providing a liberating "break with the whole concept of monogamy."[62] We can reasonably conclude that Tillich believed for the most part that his erotic life was indeed a daring way of opening up new human possibilities simply because he consistently spent his life in that manner and was aware of the danger. Being the existentialist that he was, however, he acknowledged his uncertainty about his precarious and dangerous behavior, as about everything else in his life, and was unwilling to assert categorically that the path he had chosen was the right one.

VIII

Barth's sexual life was equally bohemian, but in a very different way. Barth met Charlotte von Kirschbaum after a decade of marriage, at about the time his wife Nelly was pregnant with their fifth and last child. Charlotte, or "Lollo," as she was called, was an attractive, vivacious, 25-year-old, six years younger than Nelly. She had been a Red Cross nurse and had a keen interest in theology and in Barth. He got to know her more intimately in 1925 when she visited his summer vacation cabin at Bergli. He later visited her in Bamberg "in wonderment."[63] Lollo joined the Barth household in 1929, and under Barth's tutelege studied theology. He even "ghost wrote" one of her advanced examinations. For the rest of her life she functioned as Barth's secretary and, to some extent, unacknowledged co-author, ultimately becoming quite a respected theologian and lecturer in her own right. In Barth's own words, she became his "faithful fellow worker . . . stayed by [his] side, and was indispensable in every way."[64] She shared in his work and in much of his time of relaxation from work.

According to Eberhard Busch, who in the final years succeeded Lollo as Barth's secretary, and became his official biographer, the relationship caused the two women and Barth himself unspeakably deep

---
62 Pauck, *op.cit.*, p. 184.
63 Busch, *op.cit.*, p. 68.
64 *Ibid.*, p. 185.

suffering. In Busch's words, "Tensions arose which shook them to the core."[65] Barth's wife retreated into the background of home and children with the arrival of Lollo into the family home. Barth's mother, among other people, took offense at the arrival of this "other woman" and took Barth to task on the matter. In the face of this interpersonal tension, Barth was adamant, and insisted that he was not negotiable on the subject of Lollo. Probably in an effort to relieve some of the interpersonal tension, he and Lollo regularly moved to his cabin at Bergli for summer vacations, a move which certainly made Barth's relationship with Lollo even more transparent. Furthermore, the two of them traveled throughout Europe on numerous occasions, often with another couple, the Pestalozzis. A revealing family snapshot from 1930 shows Barth in the center with Lollo to his immediate right and Nelly on his far left, with three children interposed. Busch's biography only implies that the relationship between Lollo and Barth was a sexual one. His implications are unmistakable, but he avoids with deftness addressing the matter directly.

Most theologians have treated the subject of Barth's relations with Lollo as untouchable. Martin Rumscheidt is an exception. He is a former student of Barth's, a family friend, and one-time Vice-President of the Karl Barth Society in North America. Rumscheidt considers the question of Barth's relationship with Lollo a relevant one, especially in light of Barth's own teaching on sex and marriage. This conviction led him finally to question one of Barth's children on the matter, who revealed to him that the relationship between Lollo and his father was indeed sexual. It seems that Barth had convened a family conference in the early 1930s, several years after Lollo had joined the household, to discuss the nature of his relationship with Lollo. At that conference, which included both women as well as all the children, Barth acknowledged that his relationship with Lollo was sexual and that the sexual aspect of the relationship would be terminated.[66] Regardless of what may or may not subsequently have occurred sexually, Lollo remained in the Barth household for the rest of her life, continued to work, travel, and vacation with him, and was with him during his only trip to the United States in 1962. Whatever the continuing sexual dimensions of the triangular relationship, Lollo remained for four decades the preeminent woman in Barth's life. For this reason some Barthians, uncomfortable

---
65 *Ibid.*, p. 186.
66 Personal communication.

about Barth's functional bigamy, wish the problem had been resolved one way or another, and now wonder why the Barths did not divorce.

While Nelly remained in the background as far as the world of theology was concerned, and perhaps even in terms of Barth's primary affection, she seems to have been well-treated within the limitations of that kind of arrangement. She was hardly a wounded recluse and is said to have kept a warmly hospitable home. It should be noted, too, that Nelly had the best part of Barth's last years. Then, when he was working less, Nelly was able to claim more of him. Particularly after Barth's second prostate operation in 1964, when he wore a permanent catheter, Nelly looked after him, in Barth's own words, "as well as a nursing sister, or even better."[67] The comparison, conscious or otherwise, of Nelly with a nursing sister is a fascinating one since Lollo herself was a nurse. While Barth was recuperating, Lollo was diagnosed with an unspecified fatal, chronic brain disease, and moved to a residential nursing home in January, 1966. For anyone suspicious of the relationship between disease and the exigencies of one's personal history, the timing of Lollo's illness, and even the bodily locus of it, are highly suggestive. Lollo was Barth's "brain" and certainly the principal "other" in the arena of theological thought. We know, too, that Lollo resisted Barth's decision to slow down his prodigious work load. As his work decreased, so Lollo's share of him in their triangular relationship decreased. He wrote to Helmut Gollwitzer in July, 1962, saying he would not write the 13th and 14th volumes of his *Church Dogmatics*. "I have had my day," he wrote. "I am now invited 'in an oriental rest that defies all activists,' to look on a little and see how others plan to use the time still given them. Especially since I have in fact been a great-grandfather for a few weeks now. Lollo cannot stand this kind of thinking. She will be angry when she reads this, call me ungrateful, and try to stop me from sending the letter . . ."[68]

Even in his decrepitude Barth did not neglect Lollo in her hospitalization. He visited her regularly on Sunday afternoons, sometimes singing to her, especially when she was unresponsive. "But we had a good time, didn't we . . ." she said to him once, as he was saying

---
67 Busch, *op.cit.*, p. 472.
68 *Karl Barth Letters 1961-1968* Jurgen Fangmeier & Hinrich Stoevesandt, eds., Geoffrey W. Bromiley, trans., Grand Rapids, William B. Eerdmans Publishing Company, 1981, p. 61.

good-bye.[69] The dying process took a decade. In her invalid state she outlived Barth by seven years.

During these final three years Barth and Nelly became closer. He dedicated his last book to his wife, "with whom I am now able to celebrate a really harmonious 'evening of my life.'"[70]

To charge Barth with abusing Nelly would imply also that she was willing to be abused on a prolonged basis. More likely she made peace with the destiny that seemed to be hers. Divorce may have provided her with more dignity in middle class social circles, or the threat of divorce may even have forced Barth to rid himself of Lollo. However, it is difficult to imagine a person as willful as Barth responding to that kind of threat. The question remains whether either of those options would have brought Nelly a more rewarding or virtuous life. The very fact that she remained with him, and especially that their last years were happy ones, is testimony to the ultimate solidity of their relationship. That Barth could integrate a household of two women and five children, each of whom seems to have been grateful to have participated in his life, is also impressive testimony to his skill, wisdom, love---and, not least, his audacity.

Some have suggested that the family conference represented a point of repentence for Barth, the time from which he kept himself sexually uninvolved with Lollo. The factuality of such a conjecture cannot be either established or ruled out with the data now available, though it seems a strained one. It would require that Barth subscribed to a compartmentalized and legalistic view of sex, which is obviously not the case. His history with Lollo up to that point would tend to discredit such a conjecture. Furthermore, Lollo remained for the rest of her active life Barth's primary female relationship and Nelly remained in the background, albeit dignified background, of house, hearth, and children. Beyond that, it would seem that if Barth had undergone in this matter true repentance, a subject about which he knew a great deal, he likely would have taken more significant steps to change his life than a simple indication of no further sexual involvment with the woman with whom he was spending most of his working as well as recreation time.

A more likely motivation for the family conference and Barth's decision was simply escalating family tension. We may surmise that Barth's older children were more troubled by Lollo's presence as they

---
69 Busch, *op.cit.*, p. 472.
70 *Ibid.*

entered puberty than they might have been earlier. When Lollo joined the family the children were 15, 14, 12, 8, and 4. By the time of the family conference at least three of them, a girl and two boys, would have been in their teens and puberty would have added its contribution to the mix. The presence in the household of a younger and more theologically astute rival/colleague of their mother would likely have created especially complex oedipal issues for the boys. Barth's daughter must have had rich but complicated resources as she faced the task of forming her own sexual identity. In any case, Barth obviously had his hands full with conflicted feelings, as Busch's biography candidly reveals. (The best argument for monogamy is its simplicity.) Perhaps Barth's decision to announce the termination of his sexual relations with Lollo was a last resort in the face of the feelings of his children, in addition to whatever feelings Nelly herself had. The rationale for Barth's decision, and whether it turned out to be a permanent one or merely an ad hoc measure in the face of adolescent turmoil, is simply not known at present.

More light on the subject might be found in material in the Barth archives. However, it was reported at the 1985 Barth Symposium at The University of the South that use of the archives is highly restricted and that some of the personal material is being systematically held back. This is not unusual practice for a public figure who has many living relatives and friends who might be embarrassed by public disclosure of personal data. If data being withheld pertains to Barth's sexual behavior, that is understandable though regrettable. No subject is more difficult for the public to deal with, nor any subject more inviting to sensational journalism. As the Orthodox theologian Nicolas Berdayev put it, "No other sphere of life is so vitiated by hypocrisy and cowardice."[71]

If the archives are shielding Barth's personal life, even more significant is the fact that hundreds of Barthian theologians have made no public reference to the issue, a theological version of the emperor's new clothes. Typical is the very astute translator of Barth, John Bowden, who in his brief biography, *Karl Barth*, wrote, "In 1929 Charlotte von Kirschbaum joined him as his secretary, to stand by Barth in his work and to share his home."[72] That was it. It is nothing short of incredible how gingerly the subject is treated.

---

71 *The Destiny of Man,* New York: Harper and Row, 1960, p. 232.
72 Bowden, *op.cit.* (1971), p. 57.

IX

An examination of Barth's theological writings on sex, love, and marriage cannot ignore the details of his biography, a requirement that at least Martin Rumscheidt seems to understand. Barth's personal life does make a difference to any assessment of his teaching on sex, love, and marriage. His theology is so often read, and rightly so, in light of his courageous "No" to Hitler. So his teaching on sex, love, and marriage must be read in light of Charlotte von Kirschbaum. John Bowden has said in other contexts, "[Barth's] theology is not complete without the man himself."[73]

Barth is especially problematic in this respect because he had so much to say on the subject of sex, love, and marriage. Furthermore, he was averse to creating a philosophical system. His refusal to write "a systematic theology" was deliberate and intentional. His *Church Dogmatics* are his attempt to write a theology that is not "a system." In this sense he was, like Luther, rooted in the biblical mode. His work has a deliberately ad hoc character. Like Luther, he was very little concerned that he appear consistent. He was also very determined to keep himself unimpressed by the values of his social class. He viewed with suspicion every cherished value of the middle class, referring disdainfully to "bourgeois respectability."[74] Much of what Barth wrote on the subject of sex, love, and marriage is congruent with what we know of his personal life, but some of what he wrote is not, at least on the face of it, and bears close scrutiny. We will examine first the congruent material and then the more problematic.

No theologian in modern times seeks to be less influenced by the ideology of Greco-Roman philosophy and religion, and no one is more self-consciously Hebraic in religious posture than Barth. This is so even though, as Jurgen Moltmann points out, Barth was not entirely successful in separating himself from platonist dualism.[75] He is the theologian most steeped in Hebraic anthropology since Luther. He brooks no divinization of human life, whose creaturely status must not be evaded and whose feet must be planted squarely on the earth. This view of the

---

73 *Ibid.*, p. 117. See also Robert McAfee Brown, "Spirituality and Liberation," *St. Luke's Journal of Theology*, Vol. 24, No. 3, June 1986, p. 184.
74 *Church Dogmatics* III/4, p. 135.
75 Address to the International Congress on Pastoral Care and Counseling, Melbourne, Aug. 25, 1987.

human being as an earthly creature, and in no sense a quasi-divine spirit, is the foundation stone of Barth's approach to sexual ethics.

"The relationship between a man and a woman," says Barth, "neither requires nor is capable of any divinization, whether from below or from above, whether by eros or by the church . . . It is already blessed . . . the whole relationship is manifested in its creatureliness . . . We must leave them on earth under heaven . . ."[76] Furthermore, even to swear eternal love is a sentimental blunder.[77]

"The command of God requires no liberation from sex. Nor does it require any denial or repression of sex."[78] On the other hand, "a certain healthy limitation of the dominance and exercise of the physical sexual impulse" is required.[79]

Like Luther, Barth acknowledges that the discrimination against eros in Christian tradition is a very old mistake. He clearly and unambiguously rejects the supposed "higher perfection of celibate life," which he maintains in some sense "menaces the whole sphere of male-female relationships." An asexual or neutral humanity is a rejection of creatureliness. Such evasions are powerful temptations for some, but they are disobedience of the God who made us male or female.[80]

To be created male or female is "immediately to be completed and transcended by male *and* female."[81] The "and" is included in the "or." Barth is not alluding to the Jungian categories of bi-sexuality here, such as is promoted in the anima/animus theory. In fact, Barth had something of an aversion to psychoanalysis in general. What he is claiming here is that neither gender has a right to an autonomous life of its own, but is commanded to live only in relation to the other. Barth is thus profoundly affirming of the man-woman relationship.

In Barth's view, man and woman belong together. They must answer to each other for their existence. The relationship between the differentiated male and female, the radically different others, is a metaphor for the human fellowship into which the whole family of mankind is called. "Humanity which is not fellow humanity is inhumanity." Fellow humanity is most essentially characterized in the union of the differentiated male and female. Furthermore, Barth goes so far as to assert that

---

76 *Church Dogmatics* III/4, p. 129.
77 Karl Barth, *Ethics,* Dietrich Brown, ed., G. W. Bromiley, trans., New York: Seabury Press, 1981, p. 239.
78 *Church Dogmatics* III/4, p. 131.
79 *Ibid.,* p. 239.
80 *Ibid.,* pp. 124, 161.
81 *Ibid.,* p. 118; *Ethics,* p. 181.

the sexual union is the "image of God" in humankind because God himself exists in relation, not in isolation, and particularly in relationship with the wholly other. In light of this it should not be surprising when Barth asserts that the Hebrew requirement that everyone marry remains an obligation for Christians. The Hebrew requirement is only loosened. It is not removed.[82]

Barth acknowledges that the orientation of the sexes to one another is troublesome to many, precisely because man and woman must give account to each other for their humanity. This creates a certain unsettlement, but cannot be an excuse to retreat into single gender groups, such as men's clubs and women's circles. He chides: "Who commands or permits them to run away from each other?"[83] Idiosyncratically and typical of Barth, he labels war "a dubious affair" simply because it is exclusively male. "On either side of the trenches male cannot see female, whether mother, wife, or sister."[84]

If Barth is affirming of the man/woman relationship and even of marriage itself, he has harsh words for the typical Western marriage ceremony; "a dreadful and deeprooted error," he calls it.[85] The marriage ceremony itself epitomizes that spiritualization or divinization of the human enterprise of which Barth is so leery. For the modern Western Christian the wedding is probably the grandest liturgical event of a lifetime, certainly the most costly, overshadowing any other sacrament or liturgical event. Barth asserts that the church should get out of the marriage business as it now stands. "The so-called marriage altar is a free invention of the flowery speech of modern religion," he says.[86] He lauds a certain modern cleric, Hermann Kutter, who from a certain date flatly refused to marry his parishioners, in spite of considerations of ecclesiastical order. Barth wants to bring marriage back down to earth. What kind of ceremony would he propose? The proper form "has still to be found," but it should be rid of both its quasi-civil and its sacramental character. These Barthian teachings are congruent with the biography of Barth the man.

However, some of Barth's writing on sex, love, and marriage seems incongruent with the facts of his personal life. For example, he seems a bit prudish or conventionally middle class at points. He comments on the life of a certain 17th century Lutheran pastor, Abraham Calor, who is on

---

82 *Church Dogmatics III/4*, pp. 88-90.
83 *Ibid.*, p. 165.
84 *Ethics*, p. 187.
85 *Church Dogmatics III/4*, p. 225.
86 *Ibid.*, p. 228.

record as having married his sixth wife at age 72, only four months after the death of his fifth. Says Barth, "Some slight restraint by those passages in the Pastorals (Barth interpreted I Timothy 3:2 & Titus 1:6 as limiting bishops to one wife for life, a questionable exegesis. See above, p. 78), or a modicum of the ideal of romantic love and its possible consequences, would not have been bad for this man."[87] Calor had done nothing illicit, but apparently his urgency to replace his deceased wives Barth considered unseemly. The alacrity with which Calor remarried may have appeared indecorous by respectable middle class norms, but Calor's life story is the kind one would expect from someone immersed in Hebrew anthropology, and one we would expect Barth to approve. Besides that, in one's eighth decade a four-month wait can be half a lifetime.

Barth also demonstrates prudishness in his dismissal of D. H. Lawrence, who "left nothing to be desired . . . but definitely went too far in mentioning the unmentionable and emphasizing to the exclusion of all else, what was not customarily emphasized."[88] This is puzzling coming from a theologian who was both in word and deed disdainful of "bourgeois respectability" and himself quite affirming of the erotic in word and deed.

Other parts of Barth's writing are not only incongruent but seriously problematic in light of his biography. For example, he maintains that monogamy, even "inflexible monogamy," is commanded by Jesus Christ. He writes:

> . . . marriage, even though its form may be questionable and imperfect, is unquestionably and perfectly the full life-partnership of two human beings and therefore exclusive in relation to any third party . . . the requirement of fidelity, or rather the invitation, permission and liberation for fidelity in the strict meaning of the term . . . constancy of orientation on this chosen partner to the exclusion of any third party whatever . . . monogamy and exclusive love [are] imperiously . . . [but] not legally demanded . . .[89]

Further on he writes, "In faith we say in marriage: This woman and no other! This man and no other! In faith, we may say even in love: This partner or none!"[90] As for the polygamy of the Old Testament, Barth

---

87 *Ibid.*, p. 202.
88 *Ibid.*, p. 135.
89 *Ibid.*, p. 198.
90 *Ibid.*, p. 199.

says it was practiced quite unthinkingly. Even though no objection is raised against it in scripture, somewhere in the background monogamy seems to be envisioned as true marriage. To say the very least, this kind of writing appears to be a judgment on Barth's own life.

How Barth made the connection between his theological ethics and his own practice may never be fully known, unless further data is forthcoming. Anyone familiar with Barth knows certainly that *he* made the connection some way or another. We can, however, hazard a guess. As we have seen, Barth was not likely constrained by "what people thought." Obviously he wasn't, or he would not have moved Lollo into his home, certainly an inflammatory gesture. Had she kept her own apartment as most middle class persons would have done in similar situations, and had he not openly traveled and vacationed with her, he could better have been able to maintain the appearance of her as secretary, no matter what their relationship in private. Barth was of a different stripe. In his view there was no relationship between the monogamy that Jesus commands and the middle class practice of it, which has only the deceptive appearance of obedience. Still we are left with the discrepancy between what "Jesus commands" according to Barth and his own bigamous life.

It is important to state here that the question underlying everything Barth wrote was, "What is commanded of us by God?" About his own situation in particular, Barth must have said something like this: "Jesus commands monogamy imperiously but not legally. Within that commandment the obedient servant does what can be done in his own broken situation. However far short anyone falls does not dilute the requirements of the divine commandment. In any case, we are redeemed not by any measure of our obedience to the commandment, but only by God's mercy. The most obedient monogamist deludes himself if he thinks he escapes judgment under this commandment."

As for the suggestion that Barth should have divorced Nelly and married Lollo since the latter was *really* his wife, Barth would likely have heaped venom on such a suggestion as rooted in the desire for the appearance of morality. Barth might well have responded to such a wish by saying, like Luther, that it is better to marry two wives than to divorce one to have the other.

We can conjecture that Barth, though acknowledging to himself his own bigamous situation, continued to believe that monogamy is in fact commanded. A man of rigorous thinking like Barth would not likely permit himself shortcuts and cheap solutions in his theological thought for purposes of accommodating his own situation. If such a conjecture is plausible, we have to admire Barth's steadfastness in writing a theology that judges even its author. That is precisely the point about Barth. No one is more likely to write such a theology. (At the same time we cannot applaud Barth's lack of personal candor. We may forgive it as a disease of the times he lived in, but it can hardly be an example for our time.)

Other clues are scattered through Barth's writings that may well reflect on his assessment of his own forty years of functional bigamy. In a discussion of "relationships which cannot flower in *regular* marriage," he says,

> . . . they are not mere sin and shame . . . they do not wholly lack the character of marriage. Furthermore, in this sphere especially there is to be noted a certain zealously practised restraint against the desire or preference for strange fruit . . . They simply cannot stand in the face of God's command . . . they are simply a heap of ruins. They can be good only on the basis of God's sin-forgiving grace and within its limits. They can be regarded as relatively good only through faith. But we must not forget that the arch of the divine command spans the whole reality . . . there is here no one who is not struck by the divine judgment, [and] . . . no one who is not reached by the divine mercy and in his own way held and comforted. *Thus even where man does not keep the command, the command keeps man.*

Barth's relationship with Lollo, then, was perhaps "a heap of ruins" made acceptable only by God's mercy.

Barth was certainly thinking either of Nelly or Lollo or both when he wrote,

> . . . and if there is no perfect marriage, there are marriages which for all their imperfection can be and are maintained and carried through, and in the last resort not without promise and joyfulness, arising with a certain necessity, and fragmentarily, at least, undertaken in all sincerity as a work of free-fellowship . . . *There is loyalty even in the midst of disloyalty and constancy amid open inconstancy*." (italics mine)[92]

---

91 *Ibid.*, p. 239.
92 *Ibid.*

From Luther to the Twentieth Century's Sexual Revolution

Finally, Barth surely was speaking for himself when he wrote, "As God's creatures we are possibly nowhere so much on our own as in respect of our sexuality."[93] And in the midst of a discussion of sex ethics he says with surprising candor, "Things could be totally different from what they seem."[94]

Any attempt to speak for Barth is a problematic undertaking. Even Barthians must live permanently with Barth's own disclaimer that he himself was not a Barthian. Hardly anyone could be more difficult to speak for. It is a great loss for theology and for humanity that we have no direct word from him as to how he processed theologically and ethically his own personal history with Nelly and Lollo.

If Tillich was reluctant to make connections between his personal sexual commitments and his theological constructs for political reasons, Barth declined to make the connection probably because he considered personal experience irrelevant in light of the divine commandment. That was simply Barth's way of doing theology. In looking back on the lives and work of these two men, we can now see what they could not, that theological constructs demand connections to or at least congruence with personal experience. We can also see what they apparently could not, that the privatization of sexual behavior is debilitating and was probably a malevolent contributing factor in their silence about their own personal sexual histories.

In the examples of their lives---no small matter in religious traditions---both Barth and Tilich have presented the religious community in the 20th century with a disruptive challenge to its conventional notions of sex and marriage. In their respective lives they were harbingers of the sexual revolution to come, which arrived as their day was ending. The challenge they presented consists not of private indiscretions, but of consciously made life choices which went against the stream of the modern Western religious consensus. Each in his own way demonstrated in practice a radical critique of the Western sacralization of monogamy which must be taken seriously. Most theologians remain mute and perplexed before the biographies of these two theological giants of the 20th century. Their respective private lives may have been incomprehensible to their own generation, but that need not be the case to a generation that has lived through the sexual revolution.

---

93 *Ethics*, p. 227.
94 *Ibid.*, p. 187.

X

If Barth and Tillich participated in and by their participation furthered the cause of the emerging sexual revolution, so have numerous other lesser known theologians of both the Protestant and Roman Catholic traditions. The current literature is marked by the polarization of those who affirm and those who resist the basic implied tenets of the sexual revolution.

In the Roman Catholic tradition Michael Valente is one of the new theologians who welcomes the changes that have been taking place in sexual values. He contends that even the Vatican has made a significant step toward the affirmation of sexual pleasure for its own sake. Pope Pius XII's acceptance of the rhythm method of birth control, the use of periods of natural sterility (also known as "Vatican roulette"), is the first time in history that the Vatican has approved of sexual relations in which there is the intention not to procreate. Valente calls this "the most momentous of all decisions in the modern history of innovation in Roman Catholic sexual ethics."[95] He does not say whether he thinks this was a deliberate and strategic choice on the part of the Vatican, or a misstep. Furthermore, the Vatican itself, curiously enough, does not seem aware of the change. It continues to argue that sex is justified only by both parts of "the twofold purpose of sex---procreation and the love union."[96] The idea that a couple could legitimately engage in sexual relations with the deliberate intention of avoiding pregnancy departs from the teaching of Augustine and Thomas Aquinas, since in their view the intention to procreate is the good end upon which coitus depends for its justification. However meager this shift in viewpoint may seem to an outsider, Valente sees it as a sign of hope. Should the Vatican ever give its full blessing to sexual pleasure for its own sake, it will no doubt build on this frail beginning.

Valente himself wants to rehabilitate certain forgotten theologians in Roman Catholic history, such as the likes of Martin Le Maistre (1432-81), Thomas Sanchez (1550-1610), and Alphonsus Liguori (1697-1787), who similarly separated sex from the strict limitation of the intention to procreate, and argued that sexual intercourse had other legitimate pur-

---

95 Michael F. Valente, *Sex: The Radical View of a Catholic Theologian,* New York: The Bruce Publishing Co., 1970, p. 67.
96 See Charles E. Curran, *Tensions in Moral Theology,* Notre Dame, IN: University of Notre Dame Press, 1988, p. 75.

poses as well. Valente himself goes even further and questions whether sex should be limited exclusively to marriage. No moral valuation, he argues, can be placed on any sex act in isolation. Furthermore, he considers contraception a moral imperative in view of the world threat of overpopulation.[97]

The Catholic Theological Society of America also produced a radical volume in the 70's, the work of a committee headed by Anthony Kosnik called *Human Sexuality: New Directions in American Catholic Thought.* Kosnik and his committee proposed that the traditional purpose of sexuality be broadened, expanded from the traditional procreative and unitive (one-flesh) purposes. They sought to subject particular instances of sexual behavior to the criterion of whether they foster "creative growth toward integration."[98] The work was attacked with venom and rejected by the American Roman Catholic hierarchy. Kosnik joined the ranks of Roman Catholics who have lost teaching positions as a result of their writings.[99]

At points the work was facile, as for example when it concludes that "swinging" is probably immoral because it does not foster "creative growth toward integration." Swinging is an activity about which the committee of Catholic theologians undoubtedly knew next to nothing. Nevertheless, the work is a landmark of daring in the Roman Catholic world by the very fact that it attempts to subject particular sexual acts to such an innovative criterion. Kosnik and his committee unquestionably made a serious attempt to be faithful to some of the positive aspects of the sexual revolution. Furthermore, they produced a very significant work of reason and sensitivity whatever its flaws.

In addition to Valente and Kosnik many others have challenged the established postion of the Roman Catholic Church. Robert F. Francoeur and Andrew M. Greeley, writing from the fringe of that Church, are perhaps the most widely read.

No one has been more incisive in his critique of accepted tradition than the little known Jacques-Marie Pohier, a French Dominican. Pohier demonstrates his debt to Freud by emphasizing first that all pleasure is in some sense sexual and that, while both pleasure and sex are problematic from the outset, Christianity's attitude toward them both is itself equally problematic. He contends that Christianity has simply exacerbated the

---
97 Valente, *op.cit.,* pp. 118-132.
98 Anthony Kosnik, et alia, *Human Sexuality: New Directions in American Catholic Thought,* New York: Paulist Press, 1977, p. 86.
99 Curran, *op.cit.,* p. 76.

already conflict-ridden character of the human response to pleasure, and further, that Christians are oblivious to the problems posed by their own peculiar history in this matter. To illustrate his point Pohier compares the Christian approach to pleasure with a phobic who washes his hands fifty times a day, and who would have quite logical explanations for his actions, such as increased pollution, for example. Logical discourse with the hand-washer would be useless because his motivation lies outside the realm of logic and even outside consciousness itself. The hand-washer is not really burdened by the bacteria count but by the latent content hidden in the act of hand-washing itself. Pohier says the traditional Christian attitude toward pleasure and sexuality is similarly odd, and is an oddness no amount of logic could hope to dislodge. Something covert is at work in this odd and peculiar Christian attitude toward pleasure in general and sex in particular.

In an address to a gathering of sex educators in France on the subject of the Catholic faith and sex education, Pohier stirred up a hornets' nest of reaction. He reasoned that, as math teachers should themselves take pleasure in math and should wish for their students to take pleasure in doing it, so the same should be true of sex educators. Such brilliant insights were not appreciated by the Vatican. Pohier was suspended in 1979 and forbidden from teaching or leading conferences in the Roman Catholic Church.[100]

Pohier, of course, had gone public. How many others have sought to effect similar change secretly from within may never be known. Among the Jesuits, for example, it is rumored that a very serious and radical proposal made its way to the top echelon of that order in the late 70s. The proposal was to inaugurate a so-called "third-way" of sexual behavior in addition to celibacy and marriage. The third way was to be some kind of free sexual relationship. Oral tradition holds that the proposal was discussed at the highest administrative level of the order and was finally rejected by the Superior General who at that time was the progressive, liberal Pedro

---

[100] Jacques-Marie Pohier, "Pleasure and Christianity," in *Concilium: Religion in the Seventies, Vol. 100, Sexuality in Contemporary Catholicism,* Franz Bockle & Jacques-Marie Pohier, eds., New York: Seabury Press, 1976, pp. 103-9.

From Luther to the Twentieth Century's Sexual Revolution

Arruppe. Arruppe is said to have been very sympathetic but unwilling to back such a radical innovation.

Among Protestants, Rustum and Della Roy were the first to present themselves as theologically informed theoreticians of the emerging sexual revolution. They published a volume entitled *Honest Sex* [101] in 1968 in which they challenged from a religious perspective the demands of a sexually exclusivist monogamy. They especially pointed to the lack of justice in traditional monogamy, calling attention to the forced sexual deprivation of middle-aged single women who have little hope of remarriage. The Roys proposed a concept of "co-marital" relationships in which persons might be committed to and intimately involved with each other in ways that transcend or go beyond traditional monogamy. Subsequently many other Protestant teachers and theologians have followed the lead of the Roys. James B. Nelson and Tom Driver have been perhaps the most widely read of the Protestant theologians who boldly acknowledge that sexual, even genital gratification need not be limited to the boundaries of monogamy.

Theologians and teachers in the various religious traditions have, of course, been affected by parallel work in other disciplines that has furthered the affirmation of the erotic. That is a story in its own right. Two who have been especially influential in promoting the redemption of eros are D. H. Lawrence and Lawrence Durrell. D. H. Lawrence had as much trouble with the guardians of middle class morality as Pohier has had with the Vatican. As recently as the 1950s it was a criminal offense in the United States to possess some of Lawrence's writings. Durrell, who came into prominence at mid-century, is more subtle than Lawrence, but equally bold and committed to redeeming the erotic. He observed that the reason Western Christians kneel in church is that one must kneel to enter a woman.[102]

By the fourth quarter of the 20th century the centuries-old orthodox Protestant and Roman Catholic consensus that sex should be restricted to the boundaries of monogamy has begun to disintegrate. Though the

---

101 New York: New American Library, 1968. See also Rustum and Della Roy, "Is Monogamy Outdated?", *The New Sexual Revolution,* Lester A. Kirkendall & Robert N. Whitehurst, eds., New York: Donald W. Brown, Inc., 1971, pp. 131-148.

102 Lawrence Durrell, *Clea,* New York: E. P. Dutton & Co, Inc., 1961, p. 70. The association of knees and sexuality is a fascinating subject in itself. See Frederick Mathewson Denny, "Knees," *The Encyclopedia of Religion,* Vol. 8, Mircea Eliade, ed., New York: Macmillan, 1987, p. 339, and R. B. Onians, *The Origins of European Thought About the Body, the Mind, the Soul, the World, Time and Fate,* 1951, pp. 174-180.

The Poisoning of Eros

religious majority still gives verbal assent to the traditional view, public behavior betrays them. Enough serious, thoughtful challenges have been offered to make it clear that the traditional view is no longer credible as the standard for religious people.

Chapter Seven
Toward a New Sex Ethics Of Carnal Reciprocity

Some wearied for a sex
Like a science of known relations:
A God proved through the flesh---or else a mother.
They dipped in this huge pond and found it
An ocean of shipwrecked mariners instead,
Cried out and foundered, losing one another.

But some sailed into this haven
Laughing, and completely undecided,
Expecting nothing more
Than the mad friendship of bodies,
And farewells undisguised by pride . . .
-- Lawrence Durrell*

Sexuality is the domain of all the difficulties, all the gropings, the dangers and the dilemma, the failure and the joy . . . A serious examination of sexuality is preferable to a eulogy of love.
-- Paul Ricoeur**

Most of the Christian West since the fourth century has been dominated by a vision inherited from the Greco-Roman world of sex as a fearsome and destructive force in human life. This is a distorted vision. A certain measure of fear and awe may be appropriate in the experience of sexuality itself, as adolescents know universally in an especially heightened way. This kind of fear and awe can be no acceptable basis for a negativity toward eros such as has emerged in Western culture. A negativity toward eros now can and should be supplanted by an ethics rooted in an affirmation of sexuality. From a poisoned eros we can now turn to a new ethical vision, one which might be characterized as an ethics of "carnal reciprocity," an image taken from the philosopher Paul Ricoeur.[1]

An ethics of carnal reciprocity permits, even asserts, that sexual self-actualization is preferable to sexual innocence, abstinence, and self-denial.

---

*   "The Adepts," *Collected Poems 1931-1974,* New York: Viking Penguin, 1980.
**   "Wonder, Eroticism, and Enigma," *Cross Currents,* Spring 1964, p. 133.
1   Ricoeur, op. cit., 1964, p. 136.

This boldly sex-affirming assertion draws principally from Hebraic sources of Western culture and rejects the dominance of the Greco-Roman syncretistic sex-negativity that has been brought forward through later Christendom. An ethics of carnal reciprocity affirms as well a commitment to human mutuality, the basic rhythm of giving and receiving that is at the heart of the human community. Consequently, it acknowledges the political implications of every sexual liaison. It promotes the paradigmatic character of pair-bonding which at once both affirms and delimits the claims of any particular form of pair-bonding, as well as any particular pair. Hence an ethics of carnal reciprocity is receptive to the challenge of what might be coming into being (the so-called eschatological challenge) by acknowledging the provisional character of any particular historical form of pair-bonding. Finally, an ethics of carnal reciprocity incorporates a certain measure of fear and awe of the experience of sexuality itself.

I

An ethics of carnal reciprocity promotes sexual self-actualization as a value that stands on its own and needs no extrinsic justification. It is subject to the same ethical criteria to which any other human activity might be subject. Sexual self-actualization does not need the intention to procreate as the Stoics and most Roman Catholic ethics have claimed, nor does it require adherence to the so-called unitive principle, the monogamist one-flesh ideal limiting sexual expression to a particular couple, as many religious and non-religious ethicists have claimed. The affirmation of sexual self-actualization means that, where there are no contraindications, it is better to do it than not to do it. As the British psychiatrist, David Cooper, puts it, we should begin with the premise that "making love is good in itself, and the more it happens in any way possible or conceivable between as many people as possible, the better."[2] The present herpes and AIDS crisis has about as little to do with sex values and ethics as a spate of air crashes have to do with flying. Many people may die and many more may become frightened, but one way or another human beings will take to the air, and not just by necessity but

---

2 David Cooper, *The Death of the Family*, New York: Pantheon Books, 1970, p. 45.

for pleasure. Even persons with AIDS have learned to practice "safe-sex"---a practice that is supposed to protect their partners. Safe sex is subject to the same moral scrutiny as unsafe sex.

The preference for sexual self-actualization could be called the principle of Jephthah's daughter, the biblical maiden who on learning that she had become a candidate for human sacrifice, requested and received a two-month grace period to mourn her virginity. (Jud 11:29-40) The preference for sexual self-actualization follows the spirit, though not the letter, of Hebraic and Talmudic sex ethics which require everyone to marry and anticipates everyone's having a continuing sexual relationship for purposes of sexual pleasure. This requirement to marry, as Barth says, is now loosened but not abolished. Luther and Tillich support this principle. Even Calvin, who commissioned friends to pick him a wife, supports it, though in a less-than-exuberant manner.

Any affirmation of sexual expression connotes, unfortunately, an affirmation limited to genital sexuality, since our culture clings to a pre-psychoanalytic naiveté. In fact, the whole body and its polymorphous forms of gratification are to be affirmed. Thus in Jewish and early Christian symbols the whole body is resurrected. So also pleasurable and gratifying eating and drinking together were made the central act of early Christian gatherings. Sexual self-actualization is rooted in religious materialism, a vision of human life as created for this world. The Hebraic vision of the "land of milk and honey" is a material vision of life in this world and radically opposed to the vision of human life created for some other world, however heavenly. In the Hebraic vision spirit enlivens the body---the whole body. The Jewish author of the messianic Book of Enoch in the second century BCE unabashedly portrays a very sensuous messianic kingdom:

And then shall all the righteous escape
And shall live till they beget thousands of children,
And all the days of their youth and their old age
Shall they complete in peace.[3]

---

3 I Enoch 10:17, R. H. Charles, trans., *The Apocrypha and Pseudepigrapha of the Old Testament, Vol. II, Pseudepigrapha*, Oxford: Clarendon Press, 1913.

One could dismiss the sensuality that is implied in begetting thousands of children by claiming that the real interest here was progeny. However, the Hebraic attitude toward sex from the biblical through the Talmudic tradition consistently valorized the pleasure of sex itself irrespective of any resulting children.

Much of what passes for later Christian spirituality eviscerates the body as well as despises the earth. Pope Pius XII promoted this kind of effete spirituality in an address on sex ethics in 1958 in which he proclaimed that "man is created, first and foremost, not for this world or for his life in time, but for heaven and eternity."[4] Whatever life may or may not wait beyond the grave, a subject about which no one including the pope really knows anything, human life was created, for the time being at least, for this particular world. Created for this world means among other things, created for sex. To refuse sexual self-actualization is to deny a significant, even crucial, aspect of human creatureliness.

The assertion of a preference for sexual self-actualization calls into question the sexual situation in many geriatric institutions in the United States where genital sexual expression is policed and suppressed. Enforced sexual abstinence for the elderly is both authoritarian and misguided. That persons in their eighth or ninth decades and beyond are still able to interest themselves in sex should be a cause for rejoicing, not police action. That marriage should be required to legitimize a sexual liaison at such an age is as ludicrous as it is legalistic.

This is not to propose a categorical deprecation of celibacy or sexual abstinence in certain situations for those who voluntarily choose it, but simply and unequivocally to remove such choices from their presumed positions of moral superiority and identify them as secondary or derivative. That is to say, in the spirit of Hebraic and Talmudic tradition the burden of moral proof is shifted from those who actualize themselves sexually to those who refuse. Celibacy or sexual abstinence might for good reason be chosen in extremis, so to speak, or as an emergency option in order to achieve some other good, such as humanitarian work that might benefit from temporary sexual abstinence. Such an option should be viewed as comparable to fasting, a temporary and derivative

---

4   Address of Pope Pius XII, Sept. 12, 1958, to the 7th International Hematological Congress in Rome.

option, but in no sense "the higher life," in fact, not even as fully a form of obedience as sexual self-actualization. Just as fasting can never be as holy as eating, so sexual abstinence can never be as holy as sexual expression. Often-heard claims of certain religious authorities that those who choose a life of sexual renunciation somehow belong uniquely to God, or that celibacy is a commitment to a deeper, more universal love than sexual self-actualization, should be rejected as nonsense. The truth is, as a former Roman Catholic priest, Charles Davis, wrote, "Celibacy as it has been lived and motivated in Christian history has more often than not been an impairment of the human spirit."[5] In the biblical narrative sex was invented not by the devil but by God, and is experienced by humankind as good in and of itself. We have no warrant to refuse categorically the pleasure of sex, and even much less so to refuse it and claim such refusal as a testament to special virtue. The Jewish sage Abba Aricha (c.175-247 CE, aka Rav) was undoubtedly thinking partly of sex when he said, "Man will have to render an account to God for all the good things which his eyes beheld but which he refused to enjoy."[6] Sexual self-actualization is therefore paradigmatic; sexual abstinence is not.

While sexual self-actualization should not be subverted by the idealization of purity and innocence, it is, like all human activity, subject to moral scrutiny. First of all, it should be tempered by the judgment of what makes for creative and growth-oriented interpersonal relations and whether a given liaison is expressive of or contributes to mutual love and concern. Interpersonal exploitation, inattention to individual idiosyncrasies in personal development, and disregard for readiness and timing of the other are the negative expressions of an untempered, unreflective, and inordinately narcissistic self-actualization. Such guidelines were followed by Anthony Kosnik and his committee when they produced their pioneering and much abused study, *Human Sexuality*, for the Catholic Theological Society of America in 1977.

---

5   Charles Davis, *Body As Spirit,* New York: Seabury Press, 1976, p. 142.
6   Jerusalem Talmud, Qiddushin 4:12, Robert Gordis, trans.

Sexual self-actualization is shaped, furthermore, by its own inherent polymorphous character. Sexual activities which until recent decades have been considered unmentionably shocking, such as masturbation, homosexuality, swinging, and the like, should be tested in part by the criteria of whether they are rooted in caring, reciprocal interpersonal relations and expressive of love and concern for the other as well as the self. While heterosexual expression may be paradigmatic, it is unnecessarily rigid to expect that any particular individual will actualize the self only within the bounds of the paradigmatic. The church's historic fascination with masturbation, or what it calls "solitary sins" in the devotional literature, is entirely irrelevant and rooted in its crypto-dualistic disdain for sexual expression in any form. Some amount of masturbation may be essential in the process of nurturing self-love. It is difficult to see how one could fully value one's own sexual capacity without the experience of masturbation. David Cooper says "one can never love another person until one can love oneself enough, on every level, including the level of proper, (full, orgasmic) masturbation---at least once with joy."[7]

The only potential fault in masturbation is its solitariness, which makes it therefore the paradigmatically narcissistic sexual act. Masturbation, therefore, must be ultimately less highly valued than an interpersonal sexual encounter simply because relationship is the deepest meaning of sex. Sex is integral to the assessment that, as Genesis (2:18) puts it, "it is not good for man to be alone." So the humorous saying is true that the only thing wrong with masturbation is that "one does not meet many nice people that way."[8]

One should not be carried away by a resolve to avoid narcissism, which is essentially self-love and as such is required. The potential sin or sickness in narcissism is the loss of the radically other in relationship.

---

[7] David Cooper, *op.cit.*, p. 36. John Money claims that rhesus monkeys in laboratory experiments that are prohibited from pre-pubertal sexual play, such as mock copulation, are not able to copulate at maturity. (Address to Planned Parenthood Society of Southwest Virginia, Inc, April 21, 1988, "Love, Sex, and Medicine." See also *Lovemaps*, New York: Irvington Publishers, 1986; *Venuses Penuses,* Buffalo: Prometheus Books, 1986.) Human parents who work at protecting their children from early sexual stimulation might well reflect on such data and wonder what parallels there are in human development.

[8] Haim G. Ginot, *Between Parent and Teenager*, New York: The Macmillan Co., 1969, p. 169.

Therefore a warning about narcissism provides an appropriate monitoring principle within the task of self-actualization. Narcissism itself stands under moral judgment only because and to the extent to which the radically other is injured or neglected. A check on narcissism must not lead to the loss of the love of self. The commandment is, after all, to love the neighbor *as oneself.* Herbert Marcuse is helpful here in distinguishing between two kinds of narcissism, one which is turned inward, and the other in which self-love leads to reaching out to the other.[9]

Homosexuality, one of the variants of polymorphic sexuality, is a union with the "other" who is "not the other" but the same gender, and is, like masturbation, also vulnerable to a critique of excessive or inwardly turned narcissism. At present a heated debate is taking place in the religious as well as the psychological community about whether it is possible to make any kind of value judgment that is negative toward homosexuality. Some argue, as James Nelson does, that homosexuality is "just as natural" as heterosexuality.[10] Up to a point it is a persuasive argument, and it is supported by Freud's assertion of the basic and universal bi-sexuality inherent in all human personality. Psychoanalytic theory also characterizes the so-called "latency" period (age 6 to puberty) in human development as a homosexual stage through which developing persons pass. Stages of personal development, according to psychoanalytic theory, are never completely left behind. Such assertions radically affect the shape of the moral question. If Freud is correct, homosexuality is as basic to human development as, for example, oral dependency is. It is a well-known phenomenon that certain persons, particularly women, easily adopt homosexual behavior in prison life and often return to a predominantly heterosexual life on release from confinement. This suggests that in certain cases homosexuality for some may be simply preferable to no interpersonal sexual gratification at all. Such adaptive behavior may actually be a sign of emotional health in demonstrating resilience of character. Thus homosexual gratification can be seen in part simply as a variant of the many forms of bodily gratifica-

---

9 Herbert Marcuse, *Eros and Civilization,* Boston: Beacon Press, 1955, p. 168.
10 James B. Nelson, *Between Two Gardens,* New York: Pilgrim Press, 1983, p. 122.

tion, with no prima facie culpability. The naturalness of homosexuality has undoubtedly been the foundation on which the Episcopal Bishop of New York, Paul Moore, declared publicly that homosexuality "was not a question of morality."[11] However, such a sweeping and unambiguous declaration of a moral free zone, though comforting to some, is not persuasive.

Unfortunately, the present cultural context that is polarized by homophobia on the one side and "gay pride" on the other does not invite serious reflection on the ethical implications of homosexuality. Given the long history of homophobia, persecution, and imperialistic heterosexual politics, it is at least questionable whether a heterosexual has a right even to speak on the subject. One could question whether it is even morally acceptable for a heterosexual to raise a single word of critique about homosexuality as a life pattern without aiding and abetting those who mercilessly persecute homosexuals. The present polarized situation is like wartime where any critical judgment is inevitably used as ammunition in the war effort.

Even in the present unpromising and belligerent context the tough questions must nevertheless be posed. The principal question is of course whether homosexuality as a long-term life pattern is morally neutral and whether it holds moral parity with heterosexuality. In 1973 Seward Hiltner warned about the modern liberal drift toward reducing homosexuality to nothing more than a civil rights issue. He expressed alarm at the well-intentioned but "simple-minded approbation to all homosexual behavior that is not exploitative."[12] To consider Hiltner's abrasive challenge requires that the question of the morality of homosexuality be seriously discussed, a task not easily undertaken in the present atmosphere.

Aside from the present polemical context, the question needs to be asked whether it would really be so catastrophic were it to become clear that a long-term commitment to a homosexual life is less than what is commanded. Do we not make the same judgment of divorced persons, that divorce is off the mark of what is commanded? Being divorced offers no basis for pride or boasting, but is rather one of the marks of the brokenness of human life. Of course, unlike divorce homosexuality may be as some

---

11 Quoted in *The New York Times,* Mar. 2, 1987.
12 "Kinsey and the Church---Then and Now," *The Christian Century,* May 30, 1973, p. 628.

argue a result of genetic make-up. If that were found to be so, we should not consider it a moral issue. At present it is simply not known to what extent genetics, environment, and choice contribute respectively to a homosexual life. But even if genetics were found to be the principal origin of homosexuality, we would still not be obliged to give it parity with heterosexuality. Like drawfism, we might view it simply as a genetic affliction.

Affliction is actually an appropriate characterization of life-long homosexuality, whether by genes, environment or choice. Like divorce and dwarfism, it is not a destiny anyone would willingly seek for her children. Each of the three is outside the paradigm, off the mark of what is commanded, whether by some genetic or hormonal error or by human decision-making. However, a compassionate community surely would regard each of these as "beloved afflictions" and would provide special protection for all such people just because they are outside the paradigm. Can we not imagine how reprehensible a community would be that persecuted dwarfs or divorced persons? Those who persecute homosexuals are equally deserving of censure.

Dwarfs, divorced persons, and homosexuals each in their own way mock the paradigm. They mock normalcy. They should, therefore, be treated not only with special compassion, but also with a certain humor and irony. Dwarfs have traditionally found some of this in the circus. The spirit of the circus is not sadistic. In the circus generally a loving laughter greets dwarfs. Homosexuality should similarly evoke our affectionate laughter. As sex itself is funny, homosexual sex is even funnier! A little more circus is called for, a little more humor about the variations and distortions and twists of human existence. Such an attitude might lead to special protection and special nurture in the human community for homosexuals, as well as for others whom life has in one way or another twisted.

Human history demonstrates a propensity to abuse and destroy the odd, the queer, those outside the norm. They provide the litmus test of a compassionate community. Any community should be judged by the manner in which it treats such persons. Thus a compassionate community would form homosexual support groups, not for the purpose of promoting homosexuality as such, but to support and nurture those who, for whatever cause, are decidedly homosexual. Such support groups would assist homosexuals in "making do with" their homosexuality. A compassionate community would even provide assistance in finding appropriate sexual partners among homosexuals. Only in such a compassionate and loving context might it thus be permissible to declare that a homosexual life pattern is an evasion of heterosexuality and is probably less than what is commanded of us.

II

An ethics of carnal reciprocity suggests that any sexual act which involves more than one person has political implications, and such implications beg examination.[13] A particular sexual liaison always has some meaning or significance to other people and thereby affects the community. This assertion runs directly counter to the accepted standards of the privatization of sexual behavior that are so deeply rooted in the Protestant middle class, namely that what two people do in private is no one else's business. This is not to suggest that any and every wish or preference of the community should be imbued with final authority, much less of a tyrannical sort, over individual decision-making. One has only to witness the absurd demands of the so-called sodomy laws of the various states in the United States to see how irrelevant some public standards have been at various times. However, in spite of such aberrations, the necessity of taking into account the significance to the community of a particular sexual liaison remains.

The issue of the politics of sexuality has two foci: the implications for persons directly involved in the sexual liaison and the implications for the community at large. In other words any liaison should give consideration to a covenant that may exist between persons, and consideration should be given to ways in which a liaison may affect also the larger community, as for example, any children who may issue from such a liaison. As Jacob Neusner says of the Talmudic perspective, "There is no sexual deed without public consequences."[14] The Old Testament commandment proscribing adultery is an example of precisely this kind of politically motivated regulation. The biblical commandment against adultery has little to do with sex as such, has nothing to do with monogamy, and certainly has nothing to do with sexual purity as an ideal. The invasion or intrusion

---

13 Esp. helpful here is Stanley Hauerwas, "Sex and Politics: Bertrand Russell and *Human Sexuality,*" *The Christian Century,* Vol. 95, Ap. 19, 1978, pp. 417- 22.
14 Jacob Neusner, *op cit.,* p. 143.

into a private domain in contravention of an existing covenant is the concern that motivates the Torah's prohibition of adultery. As Paul Lehmann (following Luther) points out, the commandment means: "Thou shalt not break in and break up a marriage."[15] Neither the Jews nor Luther were concerned as we tend to be today about the specific question of sex outside the bounds of marriage. The commandment proscribing adultery in fact applied only to married women, not to men in their relationships with unattached women. Both the Jews and Luther were concerned that the community respect and protect marital covenants. Following the spirit of the Talmudic tradition and Luther we should attend to the political dimension of any sexual liaison.

It is very important to note in this context that a particular act of adultery, therefore, stands under moral judgment only to the extent of its political malfeasance. Thus, for example, adultery cannot be "adultery" when it is mutually and freely agreed upon by the parties concerned, as in open marriages, swinging, spouse-swapping, and the like. Though such activities are adultery by dictionary definition, they do not qualify as morally reprehensible when the adultery commandment is seen as a politically-based requirement.

The issue is illustrated in an actual case of a fifty-seven year-old man known to the writer who has been comfortably institutionalized for thirteen years, suffering from increasingly debilitating multiple sclerosis. He is active and mobile in a motorized wheelchair, though he needs assistance in getting in and out of bed and chair. In the seventh year of his hospitalization he learned from his children that his wife had taken a lover. His marital relationship had become increasingly distant during his hospitalization, though he and his wife were certainly not unfriendly. In fact, they continue in many ways to demonstrate tender affection toward each other. He still goes home for holidays, a very elaborate process, and he still has pictures of his wife and children tacked to the wall of his hospital room. However she visits him rarely, perhaps twice a year, in the hospital. On one occasion, with his approval, she brought her lover along, an episode that did not seem to disturb the patient. Neither the patient nor his wife has entertained the idea of divorce. During his hospitalization he has developed a series of sexual relation-

---

15 Paul Lehmann, "The Decalogue and the Parameters of a Human Future," *Association for Clinical Pastoral Education Conference,* 1981, p. 41.

ships with other patients, some of which have had durations of several years. Even though he now lacks the use of his lower extremities and is genitally impotent, he can and does perform sexually to the apparent satisfaction of his present lover. Perhaps in a more perfect world this man and his wife would have shown more continuing interest in each other, sexually and otherwise. For whatever reasons, that has not occurred in this case, and neither seems to begrudge the fact. The marriage has become something of a shell of its former self, and given the patient's extended and permanent hospitalization that development is not surprising. The relationship nevertheless continues to be maintained, and not without a particular kind of loving-kindness that they show each other. This is a case of double adultery by dictionary definition, but for both the patient and his wife their actions are politically and morally benign and therefore cannot be regarded as reprehensible given the facts as they are known.

The second focus within the political implications of sexual relationships is that of the effect on the community at large of a particular liaison, and particularly the community's interest in any children that issue from such relationships. Only in the most punitive and rudimentary ways do political institutions in the United States demonstrate an interest in the conditions under which children are reared. If children are flagrantly abused, for example, they are subject to removal from their natural parents and placed in an institution or with an adoptive family. But in large measure, this aspect of the political dimension of sexual relationships is concealed from awareness by the cultural screen of privatism and individualism, a sacred and costly tenet of the capitalist industrial world. It posits that the number of children a couple decides to bring into the world is a private matter. In fact, every child brought into the world is in a profound sense everyone's business. Stanley Hauerwas, a Duke University ethicist, is correct in critiquing Anthony Kosnik for ignoring the political dimensions of sexual behavior and attempting to build a sex ethics as if the well-being and creativity of the individual were the singular guiding principle.

An historical episode illustrates modern unawareness on this issue. According to popular wisdom today, King Henry VIII of England was driven by his sexual insatiability to marry his six wives. This is a particularly individualistic and distorted view of Henry's motivation. The truth is that, however much lust may have driven Henry, and it was undoubtedly something of a factor, Henry's deeper obsession was to sire a male heir to his throne. We forget today that in sixteenth-century England the stability of the entire social order depended upon the orderly and unambiguous transition of power from one royal generation to the next. It was a matter of utmost concern, even anxiety, to Henry and the whole nation. Failure to leave a credible heir would be comparable in the United States to the Constitution's expiring at the death of a President. Probably the most disturbing and disruptive thing a ruler could do was to leave the matter of his successor in question. Of all Henry's wives only the third was able to bear a not-very-healthy son. His wives were one after another notoriously incapable of producing a viable male child, whether by his fault or theirs. From within the sixteenth century bias against succession given to daughters, it could not be foreseen that Henry's daughter, Elizabeth, would turn out to be one of the most effective rulers in English history. The sexual life of Henry was in any case no private matter, but an urgent political concern of the entire nation. It was the primary motivating force in his rush from one marriage to the next.[16]

In a similar way, but in a different context, what happens in any particular bedroom is always potentially the concern of the whole human community. Whoever decides to have a child in some way or another affects the community because she brings into the world and shapes someone with whom the community must relate. A child born, reared, and abused in the urban slums today is one who likely will be waiting to return the abuse on some street corner in a very few years. The United States has up to now been able to afford the luxury of an individualistic and privatistic attitude toward childbirth. China, on the other hand, in the face of a desperate population explosion, has by necessity recognized and openly acknowledged that each new birth is the entire community's concern. Couples have therefore been limited to one child, and those who break the law are subject to severe civil and criminal penalties. We in the West may react with shock to such restrictions on individual prerogatives, but no one can dispute the disruptive, perhaps catastrophic social consequences had China elected to permit its population explosion to continue.

---

16 I am indebted to C. F. Allison for this insight. See also Jack Goody, *The Development of the Family and Marriage in Europe,* New York: Cambridge University Press, 1983, p. 185.

In many other national communities the catastrophic consequences of population trends are social disruptions waiting for us down the road. Mexico's population explosion, for example, is actually a burgeoning of the campesinos, the marginalized rural poor, who are flooding the larger cities and procreating in geometric proportions. It is disingenuous to pretend that these developments will fail to produce a bitter harvest. In this context the Roman Catholic Church's opposition to effective family planning is merely stoking the fires of the coming disorder that no amount of idealism can assuage.

In the United States the crisis is far less dramatic. Nevertheless, our privatistic notions of childbearing and rearing have increasingly threatened to render our larger cities uninhabitable. Large sections of urban America are even now unsafe even in daylight. Urban slums increasingly are becoming urban nurseries. The marginalized poor in the United States, as in Mexico, are reproducing at higher rates than the middle class. When an increasing proportion of the population is born and reared in poverty ghettos, where it does not share in the cultural achievements of the community, the community itself is designing radical, even revolutionary, cultural change for the future. Culturally deprived toddlers in the slums today are not likely to listen to Beethoven and read Shakespeare tomorrow. Ultimately, the coming upheaval might be even for the best, and might achieve higher cultural forms in the long run. It is important, however, for any community to be aware of the political consequences of its own sexual values and behavior, particularly so when its direction is the self-destruction of its own culture.

III

An ethics of carnal reciprocity promotes the paradigmatic character of pair-bonding. Pair-bonding thus has the force of a benign paradigm and a set of attending problems.[17] The paradigm asserts the profoundly dyadic character of human existence but at the same time refuses to elevate cosmically any particular dyad. The special ethical problems of a committed pair of any sort are partially clarified in particular ways by the works of

---

17 C. Benton Cline, "Marriage Today: A Theological Carpetbag," *Journal of Pastoral Care,* Vol. 33, Mar., 1979, p. 26.

Victor Turner, Paul Ricoeur, and Sigmund Freud, respectively from the disciplines of anthropology, philosophy, and psychology.

Pair-bonding as such may or may not take on a marital or quasi-marital character. However, for clarity's sake we must maintain a clear distinction between pair-bonding, the coming together on some basis of two persons, and marriage itself, which is a complex social institution bearing meaning that is quite variable from culture to culture, and sometimes from generation to generation. For example, Friedrich Engels has demonstrated persuasively how modern monogamy is inextricably bound with the economic principle of private property and the political principle of the modern state, and how each of these three institutions is bound to and defined by the others. According to Engels, marriage in the modern West is defined as monogamy married to capitalism and nationalism.[18]

That pair-bonding deserves the power of a paradigm at all is supported by the fact that man and woman are created physically a mutually contingent pair. Man and woman must answer to each other for their existence, as Barth says.[19] They belong to each other. Once a pair unite only estrangement separates them. Estrangement and discontinuity are struggled against in any striving to create community. This would seem to be the basis for Jesus' contention that any divorce/remarriage is adultery.

Pair-bonding as a benign paradigm emphasizes the contention that it is only a paradigm and as such must not be transformed into a tyrant. The strength or power of a particular pair-bond can therefore vary greatly in the course of an individual life and at various times may or may not be given physical expression. While a lifelong heterosexual pair-bond may be the most deeply fulfilling in terms of significance and intimacy as Ricoeur seems to argue, neither homosexual pair-bonds nor a life pattern of multiple, less than lifelong, relationships should be ruled out in principle.

The popular notion that sexual expression should be limited absolutely to the bounds of a single bonded pair has no unequivocal historical,

---

18 Friedrich Engels, *The Origin of the Family, Private Property and the State*, New York: International Publishers, 1970.
19 *Church Dogmatics III/4*, p. 167.

philosophical, ethical, or theological support. Even within a lifelong marital heterosexual relationship sexual expression need not necessarily be limited to that relationship. Open marriages in their various forms cannot be ruled out in principle. They may be painfully difficult to manage, may create time-consuming problems in interpersonal relationships, and may be socially unacceptable to the respectable bourgeoisie. But for certain bonded pairs at certain times these or similar options may be quite life-giving, creative, and humanizing. David Cooper, among others, argues in fact that pairs should not close their relationship to exclude other sexual liaisons.[20] He adds that closed pairs tend to be quite vulnerable to becoming parasitic relationships where each becomes hidden inside the other's mind. Nor should sexual expression be thought limited to its genital forms, as if to adopt a pre-psychoanalytic naiveté. However, genital expression is without doubt experienced as the ultimate intimacy, and therefore as the most problematic form of sexual expression.

The issue of sexual exclusiveness is one of the most intractable problems for any form of pair-bonding. No other issue so powerfully threatens committed relationships. The threat comes from two directions, from the anxiety created when a commitment to sexual exclusiveness is absent or becomes loosened, and from the burden of oppression experienced when exclusiveness is rigidly adhered to. An abundance of recent literature increasingly supports the viability of pair-bonding that is not absolutely exclusive sexually. One should never underestimate the personal and emotional cost of such a venture, however. Perhaps part of the tragic character of human existence is that any committed pair must choose either a measure of depression from too tight a bond or a measure of anxiety from one that is too loose. The dream of the golden mean is only a dream. (Sociopathic relationships based on the "promise anything and do as you please" principle do not warrant discussion in this context.)

From the discipline of anthropology Victor Turner has brought some significant new insights toward understanding this intractable issue in particular and marriage as an institution in general. Marriage, he says, should be understood in the context of a dialectic of "structure and anti-structure." Marriage is a social framework, which is to say, a structure. Structure is an inevitable dimension of human social life and it takes many forms. It is

---

20 David Cooper, *op.cit.*, p. 50.

the essential skeletal framework upon which any community bases its life. Presidents, kings, wives, chairmen, generals, commissars, privates, managers, and priests are all status positions within given structural formations. Structure provides the clear boundaries and the principle of hierarchy without which no work can be done and no culture can thrive.[21]

In dialectic relationship with structure is what Turner calls anti-structure, not to be construed as a negative but in fact a positive, generative pole. The substance of anti-structure is communitas, a Turner neologism, the meaning of which is significant interpersonal involvement, not a collection of people living in one area. Communitas is the quick of human relatedness, that which is between the I and the Thou. It is the emptiness at the center of the wheel, *das Zwischenmenschliche* of Buber. Communitas resembles but is not the same as the pleasurable and effortless comradeship of friends. It is rather the profound and transforming experience between persons "that goes to the root of each person's being and finds something profoundly communal and shared."[22] Communitas is not a pursuit of instincts but an act of volition rooted in awareness. Communitas floods across structural boundaries in violation and seeming disregard of them. The fruits of communitas are, paradoxically, both profound interpersonal connectedness, or love, and the reinforcement of structure and hierarchy itself. Turner's vision of human social life is thus profoundly paradoxical and dialectical. It is a vision that unites in an uneasy union the contradictory elements of structure and anti-structure.

Communitas itself is especially nurtured, according to Turner, in rituals of status reversal, which are essentially rituals of anti-structure. Turner illustrates what he means by the example of a ritual event of the Ndemba tribe in Africa. At the time a new tribal chief is elected he immediately faces a spontaneous performance in which all manner of rather severe verbal abuse is hurled at him. In this status-reversal ritual, the high is made low, and as Turner says, the power of communitas is symbolically dramatized, which at the same time strengthens the structural hierarchy. While the hostility expressed in the abusive event is symbolic and ritualis-

---

21 Victor Turner, *The Ritual Process: Structure and Anti-Structure,* Ithaca, Cornell Univerisity Press, 1969.
22 *Ibid.*, p. 138.

tic, it is also both real and intimate, more real and intimate than the normal behavior required in relation to his role as chief. Both kinds of behavior are vital to social life. The tribe needs both structure and intimacy and thus ritualizes both. In rituals of status-reversal established hierarchies such as age, sex, caste, wealth, and power are deliberately reversed in the symbolic expression of communitas.[23]

For further anthropological data Turner draws on the sixteenth century Bengali Hindu sect, the Sahajiya, and their rituals of sacramental sex. In these sexual rituals certain male initiates, simulating the lovemaking between the gods, Krishna and Radha, take female partners who in this instance *must* be wives of other men. They follow a series of liturgical actions and recitations of mantras which culminates in sexual intercourse. Turner takes this ritual action to be a symbol and ritual of communitas, in this case of a love that is both divine and faintly illicit, as contrasted with licit marital sex. "Marriage is homologous with property and represents structure in this theological-erotic language." Turner quotes the Krishna's answer to the question of how he could justify sexual relations with other men's wives: "For those who are free of egoism there is no personal advantage by means of proper behavior, nor any disadvantage by means of the opposite." Thus he defends both the liturgical adultery and also, by implication, adultery in the real world, provided it is not driven by inordinate self-interest. The meaning of the status reversal rite is twofold. Communitas is symbolically expressed in the act of adultery, and marriage is ritually defiled and paradoxically by the same action reinforced.[24]

Turner makes it clear that he values communitas above structure, but he is equally certain that communitas without structure is impossible. The dream of love and relatedness in anarchy is a naive illusion. The ultimate desideratum is "to act in terms of communitas values even while playing structural roles."[25] According to Turner, human institutions thrive only if an inner dialectic is maintained between institutional structure and communitas values, which at once threaten the destruction of the institution and at the same time provide it with vitality and a reason for being.

---

23 *Ibid.*, pp. 44ff.
24 *Ibid.*, pp. 158, 162.
25 *Ibid.*, pp. 177ff.

Turner's anthropological conclusions have important implications for any assessment of the institution of marriage in our twentieth century industrial West. In light of Turner's exposition, it becomes immediately apparent how brittle and inflexible attitudes are, at least in the United States, toward marriage as an institution. If Turner is correct, the paucity of marital status reversal rituals or any clear dialectic between structure and anti-structure in the symbols surrounding marriage should be cause for alarm. Turner's work leads to the conclusion that any brittle or inflexible institution disassociated from anti-structure symbols would be imperiled by the pressures of everyday life. His work suggests that, when it comes to marriage, we take ourselves much too seriously in the modern West and are imperiled both by our exaggerated respect for structure and our loss of communitas values.

Turner's conclusions are made even more compelling by the persistent recurrence of hitherto rather puzzling evidence in our own culture that certain kinds of tacitly approved or explicitly agreed upon adulterous relationships are experienced as beneficial to marriage. For example, a whole body of open marriage literature has emerged in the past two decades, beginning with Rustum and Della Roy's *Honest Sex*. There is also Nigel Nicholson's *Portrait of a Marriage*, which provides an intimate picture of the life of English aristocracy early in this century. It portrays widespread and tacitly agreed upon spouse-swapping by people whose marriages were seemingly quite stable and who were regarded as the pillars of society. The large, long, week-end parties at country manors which were routine for English gentry, featured single rooms for each individual, rooms that one's own spouse would not enter except by invitation, thus permitting each individual a measure of sexual privacy.[26]

At mid-century a similar pattern manifested itself in the marriages of Sir Winston Churchill and Lord Louis Mountbatten. Though both men were cuckolded by their wives on a continuing basis that made them both at the very least reluctant accomplices, they maintained throughout that characteristic British aplomb. Churchill was no doubt prepared emotionally for

---

26 See also Ronald Pearsall, *The Worm in the Bud,* New York: Penguin, 1969,
     p. 150.

such a way of life in that his mother, Jennie (Lady Randolph), was herself sexually adventurous. Among her lovers was the King of England, Edward VII.[27] Edwina Mountbatten was, of course, unusual in that she was a heroine in her own right, having done an extraordinary job of mobilizing the nursing services in the Far East in World War II. She also greatly assisted her husband in his momentous and heroic assignment as the last viceroy of India. The fact that she was concurrently having an affair with Jawaharlal Nehru does not seem to have done any harm and may have made the difficult changing of the guard easier. The marriages of the Churchills and the Mountbattens were not unusual in British aristocracy. Neither man seems to have been diminished in power or respect in the eyes of the public as a consequence of his wife's sexual adventures.

There is also the marriage of Paul and Hannah Tillich which was marked throughout by a variety of illicit sexual adventures on the part of each of them. Hannah Tillich reports of one sexual experience, a foursome, in which she felt "something of a liberation." It was experienced, she says, as "a break with the whole concept of monogamy . . . a new concept of participation without losing one's identity . . . close friends, who would embrace you and whom you would embrace without loss of personality but clear-eyed and loving---this removed the curse of neurotic jealousy from me."[28]

Then there is the marriage of Karl and Nelly Barth, who with Charlotte von Kirschbaum, lived as a sexually involved threesome under one roof for four decades. The Barth marriage held up throughout, in tension with the shadow marriage or anti-marriage of Karl and Charlotte.

Then there is the "affair" that the French have made something of a national institution. On one level it could be seen simply as the corruption of committed relationships. On another level, however, it could be seen as a national anti-structure ritual, or an embryonic form thereof. Ambiguity clouds the issue around the matter of deception that seems usually involved. If deception or covert betrayal is involved, that would seem in Turner's framework to undermine communitas values.

---

27 Ralph G. Martin, *Jennie*, Englewood Cliffs, NJ: Prentice-Hall Inc., 1971, Vol. I, p. 338.
28 Hannah Tillich, *From Time to Time,* London: George Allen & Unwin, Ltd., 1974, p. 184.

Impressionistic as it is, the writer can report from personal observation of acquaintances who have participated in swinging, among whom there seems to be a surprisingly strong pair-bond loyalty and a determination to avoid deception, which in turn seems to strengthen the pair-bond.

Though this fragmentary data is impressionistic and far from universal, it does suggest that some marriages are strengthened by the incorporation of certain anti-structure rites or patterns of behavior. Perhaps Turner has uncovered a powerful and highly significant dynamic in marital and quasi-marital relationships, namely the necessity for a dialectic of structure and anti-structure within the pair-bond itself as a requirement for the health of the institution.

No one in this generation is more affirming of the paradigmatic character of marriage nor more clear about the demonic power of an unbridled eroticism than Paul Ricoeur. Marriage, he says, with its potential for duration and intimacy, remains "the best chance for tenderness" in our modern world. Marriage stands as the "cardinal wager in our culture in regard to sex," by which he means it is the last and best hope for achieving both our humanity and at the same time a measure of erotic satisfaction. Ricoeur is equally clear about the vain fruits of a frantic eroticism which, in search of the cheapest available variety and stimulation, falls into insignificance and dehumanizes sex as "it slides from promiscuity to desolate solitude."[29] Ricoeur's hope is that in marriage eros, or sexual play, can be embraced and included in the tenderness and significance of a committed pair-bond. He is fully aware, though, that the embrace is a precarious one which involves at best suffering and sacrifice, and also has its own peculiar risks of dehumanization. The dark fact is that "tenderness and significance" are not above plotting the murder of eros. The message of so much popular humor and folk wisdom, that marriage means the end of sex, reflects precisely such an experience, the murder of eros in marriage.

On the other side, as Ricoeur points out, eros remains the serpent in the bosom of tenderness and one easily angered by attempts to trap it within the boundaries of contract or conjugal duty. This fragile balance of power is hardly one that can be comfortably stabilized. Much too easily one side or the other is lost or destroyed. It bears all the marks in

---

29 Ricoeur, *op.cit.* (1964), pp. 136-7, 140.

microcosm of the international balance of terror between East and West. In each instance our humanity is at stake. Ultimately and with a measure of poignancy Ricoeur owns up to the herculean task of creating the delicate alliance between eros and tenderness. The alliance is in a real sense undermined by the very enigma of sexuality itself.

Ricoeur reflects the influence of Freud in his vision of human sexuality as a profoundly problematic balancing act of significance and sensuality. He is, perhaps, only a little more sanguine. Freud's was after all, by his own admission, "a gloomy prognosis."[30] A man leaves his father and mother according to the biblical precept, says Freud, and cleaves to his wife. Then are tenderness and sensuality united. Such is the theory, or the dream wished for. In reality such a union is accomplished only by a very few people of culture, says Freud. He himself was apparently not one of those few since he terminated sexual relations with his wife at age forty-one and seems to have remained genitally inactive for his remaining forty-two years.[31]

Freud sees the problem as a developmental one. From his male perspective, though he was aware it applied equally from the female side, he described man as hampered in his sexual activity by his respect for women, or more specifically, his mother. The more respect a man has for his mother, and indeed the more deserving of respect she is, the more powerfully he must build his defense against the wish for an incestuous relationship with her. In turn, the greater the defense against incest, the more likely he will be inhibited or impotent in his sexual advances toward

---

30 Sigmund Freud, *Collected Papers,* Vol. 4, Joan Riviere, trans., NY: Basic Books, Inc., 1959, p. 216.
31 Benjamin Brody, "Freud's Attitude Toward the United States," *Review of Existential Psychology and Psychiatry,* Vol. XII, No. 1, 1973, p. 98. The subject of Freud's own erotic life is a matter of some controversy and remains partially clouded in mystery. By his own admission he took little advantage of the greater sexual freedom he assisted others in achieving. There is little doubt that the latter half of his life was mostly, if not entirely, bereft of genital erotic pleasure. Some of the women who gathered around him were known by him to be sexual libertines, such as Marie Bonaparte and Lou Andreas-Salome, the intimate of Nietzsche and Rilke. The evidence suggests that Freud, though very close to them personally, never was sexually involved with them. On the other hand, he was apparently quite tolerant of their sexually adventurous ways. Ernest Jones, Freud's first biographer, who was himself a libertine, describes Freud as monogamic to an unusual degree, chaste, and even puritanical. How-

other women whom he respects. Or, as Freud says, he may be sexually competent only with women whom he does not respect, who, being unlike

---

ever, Carl Jung claimed that Minna Bernays, Freud's wife's sister, confessed to him that she was sexually involved with Freud. She is said to have shared this with Jung out of her guilt. This story was first published by John M. Bellinsky, *Andover-Newton Quarterly X,* 1969, pp.39-43. Freud's relationship with his sister-in-law was a very intimate one and she was more of an intellectual companion to him than his wife was. Minna's fiance had died before their marriage and she resigned herself to the life of a spinster. In the mid-1890's she moved in with the Freuds as a permanent member of the household and functioned as nurse and housekeeper. On occasion she and Sigmund vacationed together without others present. Correspondence between them was at times "secret." Both Minna and Martha his wife referred to Sigmund by the same affectionate appellation, "beloved old man."

Peter Gay has done a thorough examination of the evidence and has concluded quite tentatively that a sexual liaison between Freud and his sister-in-law is improbable. Gay doubts the veracity of Jung's account, and identifies a number of peculiar incongruencies in it. The major source of his disbelief is that Jung had too much of an axe to grind. His own sexual life was quite libertine. His sexual involvement with his various patients is well-documented. Freud and Jung had become the bitterest of enemies, and Jung accused Freud of being neurotically fixated on sex. Thus Peter Gay thinks Jung fabricated the story for his own purposes. See Peter Gay, *Freud,* New York: W.W.Norton, 1988, pp.76, 752-3.

Late in 1988, subsequent to Gay's publication of *Freud,* the Library of Congress finally permitted access to a packet of letters between Sigmund and Minna. Gay had hoped they might provide evidence to settle the mystery. In fact the letters only increased the mystery. The letters had been dated and numbered, probably by someone in the Freud household shortly after his death. Letters #95 to #160 (April 1893 to July 1910) were missing, precisely the period when an affair between the two would most likely have begun. Gay wonders if this is an instance of the "dog who did not bark in the night." He concludes, however, that the dog probably did not bark because there was nothing to bark about. See "Sigmund and Minna: The Biographer as Voyeur," *The New York Times Book Review,* Jan 29, 1989, pp. 1, 43-45.

Gay's judgments seem judicious for the most part. However, his suggestion that a liaison with his sister-in-law would have made Freud a liar about his own failure to take advantage of sexual freedom is not persuasive. Even if Sigmund had maintained a long-term sexual liaison with Minna, his erotic life would still have seemed paltry compared to some of Freud's friends, Lou Andreas-Salome, for example.

Peter Gay also claims there is some data suggesting that Freud may even have resumed sexual relations with his wife in later years. However, given the whole picture, and even if one accepts at face value all the questionable stories, we would have to conclude that Freud was notably unsuccessful in bringing together tenderness and eros in his own personal life.

his mother, allow him to lower his internal and unconscious barriers against incest. The conclusion is that the more nurturing and affectively competent the mother is the less likely the son will manage to develop an erotic relationship with another nurturing and competent woman who combines tenderness and sensuality.

Such is Freud's pessimism. As he says: "It has an ugly sound and a paradoxical [one] as well, but nevertheless it must be said that whoever is to be really free and happy in love must have overcome his deference for women and come to terms with the idea of incest with mother or sister."[32] Of course, Freud found hope in his psychoanalysis through which one might become aware and conscious of the dilemma and thereby find a way to cope. The only real tool in Freud's analysis was that of disclosing connections, the disclosure of which he believed had therapeutic power.

On another but related level, too, Freud revealed his pessimism. On the question of how permissive and sex-affirming the environment should be for the rearing of children, he concluded that deprivation or discouragement of sexual pleasure in the early years manifests itself in an incapacity to achieve full satisfaction in later life. It is, of course, for this kind of observation that he is remembered in popular culture. What is not generally known is that he also believed that unrestrained sexual liberty from the early years led to no better results. His "gloomy view" was that the erotic instincts must be molded, but the molding of them achieves "now too much, now too little." [33]

Turner, Ricoeur, and Freud from their respective disciplines share a vision of marriage as an institution that hangs in a delicate and fragile balance. Marriage must achieve two essentially contadictory kinds of values at once, both order and chaos, faithful dependability and erotic disorder, tenderness and meaning on the one hand and primeval, libidinal energy on the other. Every pair-bond is imperiled by the unrestrained pursuit of erotic pleasure on the one hand and the restraint of erotic pleasure on the other. It is a perilous vision.

---

32 *Collected Papers, op.cit.*, p. 211.
33 *Ibid.*, p. 215.

IV

Carnal reciprocity thus does not and cannot limit itself to a pair of particular individuals. It does not in any sense sacralize the couple as a permanent, inviolable twosome. It rejects the strictures of platonic androgyny, one of the oldest and more durable myths about the meaning of sexuality. Plato, in the speech by Aristophanes in the Symposium, posits that persons as they exist in the world are really halves of an original whole that was separated by an act of god. Hence the human task is reunion with one's separated half. This myth promotes an ideology of cosmic coupling.

As a myth about intrapsychic dynamics it may have significant interpretative and integrative power, as exemplified in the animus/anima theories of Jung. In the sphere of interpersonal relations the androgyny myth is a romantic invention and is not helpful. Without warrant it elevates the couple to cosmic significance. It is a romantic illusion. The effect of the myth is to dilute the necessity of individuation in favor of a tyranny of the pair-bond. On a theoretical and practical level it inappropriately separates the couple as couple from the larger community. To those romantically in love it is an appealing myth because it reinforces those feelings of finality and forever that characterize romance. It also fosters the romantic illusion that the pair in love are alone in the universe.

In recent times Suzanne Lilar has been foremost in attempting to rekindle the androgyny myth as a vehicle for sacralizing the couple.[34] The recently popular Marriage Encounter movement promotes a similar ideology. Such evangelical efforts to fuse or reinforce the strength of the pair-bond must be seen at least in part as a defense against the unpredictability and potential destructiveness of eros. If the pair-bond can be fused in a permanent and cosmic sense, then perhaps the serpent in the bosom of tenderness and significance can be slain. However, this is a vain hope, and androgyny is a fictive and misleading construct. Just as any pair-bond must for the sake of its continuing vitality incorporate a dangerous eros that threatens to destroy it, so also the bonded pair must

---

34 Suzanne Lilar, *Aspects of Love in Western Society*, Jonathan Griffin, trans., New York: McGraw-Hill Book Co., 1965.

individually, and not as a couple, embrace the larger community which in turn secretly if not openly wishes to destroy the couple. Though far from consistent on the matter, Barth warns of the danger of androgyny: "Marriage is not permission to establish an egoistic partnership of two persons."[35]

It is noteworthy that the biblical literature does not sacralize a permanent, inviolable twosome. The Old Testament is quite attentive to both pair-bonding and the erotic, but in no instance are these relationships in any sense elevated to cosmic or ultimate significance. The continuing permission for polygamy allows for a multiplicity of overlapping pairs. Furthermore, while the Old Testament is attentive to pair-bonding and the erotic, its major concern is focused on the larger community, the people of God, in this case a community founded mainly on blood and contract. Generally one is either born or married into the Hebraic community.

The New Testament is also primarily concerned about the community, in this case founded mainly on faith and obedience. The New Testament shows little or no interest in the couple as such, never even names eros, and is relatively quiet about sex. Of course, the authors of the New Testament were not in any sense replacing the Old, but merely extending it a step further. Therefore we can assume a continuing appreciation by the New Testament authors of the manner in which pair-bonding and the erotic are valued in the Old Testament.

Carnal reciprocity thus affirms the mutuality of the sexual liaison but at the same time evades the strict boundaries of marital or quasi-marital structures. It avoids idealization of the couple and even disregards the boundaries of heterosexuality itself.

V

The religious establishment in the modern West, the most powerful institutional manifestation of which is the Roman Catholic Church, has blundered in the second millennium in choosing to sacralize monogamy, and more especially and specifically a sexually exclusive monogamy. The Jewish tradition in the West resisted this error until very late, bending only under cultural pressure from Christendom. The point here is not that monogamy was a bad choice, but that religious sanction should not be

---

35 Barth, *Church Dogmatics*, III/4, p. 224.

given to any particular historical form of pair-bonding. To do so is to neutralize and invalidate the powerful eschatological challenge---the life blood of the early church--- as it relates to marriage.

The church itself got into the business of sacralizing marriage in the Middle Ages. Having made marriage a sacrament, albeit rather late in its history, the Roman Catholic Church doctrinally locked itself in an untenable position. Orthodox Protestantism has functionally done the same thing without declaring it. Roman Catholic theologian Karl Rahner puts the best face on this theological error. He says marriage was instituted by the church "as an eschatological sign of salvation for the kingdom of God until the end of time."[36] This should be grim news to those multitudes trapped in miserable marriages, not to mention the divorced and the never-married. At least Rahner is candid in specifying that this was the medieval church's doing. Marriage as a sacrament has no basis in biblical material, and certainly none in human reason. However, there are subtle indications that Rahner may be hedging somewhat. At certain points he writes as if love itself and the physical union were the eschatological sign, rather than the institution of marriage. He even goes so far as to despise the contractual aspect of marriage. However, to eliminate the contractual aspect of marriage is to eliminate marriage itself and to be left only with love and the physical union. The sexual love/union might well be an eschatological sign of the kingdom---a splendid one in fact. If there exists anything like a literal heaven either in this world or some other, it would attract considerably more interest if it offered abundant sex rather than golden streets.

Various Protestant groups have from time to time attempted to separate themselves from an unequivocal endorsement of monogamy, but without lasting effect. Luther made an attempt to do so, and was unable to carry it through. Various Anabaptist groups and other leftist Protestant groups, such as the nineteenth century Oneida Community in upstate New York, made the same attempts. So too did the Mormons. None has succeeded for long. Marriage is to the church as Tar Baby was to Br'er Rabbit.

---

36 Karl Rahner, *Theological Investigations*, Vol X, David Bourke, trans., New York: Herder & Herder, 1973, p. 214.

Marriage in whatever form is and must remain under the judgment of what is coming into being. Marriage is thus always provisional. "Till death us do part" in the marriage rite of The Book of Common Prayer is a literalized form of the eschatological judgment of marriage, but it at least correctly calls attention to the provisionality of marriage. No particular form of pair-bonding, polygamous or monogamous, deserves sanction as the final form. This is the theological meaning of the claim that marriage stands under eschatological judgment. Symbolically speaking, sex makes it to heaven but marriage does not. Hence the long-standing tradition, a truncated and distorted version of the eschatological challenge, that marriage terminates at death.

Marriage, of course, cannot be singled out by itself as an institution to be subjected to eschatological judgment. All institutions or forms of social organization must be judged by what is coming into being. To remove that claim is to remove the essential substance of Christian theology. As Jurgen Moltmann puts it: "From first to last, and not merely in epilogue, Christianity is eschatology, is hope, forward looking and forward moving, and therefore also revolutionizing and transforming the present."[37] No one who takes such words seriously can support a sacralizing of marriage.

It is noteworthy that the Roman Catholic Church has attended to the wisdom of this claim in relation to particular organizational forms of national and political life. Thus the hierarchy in recent times has refused, correctly, to give its unqualified endorsement even to parliamentary or representative democracy. The theological claim here is that whatever the political form, it remains under eschatological judgment, the judgment of what is coming into being. Unfortunately, Christian churches generally have refused to attend to this wisdom as it pertains to the forms of pair-bonding.

One of the specific and more obvious ways in which Western monogamy stands under judgment at present is in its neglect of sexual have-nots. A single woman over forty years of age statistically stands a very poor chance of remarriage at present. Men are fewer in number, often marry younger women, and themselves die younger than women. If the wedding band is the price of admission to sexual fulfillment, we are creat-

---

37 Jurgen Moltmann, *Theology of Hope*, New York: Harper & Row, 1965, p. 16.

ing a large class of sexual have-nots in women over forty, women who might not willingly choose a celibate life. Particularly bizarre is the presumption of church or state to have a moral basis for commanding monogamy in a population that is in imbalance and where monogamy would ensure that some members of the community would be forced into involuntary celibacy. Anyone who cares about people should be concerned about this inhumane social phenomenon.

VI

I have shown how terribly wrong Augustine was in forging the identification of sin with sex in the fourth century. *"Ecce unde,"* he said, "That's the place." My thesis has been to show how the West wove a negative valuation of sex that it inherited from Greco-Roman culture and how concurrently it suppressed the positive valuation of sex that was originally inherited from biblical culture. Augustine was the principal architect of that reversal. The result is a Western religious tradition obsessed with sex, an obsession expressed on the surface as a longing for innocence but characterized covertly by a pervasive prurience. Pornography and the quasi-pornography in modern commercial advertising are simply the mirror image, the underside of a neurotic wish for innocence. Prurience and the wish for innocence in sex go hand in hand.

Evidence of the religious obsession is plentiful. In the midst of the Vietnam war, in the heat of the public debate about the morality of that national enterprise, an Episcopal bishop, the late James A. Pike, observed that "when the church talks about the 'unchanging moral law' it is apparently always talking about sex, not about war."[38]

In 1944, during the final year of the Nazi holocaust, Pope Pius XII found time to condemn the view that love or any other motivation was on a par with the intention to procreate as a proper reason for marital sex.[39] The Roman Holy Office never could find a way to be so explicit about the Nazi death camps or Jewish genocide, but it spoke in the midst of that

---

38 William Stringfellow and Anthony Towne, *The Bishop Pike Affair,* New York: Harper & Row, 1967, p. 194.
39 Address of Pope Pius XII to the Italian Medical-Biological Union of St. Luke, Nov. 12, 1944. For comment see Dennis J. Doherty, *Dimensions of 'Human Sexuality',* Garden City, NY: Doubleday and Co., 1979, p. 66.

horror with a loud, clear voice, as usual, about its fear of eros. As strange as it may seem, Hitler and the Nazis were as fearful of eros as the Pope was. If they were listening, they would have been the first to applaud the Pope on this proclamation, especially Hitler who was himself committed to a celibate image. War, genocide, and potential nuclear destruction are at times given attention by the church, but never with the same passion and consistency with which the church expresses its fear of eros.[40]

However, in a paradoxical way, Augustine---and the West in following him---was profoundly correct even while being profoundly wrong on this matter. At a different level, not at all on a moralistic level, sex is "the place" indeed. It is the one human experience that most confronts us with our creatureliness. Except perhaps for the one-time experience of dying, it is the human experience in which we feel most at the mercy of primordial powers that we do not control. The experience of our sexuality is probably the experience, or galaxy of experiences, that decides our humanity, the crucible in which we are shaped as persons. As Paul Ricoeur says, "We have the vivid and yet obscure feeling that sex participates in a network of powers whose cosmic harmonies are forgotten but not abolished," and that we become human only by plunging into that river of life we call sex. It is the one area that resists all attempts at simplification, and remains "impermeable to reflection and inaccessible to human mastery." Our sexuality is perhaps what most powerfully confronts us with the disjunctive character of human existence, the radically contingent character of human existence. Again, quoting Ricoeur, "When two beings embrace they don't know what they are doing, they don't know what they want, they don't know what they are looking for, and they don't know what they are finding."[41]

However appropriately critical we may be of Augustine, we are also deeply indebted to him. Because of him the West will at least never be permitted to take sex lightly again.

Thus the Western obsession with sex is not intrinsically wrong, but merely grossly misfocused through moralization. As an obsession it has driven into the shadows the single most problematic issue in the human

---

40 Tom F. Driver, "Sexuality and Jesus," *New Theology, No. 3,* Martin E. Marty & Dean G. Peerman, eds., New York: Macmillan Co., 1965, p. 118.
41 Ricoeur, *op.cit.* (1964), pp. 140-141.

experience. What cannot be contained in the darkness leaks out as prurience. The obsession means that we alternate between murderous rage against our sexual selves and prurient ravaging of our sexual selves---psychic murder or rape.

We cannot hope to counter the unhelpful aspects of our Augustinian inheritance by adopting a philosophy of casual sex. Our only hope is to get well from---be saved from---our obsession. Nor will any amount of moralizing save us or make us well, only the recognition that one's sexual development is both the most awesome, problematic, and delightfully ecstatic task that creation has assigned us, and can neither be evaded nor taken lightly. We may exorcise a fear of sex, but never its awesomeness and fearfulness. We may trivialize it, but it will then trivialize us. Nor can this task assigned us by creation be reduced to any moral code whatsoever, or evaded by any strategy that pretends to preserve our innocence or purity. As we go about the task of actualizing our sexual selves---using sex and being used by it---the best we can achieve is to act with creaturely compassion towards ourselves and the other, and to hope that the primordial power of sexual experience is ultimately more creative than destructive.

ACKNOWLEDGEMENTS

It is, of course, impossible even to remember all those to whom I am indebted in producing this book. I risk acknowledging my debt only to a few and ask pardon of all the rest. This work has been in progress on and off for about 18 years.

The late Seward Hiltner gave me special encouragement from the very beginning, and also goaded me for proceding so slowly. Had I been obedient to his prodding I might have finished this work a decade earlier and had the advantage of his astute consultation on the finished product. Joseph Fletcher and Norman Pittenger were also very encouraging to me in the early days. So too were Robert Francoeur, Harry Lipscomb, and my incomparable mentor, the late Armen D. Jorjorian.

I was greatly encouraged early on by the daring theological work of Rustum and Della Roy who were the first in this generation to signal the coming radical changes in sexual ethics.

Many of my students in recent years have at various stages read drafts of the manuscript and made their contributions. I mention only a few: Harold Lay, Kevin Von Gonten, Tuula Raittila Van Gaaspeck, Mike Elsasser, Richard Penrock, Bruce Jordan, Tiina Nummela, and Morten Andersen.

Alastair Reid and Jack Ashmore were very helpful at certain points in suggesting a more felicitous use of language. Charles Thobae, George Buck, Patricia Park, John Ratti, Mitsuko Tsuchiya, John Hinkle, and Ruth En-Jen Kuo also read the manuscript and made helpful suggestions. Howard Vann Pendley made a number of suggestions that improved the text, for which I am very grateful.

In the fall of 1984 I was Visiting Fellow at the School of Theology, The University of the South, where various members of the faculty read early drafts of parts of the manuscript. That was a very productive time and the consultation I received was invaluable. John Booty, Christopher Bryan, Don Armentrout, Patricia O'Connell Killen, Paul Elmen, and the late Bill Griffin deserve special thanks. Ellen Aitken was also helpful with linguistic problems. Ed Camp was very generous in making available all the resources of the theological library. Don Haymes, who came later to Sewanee, did a critical reading of the manuscript and pointed me in the right direction on a number of issues. His enthusiasm about my

Acknowledgements

work was also very encouraging. The staff of the Library of The General Theological Seminary, New York City, was also helpful on many occasions.

Portions of the material incorporated here were previously published in the *St Luke's Journal of Theology*, March, 1985, and reprinted by Paul T. Jersild and Dale A. Johnson in *Moral Issues and Christian Responses*, 4th Edition. The *Quarterly Review* also published in March, 1985, the original synopsis of what eventually became this book, many subsequent changes later. Charles Cole, the editor of the *QR,* was very helpful to me in a number of ways.

The first public reading of an early version of the full text was presented to St. Stephen's Episcopal Church, Houston, in 1985, at the invitation of its rector, Helen Havens. I am grateful for the encouraging response I received there.

My appreciation goes to Harriet Self, who patiently typed and retyped the original manuscript after the original typist resigned in revulsion somewhere in chapter two!

When I considered I had finally written the last revision in 1987, I knew the time had come for the manuscript to be vetted by the country's preeminent authority in sexual ethics, James B. Nelson. He is the author of *Embodiment*, the basic theological work on sex ethics in use today. Nelson and I have a mutual friend, Robert Tucker of Houston, who interceded on my behalf and persuaded Nelson to review the manuscript. Nelson gave the manuscript a thorough, detailed review and made a number of suggestions and criticisms, many of which I have incorporated. I am indebted to him for his careful, critical consultation and his warm encouragement.

I am happy to single out my friend and colleague, John M. Gessell, for special thanks. He has in countless ways from the beginning of this project been supportive, encouraging, and more importantly, critical. It is difficult to imagine how I could have completed this work without his continuing astute consultation. The notion of the privatization of sex that I developed in chapter 6 was a concept of his that I took directly into the text.

It should go without saying that none of the above mentioned persons who have encouraged and assisted me would necessarily agree with all my conclusions. I am equally certain that in time I will not even agree with myself on every point.

My copy editors, Dorothy Richardson and Holly Nye, have gone the extra mile to make the manuscript more readable. Anyone who reads this book should be as grateful to them as I am.

The Poisoning of Eros

Very little in this text is entirely new. The work is a culmination of the work and ideas of so many who have preceded me. If this work has value, it is in the manner in which I have pulled together the many divergent strands into a single and unified focus.

Finally, the words of the Psalmist have undergirded and comforted me throughout: (16: 11)
> You will show me the path of life.
> In your presence is fullness of joy;
> At your right hand there are pleasures for evermore.

R. J. L. jr.
Roanoke, Virginia
The Great Vigil
March 25, 1989

BIBLICAL INDEX

Genesis 1:27, 65 2:7, 7 2:18, 252 2:24, 18, 65 16:7, 31 17:17, 18, 80 19, 27 20:3, 23 25:21, 80
Exodus 19:15, 117 32:6, 35
Leviticus 15:16f, 17, 117 18:8, 37 19:34, 27 20:11, 37 22:4, 17, 117
Numbers 25:1 & 9, 35
Deuteronomy 21:15, 19 25:5-10, 26
Judges 11:29-40, 250 13:2f, 80
1 Samuel 1:9f, 80 21:5-7, 17, 117
2 Samuel 12:7, 26
1 Chronicles 1:34, 83 2:1-5, 83 2:9-13, 83 3:5, 83 3:10-15, 83
Song of Songs 5:7, 29 8:6, 36
Isaiah 7:14, 80
Jeremiah 16:1-4, 38 31:32, 26
Ezekiel 23, 26
Matthew 1:1-6, 82 1:18-25, 80 2:1, 59 2:20, 7 5:21-2, 64 8:5f, 70 10:14-5, 28 10:28, 7 14:3-12, 20 19:4-6, 65 19:9, 63 19:9-12, 68 22:23, 20 22:23f, 66 22:24, 54 26:6f, 62, 73 27:55, 63
Mark 6:3, 82 6:17-28, 20 10:6-9, 65 10:11-12, 63 12:18f, 20, 54, 66 12:30, 78 14:3-9, 62, 73 14:50-2, 71-72 15:40, 63

Luke 1:5, 59 1:26-38, 79 1:52, 82 2:2, 59 2:41f, 56 3:1, 60 3:23, 60, 80 3:24, 79 4:15-16, 56 7:2-10, 70 7:36f, 62, 73 8:1, 63 10:18, 63 20:27f, 20, 54, 66
John 1:48, 56 2:1-11, 76 2:19f, 61 4:1ff, 62 4:27, 62 8:19, 82 4:41, 82 4:57, 60 11:55, 60 12:1ff, 62 13:4-5, 72
Acts 5:36, 60 15:19, 36 16:40, 43 18:2, 53 18:8, 55 21:24, 98 21:25, 36 21:26, 98 24:26, 97
Romans 1:3, 81-2 6:12, 51 7:13, 54 7:23, 51 8:23, 6 12:1, 51 16:16, 84
1 Corinthians 2:14, 8 5:1f, 36 6:6, 51 6:9-10, 35 6:13, 49 6:15, 51 6:15-18, 35 6:16-20, 49 6:18, 51 6:20, 51 7:1b, 32 7:2, 180 7:6, 48 7:7-9, 40, 42 7:8, 41 7:9, 51, 97 7:10-11, 48 7:12, 48 7:25f, 48, 53, 55 7:28, 54 7:29, 40-43 7:31, 44 7:32-8, 42-55 8:1f, 46 9:5, 51, 68 9:25, 97 10:7, 36 10:23, 46 11:2-15, 45 14:34-35, 45 15:5-7, 74 15:44f, 8, 51 15:50, 9 16:20, 84
2 Corinthians 4:10, 51 11:2, 97 13:12, 84

Galatians 3:28, 45-6, 77
  5:23, 97   6:17, 51
Ephesians 5:22f, 50
Philippians 1:20, 51   3:21, 51
  3:5f, 33   4:3, 40-1   4:8, 98
Colossians 3:18f, 75
1 Thessalonians 4:1-8, 47-8
  5:23, 51   5:26, 84
1 Timothy 2:15, 63   3:2, 238
  3:4, 20, 78   3:12, 20, 78
  5:22, 98

2 Timothy 3:6-7, 47
Titus 1:6, 20, 78, 238
James 3:15, 7 3:17, 98
1 Peter 3:1, 98   5:14, 84
2 Peter 2:13, 36
1 John 3:3, 98-9
Jude 7, 28   12-13, 36
Revelation 14:4, 78-9   17:5, 78

GENERAL INDEX

Abelard, Peter, 3, 151-7, 166, 194
Acts of Paul and Thecla, 95
Acts of Peter, 95
Adair, Douglas, 208 n.16, 212, 220
Adams, James Luther, 223-4
Adams, John, 206-8, 214, 218
Adrian VI, 191
Adultery,
 in Old Testament, 25f
 in teachings of Jesus, 63-9
agneia, 97-8
AIDS, 248-9
Akiba ben Joseph, 29, 58
Albigensianism, 134, 147
Albrecht, Cardinal, 166
Alexander VI, 167
Alfoldi, Andrew, 112 n. 56
Albright, W. F., 68 n. 88
Allison, C.F., 259 n.16, 192 n.79
Althaus, Paul, 178 n. 37
Ambrose of Milan, 111-130
Anabaptists, 181-2
Androgyny, 65, 271-2
Anselm of Canterbury, 145
Aquinas, Thomas, 158-61, 168, 170, 198-9, 242
Aries, Philippe, 2
Aricha, Abba, 251
Aristophanes, 271
Aristotle, 170
Arruppe, Pedro, 244
Art, 197-8
Artemidorus, 12

Ashkenazim, 18
Assertion of the Seven Sacraments (Henry VIII), 190-2
Athanasius, 139
Athenagoras, 48, 84, 93, 106-7, 127
Augustine, 2, 28, 111, 118-34, 159-61, 170, 173, 226, 277
Auxerre, Council of, 138
Azzai, Rabbi ben, 38
Babylonian Captivity of the Church, The (Luther), 190
Bacon, Edmund, 208 n. 18, 210, 213
Bailey, Derrick Sherwin, 27 n.77, 30 n.87, 163 n.80
Baillie, D.M., 224
Balch, David L., 76 n.100
Barmen Declaration, 225
Barrett, C.K., 33, 36 n. 10, 37 n.11, 40, 49-51, 55
Barstow, Anne, 142, 145-6
Barth, Karl, 2, 29, 42, 64, 67, 140 n. 18, 142, 174, 185, 205, 222-6, 230-42, 249, 261 n.19, 266, 272
Barth, Nelly, 230ff
Batenburgers, 181
Baumgaertner, Jerome, 175
Baynes, N.H, 112
Beare, F.W., 42
Bede, 137
Benedict and Benedictine Order, 140, 142, 162-3

283

Benedict XV, 199
Benko, Stephen, 84-5
Bentham, Jeremy, 72
Benton, John F., 152 n.50, 153
Berdayev, Nicholas, 130, 234
Bergh, Albert E. 221 n.41
Bernard of Clairvaux, 146, 151, 194
Bernini, Giovanni Lorenzo, 198
Bigg, Charles, 135 n.3
Blake, William, 5
Blood Friends, 181
Boas, George, 12
Bogomils, 147
Boleyn, Anne, 187, 192
Bolt, Robert, 193
Book of Common Prayer, 76, 274
Bornkamm, Gunther, 33 n. 3, 44
Bosch, Hieronymous, 168
Boswell, James, 205
Boswell, John, 27 n.76, 28, 146
Bottomley, Frank, 35 n.8, 123 n.92, 134 n.1, 138 n.15, 139 n.17, 162-3
Bouwsma, William J., 185
Bowden, John, 224 n. 48, 225 n.50, 235
Boyd, Julian, 216, 221
Brethren of the Free Spirit, 164, 168
Brodie, Fawn, 208, 214, 215ff
Brodsky, Joseph, 113
Brooke, Christopher, 144 n.30

Brown, Norman O., 8 n.9, 44, 171ff,
Brown, Peter, 69 n.90, 112-3, 118 n.70, 121 n.86, 122, 125, 129, 131, 132-3
Brown, Raymond E., 60, 81 n.108
Brown, Robert McAfee, 235 n.73
Bruce, F. F., 39 n.24, 42, 54 n.63
Bryan, Christopher, 42 n.37
Buber, Martin, 263
Bullough, Vern, 15, 29 n. 85
Bure, Idelette de, 185
Burkert, Walter, 13 n.31
Burckhardt, Jacob, 112-3
Busch, Eberhard, 225 n. 50, 230, 234
Buttorff, William K., 208 n.16
Caird, G. B., 59 n.73, 78, 81
Cajetan, Cardinal, 168
Callender, James, 213-4, 217
Calor, Abraham, 238
Calvin, John, 41, 171, 182-7, 201, 249
Campbell, Joseph 155-6
Cannon, William Ragsdale, 141 n.20
Capps, Donald, 128-30
Carmina Burana, 162-3
Carnal reciprocity, 247ff
Carpenter, Edward, 224
Carr, Peter and Samuel, 210ff
Carthage, Synod of, 116
Cartlidge, David, 44, 47 n.48

Index

Catharism, 134, 147-50
Catherine of Aragon, 187, 192
Celsus, 81-2, 91-2, 104
Chadwick, Henry, 97 n.18, 111 n.46, 118 n.69
Charlemagne, 137, 141
Charles V, 175, 192
Churchill, 265ff
City of God, The (Augustine), 127
Clement of Alexander, 39, 41, 84, 104, 107-8, 110
Clement of Rome, 75, 96, 104
Cleugh, James, 163
Cline, C. Benton, 260 n.17
Coelius, Michael, 181 n.47
Cohen, Simon, 19 n.50, 29 n.84, 58 n.69
Cohn, Marcus, 22 n.66
Cohn, Norman, 169 n.10
Colt, Jane, 188
Communitas, 263ff
Concordat of Worms, 143
Confessions (Augustine), 128
Confessions (Rousseau), 204 n.7
Constance, Council of, 164
Constantine, 111ff, 136
Cooper, David, 248, 252, 262
Cosway, Maria and Richard, 209-10, 216
Countryman, William L., 68-9
Cranach, Lucas, 170
Crompton, Louis, 72 n.92
Cunningham, Noble E., 216-7

Curran, Charles E., 242 n. 96
Dabney, Virginius, 208 n.16, 209, 211, 216-21
Davies, Steven L., 103
Davis, Charles, 251
Daube, David, 66 n.85
Denifle, Heinrich, 172
Denny, Frederick Matthewson, 245 n.102
Didache, 96-9
Dillenberger, John, 197 n.1
Dio Cassius, 76 n.100
Diocletian, 21
Dionysius Exiguus, 59
Doherty, Dennis, 159
Dolenton, Jeanne, 164
Driver, Tom, 245, 276 n.40
Dronke, Peter, 153 n.53, 157
Durer, Albrecht, 169
Durrell, Lawrence, 245, 247
Edward VII, 266
Edwards, George R., 27-8
Edwards, Jonathan, 202
El Greco, 197
Eliade, Mircea, 11 n.24
Elvira, Council of, 112, 114-7
encrateia, 97-8, 100
Encratism, 91, 97ff, 103ff, 111
Engels, Friedrich, 222, 261
Enlightenment, 199ff
"Epistle of Holiness" (Nahmanides), 29
Epistle to Diognetus, 95-6, 101

285

epithumia, 64-5
Erasmus, Desiderius, 41, 188-9, 201
Erikson, Erik, 171 n. 20, 172
Eschatology, 43-9, 67, 76, 182, 248, 272ff
Euripides, 41
Eusebius, 39, 94 n.13, 111-3
Evangelical Rationalists, 181
Falk, Ze'ev W., 19 n.47, 21 n.63
Farm Book (Thomas Jefferson), 211
Farrakhan, Louis, 90 n.2
Fasting, 251
Feldman, David M. 17, 26 n.74, 27 n.75, 30
Fichte, Johann Gottlieb, 201
Fiorenza, Elizabeth S., 46, 62 n.78, 63 n.79, 73ff, 85, 104
Firth, Francis, 34 n.6
Fishback, James, 221
Flexner, James Thomas, 207 n.15
Footwashing 72-3
Ford, J. Massingberd, 39, 53, 78 n.103
Foucault, Michel, 1, 12, 70 n.91
Francoeur, Robert F., 243
Franklin, Benjamin, 205-8, 218
Franklin, William, 205
Frend, W. H. C., 94, 104 n.29
Freud, Sigmund, 122, 133, 170, 173, 222-3, 243, 253, 261, 268ff

Fronto, M. Cornelius, 93-4
Fuchs, Eric, 40 n.25, 65, 68 n.88, 159 n. 71
Galen, 91
Gershom ben Judah, 18
Ginot, Haim G. 252
gnosis, 95
Gnosticism, 6, 92, 95
Gollwitzer, Helmut, 232,
Gonzagas, Aloyisha, 202
Goody, Jack, 182, 259 n.16
Gordis, Robert, 18 n.44, 22 n.67
Gospel of Philip, 57, 85, 150 n.47
Gospel of Thomas, 57
Graham, Holt H., 98 n.21
Graham, W. Fred, 184 n.53
Grant, Frederick C., 5 n.2, 98 n.21, 117 n.67
Greeley, Andrew M., 243
Green, F. Pratt, 228 n.59
Greer, Rowan A., 121
Great Awakening, 201ff
Gregory the Great, 134, 137-9,
gyne, 51-2
Haardt, Robert, 93
Haenchen, E., 41 n.33
Hagen, Kenneth G., 172 n.22
Hamilton, Alexander, 214
Hauerwas, Stanley, 256 n.13, 258
Hegel, G. W. F., 133
Heloise, 3, 150-7, 166
Helvidius, 118, 122
Heemskerck, Maaerten van, 169

Index

Hemings, Madison, 210, n.23
Hemings, Sally, 210-21
Hengel, Martin, 9 n.14, 24 n.71, 25 n.72, 32 n.2
Henry of Huntington, 146
Henry, Paul, 6
Henry VIII, 187, 190, 258-9
Herbert, Eugenia W., 206 n.12
Herr, Moshe David, 18 n.46
Hertz, J. H., 21 n.63
Hillel, 19, 65
Hiltner, Seward, 223, 226-7, 229-30, 254
Hippolytus, 85
Hitler, Adolf, 122, 149, 225-6, 235, 276
Hoehner, Harold W., 20 n.57, 60 n.72
Hohenlandenberg, Hugo von, 167
Holsapple, Lloyd B., 112 n.56
Holst, Robert, 63
Homosexuality
    in ancient Greece, 13ff
    in Middle Ages, 140, 146-7
    as ethical issue, 253ff
Hultgren, Arland J., 66 n. 85
Huss, Jan, 161, 164
Ignatius of Antioch, 39, 54, 75, 96-7, 104, 109
Indulgences, 171-2
Innocent VIII, 166
Inquisition, 161
Institutes of the Christian Religion (Calvin), 183

Investiture Controversy, 144
Irenaeus, 28, 59, 60-1, 108-9
Islam, rise of, 135
Jefferson, Thomas, 207-21
Jephthah, 249
Jerome, 39, 114, 117, 119, 123, 126, 132, 186
Jesuits, 201-2
Jesus
    age at crucifixion, 58-61
    in Reformation art, 168-70
    marriage of, 56ff
    relationship to women, 62-3
    teaching on adultery, 63-9
    teaching on divorce, 64
Joan of Arc, 161-2
Jobes, Gertrude, 214 n.26
John of Leyden, 182
John Paul II, 199
Johnson, Paul, 21 n.63
Johnson, Roger A. 171 n.20, 172 n.21
Johnson, Samuel, 205
John XXIII, 199
Jonas, Justice, 181 n.47
Josephus, Flavius, 20, 61
Julian of Eclanum, 3, 119, 120-2, 125
Jung, Carl G., 271
Justin Martyr, 20-1, 92 n.7, 93, 105-7, 127
Kant, Immanuel, 199ff
Katrei, Schwester, 164

Kau, Ina, 228 n.59
Keifer, Otto, 11 n.26
Kelber, Werner, 46, 48 n.51, 74, 88
Keuls, Eva, 12 n.30, 15, 126 n.99
Kirschbaum, Charlotte (Lollo) von, 230-6, 241, 266
Kiss of Peace, 84-5
Klein, Isaac, 18 n.45
Kleist, Joseph A., 101 n.24
Kleming, Roland, 226 n.52
Koester, Helmut, 43 n.39, 57
Kosnik, Anthony, 243, 251, 258
Kotje, R., 117 n.68
Kung, Hans, 224
Kutter, Hermann, 237
Labriolle, Pierre de, 118 n.72
Ladurie, Emmanuel LeRoy, 147 n.39
Laeuchli, Samuel, 60, 95 n.16, 97, 99 n.23, 108, 114
Lateran Council, First, 136; Second and Third, 145-6, 148
Lawrence, D. H., 205, 238, 245
Laws, The (Plato), 14
Lazareth, William, 190
Lea, Henry C. 142 n.24
Lehmann, Paul, 257
LeMaistre, Martin, 168, 242
Leon, Harry J. 54 n.61
Leo III, 141
Leo IX, 142
Leo XIII, 199
Letter to Barnabas, 96-100

Levirite marriage 26-7, 54, 66
Liguore, Alphonsus, 242
Lilar, Suzanne, 271
Lipscomb, Andrew A., 221 n.41
Lithuanian Brethren, 182
Little, David, 183 n.51, 184
Lollards and The Lollard Conclusions, 164
Lombard, Peter, 30, 150
Lopez, Claude-Anne, 206 n.12
Ludwig, Karl 225
Luther, Katharine von Bora, 175-7, 180-1, 191
Luther, Martin, 2, 3, 41, 124, 131, 133, 142, 166-97, 200-2, 235-6, 249, 257, 273-4
Lutz, Cara, 10
McLaughlin, Jack, 208 n.18, 216
McLaughlin, Mary Martin, 151, 152 n.50
MacMullen, Ramsay, 112 n.51
Malina, Bruce, 34
Malone, Dumas, 208 n. 16, 209, 216-21
Man for All Seasons, A, 193
Mani, 103, 130
Manicheeism, 118, 125, 130
Mann, C. S., 68 n. 88
Mansi, J. D., 138 n. 15
Mapp, Alf J. 211, 216-7
Marcuse, Herbert, 253
Marius, Richard, 134, 167 n.6, 181 n.48, 188-9, 192

Index

Marriage Encounter Movement, 271
Martin, Ralph, 266 n. 27
Martyrdom of Polycarp, 94, 100
Marx, Karl, 133, 222-3
May, Rollo, 227-8
Meeks, Wayne, 37, 47, 48, 76 n.99
Methodism, 202-4
Melchiorites, 181
Mexico, population explosion in, 260
Michelangelo, 197
Middleton, Alice, 188
J. P. Migne, 21, 39 n.20, 41 n.31, 117 n.66
Minucius Felix, Marcus, 93-4
Mishna, 18ff, 33, 38-9, 65, 128
Moiser, Jeremy, 32 n.1, 40 n.26, 48
Moltmann, Jurgen, 44, 197, 235, 274
Monogamy, 17ff, 260ff
Money, John 252, n.7
Monro, Winsome, 74-5
Montanists, 110-1
Moore, George Foot, 21, 34
Moore, Paul, 1-2, 254
More, Thomas, 187-95
Mormons, 273
Moss, Sidney P. and Carolyn, 220 n.36
Mountbatten, Edwina and Louis, 265f
Mounce, Robert H., 78 n.103

Muller, Ludwig, 225
Musonius Rufus, 10-11
Nahmanides, 30
Naziism, 149, 225-6, 275-6
Nehru, Jawaharlal, 266
Nelson, James B., 245, 253
nephesh, 6f, 78
Nero, 90
Neusner, Jacob, 33 n.4, 256
Nicaea, Council of, 116
Nicholson, Nigel, 265
Niemoller, Martin, 225
Nietzsche, Friedrich, 155, 166, 222, 223
Noonan, John, 10 n.17, 135 n.2, 159 n.71
"Norman Anonymous", 3, 145
Norris, R. A., Jr., 121
Novak, David, 24 n.70
Oberman, Heiko A. 179 n.40, 180
Oden, Thomas C. 137 n.11
Ogg, George, 59
Oneida Community, 273
Onians, R. B., 245 n.102
Origen, 10, 39, 41, 82 n.109, 111
Oulton J. E. L., 97 n.18
Pagels, Elaine, 4 n.4
Paphnutius, 116
Patai, Raphael, 28
Pauck, Wilhelm and Marion, 229
Paul, 1, 31-56
Paul III, 167
Payer, Pierre J., 138

289

Pearsall, Ronald, 265
Pearson, Birger, 8
Pederasty, 69-73
Pelagius, 122, 125
Peliken, Jaraslov, 87
Pelz, Werner and Lotte, 174
Penitentials, 138
Perkins, Pheme, 44
Peterson, Merrill, 208 n.16, 216-21
Peter the Venerable, 157
Petitot, L. H., 160
Phillips, J. B., 85
Philo of Alexandria, 25, 56
Phipps, William E., 54 n.63, 57, 68 n.88, 79
Pietism, 202ff
Pike, James A., 275
Pittenger, Norman, 224
Pius XII, 225, 242, 250, 275
Place, Michael D., 102 n.25
Plato, 9, 13ff, 41, 271
Pliny, 90-1
Plotinus, 126, 130
Plutarch, 70
Pohier, Jacques-Marie, 243-4
Polycarp of Smyrna, 60, 96, 98
Polygamy, 18ff, 49, 66, 78, 272
Pontius Pilate, 59
Pope, Marvin, 29 n.84, 36
Porete, Marguerita, 164
porneia, 34-7, 47-9, 63, 78, 98-100, 107
Porphyry, 126, 131

Prisca and Aquila, 53
Prostitution, 198
Pythagoras, 9
Quinn, Edward, 224 n.47
Rad, Gerhard von, 65 n.83
Rahner, Karl, 50, 273
Raleigh, Walter, 206
Ramsey, Boniface, 170
Randolph, Henry S., 210
Randolph, Thomas J., 210-11, 218
Reicke, Bo, 28 n. 81
Reissenbusch, Wolfgang, 175
Renan, Joseph-Ernest, 41
Riasanovsky, Nicholas V., 164 n.83
Ricoeur, Paul, 6, 16, 62 n.77, 247, 261, 267-8, 276
Ridley, Jasper, 194f
Rigby, Paul, 128 n.106
Rilliet, J., 167 n.4
Robinson, James M., 43 n.39
Roy, Rustum and Della, 245, 265
Rougemont, Denis de, 66 n.86, 147-9 n.40
Rousseau, Jean-Jacques, 133, 200-1, 204-5, 220
Rubens, Peter Paul, 197
Ruehlmann, William, 217 n.31
Rule of Bendedict, 139-41
Rumscheidt, Martin, 231, 235
Russia, 164
Sahajiya, 264
Sanchez, Thomas, 242
Sanders, E. P., 9 n.12, 33 n.4

Index

Schaff, Philip, 167 n.7, 184 n.52
Schillebeeckx, Edward, 43 n.39, 44, 63 n.80, 77 n.102, 102 n.25, 120, 141 n.22, 150 n.46
Schneidau, Herbert N., 7 n.7
Schweibert, E. G., 175 n.26
Segal, J. B., 76
Seneca, 10, 89
Shammai, 65
Shepherd of Hermas, 57, 96, 99-100
Sherrard, Jani, 228 n.59
Smith, Hettie, 211
Smith, John Holland, 113 n.57
Smith, Page, 221 n.40
Socrates, 13ff
Song of Songs, 29, 36, 126
Spalatin, Georg, 180
Spencer, Bonnell, 57
Spener, Philip Jacob, 202
Spiritualists, 181
Spitz, Lewis, 172
Spouse-swapping, 265-7
Staupitz, John, 167, 175
Steinberg, Leo, 169-70
Steinsaltz, Adin, 18 n.42
Stoicism, 9ff, 25, 88ff, 186
Stoss, Veit, 169
Streeter, B. H., 99
Stringfellow, William, 275 n.38
Swindler, Leonard, 62 n.76, 63 n.80
Symposium (Plato), 13, 271

syzyge, 40ff
Table Talk (Luther), 180
Tacitus, 89-91
Talmud, 18ff, 33, 38-9, 65, 128
Tatian, 106 n.33
Teilhard de Chardin, Pierre, 4
Temple, William, 206
Tertullian, 67, 99, 102, 104-5, 109-11, 122, 148
Theodore of Mopsuestia, 3, 119-22
Theodosius, 21
Theophilus of Antioch, 105
Thirty Years War, 196, 199, 202
Thomas Aquinas, 124, 159-62, 168, 170, 198-9, 242
Tillich, Hannah, 227-30, 266 n.28
Tillich, Paul, 2, 3, 8, 202 n.4, 222-30, 241-2, 249, 266
Todd, John, 166 n.1-2, 176 n.32, 177 n. 34, 179 n.43, 195 n.88
Torquemada, 194
Towne, Anthony, 275 n.38
Trent, Council of, 197
Troeltsch, Ernst, 184
Tuchman, Barbara, 162, 164 n.82
Turner, Victor, 261-70
Tyndale, William, 189
Tyson, Joseph B. 92 n.8
Ulric of Imola, 144, 146
Valente, Michael, 158 n.67, 159, 168 n.9, 242-3
Vatican Council, Second, 140, 199

291

Vermes, Geza, 24 n.71, 56, 69 n.90, 80 n.105
Veronese, Paolo, 197
Virgin Birth, 79-83
Vives, Luis, 169
Voobus, Arthur, 103 n.26
Waldenses, 164
Walker, John and Betsey, 213-4
Wall, John N., 120 n.78
Walzer, R., 91 n.6
Warner, Marina, 161 n.77
Washington, George and Martha, 207
Weatherhead, Leslie, 82 n.109
Weinberger, Caspar, 217
Wesley, John, 202-4
Westermann, Claus, 17 n.41
Whitefield, George, 206
Wicker, Kathleen O'Brian, 76 n.100
Williams, George Huntston, 182 n.49
Witherington, Ben, 46 n.46, 47 n.49
Wolsey, Cardinal, 167
Wouk, Herman, 30
Wycliffe, John, 164
Xenophon, 15 n.34
Zwingli, Ulrich, 167, 197, 201